EMERSON, LAKE & PALMER

The Show That Never Ends

A Musical Biography

Author Biographies

Forrester, Hanson and Askew are acknowledged experts on ELP and after five years of research, they have produced a gripping and fascinating document of one of the great 70s rock bands. George Forrester also provides an erudite study of the band's complex and challenging music.

George Forrester first heard ELP's *Tarkus* at school. He has been worrying about the future ever since. A pianist who composes his own pieces, he is confident that the wealth accrued from this book will sustain him until he publishes a bestselling novel.

Martyn Hanson is 44 and married with two grown-up children. He has been an ELP fan since only a few months after their 1970 debut album. He has written sleeve notes for both ELP and The Nice. A keen runner, he has completed the famous London to Brighton road race twice.

Frank Askew first heard ELP in 1979. Being a keen drummer, Carl Palmer's playing made the biggest impact. He has since become a friend of the ELP sticksman, was a guest on ELP's 1996 Japanese tour and plays in the ELP tribute band Works 3.

There is no truth in the rumour that their next book will be called *Writing About Music For Fun And Profit*.

Acknowledgments

Special thanks to Keith Emerson, Greg Lake and Carl Palmer.
And to Chris Welch, for cheerfully supplying an excellent Forword.

George Forrester

My mum – for not understanding music!; my dad – for his deep love of music; Cathy Evason – at whose house much of the original version of this book was written; Catherine Feeny; Dave Quinn; Michael Heatley of Northdown Publishing for encouragement; Hugh Feeny for advice. Love to Laura.

Friendly machines: Tantra Computers of Bristol for the Power Mac – in the latter stages of writing, gathering photos etc., the internet speeded everything up – and not forgetting my dear old Atari 1040ST computer on which almost every word of the original version was written, and the ancient dot matrix printer!

Sean Body of Helter Skelter for accepting our tome for publication, for working on it at ungodly hours, and for coping with the three of us. I would also like to thank Sean for contributing some of his own writing on the early punk period in chapter 7, and for useful contributions throughout.

Polly Willis of The Foundry for her work on the photo section.

Robert Ashmore for his support. John Daly for music shared in many ways. Liv G. Whetmore of *Impressions*. Bill Porteous for early ELP enthusiasm – and for selling me his collection of, er, certain audio items.

Many other people were in correspondence with us in relation to the book, and on the subject of ELP in general, and to all many thanks.

The magazines *Record Collector* and *Goldmine* were essential in acquiring many obscure recordings, and long may they thrive.

Many thanks also to Paul Stump for his contribution to the final stages of the editing process.

A big Thank You to Blair Pethel for permission to use his doctoral thesis in discussion of the Piano Concerto and some other parts of the musical analysis.

Finally, thanks to my co-authors – without Martyn and Frank to push it on and improve and update it, this book might never have been published.

Martyn Hanson

Thanks to Carole and my mom for putting up with me all these years, Dale & Lee-Anne for showing me what it's all about, Lynn and Albert for the use of their computer in the early days, David Flavell – thanks for just being there, Robert Ashmore (hitherto unsung hero) for his sound advice and unstinting support, Chris Welch was very helpful and a great bloke to boot , Liv Whetmore for all her support, Adam Fenton – who sent me all sorts of rare ELP items and got me started, John Thurston, David Bentley, Mark Burridge and David Terralovoro. All ELP fans who sent me material over the years.

Finally, every word I wrote is dedicated to the memory of William George Hanson 1925–97 – Father, Friend, Fighter.

Frank Askew

Keith, Greg, Carl (especially), Brian Emerson & Tricia Beever of Part Rock, Jim Davidson, Graham Allen, Stephen Reid (for introducing me to ELP), Liv Whetmore, Jacquie Dutton, Sue Pittard, Robert Ashmore.

Geoff Parkyn (George and I first discussed the prospect of an ELP book at Geoff's house in North London in 1992. Geoff sadly died shortly after and we dedicate this book to his memory). Also all the people I've worked with who suffered my dedication to this project and who believed it would happen one day – you know who you are.

Finally George & Martyn – What can one say!

*****

Finally, George would also like to specially thank Marc Eisenoff for his time and commitment in emailing him so many great photos. It's a shame we couldn't use all of them. eisenoff@mindspring.com

EMERSON, LAKE & PALMER

The Show That Never Ends

A Musical Biography

George Forrester
Martyn Hanson   Frank Askew

Helter
Skelter
publishing

Dedicated to the memory of Geoff Parkyn

This edition published in 2001 by Helter Skelter Publishing
4 Denmark Street, London WC2H 8LL

Designed and typeset by The Foundry

Printed by Redwood Books

A CIP record for this book is available from the British Library

ISBN 1-900924-17-X

The publishers would like to thank Paul Stump and Mick Fish.

Front cover photos
Keith, Madison Square Garden, New York City 17 October 1977 *(Marc Eisenoff)*
Greg, Roosevelt Stadium, New Jersey, early 1970s *(Marc Eisenoff)*
Carl, Soldiers Field, Chicago, 2 June 1977 *(Steve Peterka)*
Back cover photo
London Features International

CONTENTS

The Definitive ELP Book?

Welcome, my friends, to the book that never ends ...

In September 1992, before the British leg of Emerson, Lake and Palmer's comeback tour, a few hardcore ELP fanatics – myself, Frank Askew and David Swift – gathered in the London home of Geoff Parkyn, now sadly deceased, who years before had been involved with ELP's original fan club. All present were unanimous on one thing: ELP were one of the greatest bands of the 70s, but probably the most wilfully neglected and unfairly reviled. No book had ever been written about this extraordinary trio of legendary musicians. There are several books about Yes and Genesis, the other progressive monsters of the period. Flick through the indexes of many books on 70s music, and you'll find them, and other prog acts like King Crimson and Jethro Tull, mentioned far more than Emerson, Lake and Palmer.

It was time to set the record straight.

On a surge of enthusiasm Frank and I embarked on writing. The subject got a grip on us, and soon we were talking in terms of the "definitive" ELP book. Dangerous talk! For years it seemed that the project would never come to fruition.

By 1995 writing was complete, but even with Carl's help we could find no publisher. The project fell by the wayside.

From 1998 Martyn contributed structural revisions and additions. Martyn's contributions reflect his engagement with things ELP at a time when I could not do so, and the comprehensive index is his. Frank put in some writing throughout, notably on Carl, and most of the legwork. I returned to the project in early 1999, and since then we have worked together to get it published.

First we tell the individual stories of Keith, Greg and Carl up to the formation of the band. Subsequent chapters deal with the albums by Emerson, Lake and Palmer, and also Emerson, Lake and Powell and Three, up to the present day, with chapters on solo work in the intervening years. Following the biographical chapters, there is a major section on the more difficult music by the band. Finally, there are lists for fact fiends – records, CDs, videos and tour dates

George, Martyn and Frank freely confess that, like ELP, they have not always seen eye to eye on everything! At times, our writing process seemed to mirror the creative struggle of the band itself. But we think it was worth it – a fitting testimony, we hope, to this uniquely dynamic, powerful and all-encompassing band. Emerson, Lake and Palmer's music needs to be celebrated as much as documented. We hope we have played our part in the re-evaluation, not before time, of one of popular music's greatest trios. They deserve nothing less.

Definitive? If not, it's not for want of trying!

George Forrester (principal author)

Foreword: When There Were Three ...

During the golden age of classic rock, few bands were more exciting and innovative than Emerson, Lake & Palmer. Their showmanship, technical superiority and competitive spirit resulted in a fireball of explosive creative energy that delighted a worldwide audience. The sound of the '70s was not just about the catchy hit tunes of Glam Rock, but something deeper and more inspired. ELP's blend of rock and the classics, jazz and acoustic music made their albums and concerts a richly satisfying experience. Who else would dare put sticks of dynamite under Mussorgsky's "Pictures At An Exhibition", re-invent the lesser known works of Bartok and Ginastera and then launch into a raucous encore with B. Bumble & The Stingers' "Nut Rocker?" Amidst all the controversy that surrounded ELP and the other bands working within the genre known as 'progressive rock' it should not be forgotten their main aim was to have fun.

They certainly enjoyed themselves on the road and in the studio as they created such astonishingly diverse works as "Knife Edge", "Take A Pebble", "Tank", and "Fanfare for The Common Man"...just some of the ballads, epics and set pieces that became their staple fare during a decade of achievement.

When Keith Emerson, Greg Lake and Carl Palmer united as ELP, it seemed like a dream ticket for all aficionados of the British rock scene. Here were three fine young players with impeccable credentials, who were clearly men with a mission. If they had anything in common, it was tremendous drive, self-belief and a commitment to excellence. Much was later made of the divisions which ultimately led to their demise. And yet as Carl once said 'We look like a group!' There were more similarities than differences. ELP shared a desire to bring great music to a wider public, to revel in eclecticism and yet keep the public turned on and entertained.

Certainly there was competition, but it was all for the good. Some of the greatest trios including Cream, Jimi Hendrix Experience and The Police, were riven by dissent yet were bound together in shared enterprises that proved enormously successful. If ELP never had an argument, never quarrelled over policy, or the next twist and turn of an arrangement, then they would have been compliant and dull and produced music to match. Instead they gave us combative, vibrant performances that have stayed embedded in the memories of legions of fans.

We remember the surging, stabbing Hammond organ riffs to a piece like "Knife Edge" from their 1970 debut album; Greg's menacing vocals and Carl's staccato drums, all wired together in an electrifying frenzy.

We remember Keith scraping the strings of his grand piano for those surreal opening moments to "Take A Pebble" and the rippling flourishes of a master pianist

7

who seemed as if he could play anything that was in God's gift. Indeed this piece epitomised all that was best about ELP, with its constantly changing moods, rhythms and themes. Listening to such music in an age dominated by machine tooled conformity, it's hard to believe that we were once regaled with brilliant piano improvisation, subtle jazz drumming, expressive vocals and meaningful poetry, all cheerfully purveyed in the name of pop.

ELP subsequently became identified with blockbuster science fiction pieces like "Tank", "Tarkus" and "Karn Evil 9" and were damned for overindulgence in long solos. It was certainly a time for excess in all areas. And yet a typical ELP concert was packed with so many twists, surprises and such a rich variety of material there was never time to get bored or distracted. The avowed intention was to explore, to improvise and experiment and yet retain a feel for melody, tunes and arrangements. They also wanted audiences to be amused, stunned and surprised. This was no denim clad blues band mournfully bashing out 'Dust My Broom'. Each member of the band had an equal part to play in the grand scheme of things, whether it was Greg surprising everyone with his tasteful song "Lucky Man", Keith pushing new technology of synthesisers or Carl developing the art of the percussionist.

All those who were fortunate to have seen the band 'live' in concert during their heyday will cherish memories of Emerson's astonishingly dynamic approach to the keyboards. When leather clad Keith was in action, tilting the battered Hammond on its side, flailing whips, daggers and flaunting the famous ribbon synthesiser that produced so many weird and wonderful noises, he seemed to be projecting himself onto another astral plane.

We remember Carl, stripped to the waist, dripping in sweat and reaching out with his teeth to clang the bell and beat the gongs that hung over his spinning drum kit, at the climax of breathtakingly fast and furious solos. We think of Greg Lake, stepping up to the microphone, bringing calm and peace amidst the mayhem with a few well chosen guitar chords and a voice as smooth as silk. Yes, it was a lucky man who saw ELP in action, from their formation back in 1970 right up to their reunion in the early Nineties. Indeed it was very satisfying for me to be able to report their progress for the eager readers of *Melody Maker*, who regularly voted the band into top place in the annual Pop Polls. It was even more enjoyable to go on the road with them and see the band at work in the studio and on stage in a variety of exotic locations.

The first time I met Keith and Greg together was in a tiny sandwich bar in Fleet Street, where there was barely room to stir a cup of tea. They explained they were still looking for a drummer, and there had been rumours that Mitch Mitchell might be recruited. However one of my favourite drummers of the day was undoubtedly Carl Palmer, who had been creating a sensation with the Crazy World Of Arthur Brown. The showman with the fastest snare drum roll in the west was now hooked up with Vincent Crane in Atomic Rooster. But he was the obvious choice for a band that would place huge demands on any drummer.

Keith meanwhile had recently broken up The Nice, a source of great distress to him, as the group had nurtured his earliest musical aspirations and brought him fame and recognition. He was also sorry to leave his old friends behind, but he had to make a career move that would give him even greater scope.

Greg had been with King Crimson, under the aegis of Robert Fripp and was itching to branch out and make use of his burgeoning skills as a singer, guitarist, composer and producer. The new group would be like a workshop, a test bed for new material, sounds and ideas. So much for the planning stage.

In the days ahead they seemed like human dynamos as they hastily worked out a set and a stage act. Their avowed intention was to be simply the best. I went to see them rehearse at Island studios when they had only three numbers and yet they had a complete set ready by the time they played at the Isle Of Wight festival and London's Lyceum Ballroom. Audiences were blown away when they unveiled massive arrangements like "Pictures At An Exhibition" interwoven with ballads and climaxed with raging drum and keyboard solos. To put it mildly, it was all very exciting.

Keith, Greg and Carl were speedy characters, who played and lived hard. Yet they were never a band to get "out of it" before or during a show. Too much depended on their co-ordination and concentration. But often their good humour spilled over into their 'live' performances, which were far from po-faced excursions into intellectualised prog. rock. Right from the moment when they fired two brass cannons on stage at their Isle Of Wight Festival debut, they were up for it.

One of the funniest and most spontaneous moments of madness came when the band were in Zurich, Switzerland during a short tour. In the afternoon the band left the theatre and went into a nearby restaurant in search of tea and cakes.

The place was practically empty, but on a small stage were some instruments belonging to the resident band. Keith politely asked if it would be alright to get up and have a play. Although they were only amateurs they promised not to damage the equipment. Greg, Carl and Keith promptly launched into a high speed performance of "Rondo" which I believe careered into a berserk "Nutrocker" complete with thunderous solos. Whatever tunes they actually played that day, their impromptu performance caused a sensation and people poured into the restaurant. The manager came rushing out in great excitement begging the boys to stay and play again. He offered them a residency on the spot. They coolly explained they were only passing through and had to get back home to England. In fact they played another show that night to hundreds of cheering Swiss fans in a theatre was so hot and sticky that Greg, Keith and Carl stripped down to their underpants to play the encore!

Life with ELP was full of odd moments. Like the time in Osaka, Japan when their show ended in a riot in the midst of a monsoon deluge. As the group fled the stage and the police began clubbing their fans to the ground, I began to wonder about the strange effect the Moog synthesiser could have on people. Even the elements seemed to be stirred up by ELP and storms and gales invariably accompanied their outdoor shows.

When the band played a concert near Boston in 1992, a huge flash of lightning lit up the pitch black skies, just as they launched into "Pirates" if memory serves me well. The great benefit of this long overdue and eagerly awaited story of Emerson, Lake & Palmer, is that at last we can out exactly what they did, where and when.

George Forrester, Martyn Hanson and Frank Askew, tireless devotees of the band and its music and history are to be congratulated on bringing together this tremendously detailed and fascinating work, which has been a labour of love for the joint authors. As George explains, it has been a task not without its difficulties, but they present a splendid and timely tribute to a band that deserves to be re-evaluated and listened to again with open ears.

Their story is the ultimate proof that working musicians can successfully call the shots and not be entirely subservient to the whims of an industry that likes to lay down the rules. ELP made a career out of being themselves, playing what they liked and always to the highest of standards. The fact that they were so successful for so long and remain so popular shows they must have been doing something right!

So now we open the Great Gates Of Kiev and plunge back into that almost mythical age, when ELP ruled the world. Let the synthesisers howl and let mighty "Tarkus" erupt....Are you ready Eddy?

Chris Welch, London, England 2000

Introduction

On August 23, 1970, the newly-formed Emerson, Lake and Palmer stepped out onto the stage of the Plymouth Guildhall. They didn't have a long set prepared, but the crowd was so impressed by what they heard that the band had to play three encores – "Rondo" twice and "Nutrocker" once.

On May 2, 1974, at the Liverpool Empire, well over two hours after they had began their set, Emerson, Lake and Palmer left the stage after what would be their last concert in their home country for 18 years. By this point, they were perhaps the biggest band in the world. A fleet of lorries was required to transport their lavish stage show, the walls of their homes were lined with gold and platinum albums, and they had an intensely loyal mass fan following across the world.

Approximately four years later, on March 13, 1978, Emerson, Lake and Palmer were at Providence, Rhode Island, playing to a near sell-out crowd. This rapturously-received two-and-a-half-hour-show would be the band's last gig before their turn-of-the-decade announcement that they were splitting up.

As the 80s dawned, many believed that Keith Emerson, Greg Lake and Carl Palmer would never again share the same stage. The three musicians seemed content to enjoy solo careers and pursue other musical avenues. As time passed however, and the post-punk years saw some of the stigma associated with 70s giants such as ELP gradually lift, the lure of the glory years began to haunt them, and two ill-fated attempts were made to revive the original band.

First Emerson, Lake and [Cozy] Powell, and then Three [Emerson, Palmer and Robert Berry] brought back two thirds of the band at a time. Each was reasonably successful, but it was the triple magic of Keith, Greg and Carl that ELP fans wanted. In the meantime, none of the original trio were getting any younger. By the time Three split in 1989, it was becoming clear that if ELP were ever going to get back together, it would have to be soon.

Finally in 1991, Emerson, Lake and Palmer's long-suffering loyal fans got what they were waiting for when the band reformed and recorded a new studio album, *Black Moon*, to be released the following year. *Black Moon* was no chart-topper, but it sold respectably and the subsequent tour saw the band given a rapturous reception wherever they played.

Nonetheless, the British press remained typically sarcastic and hostile to the band's comeback. Traditionally overlooked, undervalued and castigated by the media in their home country as representing the worst of rock's 70s excesses, ELP have always enjoyed more success in American and Europe. Away from home, the band have received better press and their financial success – which, coupled with the exigencies of the British tax system of the 70s, forced them into overseas tax exile – has never been frowned upon.

Still, charges of excess aside – which of course could be pinned on many 70s survivors – why do UK critics loathe ELP? Is there any truth in John Peel's dismissal of the band as a "waste of talent and electricity"? Are they really just "Zimmer Rock" dinosaurs?

In the older sense of the word, Peel's assessment of "waste" is accurate. For ELP have indeed "wasted" their talent – using it freely and generously and never holding anything back. The band have always worked lavishly, and in both composition and performance they have given everything they have got – all of the time.

As for the band's alleged dinosaur status, in discussing their castigation at the hands of British critics, it is crucial to place such treatment in the context of ELP's musical genre. Emerson, Lake and Palmer play progressive rock, "prog rock", or simply "prog", a form of music that since punk's 1976 musical Year Zero has been viewed as supremely unfashionable.

While the golden era of prog can be easily identified – having its roots in the late '60s, prog-rock flourished in the early-to-mid '70s – no exact definition of the form is possible. Progressive musicians borrowed and stole from every conceivable kind of music: rock, jazz, blues, classical music of every period, folk music from every country under the sun, electronic and avant-garde experimentation, and more besides. However some general observations can be made. The things one person loves about prog are the very same things that make someone else hate it: technical complexity, grandiose concepts, virtuosity, eclecticism, intensity, a variety of moods within one piece, extended instrumental passages…. Much of prog indeed is about the obliteration of categories.

Carl Palmer once described Emerson, Lake and Palmer as musician-entertainers. Showmanship, from onstage cannon and daggers in organ keys to rotating drumkits and exploding computers, has always been vital to the ELP phenomenon. Hard as it may be for some of their detractors to believe, an ELP show is fun. Fun! And yet the show's primary focus is always the music. It is compelling music, dramatic and theatrical in its implications. Even without the stage presentation it would conjure intense visions and strong emotions in the audience. In their playing and singing, these three forceful and individualistic musicians, improbably united for a while by some indefinable magic to play as a band, beckon the listener to follow them into a new and colourful world of music, full of possibilities. They speak with passion, urgency and assurance. Their musical call demands a response one way or the other, and it does indeed inspire depth of commitment in some and angry rejection in others. And when the band stops playing, the show's not over. The music lives on in the hearts and minds of those who have heard it. The music is the life of the show. It makes us feel, it makes us think, it makes us want to play the music ourselves, and to discover worlds yet unexplored.

So read on. This is one band worth knowing a lot more about. But remember, this book is just a pointer – to the show that never ends.

CHAPTER 1

From Birth To Big Time

I KEITH EMERSON

Keith Emerson lives for music. If some guy he really respected, like Andre Previn. was to compliment him on his music, that would mean more to Keith than selling a million records. He's your original loner, introspective and unpredictable, and I suspect he's only comfortable with other musicians. Keith Altham, former ELP PR

Keith Emerson has given generously of himself and his music in the cause of British rock. He has been a pioneer, a catalyst and an influence. Above all he has been one of the best entertainers, ready to drain himself of energy for public and personal satisfaction." Chris Welch, "The Legends: Keith Emerson"

Keith Noel Emerson was a war baby, born in the North of England on November 2, 1944. His parents, Noel and a then-pregnant Dorothy, had fled to the small Lancashire town of Todmorden, fearing a German invasion of the South Coast. As it turned out, young Keith was in no danger. The house of his birth, however, did not survive for long, eventually making way for a new road. He knows little of his early months except that his parents' house in Todmorden had a canal running at the bottom of the garden, and the outside toilet round the back seemed miles away.

In March 1945 when Keith was barely five months old, his family returned to the South Coast, settling in the quiet but popular resort town of Worthing in Sussex. His parents' new home was comfortable, worry-free and middle-class. An only child, he led an unusually cocooned life, in a convivial family environment.

It was in this family atmosphere that Keith received his first musical education and he continues to acknowledge his indebtedness to his parents for this. Not only were his father – who had played in dance bands while serving in the British Army – and mother, both keen amateur musicians, but his grandmother was a piano teacher.

Keith's earliest memories relate to family musical gatherings, where his father would play piano-accordion and various friends would fill in on other instruments. Keith remembers going to sleep to the muffled sounds of the get-together seeping up to his bedroom above.

Keith also vividly remembers the arrival of the first piano in his home. He used to watch in awe as his father played – particularly impressed by Emerson senior's ability to play by ear. When no one was around the young Keith used to tinker away at the keys, but it never occurred to him that one day he would master the instrument. He was so small then that his feet could not reach the pedals, and his father had to build them up for him. By the time he was eight, after about ten months of getting by playing tunes and improvising on his own, he was asked by his father if he would like lessons. Perhaps influenced by his father's strong regret at being musically unschooled, Keith jumped at the chance.

"The idea appealed to me," he later explained, "And the following Saturday a local piano teacher, Miss Marchall – she was 80 years old! – came round, and rammed all kinds of rules and regulations down my throat – like scales. I took a dislike to it at first, but I kept at it… It was something you had to do – half an hour [of] piano practice and then you were allowed out to play. I can't say I really enjoyed doing it, but those were the conditions which were laid down."

Keith got through about five local Worthing piano teachers in quick succession. At school he continued his music lessons, but even at such an early age he grew increasingly bored with the discipline of playing scales. He felt his own personality was being submerged under convention. The exhortations to "play it as Bach did" were taking their toll. The lack of room for improvisation was frustrating. He realised that if he carried on much longer, as far as the piano went, he was going to turn into somebody else. It wasn't long before he was writing his own pieces.

Not having a record player meant the only music the young Keith was exposed to was from the radio and his father. At that stage his father was playing piano in a small dance band using a stride technique influenced by people like Fats Waller. At home, when the family gathered around the radio, his father would draw Keith's attention to particular pieces and players, for example, interjecting half way through an Art Tatum song, "*This is incredible!*". Naturally Keith took all of this in.

At the age of ten Keith went through a brief skiffle phase, when someone bought him a guitar for Christmas. He rushed out and bought a Ken Colyer album featuring "This Train" and "John Henry". But from the start, he felt limited by the guitar. He could only manage a few chords and he so longed to hear the melody that he reverted to piano.

Spurred on by his tutors, it wasn't long before Keith was entering piano competitions, though with very mixed feelings. "I was about ten when I did the first one," he recalled. "You have thirty contestants and they all play the same piece of music. I remember my teacher said, 'You're number twelve, and you're going to hear eleven people play the same piece of music in a different way, but ignore them, just play it the way you've been taught.' You sat down and played before an adjudicator, and then when you finished he told you what you did wrong. I did rather well, though, coming in third in the Bach category in the first year and second the next year. The following year I went in for sight reading but didn't fare very well, because they put you in a room at the back of the stage, and bring you out and you're meant to play this piece of music that you've never seen in your life before."

Considering the presence of a large audience and a 'concert hall' atmosphere, it was a very nerve-racking experience for a youngster. But, even though Keith didn't warm to this concept, and wasn't especially enamoured with the classics at the time, he was shrewd enough to enjoy the healthy sense of competition.

As his talent began to blossom and he consistently passed his music grade exams to a high standard, Keith's piano teacher suggested he complete his studies in London. Keith however was reluctant to leave home. At the tender age of fourteen, he even turned down a golden opportunity to study at London's Royal Academy, because he had led such an insulated existence he was scared to cut off his roots. Instead he remained at school, amusing himself playing things like Russ Conway's 1959 Number One single "Side-Saddle" for his friends, and having fun at morning assembly playing organ during hymns and racing the choir to see who could finish first!

When Keith got to school-leaving age, to avoid getting a proper day job, he briefly attended the local college of further education. Music remained his main interest though, and in the free study period he used to go to the common room and play piano for the girls. When the principal got to hear of this, he had Keith expelled, though after apologies were proffered, he agreed to give him another chance.

By this time Keith had stopped having formal lessons and found himself gravitating to jazz piano. Before long he was playing his first gig at a rifle club dinner for the princely sum of one pound. Another useful exercise was playing accompaniment at his aunt's dancing school. This introduced him to a lot of different types of music and got him used to switching style or tempo at the drop of a hat.

Unusually for an adolescent in the late 50s and early 60s, Keith was not really interested in rock and roll music, though he did sometimes listen to boogie-woogie and country pianists such as Jerry Lee Lewis and Floyd Cramer. "People like Roy Orbison and Cliff Richard were making the hit parade at that time," Keith explains. "I had the attitude that I was really a jazz purist. I thought that pop music was OK, but that it had no musical value. Jerry Lee and Little Richard didn't pass me by, because I dug their piano playing, but people like Cliff and Elvis did."

Though later Keith got interested in pop music through the likes of Georgie Fame and The Animals, for now jazz remained his main passion. He began listening closely to jazz records, playing them repeatedly until he could work out the music.

The seeds of his love of rearranging the classics can be discerned in his fondness during this period for improvising with classical melodies around jazz rhythms. He had great fun taking Tchaikovsky or Bach and messing about with it. He also found Brubeck and Shearing particularly helpful, and Floyd Cramer's "On The Rebound"[1] was a major influence. Playing Debussy, often recommended by classical teachers as a way in to jazz, never inspired him.

"And then there were various jazz players," Keith recalls. "Dudley Moore was one of them. He had a TV show. At the time I was playing stride piano because I'd bought some Art Tatum and Fats Waller sheet music. And suddenly I heard Dudley Moore. He played this style that sounded great. I couldn't figure out how he was doing it. When I came to imitate him it came out like Fats Waller – or Russ Conway – in the left hand and Dudley Moore in the right." It was at this point that Keith began to appreciate the advantages of having a bass player. Before this he would play gigs with drums as his only accompaniment, because he thought bass players were only getting in the way of his left hand.

Andre Previn's jazz version of *My Fair Lady* was the next record to really impress Keith. He gradually worked out the arrangement from repeated listenings. This knack of picking things up by ear would pay dividends when Keith joined a local swing band run by Worthing Council. They used to perform Count Basie, Benny Goodman and Duke Ellington arrangements, among others.

Keith's fellow swing musicians directed him to the sort of keyboard players that he should have been listening to. Playing Hampton Hawes and Oscar Peterson gave him the confidence to form a breakaway trio with the drummer and the bass player that he named The Keith Emerson Trio.

The Trio initially performed at wedding receptions and small parties. Once Emerson had learned to read chord charts with confidence, they began to perform at larger occasions and in clubs, playing standards and current chart hits. However, the three musicians were convinced of the superiority of jazz, and included a few of their own favourite pieces in their sets. But soon they started to lose gigs as people were put off by what they saw as self-indulgent jams.

Keith found he could enjoy more musical freedom playing at sleazy Brighton dives packed with drunken sailors. He sat in with a variety of combos, such as an R&B band playing Memphis Slim and Otis Redding material and a rock band called the Black Aces which played pop hits. When the audience demanded the latest pop music he took great delight in improvising around the basic tunes. A number of other musicians used to sit in on these bar sessions, including on one occasion drummer Brian Walkeley, who played with an R&B band called the T-Bones[2], whose path Keith would later cross again. Such varied work would influence Keith's eclectic "mixed-media"[3] experiments for years to come.

While all this was happening Keith managed to hold down a day job in a bank. Although he hated it, it required minimal qualifications and had the advantage of a five o' clock finish and so didn't interfere with his more important nocturnal routine. He managed to stick with the job for two years till the manager grew tired of Keith showing up for work bleary-eyed from the previous late night bar gig.

During this Brighton period Keith began to experiment with his first electronic keyboards – though this was initially down to practical considerations. He simply got tired of playing house pianos with the hammers broken off and started to save frantically for an organ. Moreover, he was much impressed by Jimmy Smith's organ playing on "Walk On The Wild Side".

"Organs were generally expensive," Keith recalls, "although I did come across a Bird[4] organ with built-in speakers at each side of the keyboard – it looked like it was made from a Cornflakes packet! So I started saving for this instrument because it did seem quite reasonable and went off [with my father] to the Portsmouth Organ Centre[5] to buy it... When we got there we were actually shown another organ, a Hammond[6], and after trying it we both agreed it was a much better buy. My father chipped in the rest of the money – so that was how I got my Hammond L100. I got a Bedford van to do the gigs and used to play Bingo halls, 'Tico Tico'[7] and all that sort of rubbish," he laughs. "The amplification was a problem too – the amp/speaker system inside the L100 was just not enough. My father[8] got hold of an old amplifier and we fitted this into the back of the instrument. The sound still wasn't very clean and at the time I didn't even know about Leslie[9] rotating speakers."

Keith's next band was called John Brown's Bodies and used to play at the Starlight Rooms in Brighton. At one of these shows, his old acquaintance Brian Walkeley was in the audience, and on the strength of the gig invited Keith to join the T-Bones[10]. Their lead singer was Gary Farr [son of Tommy Farr, the retired top rank boxer]. Keith has since tried singing[11] but admits that he sounds "awful except when drunk".

The T-Bones enjoyed some success playing one of the Windsor Jazz Festivals and a residency at the Marquee Club in London. "After our Friday gigs at the Marquee... we'd get back to my house at 4 a.m. and try very quietly to sneak the Hammond in!" Emerson recalls fondly. "Half the time we were drunk and all putting our fingers to our mouths and going 'shhh'."

By this time though, Keith had already realised that the T-Bones' purist strain of rhythm and blues was in decline. When the band's manager tried to turn the T-Bones into something more like The Who, Keith could see the crunch coming – even though they notched up one hit single in "One More Chance". Soon after, he left to play organ for another purist blues band, the V.I.P.s.[12]

Natives of Carlisle, The V.I.P's were praised by fellow Northerner Eric Burdon of the Animals. Formed in 1964, they suffered from several label moves and two name changes in their early days (from the V.I.P.s to the Vipps and back again). When Emerson was in the group it consisted of Mike Harrison (vocals, harmonica), Luther Grosvenor (guitar), Mike Kellie (drums) and Keith on organ.

The V.I.P.s spent four shambolic months "looning" – to use Keith's term – around Germany and the south of France, sleeping in the van and generally roughing it. Keith took quite a bit of stick from the rest of the band because he wouldn't partake with as much gusto in the seedier side of rock and roll life.

Even though Keith quickly realised this band wasn't "the one", the roots of his later flamboyant stage act can be found in these early days.

"I remember one occasion when we carried on playing a concert while a fight took place in the hall," he recalls fondly. "That was the first time I got into doing a lot of nonsense with the organ – making crashing and exploding noises, and leaping and jumping around everywhere! The rest of the group said that was great and I'd have to do it again, so when I got back to England I tried it at our next gig and everybody looked at me in utter amazement! However, it formulated a kind of stage act which ended up with me playing the instrument back to front."

The other main source of inspiration for Keith's stage act was an L-100 organ player called Don Shinn [13]. "He was a weird looking guy, really strange," Keith recalls. "He had a schoolboy's cap on, round spectacles, really stupid. I just happened to be in [The Marquee] when he was playing…. The audience … were all in hysterics. Giggling and laughing at him. No-one was taking him seriously. And I said, 'Who is this guy?' He'd been drinking whisky out of a teaspoon and all kinds of ridiculous things. He'd played an arrangement of the Grieg Concerto, the Brandenburg [14] and all. So my ears perked up. Somebody else was doing these things. Playing it really well, and he got a fantastic sound from the L-100. But halfway through he sort of shook the L-100, and the back of it dropped off. Then he got out a screwdriver and started making adjustments while he was playing. Everyone was roaring their heads off laughing. So I looked and said, 'Hang on a minute! That guy has got something.' He and Hendrix were controlling influences over the way I developed the stage act side of things."

The organ was essentially an unfashionable instrument back in the mid-60s, even with Georgie Fame and Graham Bond garnering respect for it. The L-100 looked like a piece of furniture. The fact that the organist usually played sitting down contributed to the instrument's staid image. Keith set out to try and change people's perceptions and one of his first initiatives in this regard was to play standing up! Seeing Don Shinn gave Keith the inspiration to build playing keyboard into a stage act and the V.I.P.'s would give him the chance to develop it.

19

In the meantime, Keith was living in a small room in London where pigeons clattered over his head. He was so hungry he used to raid the gas meter – until he was caught and thrown out. Fortunately, a major improvement in his circumstances was not far around the corner.

The V.I.P.s were not well known at home but they built quite a following on the continent. It was Keith's first taste of being mobbed on stage, and he loved it. He had a further taste of the success to come when the V.I.P.s had an overseas hit with "I Wanna Be Free", on Island Records. The V.I.P.s had become the Island label's first non-Jamaican signing. (Emerson, Lake and Palmer would later appear on the same label.) There would be one other non-UK V.I.P.s single, "Straight Down To The Bottom".

Keith's parents were not impressed with their son's progress, fearing he was embarking on an insecure career – full of loose women and drugs! For Keith however, playing with the band was a revelation. "With the V.I.P.s I had direct contact with life for the first time," he would reflect. "I suppose you could say I was a pretty slow developer!"

Around this time, one of the V.I.P.s' roadies told Keith that Immediate Records' R&B recording artist, Pat "P.P." Arnold [15] was looking for backing musicians to tour in support of her recent batch of chart hits. Emerson promptly returned to England.

Immediate's A&R personnel trawled Soho's bars and rehearsal studios to find suitable musicians to back their singing star. The first to be signed up was Emerson's old T-Bones colleague, Lee Jackson, on bass and vocals [16]. A tough Geordie, with long swept-back hair and a heavy moustache, Lee was born Keith Jackson. He dispensed with his Christian name "due to a surfeit of people called Keith in groups." He acquired his new moniker because of his resemblance to the American Civil War soldier, General Robert E. Lee. In addition to his spell in the T-Bones, Jackson had paid his dues in the North of England and Germany with groups such as the Invaders and the Vandykes, where he'd become as adept at clouting over-enthusiastic fans with mike stands as at playing bass guitar. Jackson was instrumental in recruiting Emerson, and the two ex-T-Bones set about putting together a band for Arnold that would later become known as The Nice. Their first port of call was David O'List [17].

Londoner O'List was a classically trained trumpet player who had picked up the guitar after hearing the Rolling Stones' first album. He joined blues and soul based outfit The Attack on guitar after jamming with them on trumpet. They released a version of "Hi-Ho Silver Lining", and while it was Jeff Beck who had a hit with the song, O'List's fine guitar solo on the B-side track, "Any More Than I Do", made an immediate impression, and would be used by John Peel as the signature tune on his show *The Perfumed Garden*.

When Emerson approached O'List, The Attack had just broken up. The guitarist turned down an invite from John Mayall to replace Peter Green in the Bluesbreakers in order to join The Nice.

Chris Welch[18], a rock journalist who came to be closely associated with both The Nice and Emerson, Lake and Palmer, remembers going over to his friend O'List's home off the Earls Court Road one Saturday afternoon.

"I heard the sound of Dave Brubeck's 'Take Five', played with dazzling flair," Welch says. "As everybody was penniless and I had a car, we went for a drink at the Boathouse at Kew. Whilst supplying Keith and Dave with pints of lager, the first plans for a new group were laid."

As well as O'List, Keith recruited Ian Hague[19] on drums – Welch had sat in on drums during rehearsals but now gave way to the professionals. The band made one of their first appearances with Pat Arnold in the upstairs bar at the White Hart in Acton, West London. The initial gigs went well, though Hague was quickly replaced by Brian "Blinky" Davison [20], formerly of the Mark Leeman Five, who had also previously played with O'List as well as with Don Shinn, who had been such a strong early influence on Emerson. With Davison on board, the band soon developed their own sound and identity.

"Suddenly all the things that I'd accumulated came to the surface," Keith recalls. "At rehearsals I'd always played classical and jazz piano, just messing around, and everyone said, 'Why don't you do that on stage?' I thought they were joking. Then I realised I didn't have anything to lose..."

It was decided that the band would go on first and play a half-hour set on their own and then P.P. Arnold would come on and they would provide backing for her set. This continued for about six months, though sometimes P.P. didn't actually turn up for gigs, and this served only to reinforce the band's separate identity, showing them that they were a force on their own. All they needed now was to cultivate a fan base.

While backing P.P., Keith and co would play soul material like "Respect", "Sweet Soul Music" and "You Keep Me Hanging On". Numbers in their own spot included "A Day In The Life", "Billy's Bag" and "A Fistful Of Dollars" (These three numbers were all later recorded in sessions for John Peel's *Top Gear* programme on the then new Radio 1 pop station. Sadly the original recordings of those particular numbers no longer survive, but recently the BBC sessions did emerge on a CD which included a whole host of gems.)

Tony Stratton-Smith would become the band's manager from April 1968. Stratton-Smith was a former sportswriter who discovered Paddy, Klaus and Gibson – the band that brought Klaus Voorman to public notice – and would go on to found Charisma Records[21]. He recalled that during the early days of The Nice, "Keith would be hiding at the back of the stage, right in the shadows and behind his

Hammond. Hardly anyone saw him, but he had ideas, and gradually The Nice's part of the show became longer and longer." Miss Arnold permitted this; it eventually led to The Nice, spearheaded by Emerson, taking over.

At the 1967 Windsor Jazz Festival, in addition to a slot backing P.P. Arnold on the main stage, The Nice were booked to play their own set in a marquee off to the side. Audience interest was not exactly high. Stratton-Smith estimated the crowd at, "less than a dozen, probably all relatives". Chris Welch believes the initial number to have been even smaller. "In the early days of '67," says Welch, "the fans were more concerned with The Crazy World of Arthur Brown [soon to recruit a young drummer named Carl Palmer], Jimi Hendrix and the Cream. There was not a soul to be seen, apart from three friends, David's sisters and Baz [a roadie]."

Then Keith let off a smoke bomb outside the tent. "The crowd came running in to see what was happening," says Chris, "and found an extraordinary show, with Keith lashing a whip, Pat dancing, and the guitars and drums blasting tunes like 'Flower King Of Flies'. The tent was packed within minutes and the crowd stayed. It was the first time I had seen a group actually in the act of winning its first following in quite such dramatic circumstances." From then on the audiences, and the group, just got bigger. By the time The Nice went on to the main stage to back P.P. Arnold, everybody was shouting for them. One estimate of the audience count for that main gig puts it at about 3,500. Quite a sudden surge in popularity!

Of course it clearly presaged the beginning of the end of Miss Arnold's association with the band, and the Nice duly parted company with her in September 1967. She had been moving in the direction of variety and cabaret, which was very much at odds with the ambitions of the band. Given a contract of their own by P.P.'s label, Immediate Records, The Nice set to work on their first single, an Emerson and O'List composition, "The Thoughts Of Emerlist Davjack" (a composite name based on the members of the band). Label boss and notorious svengali Andrew Loog Oldham [22] had great faith that the band would deliver something special and insisted they work only on self-composed material. Oldham had discovered the Rolling Stones and managed their rise to the top, including their transition from blues covers to self-penned classics, so his opinion was worth listening to. Still, Immediate was run on unconventional business principles and Oldham was someone to be wary of. "If you're not prepared to be fucked," he opined, "find another business. I'm all for Art and Treachery, treachery against 90 percent of the cake. It turns me on."

"The Thoughts Of Emerlist Davjack" announced the group's arrival on the chart scene with a flourish. Though edited down from its original four and a half minute duration, it was a brilliant tour de force contrasting a vocal chorus fanfare with a slower verse on the theme of nostalgia for lost youth. There was also a short middle section featuring Keith on a slow church organ solo. The single got rave reviews on its release in November but failed to make much of a dent on a chart dominated by popular vocalists like Vince Hill and Ken Dodd.

By this time the band had finished recording their debut album, also titled *The Thoughts Of Emerlist Davjack*, at Olympic Studios in Barnes, with Rolling Stones engineer Glyn Johns. When it was all over someone scrawled on an acetate of the LP, "Nice – very".

Next, the band set off on a breakthrough autumn UK tour with Jimi Hendrix, The Pink Floyd and The Move. The Nice were consistently well-received throughout the tour and Hendrix was quoted as saying afterwards that "The Nice were my favourite group of the tour. Their sound is ridiculously good, original, free – more funky than West Coast".

Hendrix and Emerson soon became good friends and Keith recalls the guitar virtuoso very fondly: "[Jimi] had bought himself a home movie camera, and whenever we were playing I'd see him looking between the amps, filming. He was always there. He loved the act. When he'd gotten his films developed there was hysterical laughter coming from his dressing room. I poked my head around the corner to see what all the laughter was about, and they were running the film of me doing the bit with the organs. They were speeding up the film and running it backwards – it was all completely stupid. Hendrix was great."

Even in these early days with The Nice, Emerson began to be hailed as 'the Jimi Hendrix of the organ', a phrase which, though lazy, did reflect the high esteem in which his virtuosity and showmanship were held.

The UK trek with Hendrix was quickly followed in January 1968 by The Nice's first American tour, which was initially scheduled to last three weeks, but was extended to five due to its overwhelming success. After they returned to Britain, March 1 saw the release at last of their first LP. *The Thoughts Of Emerlist Davjack* included their most popular stage numbers, along with some more experimental ideas. This groundbreaking album would exert a major influence on the flood of European heavy rock and progressive bands that would emerge in the 1970s.

June saw the release of The Nice's second single, "America", a powerful rocked-up version of the show-stopping number from Leonard Bernstein and Stephen Sondheim's *West Side Story*. The Nice's version also incorporated a substantial portion of the fourth movement of Dvorak's *New World Symphony*, a fact sometimes obscured by the controversy surrounding the use of the Bernstein piece.

Clocking in at over six minutes (though stopping short of the 7 minutes, 20 seconds claimed in promotional material) "America" was then probably the longest single ever released. Opening with portentous organ and choir, backed by the sounds of perverse shrieks and whipcracks, it ended with P.P. Arnold's young daughter uttering the immortal indictment, "America is pregnant with promise and anticipation, but is murdered by the hand of the inevitable".

The single owed much of its success to the fact that it tapped into the violence and neurosis of the period. 1968 was a year of disturbance throughout the world, not just in America. In May, angry riots had broken out across Paris, leading to the downfall of the Gaullist government. The United States' own recent crises were referred to in the single's publicity material. The main promotional photograph featured the group holding three small children in their arms, the infants' faces having been replaced by those of the three great recently assassinated voices of political change: Martin Luther King, President John F Kennedy and his brother Robert. Both King and Robert Kennedy had been murdered in 1968.

Conspiracy theories abounded in the wake of the convenient removal of the very men who, by standing for liberalism and change, had posed such a threat to the conservative status quo. Furthermore, the United States of this era was a nation torn apart by race riots and an unwanted war in Vietnam. Against this charged backdrop, The Nice's savage version of "America" and their incendiary live performance of it must have seemed anarchic and threatening to the Establishment. Certainly the band aroused the wrath of the song's co-composer, Leonard Bernstein, who saw The Nice's take on his tune as a desecration – which to some extent was what was intended. Bernstein used his influence to prevent the release of "America" as a single in the US – though in later years he and Emerson became friends.

The Nice's arrangement of "America" was also responsible for the birth of one of Keith Emerson's distinctive live trademarks. "In 'America'," he explained, "I wanted to hold down two notes and sustain a fifth while I was playing another organ. I started out by using pegs, just wooden things to hold down the keys. Then I thought I could do the same thing with knives, and if I'm playing 'America' … then the knives have a definite part in it, being connected with the film and the gang fights. So I thought, yes, it has a place here; and then I used to take the knives out of the keyboard and throw them on the floor; and then probably one night I decided to throw them at the cabinets."

Tony Stratton-Smith felt that such flamboyant Hendrix-like showmanship had also grown out of Emerson's initial worries about the band's post P.P. Arnold career. "Keith, I suppose, got nervous and worried about the music holding up by itself," he reflected. "He decided that somebody had to do something and this was where the quiet side of Keith Emerson disappeared."

Amidst all the "America" controversy, The Nice were engaged to appear with a host of other artists and entertainers at a Royal Albert Hall, charity concert named 'Come Back Africa', put on "in aid of the International Defence and Aid Fund to commemorate Human Rights Year and South Africa Freedom Day". Organised by the renowned anti-apartheid campaigner Canon John Collins, the concert was opened by the Chairman of the United Nations Special Committee on Apartheid, and attended by a vast number of US celebrities, dignitaries and statesmen. Also on the bill were Marlon Brando, John Dankworth and Cleo Laine, Julie Driscoll, Brian Auger and the Trinity, Julie Felix, Igor and Natalia Oistrakh, Fou Ts'ong, John Williams and many others. It could hardly have been a more high-profile event.

Aware that Keith Emerson was planning to burn a replica Stars and Stripes on stage during "America", and concerned with effect this might have on the US contingent present, the Hall's manager, Frank Mundy, specifically asked the group not to perform the song. Tony Stratton-Smith also counselled the band against a 'flag burning' gesture, but their hype-loving label boss Andrew Oldham, scenting some publicity-generating controversy, brought a bottle of Scotch whisky to the band's dressing room and helped persuade them to go ahead regardless.

"We did the concert as a protest," says Emerson. "We were the only rock band in the show and we showed our protest by burning a painting of the American flag. The sounds of the guitar and the drums were crashing all around us from the speakers, and after I finished drawing the flag, I lit it on fire as a sign of protest. This did not go over well at all with the audience,… There was no applause at the end of the number, and a great many of them walked out."

As Emerson alludes above, amidst all the furore, it passed unnoticed that rather than burning the American flag, he only actually set light to a painting of it.

"Well no, this is one of the great myths of rock music," Tony Stratton-Smith explained. "…All [Keith] did was in fact spray on American style images on to this piece of canvas, including some red stripes and this sort of thing, but it wasn't an American flag as such. If it had been we may not have got off as lightly as we did with the American Embassy subsequently when we wanted to go to America. Now the whole purpose of that was that the band was upset, as I suppose most people were, at the assassination of Robert Kennedy, and so during their version of 'America' they wanted to make this gesture that America was just crumbling under violence, the fire of it all, and it was a purely symbolic thing, really to do."

The gesture was perceived as insulting and anarchic, and as a result, The Nice were banned from ever playing the Royal Albert Hall again – not a great concern for Emerson who later dismissed the famous venue as "a bad place acoustically". However, the attendant publicity helped push the single to number 21; it would remain on the chart for fifteen weeks. The band saw the benefits of the controversy even earlier, when the day after the Royal Albert Hall concert, they were booked into a smaller club in Norfolk. On arrival, they were greeted by the sight of a huge line of people waiting at the club. They wondered who else was in town that night, but to their amazement, it turned out that the people were queuing for them, having heard about the flag incident. This was a major lesson for the band: things can change very fast in show business.

Although the 'flag-burning', more than any other factor, was responsible for The Nice's rapid rise, Emerson soon dropped it from the act, concerned that the spectacle was assuming a greater importance in the public's conception of the group than the music. Certainly, The Nice's sound was radical and revolutionary in itself. "We were playing totally new music," Emerson explains, "Something that didn't fit any style. That was the most exciting thing about playing with The Nice. Nobody else did our blend of classical, rock and jazz." However, in a concert situation, the music alone would never be enough for the keyboard player. If the flag burning was gone, the histrionics with the organ remained – wrestling with and leaping over the organ, sticking knives between the keys, playing it from behind. Emerson would also later bring back the paint-spraying during performances of "Rondo" during ELP's 1992 tour.

"It's a natural instinct for me to perform this way on stage," Emerson has reflected. "The music is very important, but the music can only take you to certain heights. After that it's like trying to achieve the 'Diamond Hard Blue Apples Of The Moon', or whatever. You don't know quite what it is, but whatever it is you can't grasp it through music alone. You have to go one stage further, and my complete climax comes through violence. It's through exercising this violence on stage that I can be so subdued off stage."

With their first hit single under their belt, the rest of '68 saw The Nice touring incessantly. The new stage act revolved around "Rondo" – based on Dave Brubeck's Mozartian jazz hit "Blue Rondo a la Turk", and destined to become Emerson's trademark – "America", "Little Arabella", and a new magnum opus, a suite called "Ars Longa Vita Brevis". After a tour of Britain and Europe and a Marquee residency that broke the legendary venue's previous box office records, The Nice spent much of the autumn in America. However, not all these dates went as smoothly. They had a particularly tough time at Los Angeles' legendary Whisky-A-Go-Go, where all the kids seemed to be trying for a smooth Hollywood-type image and were only interested in whether the band could do Beatles numbers. Emerson got so angry he kicked the organ off the stage!

The US tour was most gruelling, however, for David O'List, who reacted poorly to the proliferation of hallucinogenic drugs the band encountered, and found a creeping depression affecting his guitar playing. However, O'List didn't find this a huge problem at the time, so it was a great shock for him when Emerson asked him to leave. Apparently Emerson was concerned that O'List was getting all the limelight and that O'List's Marshall stack was drowning him out. Emerson also claimed that O'List was trying too hard to be a great guitarist and lacked the ability. Since it was

Emerson who had brought The Nice its notoriety and who, even on the evidence of the first album, was its chief creative force, it is hardly surprising that a conflict between the two musicians would see Emerson triumphing.

David's departure divided opinion between those who wanted the original band to continue and ardent Emerson supporters. Whispers of "betrayal" could be heard. Those in the O'List camp feared that the absence of creative conflict would have an adverse affect on The Nice, and that the music world had been deprived of a budding star. The pro-Emerson faction, leaped to the support of their showman-virtuoso hero, claiming that Emerson might have been held back by the presence in the band of another strong composing talent. While there was something to be said for both these views, it would be difficult to begrudge Emerson his desire to give himself as much room as possible to communicate his unique musical vision.

"David was very young and insecure," Emerson concluded in 1971. "It got to him. He thought he was just sounding like Hendrix or Clapton or anybody else, but he desperately wanted to sound like Larry Coryell. He practised a hell of a lot, but he just didn't have the technique. You could just see him frustrated. He began to pull a lot of moodies, like once in Croydon he just didn't show up for a gig. People said we sounded better as a three-piece, so that's the way it went."

O'List was subsequently invited by Ian Anderson to replace Mick Abrahams in Jethro Tull. Unfortunately the rehearsals didn't work out and he spent a number of years in the musical wilderness. O'List took the leaving of The Nice hard and would blame a conspiracy between Jackson, Emerson and Stratton-Smith for his ousting, claiming that he never received his full credit for his part in the Nice's success. "After I left The Nice I went through a depression fit that lasted for ages and ages," he reflected in 1973. "I couldn't write or even play the guitar. I left without any money or equipment. I just didn't know what to do, you see, I wasn't expecting it. I missed a lot of opportunities. It was all because of ill-health and depression. I even broke up my friendship with Keith because I thought he wasn't friends with me any more." At one point O'List even ended up working in a belt factory. Things did pick up for him, though, and he went on to work with a wide variety of artists, including Bryan Ferry and Roxy Music, John Cale and Nik Turner, but never again would he enjoy success on a par with his time in The Nice. [23]

Whatever one's view of the circumstances of O'List's departure, one thing is certain – Emerson saw that his time had come, and seized the opportunity. Was he being ironic when, interviewed before the split, he described himself as the "referee" of the group, trying to calm any grievances? Was he being disingenuous when he said, "I can't understand people who tread on spiders for no reason. They must get carried away with their power"? These are muddy waters, but it is clear that Emerson's self-confessed early difficulty in expressing himself outside of music goes a long way to explaining any apparent contradictions in his statements about relationships and aggression.

With O'List out of the picture, Emerson immediately began looking for a replacement. "The only [guitarist] that I really wanted to work with ... was Steve Howe," said Emerson. "He came and auditioned and was very talented. We begged him to join. He hummed and hawed at that. The first day he said yes, but then he said he couldn't refuse an offer to start his own band... [Then] he disappeared for two or three years. Next thing I heard, he was playing in Yes." Disillusioned, Emerson determined to get used to working without guitarists. After Howe, an American guitarist, Gordon Longstaff [24], was tipped as O'List's successor – and a picture even appeared of him recording with the band at Pye's studio – but the following week it was announced that The Nice would stay a trio.

The second Nice album, *Ars Longa, Vita Brevis*, strongly featured Keith Emerson's interest in classical music. Alongside a few groovy psychedelic numbers – one of which, "Little Arabella", ranks among the best short songs that Emerson has been involved in – there was a nine-minute arrangement for group and orchestra of the Intermezzo from Sibelius' "Karelia Suite" and the side-long title piece, which included as its third 'movement' an arrangement for group and orchestra of the last movement of Bach's third Brandenburg Concerto. The first movement was in fact an excellent drum solo, and the second, "Realisation", gave Keith a chance to stretch out on driving, jazzy piano with an ostinato bass.

Though not as big a success as their first album, *Ars Longa...* helped establish the group in both Europe and America. This accomplished, they took a more conventional approach for their third album, *Nice*, in 1969.

Nice opens with "Azrael Revisited", an updated and extended take on "Azrael", the B-side of the band's first single, which clearly demonstrates Emerson's confidence in his new direction for the group's music. Whereas the earlier version, with O'List's guitar, had been heavy psychedelic bad-trip stuff, this was slightly quicker, more precisely played, and featured an interesting interplay between Emerson's detuned piano and Jackson's warm, jazzy bass. In the middle of this passage, Emerson cleverly takes the bass line and turns it into his favourite ostinato device, improvising on top, with Jackson eventually coming in on scat vocals. The subsequent three tracks all featured substantial jazz-like improvisational sections. Side Two comprised two tracks recorded live at New York's Fillmore East: "Rondo 69", by now a very familiar crowd-pleaser, and Bob Dylan's "She Belongs To Me" here used as a vehicle for a brilliant and humorous instrumental tour de force, on which the whole band pulls out all the stops. Massive crescendos are subverted by sudden lulls, and Emerson throws in witty musical references throughout.

Yet in the end the impression is very definitely left that by now The Nice, though far from a one-man band, is mainly one man's band. It is becoming increasingly obvious that Jackson's vocal range is limited and O'List is certainly missed. While *Nice* is artistically superior to *Ars Longa*, the album was again less commercially successful than the first one.

Undeterred, Emerson began working with the American composer and conductor Joseph Eger on "mixed media" projects aimed at merging orchestra and group together. It would mark the beginning of The Nice's most ambitious and experimental period. The Nice would perform new material in conjunction with Eger's 40 piece orchestra, The Sinfonia of London. Often it was a case of musical competition rather than integration, with band and orchestra mostly playing alternate passages. While these experiments did not always work, the concerts were never less than exciting.

One of the first of these collaborations involved a piece Emerson was commissioned to write for the Newcastle-on-Tyne Arts Festival of 1969 – "Five Bridges Suite" for which Newcastle-born-and-bred Jackson wrote and sang some lyrics about his home city. "I got inspired flying up to Newcastle by the noise of the engines," Emerson later explained, "so I wrote the first five bars on the back of an airsick bag." While the piece has been adversely criticised, it actually contained some of Emerson's most rhapsodic and lyrical writing, and one of the best pieces he has ever composed for solo piano, the High Level Fugue. The recording made available to the public on the *Five Bridges* album showed that the audience was pretty impressed too.

"It was the highlight of The Nice for me because it took such a lot of hard work," Emerson later reflected. "Looking back on it, it was an impossible feat. I wrote and scored it in a week for orchestra. It was one of those totally inspired occasions when I'd get up at nine o'clock in the morning and I'd write constantly until three in the morning every day."

It would represent The Nice's last great flourish of creativity, for the band split up in April, 1970. "It got to a point where it was just me..." Emerson told American magazine *Crawdaddy* the following year. "That could be cool for somebody's ego, but .... I like to feel that other people are working and sometimes I like to feel that I can play with them or play behind them if necessary. With a band like The Nice you get to a point where you think, Well, I've done this, what the devil do I do now?, and you realise that you're on your own, you can't go to somebody and say, 'Look, I don't know what to do next, you got any ideas?'. There was nobody in that band that could help me.

"I think that's basically how The Nice came to work with orchestras, because we were working together and playing music, and each time we did something I felt we were going to do something new, and we can't do it with this band, so let's get somebody in to play with us... Then after working with orchestras I was left with one decision: to fall back on the original format of a three man band, but there was nothing there that could inspire me, nothing new, nothing fresh. We tried it, we discussed the problem, we tried to make it work again, but you just couldn't get away from the fact that it was just the same, and I had to work with more inventive people."

The Nice played their last show at the Berlin Sportspalast on March 30, 1970. As at the time of David O'List's departure, the split was not entirely amicable. Jackson, for one, had at least seen it coming, "I had a premonition in America when I walked into a club and Keith and some other musicians were all in a huddle in the corner," he explains. Davison was initially philosophical: "Keith wanted to move on and that was OK – we respected him." However, when Davison discovered Emerson was planning another trio "rehearsing in the same way", he felt let down.

Still, as Lee Jackson admitted: "There was no possibility of us continuing without Keith. When it's over, it's over."

Though sympathetic to his former colleagues, Emerson had made up his mind the previous year that it was time to do something new.

"It is always difficult to make a split, even more difficult to talk about it for print," he explained. "It's like when you split with a girl. If you can still talk together afterwards, well.... As with any relationship each one has to be different. So it is with music. Each new musician gives you a different buzz..."

Apart from compilations, there would be one more Nice album to come, *Elegy*, though it was made up of longer versions of pieces which had either been recorded before or played live. Released in 1971, well after Emerson, Lake and Palmer had got into their stride, it showed off The Nice as a tight vehicle for Emerson's virtuoso talents; it is filled with excellent piano and organ work and shows a confident compositional awareness. Comparison with the earlier versions of the material showed just how much Emerson's ideas had progressed. Fittingly, the final track is a live version of the song that shot them to fame – "America", here performed live at New York's Fillmore East.

Meanwhile, Lee Jackson formed Jackson Heights who went on to release five musically strong albums that failed to sell. Later he teamed up with Davison and Patrick Moraz for one impressive album with the shortlived Nice-replica Refugee. Eventually both Jackson and Davison would leave the music industry, with Jackson going into interior design and Davison becoming a peripatetic music teacher.[25]

Back in 1969, when Emerson had first made his mind up to disband The Nice, he had already started to think about alternative bass players who could sing. When he asked Tony Stratton-Smith who he thought was the best bass player in Britain,

Stratton-Smith suggested Greg Lake, then touring the US with King Crimson. As luck would have it December 10, 1969 saw The Nice and King Crimson on the same bill at San Francisco's Fillmore West. It was a momentous day in the early history of Emerson Lake & Palmer.

II GREG LAKE

The diversity of his styles of playing is almost schizoid. One minute he could be hammering away some powerhouse bass and the next he could be slowly picking a soft, gentle ballad like "Lucky Man". Sounds, *27 July, 1974*

Greg is a large friendly man quick to smile but a sufferer from that malady common to the group – perfectionism. Sounds, *21 May, 1977*

The not-so-secret weapon of the band is still guitarist and singer Greg Lake. Lake is a fine bass player, underrated guitarist and writer of some of the bands less pompous material. Boni Anthony Johnson, music journalist February, 1992

Gregory Stuart Lake was born on 10 November, 1947 in the kind of draughty asbestos pre-fabricated building constructed in response to the massive post World War Two housing shortage. It was a humble upbringing, and it would leave its mark on the young Greg.

His father and mother came from opposite sides of the tracks. "Strange, my father came from a very poor background," Lake explains, "and yet my mother was comparatively well-off. We had two different points of view going. My father's was that I should attain security, and therefore he wanted me to be a draughtsman. He wasn't prepared for me to take a gamble, but my mother [was]. My father was liberal enough to say that it was my life and 'Do what you want to do, but this is my advice'. He accepted it when I told him I was going to be a musician, and they really grafted for me. There were times when I was hungry and they gave me money and sent food parcels."

Lake felt drawn to music from a very early age. He believes pieces he heard at a very early age influenced his musical development, and can still remember hearing one song in particular, 'Charmaine', when he was only about three or four.

His main early musical influence was his mother, who was a pianist. She bought him a second hand guitar and booked him lessons for about a year. However, all he was taught was Bert Weedon's style, when what he really wanted to learn was Hank Marvin's. He also remembers learning old Thirties tunes, and though he wasn't enamoured by them at the time, he can look back and acknowledge how the subtle chord changes in such material helped his technique considerably.

"I don't rate Hank Marvin as a great guitarist," Lake says, reflecting on his early role models, "but he was certainly an influential one. Hendrix listened to him, I can promise you that…. Hendrix was the next guy who did it for me. Obviously the Beatles were an influence on everybody, but they were musically so positive and definite, if you played something from the Beatles it would come out so positively Beatles that you couldn't use it. Also, Cream missed me by a mile, and I think that was because once you'd seen Hendrix you'd seen the thing done properly, if you know what I mean."

In 1963, after a "secondary modern education that was a disaster", Lake took a few non-musical jobs, including some particularly back-breaking lifting work at Poole Harbour, before starting to gig with semi-pro Bournemouth bands, beginning with Unit Four, a group of local schoolboys who played hits by Cliff Richard and The Shadows and The Beatles. Greg was on guitar and vocals, with Dave Jenes also on guitar, Kenny Beveridge on drums and John Dickerson on keyboards. In 1965 Lake and Jenes moved on to form the Timechecks – with Tony Batey on drums and Bev Strike on bass – playing pop covers in beach venues till 1966.

In 1967, as the flower power era dawned, Greg formed The Shame with his old friend and former Unit Four member, John Dickerson. The line-up was completed by Billy Nims on drums and Malcolm Braiser on bass. In September of that year, The Shame released their one and only single, a cover of Janis Ian's "Too Old To Go 'Way Little Girl" backed with a band original, John Dickenson's "Dreams Don't Bother Me". Greg sounds Lennonish on the A-side, and the song itself is rather reminiscent of *Revolver*-era Beatles. It had limited local success in Dorset, but like so many unsung singles of the period it deserved more widespread attention. Indeed, Andy Ellison of contemporary band John's Children, remembers The Shame as "an amazing band".

Next Lake spent a brief stint with The Shy Limbs – along with future King Crimson drummer, Andy McCulloch – supplying, amongst other things, a wonderfully pneumatic bass riff for "Love", the B-side of their first single, "Reputation", in early 1969. Money was short, and The Shy Limbs would rough it from town to town, sleeping in the van and living off hollowed out loaves of bread packed with chips and washed down with a pint of milk. Before long, Lake contracted pneumonia.

"You keep going as long as you can," he explains, "but eventually you become aware that you're more than just ill, you're seriously ill. This was in Carlisle, but the guys didn't want to drive back overnight, so we slept in the van, and it was well below freezing. I woke up blue! When we got home I was nearly dead. I literally fell over and went into a coma. My mother got a doctor and he pumped me full of oxygen and penicillin. That was probably the worst I went through."

By the time The Shy Limbs had released their second and less successful single, "Lady in Black", Greg had departed for pastures new, in this instance The Gods, on bass and lead vocals in the first line-up. Ken Hensley, on keyboards, drummer Lee Kerslake and guitarist Joe Konas made up the rest of the band.

"In The Gods we were making our own [music]," Lake explains, "But [it] was horribly similar to others. It was the first stage for me between playing other people's material and my own. It was a stage of compromise, when you write your own material but you make sure it sounds like somebody else's, not consciously, but it lands up that way." Unintentionally, The Gods' compositions kept turning out remarkably similar to songs by Cream. Pretty soon, Lake was on the move again. The Gods replaced him with John Glascock, later of Jethro Tull, on bass and vocals and released their first album in 1968. In 1970 The Gods played as Toefat with Cliff Bennett, Hensley went on to join Uriah Heep, followed a couple of years later by Kerslake.

By the time Lake left The Gods, he was holding down a day job as a draughtsman. He knew he didn't want to spend the rest of his life doing anything as regimented and realised that his only alternative was music. Music would have to be his ticket out of the nine to five existence. Fortunately, Lake's first full time band was just around the corner.

Lake had known fellow Dorset musician Robert Fripp for years. When the two first met, Fripp was by far the better known guitarist.

"He started hearing about me and came along to a gig just to check out that I wasn't any competition for him," Lake remembers. The two players kept in touch and shared the same guitar teacher [26] .

"I [had] dabbled on bass with the Gods," says Lake, "But for eleven years I played guitar. When Bob started to form [King Crimson], he needed a bass player because he couldn't find anybody he could play with. So he said to me, 'Would you like to play bass?' I said, 'No, not really', and he said, 'Yeah, but if you don't, we'll never get it off the ground.' So I said, 'OK, I'll play bass for you'."

Fripp's new band had grown out of an earlier trio, Giles, Giles and Fripp, and in addition to Lake, it was to include Ian McDonald on keyboards and Michael Giles on drums, with Pete Sinfield as a non-performing lyricist.

Lake's switch to bass had a dramatic effect on both his guitar technique and his writing. His first instrument with King Crimson was a Fender Jazz bass, which he has always considered one of the best in existence. From the beginning, he used a thin triangular guitar pick, convinced it was the only way that any real speed could be achieved on bass. Hitting bass strings straight on with the pick, gave Lake the ability to strum rapid up-and-down strokes – a major foundation of his technique.

"In a way, I developed a style of playing for myself," he explains. "The thing with fingers is for your 'boom-boom' bass players, people into the Motown type of bass playing. That's a fine style, but I was really looking for something a bit new from a bass guitar…. I tried to get as close as possible to the bottom end of a Steinway piano, as far as the sound goes, and it's upon that that I tried to develop my playing."

King Crimson were unveiled to the public on July 5, 1969, supporting The Rolling Stones at a free concert in London's Hyde Park just after Brian Jones' death. They received a favorable reaction from the crowd – possibly as many as 650,000-strong – and *The Guardian* considered King Crimson to be the only band who made a good impression. A few months later, reviewing their Fillmore East show of November 21st, 1969, US music industry journal *Billboard* painted a compelling portrait of the band: "King Crimson can only be described as a monumental heavy with the majesty – and tragedy – of Hell. Greg Lake, who snaps a cathartic bass guitar to the fore of the music, also sings lead like a hoody choir boy, but with all volume controls open, both his bass line and voice resound like thunder in the night."

Over thirty years on, it's hard to comprehend how disturbing the new phenomenon of high volume in popular music really was. The *Billboard* reporter was particularly fascinated by this aspect of King Crimson's performance: "The group's immense, towering force field, electrified by the energy of their almost frightening intensity, either pinned down patrons or drove them out. Volume is the total affirmation of their music just as no volume is the negation of rock, so threatening the sound barrier is part of their act of harnessing the hell of machines – in this case, amplifiers – gone berserk…. The presence of King Crimson – and it will be very hard to miss them – has made hard rock a little harder."

The first King Crimson album, *In The Court Of The Crimson King*, wouldn't possess half that intense, hellish power, however, without Lake's unusual, compelling Southern English tones. But the first time we hear him, his voice is horribly distorted, in keeping with the barbed-wire lyrics of "Twenty-First Century Schizoid Man". The next track, "I Talk To The Wind", is in the greatest possible contrast, finding Greg in pastoral folkie mood. "Moonchild" reprises this wistful tone, providing relief between "Epitaph" and the title track. Incidentally, the band also rehearsed Lake's "Lucky Man" – later to be made famous by ELP – but dropped it.

In The Court Of The Crimson King is an album of dramatic and carefully judged contrasts, and Lake's sensitive vocals are critical to its success. When the gentle improvisation at the end of "I Talk To The Wind" segues into "Epitaph", Greg's singing beautifully conveys the sense of loneliness and ominous fatalism in Pete Sinfield's lyrics. The whole album has the quality of a dream-nightmare in which Greg plays the role of the dreamer – a lone human voice ultimately yielding to the unstoppable tide of the music. Lake's bass playing is also remarkable, from the busy blast of "Schizoid Man" to the clear, simple lines on the title track.

When the album's title track was released as a single, P.P. Arnold, former front-woman to Lake's future collaborator Keith Emerson, reviewed it for a music paper, commenting presciently, "They remind me of The Nice a bit, but they are not quite as aggressive."

In The Court Of The Crimson King caught the public's imagination and in November 1969, it climbed to Number 5 on the UK album charts. However in spite of this commercial and creative triumph, Crimson were beset by internal problems. From the beginning, Lake felt that McDonald and Giles were of a different temperament to him and Fripp.

"Crimson was a very strange band," Lake explains. "There were four musicians who each had an energy of their own. As musicians we were totally unconnected but we managed to gel for a short period of time. With Giles, McDonald, Fripp and myself it was fifty percent musical incompatibility and seventy-five per cent as people. I felt closer to Bob but respected their talent."

Any tensions in the relationship were exacerbated by the amount of time the band spent together.

"I lived with Fripp when I was in Crimson," Lake explains, "And I don't think anybody else in the world could live with Fripp, or me for that matter. It was only for three or four months, which may not seem long, but when you're in a group and working together too, it's like living in each other's pockets all the time."

King Crimson toured America in November and December 1969. By the time they ended up sharing the bill with The Nice at San Francisco's Fillmore West on December 10, 1969, their internecine problems had been exacerbated by weeks on the road. Even though the band were on a roll, it was a good time for Keith Emerson to approach Lake about forming a new band. Still, all did not run smoothly.

"My first impressions of [Greg] were confused," Emerson recalled, "Perhaps because both of us are Scorpios. A lot of the opinions he had, I didn't agree with, and vice versa, but the guy had a hell of a lot to offer. His background was very similar to mine. We both liked the same pieces of music, mainly classical."

While Lake did not accept immediately, it was an intriguing proposition, and the two musicians agreed that on their return to England, they would discuss the prospect further.

Meanwhile, Lake was not the only member of King Crimson thinking of jumping ship. On the band's return to England, McDonald and Giles split to play as a duo. Lake felt at this point that they should consign the Crimson name to the dustbin and start a new band. Fripp, however, wanted to recruit new musicians and continue the band.

35

"Bob wanted to work in a situation where he was in the driving seat over other musicians, which I can dig, but [it was] not for me," Lake explains. He was also concerned that he wasn't getting due credit for his musical contributions to the band.

"Most of the songs on that [first] King Crimson album I had a large part in creating," he maintains. " 'Schizoid Man' – I wrote the riff and song; 'Epitaph' – I wrote the melody line for 'In The Court Of The Crimson King'." Uncertain about the future of a Fripp-dominated King Crimson, and with Keith Emerson's invitation to join a new band already in his mind, Lake quit the band around Christmas 1969.

"Weighing everything up," he reflects, "I saw a whole future with Keith and myself, whereas I saw a lot of trouble in the King Crimson thing."

As a favour to his old friend, Lake agreed to stick around long enough to help with the follow up to *Court*. His departure was not announced, but he couldn't begin work with Emerson anyway, because the keyboardist was tied up with The Nice till the end of March 1970. In the meantime Fripp recruited childhood friend Gordon Haskell [27] as the replacement singer.

The second King Crimson album, *In The Wake Of Poseidon*, was an obvious attempt to repeat a formula, though neither music nor lyrics are generally up to the standard of its predecessor. It's another "concept" work, but less well conceived and executed, lacking the sweeping vision, dramatic power and balance of the first album.

The album is framed by two rather banal tracks, "Peace – A Beginning" and "Peace – An End" (there's also a Fripp acoustic solo, "Peace – A Theme"). These and "Cadence And Cascade" are the equivalents of *Court's* "I Talk..." and "Moonchild" on the first album, but they're less interesting and Greg's flawed opening vocal on "A Beginning" would no doubt have been re-recorded if he'd stayed with the band. High points are the urban-nightmare "Pictures Of A City" and Sinfield's processed food protest, "Cat Food". Both tracks showcase some great Lake bass playing and his voice suits the songs perfectly.

King Crimson was a defining period for Greg Lake, and he remembers those days fondly. It was the first time he had worked with really professional, talented musicians, and the first chance he had to really express himself musically.

"When I originally joined the groups," Lake explained, "It was a way of getting the birds, of being recognised, when you're young that's what you want. And it was only when I got to the age of 18 or 19 when I started to play with King Crimson and we had this record *In the Court of the Crimson King* [that] I could see that music was quite a serious thing if it was done properly and it was done with enough care... And from that day I started to work at it as a career."

"Crimson for me was probably a refining process," he told another reporter. "Because I was very raw. With them I began to appreciate the subtleties of music.

When I joined I was very much out of my depth. It was strange, because they were at that time so much better than I was. I feel it evened out later."

Having given his notice to Fripp, Lake got together with Emerson early in 1970 with the aim of recruiting a drummer. The first big name they approached was Hendrix's drummer, Mitch Mitchell. Mitchell was extremely enthusiastic and, aware that Hendrix admired Emerson, he suggested Jimi came along too. Emerson initially thought this was a great idea, but he soon began to fear that Hendrix would hog all the limelight. In the end such fears proved academic, as the plan quickly fell through. Emerson, Lake, Hendrix and Mitchell would remain one of rock's great What Ifs.

After a series of unsuccessful auditions, someone – Tony Stratton-Smith according to Emerson, Robert Stigwood according to Lake – suggested Carl Palmer of Atomic Rooster. Emerson and Lake bought Atomic Rooster's eponymous debut album and, liking what they heard, approached Palmer.

III CARL PALMER

*A superlative percussionist whose speed, invention and dexterity with Emerson, Lake and Palmer put him in the front rank of world drumming."*A-Z Of Rock Drummers, *1982*

"The first Emerson, Lake and Palmer album established Carl Palmer as one of the finest drummers of all time" Hurricane Magazine, *1986*

"Plenty of drummers do solos but only certain ones become known as legendary soloists. Carl Palmer is one of those few." Modern Drummer, *1983*

Carl Frederick Kendall Palmer was born in Handsworth, Birmingham on March 20, 1950. Music and showbusiness were deeply rooted in his family. Carl's paternal grandfather was a versatile percussionist, and he had a great uncle who taught at the Royal Academy of Music, but it was his father – a comedian, singer and tap dancer in the local clubs – who was his real musical inspiration.

Young Carl's first musical foray involved a few months learning the violin, though he never really took to it. He considered trying his brother's guitar next, but fate intervened. One day while driving through Birmingham Town Centre with his family, they went past the famous Yardleys Music Store. Young Carl caught a glimpse of a red glitter snare drum (an Eric Delaney model made by toy company Chad Valley) – and that was that! He wanted it immediately, though he would have to wait until Christmas. Apparently it was the colour that fascinated him, not the drum, and after all the Christmas activity it was in danger of being overlooked.

"My father was always interested in drumming," Carl explains, "and he started messing about on it one day, and being like a selfish child I said, 'Leave it alone, it belongs to me!' He said, 'If it does belong to you, you should play it.' I said, 'OK, then.'

"So he happened to get out an Art Tatum or a Lionel Hampton or even a Buddy Rich record, I can't quite remember. The drummer on that record was playing time, ting-ting-a-ting, and my father said, 'That is generally what they play.' So I got behind my drum, picked up the brushes and just started playing, which knocked him out. I thought that was a bit silly, because it was so easy."

Carl's earliest musical influences were his father's dance band records – Harry James, Glenn Miller and Benny Goodman. Rock 'n' roll did affect the young Carl, but he never wanted to play it, though his first hearing of Elvis Presley left him stunned. After hearing some American jazz bands he began to realise there was more to music than Glenn Miller et al and tried jazzier things. The first record he bought was of Buddy Rich (not drumming, but) singing Tony Mercer. At that stage he didn't realise Rich played drums as well. Rich was to become one of Carl's key drumming influences. Another major influence on the young Carl was the Gene Krupa biopic *Drum Crazy* (known in the US as *The Gene Krupa Story*). Carl saw the film at the age of 11, and after buying the soundtrack became firmly hooked on drumming.

When he was twelve his father bought him a small Olympic [28] red glitter drum kit. He seemed to have a fascination for red glitter. Around this time he played his first gig, backing an accordion player and his wife. It was quite exciting for him until he had to play a waltz – up until then he had been used to playing four beats to the bar. No matter, it was all part of the learning process. It's a shame that no photographs exist of this gig, as Carl had to wear a kilt!

By this time Carl was obsessed with music to the complete exclusion of everything else. Each day, he would rush home from school straight into the bedroom and practice for four hours. He was smart enough to realise early on that as he was no good at school he had to throw everything into the one thing he excelled at. His natural aptitude, along with his parents's support and encouragement, certainly gave him an early edge.

Before long, while still at school, Carl was soon making good money.

"I was getting fifty bob a night in working men's clubs at weekends at the age of twelve," he recalls – about twenty times the average child's pocket money at that time.

During these early school days, Carl would have his lunch at home listening to bands like the Jerry Allen Trio on the radio show, *Lunch Box*. Allen's drummer was Lionel Rubin, from whom Carl was later to take lessons and whose old drum kit he had just bought.

Carl's first teacher, though, was Tommy Cunliffe.

"He was the best in town," Palmer recalls with pride. "[He] played on the radio in the Midland Light Orchestra. I went to him for about two and a half years. I was taking these lessons in Birmingham till I was fourteen." Palmer's natural talent and his fierce dedication to daily practice saw him rapidly improve and eventually Cunliffe was forced to acknowledge that his pupil had outstripped his teaching ability.

"He knew I was better than him," Palmer explains, "and he said to my parents that it was time for me to move on. Then I started to come to London every week for lessons in Denmark Street, off Shaftesbury Avenue. I went to a cat called Bruce Gaylor for a further twelve months."

By this time Carl had his first regular paid engagement with a Mecca dance band, earning £25 per week. Dressed in a "horrible" red jacket festooned with cigarette holes, courtesy of the previous incumbent, he spent six months or so keeping time for waltzes, foxtrots and tangos.

Next Palmer joined the Central City Jazz Band. It brought him into contact with one of the big figures of British jazz. Carl remembers fondly: "I did a gig opposite Humphrey Lyttelton, his drummer was taken ill. I went up, as bold as brass, and asked if I could sit in. He said, 'Can you read?' I could, so I sat in for three quarters of an hour, and he said it was OK. That was some experience."

However the Central City Jazz Band's music didn't really excite Palmer and he quickly moved on. Confident that drumming would be his life's work, he left Handsworth Wood Boys Secondary Modern School at the age of 15 and turned professional. His first audition was with a group called the King Bees [29].

"I went along and got the gig," he remembers. "They said they didn't get much money, a couple of quid per gig, more if they went out of town, and maybe two or three gigs a week. I thought this [was] a bit heavy because I was already getting twenty a week in the Mecca band – and at the age of fourteen."

Nevertheless, Palmer still joined the band, mainly because he liked the R & B material they were playing. He stayed with them for about a year.

"The King Bees was my first group of any quality," Palmer would later reflect. "It was mainly a blues band. We went through Motown stuff to recording our own material. We actually got into the charts in France. The band had a degree of punch, and when I was young I thought the band was going to make it. We ended up sounding very much like The Who... Geoff Brown and Richard Parnell wrote the material. I never got into writing, because I was too interested in what I was playing to think of writing something."

The music scene in Birmingham was vibrant during this era. The young drummer came into contact with a number of talented performers, the first of which was a young, pre-Spencer Davis, Steve Winwood. "He used to play piano in the

39

Chapel Tavern pub," Palmer recalls. "On Sunday morning I used to go along there and everyone could sit in, and every time I used to sit in he was playing. He was doing this jazz thing which I really dug because I was a real jazz freak. But he never really wanted to know me."

Some time later, Carl was sharing a bill with Winwood – and that night turned down a remarkable career opportunity. "I was then nearly sixteen, and there was an all-nighter at Birmingham Town Hall," he recalls. "On the bill were the King Bees, Spencer Davis, Brian Auger and the Trinity (with Rod Stewart) – and Chris Farlowe and the Thunderbirds... We, the King Bees, went on first, and Chris Farlowe had just turned up and was watching us from the side of the stage. When I walked off stage Chris asked me whether I'd like to join the Thunderbirds. I said no! We had just made a record [30] and were due to appear on *Thank Your Lucky Stars* [31] that next week – everything was happening. Of course, Chris was well taken aback."

Needless to say, the King Bees' record never made it. Disheartened, some members of the band went back to university, and the band broke up. At a loose end, and with nothing to lose, Palmer gave Chris Farlowe a call. "He remembered me," Palmer recalls, "which was a little surprising, because by that time he had had his Number One, 'Out Of Time'. I asked whether he still needed a drummer. The answer was yes, but I'd have to audition. I thought this a little strange, because he'd previously offered me the gig. I realise now that he was leading me on and making it tough, which in retrospect was a good thing."

Farlowe's road manager drove Palmer to Farlowe's parents' house in London, where they gave him the basement flat. Things didn't start swimmingly:

"Chris didn't turn up for a couple of days," Palmer explains, "And I was getting worried – I'd given his mother four quid, and there I was in London with only another four in my pocket. When he did eventually turn up we went to audition, or rather rehearse, at the Bag O'Nails. As I'd bought his albums beforehand and learnt them, I was really in business before I got there. I had a great time with the band and also did a lot of session work."

One story illustrates just how confident the young Palmer was. While in London, in his Chris Farlowe days, he heard that Buddy Rich was staying at the Dorchester Hotel, London. Carl went to reception and asked to see his hero. Just at that moment, the great man came out of the lift.

"We had an introduction," Palmer remembered, "and he asked me to come back the following day for a chat – which I did. In the room were Jack Delaney, Ronnie Verrell, Jack Parnell – and I'd brought my sticks along. I talked about a couple of techniques I thought I was playing incorrectly, and he showed me some tips – it was great." After this initial meeting, Palmer and Rich became friends – something that was tremendously important for the young drummer.

"When I was younger [Rich] gave me a big goal to strive for," Palmer reflected. "Hearing him play, I couldn't match anyone else with him – he kept coming up with the magic. Regardless of how his style dated by the time I began playing, his superb technique [was] obviously capable of covering anything – he [played] great rock and roll. My ambition was to try and play as fast as Rich," though Palmer added, "I'd like to bridge the gap between Elvin Jones and Buddy in a rock group."

The Chris Farlowe band had quite a line up, comprising Albert Lee on guitar, Dave Greenslade on organ, and Bugs Waddell on bass. They were mainly a live band; though Palmer can be heard on the odd single.

Still, all this talent was not enough to keep Palmer on board. When he got a call inviting him to join The Crazy World of Arthur Brown he accepted.

Former teacher Arthur Brown had formed his band with organist Vincent Crane and drummer Drachen Theaker. The band got their big break when Pete Townshend spotted them at the renowned UFO club and persuaded Kit Lambert to record them on Track Records. Theaker left after a US tour, and in addition to the recruitment of Palmer, the new band included another Farlowe alumnus, Pete Solley (who took over from Greenslade in 1967) on organ.

"It was a very weird band," Palmer reflects, "and meant cutting myself off from any other contracts – when with Arthur Brown one just played with the band."

Initially the band was immensely successful, notching up a number one album and single, "Fire", in America. Palmer arrived too late to play on either record, though he was the drummer by the time the band went on TV to promote "Fire". *Top Of The Pops* had never witnessed anything like The Crazy World of Arthur Brown! Arthur appeared in flowing robe and flaming helmet, and the band were dressed as demon serfs – Palmer playing drums wearing a skull mask. Unfortunately all these theatricals did somewhat detract from the musicians' enjoyment. "I didn't know how the audiences were", Carl lamented. "I couldn't see them with Arthur Brown. I was wearing too many masks, There were too many strobe lights, it was very hard to tell....And with Arthur being so visual you never got a chance in that band. Audience anticipation was all Arthur's. He was the only one that got them all. If anything got to them. So musically I was left behind."

Palmer and Crane were tired of unenthusiastically cranking out the old material. Crane was especially fed up with Brown hogging all the limelight and Palmer was wondering where all the money was going. Both musicians left on the same day, Friday 13th June, 1969, while the band was in New York on the third American tour playing poorly attended gigs. The only recorded Crazy World track which definitely features Carl's drumming is "What's Happening?", the B-side of the follow-up single, "Nightmare"[32].

Palmer and Crane had become friends during their Arthur Brown days and resolved to put together a new band. Nick Graham came in on bass and vocals, and Atomic Rooster was born. The first Rooster single, "Friday The 13th", was named after the date of Crane's and Palmer's departure from the Crazy World. Their eponymous album [32], released in early 1970 on B&C Records, featured the first major recorded examples of Carl's drumming. With a kit that combined Gretsch, Zildjian and Paiste components, he showcased the fierce snare drum technique which in later years would become such a trademark. Palmer's solo on the 6/8 time "Before Tomorrow" was particularly remarkable.

With an acclaimed album in the can, a well-received Isle of Wight festival performance under their belt and a growing live following, things were shaping up nicely for Atomic Rooster in 1970 . And then Palmer got a call from Keith Emerson and Greg Lake. The former members of The Nice and King Crimson were forming a band, and having a terrible time finding a drummer. Palmer agreed to meet them for a rehearsal, though at first he wasn't very enthusiastic.

"I didn't really want to be a part of something that had been done before," he explained. "Keith had been so much into classical music and had just broken up a three-piece band, and it seemed strange that he was thinking of forming another one. This disturbed me a little, so I said no to them at first, because Atomic Rooster was my band and my first big success. I'd started it and worked really hard to get it up to two hundred pounds a night....

"I didn't want to give it up. It didn't mean anything when Greg said he and Keith were going to be big and 'You've got to join'. My attitude was, I've got my own band, we're earning two hundred pounds a night, so stick your job up your arse! However, they wanted me to join so badly, which I was quite pleased about, but didn't make out at the time. Then Greg phoned me up and he said a classic line that just freaked me. I'll never forget it: 'If you don't join this band you're not only damaging yourself, you're damaging me and that's heavy'." On the receiving end of this psychological strategy, Palmer made a timely phone call to his father, who, struck by Lake's audacity, came to the correct conclusion that "the guy must have something".

"Then it clicked that the musicians in the Rooster weren't of the right calibre for what I really wanted to do," Palmer explained. "So the next day I went round to have a chat with Greg, who incidentally I'd not heard of at the time, but he did have a certain aura about him that came on like a ton of bricks! I then got together with Keith, who was very inhibited as a character – he didn't say much, only 'Hi, man – let's play'. That's what I liked about Keith, he came in on a pure musical thing. He was challenging musically, and I love a challenge. I'd say, 'Whatever you wanna play', and that'd knock them out, because apparently other drummers had said let's play this and that but I told them, 'Just count me in', and they loved it. It began to get very exciting. And that was it, really."

There were some legal formalities to sort out, so for a while Palmer was rehearsing with Emerson and Lake during the day and playing with Atomic Rooster at night. Released from his contractual responsibilities to Atomic Rooster at the beginning of June, Palmer found it highly amusing that his final gig on May 31st had been thought a big enough deal to merit the billing "Atomic Rooster – Last performance with Carl Palmer".

With the last Atomic Rooster show out of the way and the legal work sewn up, Palmer was free to concentrate on the new band full-time. Named simply after the three members, Emerson, Lake and Palmer were now ready for work.

Notes

1 Years later, Keith recorded this Floyd Cramer number, originally released by Cramer in 1961. Emerson's version can be found on the album *Music from Free Creek* (See discography). The Cramer style clearly influenced the piano playing in 'Jeremy Bender' on ELP's *Tarkus* album.

2 Brian Walkeley can be heard on a Gary Farr and the T-Bones compilation album (London 1964l65X, see discography). CHARLY CR300015

3 Many late-60s bands were into "mixed media". The vogue for combining all manner of different and conflicting art forms and seeing what happened lasted for some time, and was one of the factors in the rise of "progressive" music. It was just part of the growing freedom sensed by many people in the late 60s. There was a feeling of openness throughout society, including the media. Sadly, it didn't last; by the early 70s the tide was beginning to turn.

4 Made in Poole, Dorset in the 60s and early 70s, the Bird organ was a far cry from the Hammond in appearance and capabilities. Its construction was rather rough and ready, with a piece of 3-ply bolted on to each end of the keyboard, and it was supported by four short legs, two on each side. Its performance was let down by frequent cipher difficulties, i.e. notes would sometimes continue to sustain after release. Although there was a console model developed in later years for church work, Bird organs have been out of production for about thirty years. Even if Emerson had bought one he would soon have found it hopelessly impractical for regular gigging – not to say maltreatment. Thanks to Jeff Walker of Courtney & Walker in Poole for this background information.

5 This shop no longer exists.

6 Invented in 1933 by Laurens Hammond, the instrument used by Keith Emerson is the same in most essentials as the original version. Tones are produced by ridged wheels (Tone Wheels) revolving in a magnetic field, producing sound-waves which can then be amplified. The player can alter the relative strength of overtones, or 'harmonics' of each key by adjusting the positions

of "drawbars", making it possible to produce and extremely wide variety of timbres. Echo, reverberation, chorale and tremolo effects are also available, in addition to the pedal volume control.

The first Hammond (Model A, serial no 1) was first used as a demonstrator around the American Midwest for a number of years after it was built by the Hammond Clock Company in 1935. It was eventually purchased by the Paseo Methodist Church in Kansas City for less than $1,000 It remained there for 11 years, being used again as a demonstrator model after leaving the possession of the church. The organ now resides in the Smithsonian Institution.

7   Composed in 1943, this was a Brazilian song which features in three popular films, including one in which it was played by the organist Ethel Smith. With Bando Carioca, she released it in 1944; it rose to 14 in the Hit Parade. Although there were other versions, Ethel Smith's organ recording was no doubt of greater appeal to the young Keith Emerson, who would certainly have been aware of her book 'Hammond Organ Method'.

8   Noel Emerson had played a massive part in his son's attempt to establish himself. Keith dedicated his 1988 record *The Christmas Album* "TO THE MEMORY OF MY FATHER NOEL EMERSON".

9   A speaker originally designed for Hammond organs, housing two speakers on a drum which rotates, causing subtle modulations of pitch and volume to create a rich chorus-like effect.

10 The other original members of Gary Farr and the T-Bones were Winston B. Whetherall, Andy McKechnie, Stu Parks and Andy Steele. They quickly got residencies at the Crawdaddy Club in Richmond, and the Marquee in London, as well as plenty of other work. In November they released their first single for Columbia, who had signed them recently This and the next two failed to dent the charts.

Then Steele left the band, and was replaced on drums by Brian "Legs" Walkeley (mentioned earlier by Keith in his narration of that period). In late 65/66 the band changed radically. Only Farr and Walkeley remained from the original line-up. Enter Keith Emerson on keyboards, Lee Jackson on bass and "Cyrano" on guitar. The line-up probably lasted until early 1967, when the band split up. A single, "If I Had A Ticket", is rumoured to have been recorded by Chris Barber and Kenneth Washington for CBS in 1966. The backing band are said to be Farr, Emerson, Jackson, plus Alan Turner and David Langston.

Other than this, much remains uncertain about the identities of the players on the tracks cut by the band. Farr went on eventually to cut three solo albums, none of which were big sellers. The last was recorded in America, to where he had emigrated, in 1973. The T-Bones were very nearly as good as those bands which did make it big out of the mid-60s R&B boom. It is interesting to speculate about which tracks Emerson et al are playing on, but impossible to be conclusive.

11 Apart from some backing vocals in the early days of The Nice, a little tomfoolery at the end of 'Are you Ready Eddy' on the *Tarkus* album, a snigger at the end of the "Benny The Bouncer" on *Brain Salad Surgery* and some bad pub singing called "Intro-Juicing" on the solo album *Honky*, Keith's vocal contribution to recorded music has thankfully been limited to one song, a version of Steve Winwood's "I'm a Man" included on the *Nighthawks* soundtrack album. However, he was ironically cast as the voice of the Bridge Computer on "Karn Evil 9", 3rd Impression.

12 Had Emerson remained with the V.I.P.s, he could have found himself playing with a band called Art, for the band changed their name on completion of their first album, *Supernatural Fairy Tales*. A further name change followed when Gary Wright joined on keyboards and Spooky Tooth was born.

Emerson became a friend of Gary Wright and co-wrote some children's songs with his wife, Lorna – "My Name is Rain" (from the Various Artists' album *Songs For A Modern Church*) and "Captain Starship Christmas" (from *The Christmas Album*).

13 Don Shinn released an album, *Temples With Prophets* (COLUMBIA SCX 6319), in 1969. The brief sleevenotes describe him as "a slight gnomic figure", and the album as "a tour de force of inspired improvisation". In retrospect this goes too far, but the LP is certainly a freewheeling and eclectic mixture of styles and influences, from Bach to Eastern music.

14 "Brandenburger", an arrangement of the first movement of Bach's third Concerto, used as the basis of the third movement, "Acceptance", of "Ars Longa Vita Brevis", from the eponymous album on IMMEDIATE IMSP 020,1968

15 A native of Los Angeles, Pat Arnold (b.1946) sang in local church choirs from the age of four As a teenager she joined Ike and Tina Turner's backing group, which became known as the Ikettes. When they visited London in 1966, Pat realised that she could make a name for herself in Britain (Ike and Tina were much bigger stars in the UK than in the States, where there was a lot of competition for soul acts). She made the big decision to leave the Ikettes and pursue her own career in London.

The nickname "P.P." was suggested by her agent, Gered Mankowitz. Blues singers like B.B. King and O.C. Smith had established the trend, and he liked the idea of associating her with these giants. Pat wasn't so sure, but she agreed, and of course it stuck forever. Andrew Oldham's Immediate Records signed her, realising she was a potential star. she was sent into the studio with big names of British R&B – Jimmy Page, members of the Rolling Stones and the Yardbirds. Four hit singles resulted. The biggest, "The First Cut Is The Deepest" by Cat Stevens, reached Number 18 in the UK chart in the Summer of 1967. Her debut album, "First Lady of Immediate", was produced that year by Mick Jagger and Mike Hurst.

After the Nice left to become stars in their own right, P.P. released another album, *Kafunta*, in 1968. This yielded the Top 30 hit "Angel of The Morning". in 1969 she starred in the rock musical *Catch My Soul*, then in *Jesus Christ, Superstar* the following year. In the 70s P.P. Arnold returned to the USA and did TV work, appearing in such series as *Fame*, *T.J.Hooker* and *Knots Landing*. When her former Immediate stablemates, the Small Faces, reformed in 1978, she toured with them.

In 1984 she contributed to the *Electric Dreams* soundtrack, and returned to the musical stage to star in Andrew Lloyd Webber's *Starlight Express*. In recent years she has become highly sought after by dance musicians. In 1992 she was heard and seen with The KLF in their hit single "Justified and Ancient". She helped out The Beatmasters on "Burn it Up". She returned to musicals in 1994 with *Once on This Island* and has recently recorded with Ocean Colour Scene.

P.P. Arnold had, and has, a wonderful voice. She deserved to achieve greater fame – but she hasn't done badly!

16 Newcastle-born Lee Jackson (b.8/1/43) went to St. Mary's Technical School, Newcastle, but had no formal musical education. Before The Nice, he worked as a salesman for Burton's Menswear for some time, while playing in various small bands.

17 David O'List (b.13/12/48) was born in Chiswick, London. He went to St. Mark's School, Fulham, and in 1960 received a scholarship to the Royal Collage of Music, where he studied trumpet, with piano as second instrument, for four years, performing with the London Schools Symphony Orchestra at, among other places, the Royal Albert Hall.

With four friends he formed a R&B group called the Little Blue Boys, which he left to finish exams. In early 1967 he was briefly in a soul band, making his professional debut at a club in the Earls Court Road. After this, while working in Sainsbury's supermarket in Earls Court, he met Gerry Henderson, also working there, bassist with The Attack. Chris Welch cottoned on to him and included him in an article called "Group Scene '67" in which David acknowledged George Harrison as his first idol.

18 Rock and pop journalist and author Chris Welch is also a drummer, and was in at the formations of both The Nice and ELP. He has been one of the most important public advocates and defenders of these bands, as well as being possibly their fairest and keenest critic. In 1976 Keith played "Promenade" from "Pictures At An Exhibition" at his wedding. Welch founded the excellent but short-lived weekly *Musicians Only*, which was the first to report ELP's split. He was most recently editor of the monthly magazine *Rock World*, which gave ELP's 1992 reunion a high profile.

19 Ian Hague played with Chris Farlowe at about the same time as Carl Palmer. He also recorded with soul artist J.J. Jackson, and can be heard on the album J.J.Jackson's Dilemma (RCA SF8093, 1971)

20 Brian Davison (b.25/5/42) first played drums in a working man's club at the age of thirteen. At the time of the formation of the Nice he was the only married member of the group, with a young daughter, Julie. He started off thumping along to Jimmy Shand records, and progressed to three hours' practice a day on a battered old kit.

Davison had been with a very fine band called the Mark Leeman Five before joining the Nice. Leeman was a singer in the Paul Jones mould, but was sadly killed in a car crash. When the group broke up Davison entered a depressing period. At one time he was doing manual work and considering selling his drums. He occasionally gigged with the Mike Cotton Band, with David O'List in the Attack, and in London discotheque bands. He played briefly with a band called the Habits, and interestingly, also with the band backing Don Shinn, who was such an influence on Keith Emerson's stage act.

21 For eleven years Tony Stratton-Smith (1933-1987) was a sports journalist, latterly writing for the *Daily Express*. By the early 60s he was establishing himself as a freelance writer and journalist, but his many planned books never got published except as serialised newspaper articles. He whiled away a lot of time on Copacabana Beach after the 1962 Chile World Cup, and there met composer Antonio Jobim, who suggested he pursue a career in music publishing. Strat's early doubts about this were well-founded: he wasted a lot of money and gave up, disillusioned.

While writing *The Rebel Nun*, a biography of the martyr Mother Maria Skobtzova, (which he published) he met the Beatles' manager Brian Epstein, who was looking for someone to ghost his autobiography. Although he turned it down eventually, the meeting was inspirational. Stratton-Smith discovered a band called Paddy, Klaus and Gibson in 1965 and set about the business of managing them. They had major potential but never made it big; Klaus (Voorman) later designed the Beatles' *Revolver* album and played with Manfred Mann.

Next came unpredictable Liverpool singer Betty Marsden, and then The Creation and The Koobas. In every case Stratton-Smith lost money. He abandoned the music business and returned successfully to books and film scripts. But then along came The Nice. They were obviously going places. However, Andrew Oldham had left a legacy of problems.

"My last meeting with Andrew Oldham was at The Speakeasy when we threatened to have a punch-up as a result of the way he was failing to give any support when The Nice badly needed it in America...We couldn't get any action on the records. It was one of the most frustrating years of my life.

"I don't think he ever really had any faith in them. He didn't try hard to help the band, or even to hang on to them. I think he totally underestimated what The Nice were about. That's why they brought me in. They wanted somebody who would pick up their career by the scruff of the neck and slam them into the concert halls. Happily, I was able to do that for them, with their help."

When The Nice disbanded, Stratton-Smith was deeply upset. "The Nice were genuinely exciting, innovative and moving. There were nights when they were so good, they could bring you to tears. In fact, one of the few times I broke down in tears in this game was when I realised it was all over. I knew it was a mistake – they should have given it a couple of more years." The Nice would have split even earlier had Strat not persuaded them to do a farewell British tour. Their last two albums helped establish Charisma in the record industry. Tony Stratton-Smith was responsible for the developing careers of an extraordinary number of big name artists. By the early '70s Charisma had established itself as the home of underground music. Genesis, Lindisfarne, Van Der Graaf Generator, Patrick Moraz, Bo Hansson, Brand X, Rick Wakeman, Hawkwind, Audience, The Bonzo Dog Doo-Dah Band, Clifford T. Ward, Monty Python, even Sir John Betjeman and psychiatric guru R.D. Laing – these and many more were helped along by one of the most important and most likeable rock entrepreneurs of the 70s.

In 1986 he sold Charisma to Virgin, anticipating his death from stomach cancer in March 1987. The memorial service at St. Martin In The Fields in London was attended by everyone you can think of in the music industry. Keith Emerson played a specially-written piece; in 1988 this song, "On My Way Home", for which he wrote both music and lyrics for the first time, was included on the album *To The Power of Three* by Three.

22 Andrew Loog Oldham (b. 1944) was born in the same year as Keith Emerson. The middle name was given to him by his Dutch father. Before he was a teenager he had visited London's 2 I's coffee bar in London, famous for being the launching pad of many of the biggest names in British rock 'n' roll, including Tommy Steele and Cliff Richard. The experience altered the course of his life. Leaving school after 'O' Levels, he made contacts in the fashion and music industries, even recording some singles under assumed names. Realising that his talents as a pop singer were heavily outweighed by his gift for self-publicity and people management, Oldham tried his hand with current idol Mark Wynter. He was eventually hired by Brian Epstein as publicist to Gerry and the Pacemakers and Billy J.Kramer and the Dakotas. He tried for the Beatles, but they were in another league, so he moved on again. His encounter with Phil Spector taught him a vital lesson in music business economics: never record on the premises of your record company, or they will own your master. Taking Spector as his role-model, even down to the dark glasses and gangster suits and limos, he was at first set on production, but soon realised that management could reap richer and quicker rewards.

Oldham saw the Rolling Stones at the Crawdaddy Club in Richmond. He managed to persuade them to leave their current management, found a financial backer, and on May 3, 1963 signed them to Impact Sound, the company he had formed with his financial backer Eric Easton to supervise recording sessions. The company was aptly named, because Oldham certainly made a splash for the group whenever and wherever they performed. He was behind most of the attention-grabbing headlines and disruption of press conferences which set the media in a spin about the band, and was quick to capitalise on events which he had not engineered. Teen hysteria and violence and certain minor outrages by the group, such as urinating in public, were loved by Oldham. "Would You Let Your Daughter Go Out With A Rolling Stone?" asked one preplanned headline.

Dumping Easton and joining with Allen Klein removed from Oldham the day-to-day responsibilities of business management. But now some of his grander schemes for the Stones began to fail; he chose to return to the musical side of things. His greatest ambition, to be the British Phil Spector, could most easily be achieved, he believed, through record production and company ownership. In 1965, Immediate Records was the result.

The new label, with its typically grandiose motto, "Happy To Be A Part of The Industry of Human Happiness" (purloined from an international industry body), was Britain's first major independent record company. Its first release, "Hang On Sloopy" by the McCoys, made the Top Ten, and by summer 1966 Chris Farlowe had a Number One with "Out of Time".

Immediate was hardly run on traditional business principles; hype was the watchword. For example, Oldham went to America and bought, at inflated prices, the rights to records that had been hits there and were sure U.K. hits. By purchasing instant success and a high profile, he attracted a large number of artists who were either beginning to enjoy fame or were on the verge of it.

In 1967 came the long expected split from the Stones. After the Stones came the Small Faces. Immediate brought them a string of hit singles and a number one album. But studio indulgence and further financial complications lost them a lot of money, and they split at the end of 1968.

Oldham briefly attempted to manage the Herd. Next came P.P. Arnold, who was to have some major hits with Immediate. Her backing group, The Nice, became a sensation on both sides of the Atlantic, but Oldham could not profit as much from their success, or Humble Pie's, as he wished, because Immediate was now in big trouble. In April, 1968 the company went into liquidation and the Nice appointed Tony Stratton-Smith as their new manager. Oldham remained in the music business and had some success in the U.S.A. as a producer. In the early '70s he married a Colombian actress and settled in Bogota. An attempt was made in the 80s to get Immediate going again, but without success. Oldham's importance in Keith Emerson's career was crucial. He was the ideal manager for the Nice, given their theatricality, though they would have achieved success with any manager.

Tony Stratton-Smith's feelings about his rival were understandably mixed. "Oldham's Immediate was brilliant. They had a marvellous A&R policy, they developed some great artistes. But unfortunately they had no genuine commitment with what they were trying to do...I had a love-hate thing for Immediate, I learned a lot of good things from it, creatively, but, as the way they went down at the end tended to prove, there wasn't a lot of integrity there".

It has to be said that Oldham divides opinion, however. Others see him as the sixth Rolling Stone, even their virtual creator, and as the great pop Svengali of the mid-60s. In May 1993 *Rock World* magazine carried Oldham's announcement that he and his original partner Tony Calder were to revive the Immediate label and logo under the name Immediate 3. The intention was to both re-release old material and to sign new acts. According to Calder, "We've got an option on a film...and we are helping some people do a documentary on Immediate."

Oldham's autobiography, *Stoned*, was published by Secker and Warburg in 2000.

23 In February 1969 David O'List joined Opal Butterfly (not CBS' Iron Butterfly, later to include future Hawkwind members Lemmy and Simon King, but another group on the Fontana label). In March, at a disused linoleum factory in Staines, a remarkable super-session jam took place, with the likes of Eric Clapton, Roland Kirk, Buddy Guy, Colosseum and Led Zeppelin on stage together. Although O'List was invited to play, he never appeared in the resulting film. However he can be seen on the video of the occasion, *Supershow* (see Videography), playing with the Misunderstood. This led to him playing on their third single, "You're Tuff Enough".

After the Nice split, an attempt was made to form a band with two ex-Downliners Sect members. Pointedly christened The Nasty, it fell apart after two members of the group were beaten up by skinheads and David's new amplifier was smashed. Later, David played with Brian Ferry in Roxy Music's first line-up and on two of his solo albums. He plays on "The In Crowd" on the *Roxy Music: Total Recall* video. In 1975 David formed Jet with a couple of ex-Sparks players, releasing a single, "My River", which should have been a hit. The next album was not so good, lifted only by O'List's superb guitar work. Had the band not split before the completion of the third album, however, they might have gone on to greater success.

Among the many people with whom David O'List later worked was his old partner in the Nice, Brian Davison. Little was heard of him through the 80s, though he notably played with John Cale and Nik Turner. He became a sound engineer and keyboard player for psychedelic reggae outfit Urban Shakedown – "complete with Caribbean shirt!" In 1987, an album of early Nice material, basically the first Nice album modified and re-packaged as "The Nice featuring Davy O'List – Twentieth Anniversary Release", popped up in record stores. Styling himself "The Big Seal", O'List credited "The Thoughts of Emerlist Davjak"[sic] to "O'List/Emerson" rather than the other way around as originally, and "The Cry of Eugene" to "O'List Jackson/Emerson/Davison" rather than "Jackson/O'List/Emerson". Credits were also reversed for "Bonnie K" and O'List was shown to have had prime input to the composition of "Dawn", whereas only the other three members were originally credited, and the sleevenotes were interesting, to say the least.

Davy O'List's most recent project was Fax. The solo LP of synthesiser and dance music was given one unjustifiably bad review in *Q* magazine, and fell by the wayside. One hopes this sensitive, fine musician, currently also studying film in London, may soon find success again.

24 Longstaff had already played with Jackson in a Newcastle band called the Kylastrons.

25 Patrick Moraz quit Nice-clones Refugee to join Yes after just one well-received album and a short tour. For Jackson, this was "a sickener – more or less the end of me and music".

Eventually he married an American, settled in Los Angeles and turned his longtime hobby of interior design into a full-time job. "I'm lucky – to be able to do something else which I love just as much. The visual arts to me are a lot of fun. I remember the opening of a rather amazing bank I did in Santa Ana where they'd found out who I used to be, produced a bunch of records and played them during the opening. I walk in and there's Rondo thumping away!" In 1983 there was a brief onstage reunion of Emerson and Jackson, prompting speculations (as yet unfulfilled) about a Nice re-formation.

Immediately after the Nice split, Brian Davison formed the jazzy Every Which Way with Graham Bell (ex-Skip Bifferty). They recorded one Charisma album, and lasted about eighteen months. After Refugee came a brief spell with German spontaneous jazz-rock band Etcetera. Today Davison is a peripatetic music teacher in the South-West of England. "I look out of the kitchen window to Lundy Island." More recently he has divided his time between teaching drums in schools, giving his own "rhythm and improvisation" workshops and playing the occasional modern jazz gig in London with the Nick Stephens Septet.

26 Lake and Fripp were taught guitar by Don Strike, father of Bev Strike from the Timechecks.

27 Haskell had a post-Crimson solo album; more recently he has released two truly wonderful solo albums on the label which has also reissued Pete Sinfield's solo album. *Hambledon Hill* and *It's Just A Plot To Drive You Crazy* (VOICEPRINT VP127 & VP118) are classics which deserve as much promotion as they can get, and 1998 saw the release of *Butterfly in China* (BLUEPRINT BP-287), another great album.

28 Olympic drums were made by Premier – the Leicester based drum company

29 Not to be confused with David Bowie's early band of the same name. Carl's group changed their name to The Craig for their first single. See Discography.

30 See Discography. Under the name of The Craig, they cut "I Must be Mad"/ "Suspense", both credited to Geoff Brown. It appeared on the Fontana label, which distributed Larry Page's Page One Records in 1966. FONTANA TF715.

31 A weekly Independent Television music show, similar to *Top of the Pops*.

32 See Discography.

CHAPTER 2

From The Beginning

I want someone in 200 years' time to pick up an ELP album and say, "Christ, that's a gas!" Greg Lake, 1970

Emerson, Lake and Palmer was a seed sown in fertile ground. The Nice, King Crimson and Atomic Rooster were just a few of the late 60s' bands who had planted a desire for technically accomplished, complex and eclectic rock music. The new band's musical ambitions also coincided with rapid advances in recording technology and instrument design – which would help them fulfil their vision.

ELP spent most of the summer of 1970 rehearsing at a church in Shepherds Bush, London for 4–5 hours a day. Initially they worked on The Nice's "Rondo" (retained, as Keith had promised the fans), King Crimson's "21st Century Schizoid Man", "Tank" (which would be the platform for Carl's drum solo) – and "Pictures at an Exhibition" – a rock arrangement of Russian classical composer Mussorgsky's virtuoso piano showpiece. They soon graduated to the studio to begin work on their debut album, beginning with a new track, "The Barbarian".

Emerson was confident that this new band would enable him to expand on the musical possibilities of The Nice. His orchestral experiments towards the end of the latter group's existence had alienated the rest of the band. But now, not only were Lake and Palmer more accomplished musicians than Emerson's previous colleagues, they were ready and eager for the journey. There were, however, a few initial hiccups.

While Palmer seemed happy that ELP were picking up where The Nice had left off, Lake was worried that the new band would be no more than a glorified version of Keith's former outfit, a concern compounded by the inclusion of "Rondo" in their set. Lake would strive to ensure that ELP really did take a new direction, offsetting some of Emerson's classical excursions with experiments of his own.

Another initial worry was that while Emerson and Lake had both played in progressive bands and were used to extremely complicated arrangements, Palmer, though talented and extremely willing, had never played music like this before.

"I went to see them rehearsing when Carl was particularly concerned about playing '21st Century Schizoid Man', the tricky King Crimson number they were trying out," Chris Welch recalls.

"I wore out the LP trying to learn the drum part!" Palmer later confessed. In the end the song was dropped from the set. Palmer also initially struggled with the technicalities of playing "Pictures At An Exhibition". "'Pictures' is a hard one to play because there is so much to remember," the drummer explained. "There are lots of different moods and tempos. I've never worked on this type of arranging before" However, Palmer soon got the hang of more subtle playing, and enjoyed experimenting with different drum techniques such as jazz brushwork.

The rehearsals soon saw the band gel. "I remember Greg and Keith smiling proudly when Carl launched into a drum solo at the speed of light," says Welch, "And the feeling was of quiet confidence and eager anticipation. ELP were going to have fun, play to the maximum and conquer the world."

Meanwhile, away from band rehearsals, Palmer would also continue to practice drumming for a couple of hours day, motivated by a rare desire to become the complete percussionist.

While ELP were soon combining to create a unique sound, they did not mix socially. The musical environment they created for themselves was stimulating, maddening, frustrating and rewarding, and it saw the three musicians push and pull the band in all directions. Away from the studio, they perhaps healthily decided to opt for a less intense atmosphere.

The personalities of the three musicians that made up ELP were not easy to bind into a unit. Carl was different to Keith and Greg; he had never really struggled to make a living as a musician. "All the time people have given me money, so I've never really hustled," Palmer admitted. Emerson and Lake on the other hand had paid their dues over the years in dodgy transit vans up and down motorways. Years of adversity had helped make both musicians more assertive individuals than the laid back drummer. Consequently, Palmer's personality was to pay dividends as Emerson and Lake had their battles over musical supremacy.

As the band toiled in the studio, outside expectations were extremely high. The media bestowed on them the unwanted tag of "supergroup", which the group found quite nauseating. By the time their first shows came around that August the pressures and expectations had grown to almost unbearable levels.

"I'm dreaming of gigs, man," Palmer told the press. "I wake up thinking I'm gigging somewhere. It's two months since I played in public, and for Keith it's even longer. I don't think Greg has done a gig since last Christmas."

The much anticipated debut concert finally took place at the Plymouth Guildhall[1] on August 23rd, 1970 – a warm-up for their appearance at the Isle of

Wight Festival on August 29th. Carl had a picture of the children's book character Noddy[2] on the bass drum of his Gretsch drum kit.

The band had deliberately selected Plymouth as the setting for a warm-up gig because of its distance from London. Having only rehearsed for a few weeks, they were still lacking in confidence. "Getting ELP together was a worrying time," Emerson would later explain. "You began to think after a while that people have forgotten about you – it gets as bad as that. Getting towards the first gig, we couldn't sleep at night, because it had been so long before we'd even faced an audience."

They needn't have worried. After Emerson's concise introduction, "This is what we sound like", and a shaky start, the band quickly won over the audience.

The initial set comprised "Barbarian", "Take A Pebble", "Rondo", and a full forty minute version of "Pictures At An Exhibition" – everything they had rehearsed apart from "Schizoid Man". Encores were demanded; even after hearing "Rondo" for the third time, there was a quarter of an hour's shouting for "more, more, more". In the end ELP returned for "Nutrocker". By the following week the act had tightened still more; just as well, as their next public appearance would be before a rather larger audience.

The third Isle of Wight Festival was as high-profile a second appearance as any band could hope for. Still remembered as "The Last Great Event", the Festival was attended by a quarter of a million people over five days. It was promoted as "the largest and most spectacular Festival ever", with "the best available progressive music in the world". One of the modern commonplaces of rock festivals was also being experimented with: each concert was to be relayed in colour on a giant video screen [3]

Everybody remembered Atomic Rooster's excellent performance at the previous Festival, and expectations were running high for the new band.

On the evening of Saturday 29th Emerson, Lake and Palmer stepped out on stage, and though still working with a short and under-rehearsed set, they made a major impact. During "Pictures", Lake and a silver-blue-glitter-suited Emerson let off two small cannon on stage. Keith's idea for the cannon came from Tchaikovsky's masterpiece of proto-ELP orchestral bombast, pomp and circumstance, the *1812 Overture*. Emerson thought, why not give Mussorgsky the same flavour? Two days before, the band had found a pair of cannon in a Kings Road antique shop. They persuaded the owners to lend them and went to a field to test them. Everything seemed fine. On the night, just as "Pictures" was reaching its climax, Emerson was about to hit his foot switch which would detonate the charge when he noticed an Italian photographer leaning over too far in order to get a good shot. Quickly Emerson signalled him to "fuck off", and hit the switch. Too late! The keyboard player looked on in horror as the blast blew the hapless lensman into the crowd.

Beginning a pattern that was to continue for most of Emerson, Lake and Palmer's career, the audience loved the performance, while some more sober-minded critics were far less impressed. Some sectors of the press made unfavourable comparisons with The Nice, dismissing ELP as "over-technical" and "lacking in warmth and spirit". From the word go, ELP's music divided people. You either loved it or you loathed it. John Peel was in the latter camp: "a tragic waste of talent and electricity", he said; and the scornful headline in the microscopic local Midlands rag *The Kettering Leader* of 25th September 1970 was, "The Rubbish Some Pop Polls Do Produce", perhaps one of the most preposterously irrelevant notices in the history of music criticism. Others were kinder. One reviewer, responding to Peel's execration, pointed out that Keith, Greg and Carl, with their combined reputations to live up to, were perhaps just too keen to impress.

In spite of the critical hostility, ELP quickly earned themselves a reputation as one of the best live acts around, "hitting everybody in the audience on several levels," as Palmer explained. Their stunning shows further heightened the anticipation for their debut album. Titled simply *Emerson, Lake and Palmer*, this record appeared in December, 1970 and duly silenced those who felt the band were merely The Nice Mark II. The trio's recorded debut featured a slicker production and a more momentous sound by far than anything Emerson had recorded previously. The sound hadn't come as easily as the record might suggest. "Greg kind of automatically seated himself at the mixing desk," Emerson later recalled. "I'd be out there twiddling with the synthesizers or whatever... and Greg would be at the desk. When it came to mix things down, we'd all be in the control room, but Greg, having swiped the chair in front of the desk, would still be occupying the position a producer would occupy. We'd all be there to say when we didn't like something, and we'd all end up with our hands on the faders. We had mutually worked it out that Greg would be credited as the producer, but Greg acknowledged that we were all producing the albums. We'd all do the typical thing, where you know this great lick is coming up and you have to make sure everybody hears it, so you push the fader all the way for that second or two. And of course, when we heard it back, this thing would come out of nowhere and go *"raaahhhhh!"* over the top, and everybody would look at whoever had done it and give them the evil eye or something. The poor engineer would be riding the master gain fader throughout the mixing session, and after four or five hours he'd have brought it down to nothing because we'd all been trying to make sure our licks got heard, and we'd have to reset the whole board and go back to square one."

Emerson would always maintain that Lake's role as producer was never decided democratically, but that perhaps overall, he was happy to have Greg in the chair. The pressure he felt as The Nice's only creative force had frustrated him. Naturally, in giving up some of his power there would be problems but right from the word go he had told the other two that they would all be equal. As Lake had more experience in production than his bandmates, it made sense for him to take this role.

ELP's debut LP formulated most of the winning elements that would drive their career: the fierce riffing; the soloists' battles contrasting with unison discipline; Lake's lyrical world of myth, war, love and loss. They showed they had what it took to write and perform great and unusual music, both as a band and individually. The jazz stylings and classical adaptations would appeal to Nice fans. The by turns gentle and tortured lyrics owed more than a little to Pete Sinfield and early King Crimson. Finally, Carl Palmer had brought his distinctive drumming from Atomic Rooster. Although some fans of Nice, Crimson and Rooster still harboured grudges over the breakup of three acts, the new songs were distinctive enough to woo new converts, and were obviously crafted to make good live material.

Crucially *Emerson, Lake and Palmer* was also the first record to introduce the synthesiser to the rock world, first in the coda of "Tank" and more famously in the groundbreaking solo on "Lucky Man." Emerson had used a Moog synthesiser on stage during the late Nice era – surprisingly, considering Dr Moog invented the initially unwieldy instrument specifically for the studio – but this was the first time he'd committed the revolutionary sound to record.

Emerson's first encounter with the Moog synthesiserwas in a record store, in the late 1960s, listening to Walter (later to become Wendy) Carlos's *Switched-On Bach* LP. "That's when I heard the Brandenburg Concerto, which we'd already been doing, played on a Moog synthesizer," Emerson explained. "I didn't honestly like it. The guy asked me what I thought of it. I said it sounded horrible. It was too boggy, too laid down. But there was a picture of the thing it was played on, and I said, 'So what's this?' And he said it was like a telephone switchboard. And I said, 'Oh, that's interesting.' So I bought the album. I couldn't wait to see one of those instruments and found that Mike Vickers, who used to be with Manfred Mann, had one of the first Moog modular systems in his flat in London.

"I went round to see it and asked him if I could use it for one of my performances with the orchestra. He told me that it wasn't really meant to be moved around, that it was really for studio rather than live performance. Anyway, he was willing to have a go, so what happened was that he hid behind the instrument while I played it live, jumping up occasionally to make the necessary patch changes. It amazed everybody, because of all the new sounds that were coming out. They said, "What the hell is that?. So I became the first person to use a synthesiser on stage and obviously wanted to get hold of a Moog instrument for myself. I wrote to Bob Moog asking for all the specs. He told me there was no 'live' model, but he had produced a new version which had a pre-set box, which might make live performance easier.

"[Four thousand pounds later] all this stuff arrived over from America and I had it in my flat and didn't even know how to start to get the thing working! There was no instruction manual. In desperation I called Mike Vickers who had it at his place for three days and finally got it going. I didn't understand exactly where the noise started from, it was as simple as that. Mike Vickers worked on it and set up this patching arrangement, I used that for a bit."

Emerson sought instruction from an electronics professor in Devon. Dag Fellner of Feldon Audio also came round and gave him a hand. It took Emerson practically two years to master the Moog, and even then he was at the mercy of the machine's humidity-related volatility. Fortunately the technology progressed apace and portable versions soon appeared.

Emerson's own role in the development of the synthesiser cannot be overstated. Dr. Robert Moog recalls, "In the summer of '70 we were commissioned to build a quartet of live-performance modular synthesizers for a concert series to be held in the Museum of Modern Art in New York City. It was called 'Jazz in the Garden'. We built these four things out of standard modules, and we designed pre-set boxes so that, instead of changing all the knobs and re-routing patch cards, you could just press a button and get a new pre-set.

"After the concert, we wondered what the hell to do with these things. We let our representatives know that we wanted to sell them. One of them, a Londoner named Dag Fellner, told me that maybe he could sell one to a young musician by the name of Keith Emerson, because their new group was doing an album. That winter I visited Dag. By that time, Keith already had this damn thing in his possession. Dag asked me if I wanted to meet this guy, and of course I said yes. I found out later the group was right in the middle of making *Emerson, Lake and Palmer*." Moog and Emerson met and hit it off, leading to a close association that would involve Emerson in the role of Moog's official "test pilot". The keyboard player's help in the development of the synthesiser was crucial. "In general, everything we've ever done has been in collaboration with musicians," Moog explained. "It's not something you can do out of a formula book or in an ivory tower, there's constant experimentation. Keith was the first guy who really, in a professional and businesslike way, took a large modular system on stage and made it work. That synthesiser of his is one of four instruments that we made that were the first pre-set instruments ever. We had no idea what the problems would be on stage, and what would be more convenient than the first arrangement we had. ...

"The range of pitch which you would want to pre-set and the accuracy with which you would want to pre-set it is something that we didn't know precisely. Keith went out and developed his own technique for tuning the instrument up with one hand while playing the organ with another. That was the damnedest thing I'd ever seen, and only at the highest level of professionalism could someone do that, to have the discipline to do it effectively in front of ten thousand people."

As a virtuoso pianist, Emerson was quick to answer those who saw the synth as not "real" playing. "Well, I think people are wary of new inventions," he reasoned, "And this has happened right from the time of the electric organ. Fats Waller and Jimmy Smith were both looked on as a joke, and it took a commercial record as such to get it known, and that was probably 'House Of The Rising Sun' by the Animals.

"As far as the Moog is concerned, well, I may be wrong, but I think some people get the idea that the Moog is playing itself. Sure, it can be programmed that way, and I do it in the act to show the possibilities of the Moog, but it's well in control. And everything I put into it comes out of it. It cannot play itself. You see, they see all those flashing lights and they think, 'Oh yes, he's got completely lost in the wires', which just isn't the case."

The opening track on *Emerson, Lake and Palmer*, "The Barbarian," was based on Hungarian composer Béla Bartók's "Allegro Barbaro", the first of many ELP classical adaptations and typical of their early approach. Bartók's forbidding, aggressive style, had led contemporary critics to brand him, along with fellow Hungarian composer Zoltán Kodály, a "young barbarian" in 1910. He responded the following year with "Allegro Barbaro" for piano, a piece of greater ferocity than anything he had yet composed. Although it represents only one aspect of Bartók's style, he was characterised by some critics as brutally iconoclastic. As early as 1915, one critic likened his piano works to "uncaring bunches of notes apparently representing the composer promenading the keyboard in his boots... some can be played better with the elbows, others with the flat of the hand. None requires fingers to perform, nor ears to listen to". The name Bartók came to symbolise everything that the bewildered layman hated about "modern music", in much the same way as Picasso symbolised "modern art".

Emerson had been practising the Allegro in the studio when Palmer heard it. "He had been listening to one of Bartók's piano concertos anyway," Emerson explained, "and when he heard me playing the 'Allegro Barbaro' he wanted me to do a version of it."

"We called it 'Barbarian' because of the aggression," said Palmer. "There is a real hate thing going on. It always reminds me of violence, which is very easy to express in music. I like this track for its intensity – it doesn't let up for a second."

In the early days this cut was the opener on stage.

Controversially the band did not credit Bartók as co-composer on the album. This resulted in the first of ELP's problems over copyright when the Bartók estate let its disapproval of the piece's treatment be known. (Similar difficulties cropped up with the third piece on the album, "Knife-Edge".) "At that time I thought the record company sorted out copyright"[4], Emerson later explained, "And we just played the music. In fact I thought that until I had a letter from a Mrs. Bartók..."

The reason for Mrs. Bartók's concern was that ELP's version was diametrically opposed to Bartók's intentions. "The main task of the performer is to avoid making the piece an avalanche of relentless noise," says one writer... Another remarks that were it not for Bartók's compositional "checks and balances" (few of which were observed in the ELP arrangement!), the piece "might have degenerated into a machine-like percussion"!

After such a powerful group showcase, the album's second track is a simple and charming Greg Lake song demonstrating Emerson's piano playing talents and featuring a beautiful acoustic guitar solo by Greg.

"I wrote 'Take A Pebble' after Christmas 1969 with Keith," Lake explains, "when there were just the two of us and Carl hadn't joined us. It started out as a folk guitar thing, then Keith added piano and I used a bass. The solos weren't there to start with, but Keith wrote a solo and I decided to put in a guitar solo as well. It was a solo I had written about five years ago and never had a chance to use." The song was to be the band's piano showcase for many years, fulfilling the same function in the band's live set as "Hang On To A Dream" had done for The Nice.

Side One of the vinyl album climaxed with "Knife-Edge," a rip roaring heavy workout showcasing Emerson's Hammond in full flight, which was soon to become one of the band's most popular live numbers. It was inspired by the joyful and triumphant fanfare opening of the Allegretto from Czech composer Leos Janácek's *Sinfonietta*.

"'Knife-Edge' was written right at the end of the album," Lake explained at the time. "For most of the album the direction of the group was still being formed, and this track is an indication of what we'll be doing in the future." Lake's lyrics, co-credited on the sleeve to the enigmatic "Fraser"[5], are packed with inner turmoil, religious imagery and doom-laden portents of a future world of darkness and madness, making the piece reminiscent of "Epitaph" and "In the Court of the Crimson King" from his Crimson days. The song concludes with a screaming headlong rush into the abyss – created by slowing the tape down. Keith remembers that his solo "was a one-off thing. Greg was very good at choosing which solos were all right. He always persuaded me in the end. There were times when I'd say, 'God, that was terrible, let me play another solo,' and he'd say, 'No, I like that, let's keep it.' So I'd live with it for two days and come to accept it. By the time we were done with the album, there wasn't another solo that could have been more right."

The second side of the album comprises three solo showcases. "The Three Fates" is a virtuoso Emerson display, while the keyboard player composed the music for "Tank" as a vehicle for Palmer's percussion solo. Finally, Lake's "Lucky Man" started life as a very simple acoustic song.

The three-part composition "The Three Fates" was based loosely on the Greek legend of the three goddesses of fate – Clotho, holder of the distaff which spun the thread of life, Lachesis, who mixed good and evil with it, and Atropos, who cut the thread at the appointed moment. The organ parts were recorded at the Royal Festival Hall and St. Mark's, Finchley. "We had to take all the recording gear around with us," says Lake. "The Festival Hall organ was distorting at the lower end of the pipes, and that was why we went to the church as well." Along with "Take a Pebble", the track illustrated the kind of freedom big-name musicians were allowed during the era. As Emerson has recently mentioned, in the 70s one could go into a studio and do anything one wanted, and then play it to the record company executives, with minimal marketplace pressure.

Another distinguishing musical feature of concerts in the late 60s, and early 70s, was the much derided "drum solo". Among the earliest examples of this perhaps unfortunate trend was Ginger Baker's "Toad", which featured a solo almost fifteen minutes long. Audiences soon tired of such live indulgences, and drum solos on studio records remained rare. Unlike most such pieces, ELP's effort, "Tank", was exhilarating. Set against a jazzy backdrop, Palmer's drum solo – which he was then performing live during "Rondo" – underlined his frightening speed and technique and drew comparisons with his hero Buddy Rich. Years later Emerson would introduce "Tank" to the audiences as Palmer's "chance to have a bash", adding under his breath – with admirable irony – "We'll never hear the end of it otherwise."

"Tank" was perhaps most revolutionary however, for featuring a Moog synthesiser towards its finish. A brass-like accompaniment underpins a lead synthesiser line which sounds something like a piccolo. The piece fades out, like a military band passing into the distance.

"Lucky Man" is an anti-war protest Lake originally composed at the tender age of twelve years old, though it's difficult to imagine a young boy coming up with lines like "a gold covered mattress on which he was led." "Lucky Man" was Lake's first acoustic piece and quickly became an important part of the band's eclectic live armoury.

Lake's instincts as a producer also paid dividends on this track. With all the music completed, both he and Emerson agreed this would be an ideal vehicle for the Moog synthesiser that the keyboardist was experimenting with at the time. Emerson started dabbling, while Lake had engineer Eddie Offord[6] roll the tape. The first attempt was just what Lake was looking for. An amazed Emerson insisted he could do better and wanted another go. Lake held out and his firm stance was justified by listeners' enthusiastic responses to the now famous concluding solo.

Emerson's first recorded synth solo was very much a departure from how the instrument had been used before. Walter Carlos had used the Moog to replicate other instruments. Emerson described his own use of the synthesiser as "basically all effects."

"It's just been a matter of trying to get new sounds that you wouldn't hear on any other instrument," he explained. "It's got to have a definite characteristic that's obviously a synthesiser.... I've never used the synthesiser to copy. There's no real point in it if you can't tell if that's a guitar playing or a Moog. With me you say, 'That is definitely a Moog'."

Although "Tank" was the first track in the running order of the record to employ the synthesiser, it was this number which brought it to the attention of millions of people. Many people who heard it, including Dr Robert Moog himself, were astonished by this strange, and even physically disturbing, new noise. As Greg says, "The Moog at the end goes down to twenty-one cycles, which is lower than most ordinary speakers can go. If you listen to it in a bass speaker, it makes your stomach rumble!" Emerson was less enthusiastic. "I put a few lines onto the song and Greg said, *'Great, great!'* I didn't think much of the solo. Honestly, it's a lot of shit. But it was just what he wanted. I just did a rough setting on the synthesiser, went in, and played something off the top of my head."

Thus was born the most celebrated solo in synthesiser history.

When the album was released, the critics were generally pretty scathing. However, *Melody Maker*'s reviewer considered the debut, "A triumph for ELP." Aware of the hostility all around, the reviewer continued, "They have so much to say and offer, it would be a tragedy if they were stifled or discouraged by the knockers. Give them an 'elping hand and listen!"

Looking back at the first album with the benefit of a decade's hindsight, Keith would feel that the adverse critical response had actually affected the music and, ironically, helped them along. "The first ELP album was totally unlike anything being played on the radio stations at the time," he explained. "We were in a completely different category from the heavy bands like Led Zeppelin and Cream. The slagging we got at the beginning probably did us a lot of good. It made us more introspective, and the result has been some very aggressive music. In fact I don't think we would have made it if there hadn't been that high level of aggression, because that was what attracted people initially. There were two arrangements of classical pieces on that album, and rock people weren't supposed to be into that at all.

"The album isn't perfect," Emerson would conclude, "Because at that stage we weren't really playing together as a unit. We were just a trio of individuals."

But the band profited from the experience, and remarkably, by the end of January 1971 had already completed the follow up record. On March 4th ELP embarked on a month long tour of the UK. Shortly afterwards they went to the States, including a show at the Carnegie Hall.

By the summer the second album was ready for release. The debut album, as Lake saw it, still had one foot in the past. However, just round the corner was *Tarkus* – a milestone in the history of Progressive Rock. Its like had never before been heard.

Notes

1 Over the next month, Plymouth's Van Dike Club saw (non debut) performances by two other new groups led by ex-Nice members; 11 September – Lee Jackson's Jackson Heights and 10 October – Brian Davison's Every Which Way.

2 Non-British readers may not know of the series of children's books, set in Toytown, about Noddy and his friends, written by Enid Blyton.

3 Most of the festival was filmed and recently some performances have been released on video – Jimi Hendrix and The Who. Only a short clip of ELP's performance survives.

4 Since then he has checked with the Performing Right Society, who analyse cover versions and grade them. A Grade One rating means sufficient disparity with the original theme that a work can be classed a musician's 'own composition'.

5 There were some additional lyrics from Alex Fraser. Greg explains: "He was a roadie, a roadie's roadie, called Dynamite Legs. We got to be friends with him. He helped one day with the words, so we gave him credit. (Pause) We only gave him credit, we never gave him any money." Fraser also contributed to the lyrics of "Pictures at an Exhibition".

6 One of the most celebrated of the rock record producers/engineers of the 70s. Eddie Offord was credited as engineer on the first four ELP albums. He was even more closely associated with Yes, for whom he produced six albums – *Fragile*, *Close to the Edge*, *Yessongs*, *Tales from Topographic Oceans*, *Relayer* and *Drama*. He also produced Steve Howe's *Beginnings*. The Dregs, Baker Gurvitz Army, Lindisfarne, Terry Reid, David Sancious and Billy Squier have all profited from his work and without his help, the 1984 Pallas album *The Sentinel* would not have been one of the classic examples of the new wave of progressive music.

CHAPTER 3

Battlefield

Unusual time signatures abound, rapid tempos call up the musicians' fleetest fingering, and a slight but attractive jazz tinge colours the proceedings. It's hard to categorise, but it has a remarkable ability to mix trippy rock sounds with significant musical content. And that is not exactly what one finds in your run-of-the-mill rock recording. Stereo Review, *1971*

You have to be self-indulgent to do something new. Keith Emerson

When they returned to the studio in January, 1971, ELP took two weeks – one week per side – to record *Tarkus*, the album that would take them to the top of the album charts and ensure that they swept the year's music paper polls. Even bearing in mind that Emerson had mapped out all the arrangements beforehand, it's sobering to realise that such a piece of work could be fashioned within such a short timescale. Emerson admitted the LP was the quickest he'd ever committed to vinyl. And yet it has the most varied ideas, from country to boogie and honky tonk piano. Though the music was complex, this fast recording process ensured the record retained its freshness. As producer, Lake was keen to retain the buzz a musician gets when playing an exciting new piece.

On release, the album polarised opinion. Press criticism was more divided; some was much more hostile. However there were certainly plenty of positive reviews, and the belief that ELP always attracted the critics' bile is misplaced. *Sounds*, for one, felt *Tarkus* saw ELP "get[ing] to grips with their myriad of instruments." More importantly, this time around, ELP showed that they were winning fan loyalty of an exceptional kind. The major composition "Tarkus" itself was an extraordinary *tour de force*. With its constantly changing time signatures and biting, hard-edged sound, it could not fail to make an impression – and by now Emerson was using the Moog synthesiser liberally and with great inventiveness on such tracks as "Aquatarkus."

Emerson had written most of the music, and his cohorts completely lived up to his creation. It was a "concept" album, built around a science fiction theme. The sci-fi vision of a violent world populated by fearsome bio-machines clearly announced the band's intended new direction, previously hinted at on "The Barbarian", "Tank", and "Knife-Edge".

Some of the pieces on the second side, while unrelated to the title piece, which filled Side One, very much contributed to the overall atmosphere of the LP. Like "Tarkus" itself, "Bitches Crystal" and "A Time And A Place" were close in spirit to "Knife Edge" from the first album, and "The Only Way" was just one of the songs which elaborated Greg's religious preoccupation. "Infinite Space" was a repetitive bash descended from earlier ostinato-based pieces by Emerson while in The Nice and on the first ELP album. The other numbers at the beginning and end of the second side, were fun items and gave Keith a chance to play country piano like his long-time hero Floyd Cramer ("Jeremy Bender"), and crazed rock and roll ("Are You Ready Eddy?".)[1]

Keith explained how it all came about : "The main idea for "Tarkus" came from an improvisation I was playing one night on tour. I developed the idea on the piano at home when we had some time off [years later Keith gave some credit to Frank Zappa for the inspiration to write Tarkus]. I found myself playing a new kind of music that I couldn't relate to anything else. When the group met up again after two weeks I played it to them and Greg and Carl had the horrors. We had a big discussion about self-indulgence. Greg said, 'I can't play that kind of music. If that's what you want to play then I think you should look for someone else to play with.' This kind of shocked me, because I was excited about the new piece, but I told him that if that was what he wanted, I'd find some other musicians. Eventually everybody agreed that you have to be self-indulgent to do something new. So we put it down and everybody liked it. Carl was in his element and we worked well together." Indeed Palmer was absolutely critical in reconciling Lake to Emerson's vision of "Tarkus". If he hadn't been fully behind the project, the band might well have split.

There were plenty of "concept" albums around in the late 60s and early 70s, but *Tarkus* was probably the most striking yet, as much for the gatefold LP sleeve design by William Neal as for the extraordinary music. Without Neal's paintings – most importantly the design of the star of the show, the Tarkus creature itself – the album would lack a level of symbolic depth. While the music can of course stand alone, this is the only ELP album where one actually needs the sleeve art to begin to fully comprehend the band's artistic vision. Both the music and the paintings combine to conjure up a remarkable fantasy world.

For all this synchronicity, the artwork actually came about by a stroke of luck. Neal was an art student who used to hang out at Advision Studios with his paintings of semi-mythical scenarios. At that stage the band didn't have a title; Emerson was impressed by Neal's work and realised it bore more than a passing resemblance to the music he had written.

In the first picture on the inside of the gatefold sleeve, the Tarkus – half-armadillo, half-tank – hatches from a giant egg on the slopes of an erupting volcano.

It then sets out to do battle with four creatures. The first, an indescribable rocket-firing creature filled with rockets, is blasted to Kingdom Come by the Tarkus's cannon. The same fate is met by the next beast, which is half-pterodactyl, half-warplane, and also by the third, an ingenious combination of lizard and armoured vehicle. The Tarkus seems to be unstoppable, until it finally meets its match in the Manticore – a mythical animal traceable to ancient Greek writings possessing the body of a lion, the quills of a porcupine, the head of a man and the tail and sting of a scorpion. Perhaps significantly the Manticore features no machine element at all. When the Manticore gashes the eye of the Tarkus with his sting, the Tarkus swims, defeated, out to sea. The backdrop of the white cliffs of Dover tell us this has all taken place in England!

One of the work's main themes is the futility of war – still a major theme in rock lyrics in the early 70s. Lake wanted to ask questions about violent revolutions. " "The first song ('Stones of Years'), … asks the question, 'Why can't you see now...?' – how stupid it is, conflict." Lake explained. "The next song ('Mass') is about the hypocrisy of it all, and the last song ('Battlefield') is the aftermath, the conclusion of it. What have we gained?"

Emerson had a different interpretation, seeing *Tarkus* as about "a reversal of how life is supposed to have begun on the planet. It's evolution in reverse after the final nuclear explosion". That's why in "Aquatarkus" Emerson's Moog replicates a snorkel as Tarkus returns to the water – where life originated.

Predictably, when the album came out there was a lot of speculation over the meaning of the lyrics. The ambiguity that allowed two of the band to hold diverging interpretations helped to imbue "Tarkus" with a mystique in the same sort of way as Peter Gabriel's relatively impenetrable words did on Genesis's *The Lamb Lies Down on Broadway*.

In 1997 in his history of progressive rock *Rocking The Classics*[2], Edward Macan recounted one of the less convincing interpretations that had been put forward – that the beast represented imperial America using its military might to bend the world to its will. "Battlefield" is thus about the Vietnam War and the story ends with the Tarkus (America) getting its comeuppance. Although fanciful, this interpretation would tie in with the end of The Nice's version of "America".

Bill Martin, in his prog analysis *Listening to the Future* [2], (also published in 1997 – a bumper year for prog books that also included Paul Stump's *The Music's All That Matters* [2]) identifies *Tarkus*' theme as technology out of control, drawing debatable parallels with James Cameron's movie starring Arnold Schwarzenegger, *The Terminator*. There is a good case for seeing a message in the story about the ultimate victory of a "natural" being over horrifying machine creatures presumably created to wage war. The Manticore could be taken to represent MANkind – it does have a human face.

Another dimension to *Tarkus* is its attack on the church's involvement in politics – the Cardinal of grief, the pilgrim committing every sin. In this "war" there is no doubt the church is heavily involved in the power structure.

Lake has devoted quite a lot of his lyrical work to the subject of religion – most of the songs on *Tarkus* refer to it in some way, including the jokey "Jeremy Bender". It's one aspect of Lake's search for intense experience and expression, which would later reach its apogee on *Works Vol 1*. ELP's stage presentation, too, with projected slides of stained glass windows during "Pictures", reflects the exorcising of their personal demons. And there's something about Lake's still, calm presence at centre stage, between two musical hurricanes, that's bound to stir religious instincts in an audience. An ELP show has a lot in common with a religious ceremony. Interestingly, they had originally floated "Trinity" as a name for the band.[3]

Later the following year, when Lake was listing some of the people he respected, alongside Prince Rupert Loewenstein, Al Oerter, Muhammad Ali and Bertrand Russell, he namechecked, "Jesus Christ, who," he continued, "was one of the highest-level entertainers of all time. He went out with his twelve roadies, and some of the stunts that cat pulled would blow your mind. He was a real heavyweight – I mean, they're still turning out to see Him, every Sunday, and He doesn't even appear! I wouldn't mind playing Jerusalem myself some day." Though this was tongue-in-cheek, it gives a clue to why Lake – who explained in the same interview that his personal philosophy was "based on transformation of energies" – finds religion an interesting concept.

Musically, what is obvious to anyone familiar with its predecessor, is how *Tarkus* is more of a band album. ELP's debut was a balance of individuals that in some ways anticipated the much later *Works* period.

"I prefer to think of *Tarkus* as being the first album we cut as a band," Palmer would confirm. "We were so much together on those sessions and playing without any pressures, whereas our first album was more or less a proving point to initially show what we were capable of doing. On *Tarkus* we did it."

"*Tarkus*...showed that we could play together," Keith acknowledges. "It's more musically mature, I think. Also, the first side of that album has got some screaming solo organ and synthesiser lines on it, and that showed that a keyboard player could do more than just lay backing chords under guitar solos."

Certainly *Tarkus* made quite an impression. At the end of 1971, Emerson, Lake and Palmer – as a band and as individuals – received no less than seven awards in the prestigious poll of readers of the rock and pop paper *Melody Maker*. They also fared well in the polls by *Sounds* and *New Musical Express*. *Tarkus*, both as a piece of music and as an album package – set ELP on their ascent to the being one of rock's top attractions.

However, back in these early days, audience capacities aside, some of ELP's very best gigs were raw and basic. In 1992 Dr. Robert Moog recalled the first time he saw the band in concert. "In 1971, I got a call from Keith saying he was going to be on tour. It might have been their first American tour. I was still in upstate New York, and the closest they were going to get was New York City. I tried and tried to find out where Gaelic Park was. Nobody at the New York City Parks Department had heard of it. Finally, somebody found out that Gaelic Park was a little soccer field way up in the Bronx or Manhattan. In fact, it was at the end of the subway line, because there was an elevated track all the way around it, where the train looped around before going back.

"Keith had invited me to come wherever backstage was. He and I piled into his mandatory limousine and we went through the mud, rocks and broken glass – which is what you expect to find under the tracks of a New York City subway train – onto the soccer field. He got out with the rest of the group and they walked onto the field up to this wooden platform stage out by one goal. At the other end of the field there was a line of ten or twelve portajohns.

"There were about 10,000 young white males packed in there. I don't remember any seats; people were just trampling on the soccer field...lo and behold, who do I meet there but a customer friend of mine, Gershon Kingsley. Gershon was a successful middle-aged professional studio musician who had lived in Israel and Germany. ... Anyhow, I meet up with Gershon by the row of portajohns, and he's completely disoriented and freaked out. In back of us, you can smell all the shit and piss and the doors to the johns are banging open and closed. And in front, here's this guy throwing an organ around, making keys fly off, and making the instruments scream. All of a sudden, Gershon shrieks, 'This is the end of the world!'"

Which was probably the generally desired effect

ELP took a huge replica of the Tarkus 'tank' on stage; it was designed to shoot foam at the audience. Unfortunately, it was not entirely reliable. Carl Palmer recalls one occasion in Brighton when it went wrong: "That night we had it aimed in the wrong direction, and it poured all this stuff straight out into the grand piano! Filled it up! We had to stop the show, and on came the roadies with the dustpans and the hoover to clear it out." The band also experimented with replicas of other monsters from the album sleeve, including the half-pterodactyl, half-warplane creature, causing some odd juxtapositions. In his review of the Odeon, Hammersmith concert of November '72, Chris Welch observed, "... a rather comic bird on a wire ... flapped menacingly over Keith Emerson"!

Emerson, Lake and Palmer's gleeful critics never hesitated to draw the obvious parallels between the fictional Tarkus monster and the band itself. The day would come when someone started describing ELP and the other equipment-heavy progressive bands, as "dinosaurs" with the implication that they would soon be extinct. But for now Emerson, Lake and Palmer were under no threat. To their many fans they were untouchable.

Notes

1   Originally "Are You Ready Eddy" was not going to be on the album. It was mooted that a live version of "Nutrocker" was going to be used. It seems that at that stage they were unsure how the *Pictures* album was going to look.

Incidentally, at the end of "Are You Ready Eddy", there is some jokey banter, and Keith shrills the words "We've only got ham or cheese" in a Pythonesque voice. This relates to the canteen lady at Advision Studios. When asked "What sandwiches do you have?" this is what she replied.

2   For years progressive rock has been vilified. These books are important ammunition in establishing the genre's place in music history. In late 1998 news leaked out that Edward Macan's next book is to be about ELP – we await its publication with bated breath.

3   ELP and other progressive bands touch the religious impulses in their audiences. (Edward Macan refers to "the whole hermetic ethos of the psychedelic era".) The similarity between ancient religious rituals and the staging and atmosphere of progressive rock concerts is striking. As in Gnostic religion, progressive rock can be seen as having its Outer Mysteries (for the casual fan) and Inner Mysteries (for the devoted night-after-night follower) which are only perceived after closer study and long acquaintance.

CHAPTER 4

Pictures From Newcastle

We were playing in Budapest, doing Pictures, and this chap was standing in front of the stage with tears rolling down his face. I found him after the show and asked him if anything was wrong. He said 15 years ago he'd been put in prison for three months for owning a copy of the Pictures *album. Greg Lake, March, 1993*

In December, 1971, just six months after the groundbreaking *Tarkus*, another ELP album hit the stores. *Pictures At An Exhibition* was a live recording of the Mussorgsky classical piece that been a part of the band's live repertoire since its inception.

The great Russian composer, Modeste Petrovich Mussorgsky (1839-81) studied unsystematically and composed erratically, dying of alcoholic epilepsy one week short of his forty-second birthday. *Pictures At An Exhibition* (1874) was the first great Russian solo piano masterpiece, though upon its publication, many thought Mussorgsky's startling harmonic and rhythmic innovations were evidence of incompetence.

The pictures which inspired Mussorgsky were from an exhibition of the work of architect Victor Hartmann, a long-standing friend who had recently died. In fact, only three were from the exhibition of Hartmann's work; Mussorgsky saw the others at Hartmann's home. Most of the pictures have not survived.

While the composer was content to leave *Pictures* as a piano work, its orchestral nature led to it being arranged for many instrumental combinations, with the technicolored orchestral arrangement by Maurice Ravel (1875–1937) introducing it to a far wider audience.

Emerson first heard the piece in its orchestral form at London's Festival Hall.

"The next day I went to the music store," Emerson explained, "And asked for a copy of the score, and when it turned out to be a work for piano solo, that thrilled me, because there it was in a form that I could play. Later, when I approached Greg and Carl about performing it, they were agreeable. So we put a version of it together, added a few cuts of our own, and took it on the road. I wanted to use it sort of as an educational piece, exposing our audiences to this great work of classical music."

Although ELP's "Pictures" often sticks pretty faithfully to the Mussorgsky original, it's in no way a complete transcription and arrangement in the way that, to make the most obvious comparison, Tomita's later fully synthesised version was. There are only four of the composer's eleven pictures (the first two and the last two), and three of the five versions of "Promenade". For a more detailed study of the piece, see Appendix 1.

Though the piece was now a live favourite and had been recorded before *Tarkus* it had not been considered for a record release because it was not primarily ELP's own work. In the end the band buckled to "popular demand." The recorded performance took place at the Newcastle City Hall on 26th March, 1971.

"We were in a strange predicament with *Pictures*," Carl would explain, "Because we didn't want to rob people of having it…. And to record it live seemed to be the only way to capture the energy, enthusiasm and spontaneity that a band should have playing a piece of music like that. Because it's a classical piece it doesn't mean it should be played in a rigid fashion. Playing it on stage one can open up certain areas. I used to say to myself, I enjoy playing this piece of music immensely, and because I'm European, it's in my blood anyway I always enjoyed the classical piece. As players we wanted to entertain rather than educate people, but if you can do both, then that is fantastic and that's what we did."

Earlier in February of that year, a movie of ELP's performance of *Pictures*, taken from their 9th December 1970 show at London's Lyceum Theatre, was given a theatrical release along with films by the Strawbs and the Scaffold. The movie was shot by the band's friend Lindsay Clennell, for Visual and Musical Entertainments. During the sold-out concert there was a power cut, and electricity for the performance was provided by the TV generators.

The movie featured some strong performances, but the music sometimes sounds disjointed. Also, a great many of the most interesting moments were obscured by the ubiquitous psychedelic coloured blobs so beloved of pop film makers of the time – perhaps to conceal the uninspired camera work. The movie was not a commercial success and the band quickly distanced themselves from it.

"What I object to about the film is that they're charging too much for people to see what I feel is basically a bad production," Lake commented at the time. "I really have no responsibility to the kids over the film. It wasn't me who made the film. I would prefer to say that I salvaged what was there of the sound rather than produced anything. On the Lyceum recording, which is with the film, [the film crew] presented me with an eight-track tape. They'd run out of tape half-way through, and quickly had to chop one tape on and one tape off, with bits missing, and they said, 'There's your tape'. There was overspill on every track: the drums were on the piano track and the bass was on the organ. It just went on and on and on. So I did the best I could with it. I would have chosen not to have had a producer's credit. What they had on the billboard in Piccadilly, 'Their first full-length movie', or something like that, I wouldn't have chosen. You've got to know that we wouldn't say things like that. Somebody did it and we weren't happy. It went out. I'm pleased it's not doing very well. I tried to stop it going out completely."

"The film in my opinion is shocking," Palmer complained. "It is a sort of 1959 rock and roll film, because the modern filming technique put into it was nil. There are lots of basic shots of the band... we had a lot of ideas about modern filming techniques which we wanted to see done, but instead... it was done as a straight film, like early Beatles films, it was so straight... Because a friend of ours is doing it is the only reason we let him release it."

As with Lake, Palmer's main objections were to the sound, blaming the absence of the band's engineer, Eddie Offord, for its general poor quality. "I think there was something wrong with the organs too," Palmer added. Faced with the demand for a soundtrack album, drastic action was called for.

"The original soundtrack has gone out with the film," Palmer continued. "It could have been changed, but the people didn't want to spend any more money on doing it. So we said, OK, we can't release an album like that, so we spent more money, we'll pay for it ourselves, and we'll get a unit up to Newcastle with all the tape recorders and things, and our own engineer and we'll do the best we can."

"I think we got a live recording that is worthy to go out as a 'live' album," said Palmer, who was dubious of the merits of live albums in general. "I think most 'live' albums, even if people have been very careful, are really a glorified bootleg. There was a lot of pressure put on us at the Lyceum that day because of the film, so the music didn't hit it off. It wasn't that bad , but it was bad to us in the group to release it as a 'live' album. That was why we held back, and we got a lot of letters and we were slagged for that."

With a satisfactory recording of *Pictures* captured on tape, the "live" project was then put on a backburner until after the release of *Tarkus*. "Originally it was going to be a double album," Palmer told the press, "with *Pictures* and the new album we have just started. But because we kept people waiting so long we just had to release it. There has been pressure as well from the record companies, because they wanted it."

Like *Tarkus*, *Pictures* came housed in a fascinating sleeve. Each section of the piece is given a separate name and is illustrated by a painting by *Tarkus* artist William Neal. On the outside the paintings are unfinished, while inside they are complete. Neal's striking artwork is reminiscent of his work on *Tarkus* and very different from the Hartman pictures that originally inspired Mussorgsky. Hartmann's drawing for "The Gnome" featured the complete figure of a dwarf tottering on crooked legs. His picture of "The Old Castle" belongs to the Italian Middle Ages in contrast to Neal's sci-fi landscape. For Baba Yaga's hut, Hartmann has a clock-like structure standing on hens' claws. As for "The Great Gates Of Kiev", (the word "Gate" is not in the plural in the original, by the way), the city never had any form of entrance gate; Hartmann entered his design into a competition to build one, but the competition was called off, and no gate was built. No painting existed to represent the "Promenade"[1]; it is the thematic equivalent of the composer's gaze at each painting as he passes.

In addition to "Pictures", the album featured the live encore, "Nutrocker", ELP's lighter, jazzy version of Kim Fowley's chart-topping take on the March from Tchaikovsky's "Nutcracker" ballet.

The album burns. Particular highlights included Lake's storming bass playing and complex acoustic guitar picking. Quite apart from the performance, it was one of the very best quality live recordings ever made, and came to be used as a demonstration disc in hi-fi shops. "Pictures" would also remain the only ELP piece to be played, at least in part, at every concert until 1998.

To underline the fact that the band didn't consider *Pictures* to be a proper ELP album, it was sold at a special discount price. "Selling it cheap and slipping it out," Palmer would say, "and not making a big issue of it."

"We don't look on it as a third album," Emerson told the press, "just a good vibe."

Press reaction was typically mixed. However, *Sounds* deemed it a "Thundering ELP Suite," and considered it "certainly time 'Pictures' was available to the public", while *New Musical Express* saw it as "Just Emerson, Lake and Palmer at their very best." Ironically, considering its low key launch, *Pictures* became one of ELP's most popular records – perhaps partly because of its low price. While it failed to follow *Tarkus* to the number 1 spot on the album charts, stalling at Number 3, it quickly became ubiquitous in record collections of the era.

It also led to something of a Mussorgsky revival. "The classical versions began to sell," Palmer noted with pride, "And the kids realised there were classical pieces they would enjoy." ELP's version also inspired a spate of alternative modern takes on the piece, most notably one by Japanese synthesizer wizard Tomita, in 1975.

For ELP to have put out two hugely influential top three albums within six months was quite a feat. They were now firmly at the head of progressive rock's vanguard.

Notes

1   The original William Neal paintings "The Gnome" and "The Sage" were put up as lots 32 and 33 in the Sotheby's Rock and Roll Memorabilia Auction on Wednesday December 22, 1982. A price of £800–£1,000 each was hoped for, but in the end they remained, embarrassingly, unsold.

CHAPTER 5

Tomorrow … The World

ELP's first public outing of 1972 was a two month trek across the US. It was their third visit to the States and would see them finally achieve major American success. The tour included an appearance at Puerto Rico's Mar y Sol festival along with The Allman Brothers, John McLaughlin and BB King. By the time they headed off across the Atlantic, they had already recorded the studio follow-up to *Tarkus*. Unlike *Tarkus* and *Pictures*, *Trilogy* was "just a collection of songs, really" as Emerson dubbed it.

The opening cut "The Endless Enigma" begins very quietly with a then-fashionable heart beat effect on the bass drum. However, it isn't long before the band are in headlong flight. The action quietens down with a piano trio piece, "The Fugue."

A fugue is a highly ordered contrapuntal piece of music in two or more parts (or 'voices'), built from a theme ('subject') which is stated imitatively at the beginning and recurs in whole or in part, and with alterations, at points throughout the piece. In this century, composers have often deviated considerably from tradition; Emerson is aware both of classical practice and of contemporary harmony and rhythm, and adopts a looser approach to form.

Emerson has dabbled with contrapuntal technique throughout his career. While with The Nice, he heard the "Prelude and Fugue" by Friedrich Gulda, a Swiss pianist and composer whose works successfully integrate jazz and classical approaches. Combining the Gulda influence with Bach's "The Well-Tempered Clavier," he came up with the wonderful "High Level Fugue" for the *Five Bridges* album – though this piece owed much to strict fugal methods, Emerson acknowledged in the sleeve-notes that its infectious foot-tapping rhythm was partly attributable to his use of the boogie-woogie techniques of Meade Lux Lewis and Jimmy Yancey. Imitative and fugue-like techniques recur regularly in Emerson's work and he has also utilised preludes and fugues by other composers (especially Bach) within his own pieces, including the "Prelude no. 6" in "The Only Way" on *Tarkus*.

For someone who naturally favoured playing by ear, "The Fugue" represented something of a departure. "[It] was literally written out on paper before I ever played it," Emerson explained. "I couldn't work out a fugue any other way. Some people are very clever and can improvise them. It's great to be able to do that. But as for me, I have to write it down, look at it and work it out."

Emerson had recorded a short Friedrich Gulda piano piece called "Prelude and Fugue", back in November, 1971. The inclusion of "The Fugue" as part of "The Endless Enigma", recorded the following January, led to the Gulda piece being consigned to the vaults, though Emerson would use Gulda's fugue for the improvisational section of "Take A Pebble" on *Welcome Back My Friends*. (It eventually surfaced on the 1993 box set, from which one may speculate that its omission from *Trilogy* was due to Emerson being less than satisfied with his performance.)

The piece ends with a reprise of "The Endless Enigma", which closes in an impressive fanfare of [Moog-generated] trumpets. This opening cut is packed with ideas and incidents, but, while constantly exciting, it comes over like a lot of good bits put together and is probably the least satisfying of ELP's longer compositions.

"From the Beginning" gives Lake another chance to show his talent for acoustic ballads. Lake's guitar is marvellously languid, while Palmer's percussion is revolutionary. Emerson's Moog solo is very reminiscent of "Lucky Man," if somewhat more restrained. This track provided the band with their biggest hit single and US audiences would come to associate ELP with this Moog-augmented acoustic sound.

The final two tracks of Side One of the record see the band looking toward the Wild West. "The Sheriff" kicks off with Palmer's rallying drum intro. Lake's lyrics tell the story of bad guy Big Kid Josie. It's another of the band's more lighthearted efforts and rolls along humorously to the rip-roaring syncopated solo at the end. The song's cowboy feel is reinforced by Palmer's temple blocks, and Emerson coaxes a clip-clop sound out of the Hammond. This leads us nicely on to a different side of the Wild West in a rumbustiously rhythmic Hammond-dominated take on Aaron Copland's "Hoedown".

As well as being a conductor, a pianist, a lecturer and an author, Aaron Copland (1900–92) was the foremost modern American composer responsible for what critics have seen as a distinctly American strain of modern classical music, as evidenced by his hugely popular score for the 1942 ballet *Rodeo*. Like all his orchestral music, "Hoedown" is full of vivid textures, strongly contrasting colours and bold rhythms. It alludes to old American folk tunes, making special use of the old fiddlers' breakdown "Bonyparte" – a tune Copland found in the book *Traditional Music Of America* – and incorporating a jazz influenced extract from the Scottish "McLeod's Reel." [1]. Emerson was hugely influenced by Copland and would even name his elder son after him.

The arrangement was credited to ELP, though Emerson was probably responsible for all of it except the drum part – "I've adapted the percussion parts that the orchestra would have played as closely as I could put them on the drums," Palmer explained in his book *Applied Rhythms*. Although in many ways Emerson stays close to Copland, he isn't afraid to use the original as a launch pad for a distinctive and uniquely ELP instrumental which sums up one side of the band's musical personality, and soon became one of their most popular live numbers.

The album's title track is immensely varied. From the soft, synthesised strings of the very first bars to the jokey tag at the end, however, this (unlike "The Endless Enigma") is one of the most musically unified of all ELP's pieces. The strings are easily mistaken for a Mellotron, though in fact they were produced by the Mini-Moog. "I refuse to play a mellotron on the grounds that it just doesn't agree with my principles," Emerson maintained. "Because another violinist has had to come in to tape record it and what you're playing is a tape recording – I refuse to play a mellotron under those situations." Emerson nevertheless added, "Greg has a Mellotron – I don't mind *him* playing it. I'm very two-faced, aren't I?"

The first part of "Trilogy"'s tale of relationship breakdown could have been adapted from a Lake ballad, though it is made more effective by Emerson's moog and piano sweeps. Lake's faint cries of "*goodbye*" usher in the ferocious climactic part of the piece. Above the riff, the original melodic theme of the song is radically transformed, becoming the jumping-off point for a brilliantly wild lead synth improvisation. Emerson's big brassy synthesiser sound and the power rhythm section of Lake and Palmer – in particular Palmer's ferocious one handed high-hat work – make this dissonant music some of the most brashly aggressive ELP have ever produced – it wouldn't have been out of place in "Tarkus"; and is in fact in the same time signature.

"Living Sin"'s debauched lyrics are accompanied by the most ferociously exciting music from any of ELP's short songs, with the power coming from an organ theme played in octaves, a brassy synthesiser middle section and Lake's unusual vocal performance. The excitement on this lesser known number gets whipped up further in the instrumental conclusion. While, unlike many hard rocking bands, ELP rarely referred as explicitly to sex as in "Living Sin", matters of the flesh were regularly present under the lyrical surface and in the music.

The final cut, "Abaddon's Bolero", is one of ELP's most interesting pieces. Like most boleros, it's developed from a single idea; this one is Emerson's longest and perhaps most intriguing thematic invention. While the piece's direction has a logic all of its own, it remains entirely satisfying, precisely because of the abrupt changes of tonal centre and lack of conventional modulations. This adds to the sense of cold and tenebrous remorselessness conveyed in the title, Abaddon being the name found in Hebrew for destruction, and in Greek for the angel of the bottomless pit, namely the Devil.

"It frightens me, the fact of where [inspiration] starts, because I can't pin it down to anything," Emerson explained. "It can happen at really weird moments. 'Bolero' happened to me when we were packing away after rehearsal and I just started playing it and everybody looked round. They said, 'What are you doing?' and I said, 'I don't know, but stop packing away your instruments and get them back together again now, because something's happening now, and I don't know what the hell it is!' And we did, and it started building from there."

The piece shares no great similarity with Ravel's famous *Bolero*, a rather stately orchestral crescendo, in comparison with Emerson's insistent martial beat. Emerson's composition demonstrates the variety of sounds now available from the synthesiser – he acknowledged that it was an atypical "attempt to copy the Walter Carlos thing. That was one occasion where I tried to copy trumpet sounds and the like." In the way it used the expanding potential of studio overdubbing, it stole a march on Mike Oldfield's *Tubular Bells* by a year. Indeed, there are up to 24 instrumental lines. When, years later, Emerson arranged the piece for orchestra, he scored it for 2 piccolos, 2 flutes, 2 clarinets, 2 bassoons, contrabassoon, 4 horns, 5 trumpets, 3 trombones, tuba, 4 percussionists (playing timpani, side and snare drums, suspended cymbal and gong), harp, and a large string section.

The work was not originally conceived as a bolero. "I had picked out this little melody that I liked, and I put it down on tape," Emerson explained. "After listening to it several times I began to put down overdubs, and it struck me that this was the perfect thing for the kind of piece which begins at nothing and grows to everything. I took it in to Greg and Carl, and we played it through several times. I told them what I had in mind, so we just started with me playing the melody on a little flute sound that was programmed into the synthesiser. Each time we repeated the theme, I added something, Greg added something, and Carl added more sound on his drums. There wasn't any bolero rhythm at this time; Carl was just beating time and increasing the volume with each repetition, and we just kept on building the sound, and almost instinctively knew when the piece had reached its peak. I looked at Greg and Carl, and we cut off exactly together." After discussion, Emerson hit on the bolero rhythm, and the piece came to be recorded in the form we know.

It is clear from Emerson's words above, that the orchestration of the bolero had a lot of input from the other band members. In spite of the public conception that Emerson was the band's "maestro", ELP were a real working band. By 1972, they were collaborating increasingly successfully, and *Trilogy* was in many ways their most musically integrated and advanced album to date. However this would bring its problems in lack of scope for the three members' individual expressions.

A rumour circulated in advance of the album's release that it would feature new cover art painted by the surrealist artist Salvador Dali. Coincidentally, Dali had painted a picture called "The Endless Enigma", but he was never approached by the band. Other rejected cover concept ideas included a reindeer snowscape.

Trilogy was released to more mixed reviews, though some critics considered it their best yet. One critic even picked up on the sheer entertainment value of the album, placing ELP in the tradition of Liberace(!), light opera, vaudeville and Bernstein. "They're showcase musicians, slick, brash and popular. Once you work that one out, you can start to dig what they're doing." The fans' reception was overwhelmingly positive and it was an instant commercial hit. While it didn't reach the number one spot, it would go on to be one of ELP's bestselling albums.

In one respect, however, *Trilogy* was the band's biggest failure. ELP had always composed music with stage performance in mind. In this respect it really didn't work. The album's three big tracks, "The Endless Enigma", "Trilogy" and "Abaddon's Bolero", were all exceptionally difficult to reproduce live. In fact, the title track of the album was only attempted once. They had problems with "Abaddon's Bolero" too and it was subsequently dropped (though briefly resurrected with the orchestra in 1977). "The Endless Enigma" was only played in 1972, and then dropped. Concert tapes reveal it sounded a little ponderous live; nonetheless the studio version remained immensely popular with fans. In the process of attempting the new *Trilogy* material, the band began to truncate their most popular live number, *Pictures*, and would later relegate it to the encore section. Certainly, the new songs were better received than has subsequently been inferred, but it was clear from the start that the fans were far more enthusiastic about the older, more familiar, material.

Still, ELP remained intent on entertaining at their concerts. When they took the new material on the road across Europe that summer, it was with a massive retinue of roadies and truckloads of sound and lighting equipment. For this tour they came up with an impressive new opening for their stage presentation. On each side of the stage they sited four giant slide screens. As the lights went down at the beginning of the show, a sequence of coloured stills was shown, accompanied by "Abaddon's Bolero" on tape. The band walked on stage through the rapidly changing rainbow colours, and launched straight into "Hoedown".

As ELP's stage show set grew more grandiose, so did Palmer's drum kit. Gradually he introduced bongos, congas, tubular bells and glockenspiel, taking it further and further away from the basic rock set up. The process would reach its natural apogee with Palmer's steel drum kit, of which more later.

"When I joined ELP I noticed I was playing so many things in unison – and on the conventional kit," Palmer explained. "I thought having one mounted and one floor tom-tom was rather limiting because guys have had that since 1920. Anyway, Ludwig market a range of eight drums called Octoplus – 6", 8", 10", 12", 13", 14", 15" and 16". Their sound and tonal range are incredible. Musically it added up, because there were four root notes for one chord, and four for another chord – a high and a low. This gives me treble and bass to the kit immediately. The old concept is like giving someone a piano with just one octave and asking them to play everything within that – you can't. Of course, there are people who gather drums around them which are all of a similar size – that's ridiculous as well. But if you have a range, then you can draw more musical qualities from percussion."

Another piece of ELP live showmanship involved Emerson's remote Moog controller – a wood and metal device containing a metal ribbon and a number of switches. With this device, connected by a lead to his Moog, Emerson could make a dash into the audience, from where he could still trigger the main instrument, producing all manner of whoops and whistles. When he pressed one of the switches a pyrotechnic display was produced, shooting out sparks. It was always an unpredictable beast. "Keith's roadie Rocky," says Will Alexander, Rocky's replacement, "would load the pyro-launcher, which was basically copper tubing inside the original ribbon controller ... The pyro-launcher was loaded with glow plugs that heated up when Keith pushed the switches; the glow plugs would fire the gunpowder and shoot out the flash-paper stuffing. Keith would get more and more ambitious, wanting to make it bigger every time. One time he was playing, it blew his thumbnail off."

On one occasion, Emerson picked the controller up the wrong way round and fired the pyrotechnics directly at the front row, to immense cheers from the rest of the crowd. Audiences loved it all, and ELP responded in kind by expanding the visual elements of their live show. Certain corners of the press, however, reacted with hostility; media assessments were beginning to turn negative. As ELP's live shows became larger and larger both in scale of stage sets and audience numbers, the press commensurately found more and more to criticise them for.

The rest of the year would see the band consolidating their growing following in the US and Europe and in July, making their first expedition to Japan – their only Japan trip before their later reunion. They chartered a JAL Boeing for the trip East, flying via the North Pole for two well-received shows in Tokyo and Osaka. The two week trip also gave the band time to relax, and Emerson even managed an impromptu jam session when he went to the Tokyo Tower TV station to be interviewed. Discovering a piano in the corner of the room, he proceeded to delight his hosts with half an hour of virtuoso playing. Sadly it was not broadcast. The short trip was marred by thunderstorms – humidity playing havoc with Emerson's Moog in Tokyo – and problems with the Osaka police.

The Osaka show began well, though there was a chaotic incident relating to Emerson's ribbon controller. The keyboard man had forgotten that the length of the connecting cord has been cut from 100 feet to 25 feet. "The band was playing in

Osaka at a baseball stadium," Will Alexander explained. "They were set up in the outfield and the audience was about 150 feet away, up where home plate was. So Keith started playing with the ribbon controller and he went running at the audience, when all of a sudden he reached the end and it knocked him down! It made the Moog go berserk. He got up, turned and bowed to the audience, and went running back to the stage."

However it was the audience's great distance away from the stage that contributed to the later trouble. Student unrest was rife in Japan at the time and as fans jumped the barrier to get a closer view of the band, the police moved in with a baton charge. As Emerson picked up the mike to try and control the situation, the promoter turned off the power. In the end the concert went on, but it left a nasty taste in the mouth.

After the Eastern trip, the band resumed touring in the US before they could enjoy a couple of month's rest in anticipation of their November UK tour. Between these two treks they performed at the *Melody Maker* poll awards gig at the Oval Cricket Ground in South London.[2]

Rumours of internal dissension soon surfaced. The new material, it was said, didn't give Emerson, Lake and Palmer the same scope for satisfying individual expression that their previous work had. After releasing four successful albums in eighteen months, they neither had time to record or compose new material which would give free reign to their improvisational powers. Also, they were still under immense pressure to produce something even more spectacular than *Trilogy*, if it were possible. Before long, the talk was turning to solo projects.

"All bands go through this kind of lull," Emerson maintained, "In the past we've always had something ready in the bag. When we did *Pictures* we already had *Trilogy* recorded and ready. Now the recording gap has caught up with us... The thing is, not to panic."

Emerson was the first to put his solo plans into action. He went into the studio without Lake and Palmer to record some jazz pieces with drummer Jon Hiseman and other jazz musicians. Hiseman had no idea the tracks were meant for Emerson's first solo album, but he enjoyed the sessions. The musicians collaborated on "Walter L" – an unrecorded piece by big band leader and vibes genius Gary Burton, Charlie Parker's "Au Privave" and "Honky Tonk Train Blues" by Meade Lux Lewis.

"I am going back to the past in a way," Emerson explained. "Before I went into the music business I used to listen to jazz at home. And I always used to listen to Jazz Club on the radio and hear Don Rendell and guys like that. And I longed to play with those guys." It was Emerson's intention to present "different aspects of my playing in their original forms. I want to make it look like, here's Keith Emerson the jazz pianist, and Keith Emerson the classical pianist, and so on. My style with ELP is a heavy integration between classical music, jazz, country music, and any style you want to name. It's so heavily integrated into one thing it gets difficult to pick out whether I'm playing jazz, classical, ragtime, stride piano, boogie woogie or what. But I know where my influences lie. So the object of the solo album is to play my influences in the original form. You see, if I go out for an evening's entertainment I'll go to a club with the right vibes and just get up and jam with other musicians – there's one in London called Gulliver's. And I find great enjoyment in this, because it reminds me of when I played in pubs with local jazz musicians – and that's where my roots are at."

Emerson made it clear at that he wanted his solo material to have nothing at all to do with the band. "I'm going to arrange it for other guys. So I'm not going to play anything off my solo album on stage, because it just wouldn't be fair – it wouldn't be ELP."

The idea was that ELP would remain the focus for the group members, while allowing them to go off and do their own projects when it suited them. "ELP could be known as just a central working point for possibly branching into different things," Emerson expanded, "maybe even doing concerts individually. But still keeping ELP as the nucleus."

Questioned as to whether he thought the reason they all needed to do their own particular things was that there was less and less freedom within the musical structure of the band, Keith was perhaps a little defensive at first. "Yes, I know, it has become extremely tight, I must admit. But we are striving for perfection and it's obvious that when you are, this feeling of discipline, lack of freedom if you like, is going to come about. But musicians like Oscar Peterson have been criticised for being so mechanical, and it doesn't dispute the fact that he's an excellent musician.

"You see, I don't know – I like the whole thing being so tight. A piece of music like 'Tarkus' for instance was meant to be very machine-like, like a big mechanical monster. And when you have machinery the only way to imitate it is through being that tight. I mean, I do miss the sense of freedom to an extent, but even with ELP there are sections within the band's music where there are pieces arranged for pure improvisation – like 'Take A Pebble', which has grown so much since we recorded it on the first album."

Emerson clearly still enjoyed working with ELP and simply wanted an additional outlet for his music. "I'm only happy when I'm working," he insisted. "I get bored stiff sitting round on my arse doing nothing." However, it wasn't long before Emerson had gone rather soft on the idea of a solo album. Certainly he quickly retreated from the idea of keeping solo compositions separate from the band.

"From my point of view everything I write gets used for ELP, so there's not very much point in me doing a solo album," Emerson explained. "The thing is now when

I write I have to think where I'm going to put the song – on the solo album or for ELP – and it gets extremely difficult. So now when I write I have to decide if anything can be done with that number on stage and divide the compositions that way, between what would work best on stage, and what would work best as a purely recorded piece."

Despite the strong musical bond between the band members and a co-operative atmosphere, the post-*Trilogy* period was a problematic one. The mooted solo projects were not really helping. After three years of constant writing, recording and touring, rumours of a split began to circulate. Emerson had said as far back as 1970 that he felt "three years is about the natural life-span of a group". As 1972 drew to a close, ELP fans had some reason to worry about the future of the group.

Notes

1   Thanks to Blair Pethel for this folk tune information in his dissertation (see acknowledgements).

2   This was the first time comedian Jim Davidson would see the band – he would later become a friend and collaborator to members of the band.

CHAPTER 6

Glory Is Ours

Emerson, Lake and Palmer's first initiative of 1973 was to establish their own record label in order to have complete control over the way in which their music was released to the public. In the words of the new company's press release, the company, "enabled [ELP] to continue relentless pursuance [sic] of their uncompromising musical ideas". The band also planned to release music by other acts. The new label was named Manticore, after the mythical beast which gave its name to one of the songs in "Tarkus". One of the parts of the creature was the sting of a scorpion; both Keith and Greg have the astrological sign Scorpio, so it seemed quite appropriate. "We're both Scorpios, but we don't ever fight," Emerson had said playfully in 1971. "Carl just kind of fits in. He's Pisces." The company's logo was a silhouette of a Manticore.

The label set up in London in a converted theatre at 16 Curzon Street. They also had offices on the Upper East Side of New York City. Distribution was initially charged to Island, but the band quickly switched to WEA. US distribution was handled by Atlantic Records.

Fortunately the band now had a manager, Stewart Young, to help them with all these corporate matters. Young has always maintained a shadowy profile and is a very different figure from impresarios like Stratton-Smith or Loog Oldham. Until Young came across ELP, he had never been involved with the rock business.

Young was working as a chartered accountant in practice with his father when a band walked into the office to seek advice for some taxation problems. Stewart's father rang through to say he had three "rather scruffy" individuals called Emerson Lake and Palmer in his office and asked Stewart if he had ever heard of them. Stewart apparently replied "No, but I will look them up", thinking his father was talking about a firm of solicitors! When Young finally saw the band in concert, he was "totally amazed". Shortly afterwards he became their manager and was instrumental in the setting up of Manticore Records. (In fact the headed notepaper shows both Stewart and his father as directors).

Other Manticore acts included PFM (Premiata Forneria Marconi) and Banco (more fully, Banco del Mutuo Soccorso), two splendid Italian progressive outfits that ELP had seen in Europe, plus songwriters Keith Christmas and Pete Sinfield. "There was a time when certain styles of music really couldn't get on to major labels, and because we were unusual ourselves, playing sort of classical music and sort of progressive things, we identified with them," Lake reflected later. "We thought we'd have this little label to try to bring these new bands in."

A few weeks after the formation of Manticore was announced, February 1973 saw ELP embark on the famous "Get Me A Ladder" tour of Europe. A 30-man television crew accompanied them on part of the trek, shooting footage for a documentary to be screened in the UK on Boxing Day of that year. The highlight and central focus of the film was the concert ELP played to 50,000 enthusiastic fans at Milan's Vigorelli Stadium. It had been their third attempt to play the gig, the first postponement being due to bad weather and the second due to Greg Lake contracting severe laryngitis. This second cancellation had almost caused a riot.

"I was in the Milan Hilton, and this crowd of people arrived outside, quite orderly, and they just wanted to know why the gig was cancelled," Lake recalled. "As we went on it got a bit more riotous and a bit louder. I still didn't know why all these people were downstairs and I asked somebody to look out of the window and find out. One of the roadies said, 'Someone famous must be arriving'. Then the Police Commissioner came up and said that they were there waiting for me. By this time they were throwing stones and everything, which was really heavy."

ELP were not the first band to play stadiums, but they were pioneers in the idea of taking a huge self-contained set from country to country. It was this European tour that saw ELP become the first band to carry around their own stage – the legendary (and to some, notorious) proscenium archway. This required a battalion of over 40 roadies – an unprecedentedly huge retinue in those days. The scale of the touring party soon bred a thousand stories of excess and the press had a field day. It's no coincidence that the bile generated by the band got more and more poisonous as the dimensions of the stage show grew.

While in Switzerland Emerson became interested in the work of a controversial designer, Hans Rudi (H.R.) Giger, who was making a big splash in Zurich with his surreal, gothic sci-fi paintings. Some saw his work as inspired and erotic, others dismissed him as vulgar, middlebrow and depraved. Emerson decided that the band should commission Giger to produce the artwork for their new studio album.

Giger was born in the Graubunden town of Chur, high in the Eastern Swiss Alps. Recurrent nightmares in his early twenties led to his sketching out the images that tormented him. After qualifying – tellingly, given the nature of his later figurative work – as an industrial designer in 1966, he became a freelance painter and designer in 1967. Exhibitions of his work have taken place throughout the world every year since.

Giger was already an ELP fan and the band's music was among the sources of inspiration for his controversial triptych *Landscapes*.

"This time period was my most productive and creative phase as a painter," Giger recalled. "It was then that I received the news,... that ELP was interested in having a record cover done by me and that the group would be playing in two days at the Hallen Stadion [April 15, 1973]. On this occasion an expert opinion about the design could be given. This was already my second contract for an album cover, and I began with enthusiasm on the work...

"The title was supposed to be *Whip Some Skull On Ya*," Giger explained. "Basically, the phrase is a euphemism for fellatio and the obvious thing was to combine lips, penis and skulls. It is possible to make out the outline of a penis approaching the female's chin on the outer cover. The graphic artist for ELP had the idea that the cover should be able to be opened up like a gate; not a good idea, as would later become apparent when they were stacked..."

After the show, Emerson met Giger at the artist's house. "I was terribly excited. As I had never stood directly across from a pop star and the house, as it happened, was also full of people.... I was ceremoniously showered with compliments on my work. Nevertheless, Keith suddenly informed me that the title of the album was now going to be *Brain Salad Surgery*. I was dismayed until he explained to me that this expression, likewise, connoted fellatio." As it happened, the new title came from a Dr. John song.

Emerson: "As I remember [Giger's house] was a fairly modest 'bungalow' from the outside until you went in. Straight away Giger struck me as *heavy* to say the least. The interior decor was overpowering, Gothic to the extreme. From floor to ceiling his unique airbrush technique had transformed a simple room into a cathedral, and it was all around you. If this was not enough Giger had gone three-dimensional. His toilet had arms coming out, almost engulfing the sitter. I noted the arms had 'drip feeds' going into them. Other decor consisted of gas masks.

"He showed me his *V.D. Landscape* which looked very science fiction until he told me the subject had been taken from medical photographs. I was both shocked and fascinated at the same time. It was very dark and foreboding, and for me it represented ELP's music; I suggested that Greg and Carl view it all. I finally persuaded Greg and Carl to come to Giger's house. They unanimously agreed on two of Giger's existing works, though after much deliberation with the record company, the band had to reluctantly appeal to Giger to 'tone down' the phallic object in front of the cover woman's mouth until it looked like a 'shaft of light'."

Giger found worldwide fame, and later went on to win an Oscar for his designs for Ridley Scott's movie *Alien* in 1979.

When the "Get Me A Ladder" tour came to an end, ELP adjourned to the studio to record *Brain Salad Surgery*. While they had already premiered some of the new album on that tour – notably "Karn Evil 9 First Impression" and "Toccata" –

the recording process would take much longer than previous ELP records. The release date was accordingly postponed a number of times. They finished the record in early autumn.

Readers of the *New Musical Express* had already had something of a taster in the shape of a new track "Brain Salad Surgery" – not on the album, but recorded especially for a flexi single to be given away with the paper. However, while the piece is made up of three or four jams the band recorded in left-over studio time from the sessions, it is played fast and loose – far from the style of the album and not very representative of what was to come.

On the flexi's flip side there were short extracts from all the album tracks. In the accompanying interview Lake made a historic, if tongue-in-cheek, *faux pas* by saying he'd love to play with Clapton "just to see if he could keep time"!

When the album itself finally emerged in December 1973, it transcended all expectations. "We felt we needed a bit of time to consider things and not let everything go to our heads," said Emerson of the long gap between *Trilogy* and the new album. "I think it was worth the wait, because a lot of people think *Brain Salad Surgery* is just about the best thing we ever did. I think that 'Karn Evil 9' proves that. Again, the most important thing was the way we were playing together as a band."

In addition to the innovative Giger artwork, the album marked a vital advance in synthesizer technology, featuring one of the prototype polyphonic synthesizers, the Moog Polyphonic Ensemble, as well as the new percussion synthesizer which was still in the early stages of development.

"The Moog system was expanded considerably and I had a sequencer and another row of oscillators," Emerson explained. "It got so big I couldn't even reach up to it and tune the damn thing any longer! I used the sequencer basically just for the gimmick value it offered on ELP's *Brain Salad Surgery*. I'd written this music about computerisation with very heavy lyrics, and the idea was that the instrument sort of took over in the end. The sequencer would be programmed to go through this change of notes and speed up until it blew up."

A few years later, one critic [1] described ELP's music as "the cosmic soundtrack for an ultra violent age of endless struggle between man and machine" – a comment particularly apt for *Brain Salad Surgery*. However, for all the technology on display and the controversy of the Giger contribution, the new album began with an arrangement of the popular hymn "Jerusalem", with words by poet-artist William Blake and music by Hubert Parry.

"I had always loved the tune," says Emerson. "The opening chord progressions sound a bit like 'Pictures At An Exhibition', and everyone in England knows that hymn. It's a traditional, patriotic tune that evokes good feelings in every Englishman. I had originally wanted to do it with The Nice, but we never got around to working it up."

Still, even approaching such a traditional tune was controversial. The very idea of rocking up a song that ranked with the National Anthem and "Land Of Hope And Glory" in national significance was anathema to the BBC, who banned ELP's version from the airwaves. Backed by "When The Apple Blossoms Bloom...", it had been released as a single in Britain just before the album. With airplay it would certainly have charted. "Although we tried to get a very orchestral feel," says Carl in *Applied Rhythms*, "as with all pieces of music that we played with Emerson, Lake and Palmer, it was still labelled as a piece of pop music...the BBC thought we were degrading it."

Notwithstanding this reaction, there was no getting away from the irony of including "Jerusalem" on the same album as "Karn Evil 9". "Jerusalem" sets a mystical, triumphal mood, with words of aspiration to an ideal society, whereas "Karn", the work which occupies most of the album, ends bleakly with a vision of a wholly dehumanised world. "Toccata", the track directly following "Jerusalem", also seems to belong to the same landscape as "Karn Evil 9".

Blake's romantic words in "Jerusalem" alludes to the idea that Jesus might once have visited England. The inclusion of the hymn thus naturally provoked press speculation on the band's interest in Christianity, a subject that particularly interested Lake. "Its release [as a single] had nothing to do with the fact of other religious type songs having made the Hit Parade in the last year or so," the bassist told one reporter, rather defensively. "As I said, to us it was a beautiful song and that's it.

"I can only remember going to church once in my life, maybe twice," he continued. "I recall receiving one of those cards on which they put stars to record attendance. Trouble was, my first visit saw me beaten up by a mob – not the best of introductions!

"What I've done since is brush up every now and then with religion. We're not buried into the religious thing too much, yet, you know, it's something which has always upset me to a degree. This upsetting comes from my belief I can see through the Church. I'm an entertainer, and I can relate to the kind of show the Church presents. You have the priest, the beautiful shaft of light on his head, the collection, it's always something that disturbs me a little. I think it's based on fear. When you're small you're indoctrinated with the thought if you don't believe in the Almighty there is a terrible penalty to pay. At the age when I could think things for myself, what I found myself believing is expressed in my [earlier] song 'Black Mass'[2].

"I don't believe it, I don't subscribe to it. I wish there was something. I think if I did have blind faith, then it would make me much happier, giving me this security and feeling that whatever happened to me it would be all right."

In his subsequent lyric writing with Pete Sinfield on *Works, Vol 1*, Lake lays greater stress on inner spiritual experience than hitherto; only with Emerson, Lake and Powell's "The Miracle" did the vivid religious imagery of resurface.

As mentioned above, "Jerusalem" was followed by a version of the fourth

85

movement of twentieth-century Argentinian composer Alberto Ginastera's 1st Piano Concerto, "Toccata," a remarkable tour de force that represented one of ELP's best classical adaptations. One critic dubbed it, "Dr Who meets Ginastera"! "It's really the ultimate in funk," said Emerson, somewhat fancifully.

The Ginastera *Toccata*, like many modern toccatas, is very fast and percussive, with highly aggressive rhythms. It also integrates some characteristics of Argentinian dance. This adaptation was something that Emerson had had in mind ever since the latter days of the Nice. "I was in Los Angeles doing one of those spectacular Hollywood television productions [*Switched-On Symphony*], which was being organised by Jack Good," Emerson explained. "It was about the time that mixed media was all the rage and everyone was getting into the thing that rock groups and orchestras were all the thing, let's do a television spectacular on it.

"While I was over there I met Zubin Mehta, Daniel Barenboim and Jacqueline Du Pre and lots of other people. This particular piece was being played by the pianist who did the world premiere of Ginastera's First Piano Concerto, a Brazilian pianist named Joao Carlos Martins. He played it with the L.A. Philharmonic and I heard it from my dressing-room. I went and stood off-stage to listen to the work, and after the concert I went to Martins' dressing-room, introduced myself, and told him how much I liked the piece and his playing. It was very interesting to look at the part.

"He happened to have an extra copy of the music, and when I got back to England I got a copy of the recording and I just worked on it in my leisure time, not really intending to do it – it was just sort of something to play. Carl had always wanted to do a percussion piece which was well arranged, and it wasn't until we were getting this new album together that I realised that this was the ideal number, because it's very percussive anyway – in the original there's lots of pounding piano – it's a very hairy piece of music.

"So I rang him up and played it to him on the telephone and he liked it quite a lot, and at rehearsals I played it on the organ and everyone was well into it. So I talked about arranging it, making strict observations on how Ginastera himself had written it, and the rules that he had laid down. The thing that came across to me was that it can only be performed with the timpani set up here, and the pianos were set up here and everything was laid out on this chart. The actual movement which I was arranging was well laid out to the number of bars and the whole thing was in rondo form, so in arranging this I had to adhere strictly to the rules. I didn't want to adulterate his music in any way....

"We knew immediately that we couldn't do the entire last movement, so we just took the first four or five pages and used them as the basis for what happened next. Carl's percussion movement wasn't planned; it just came into being as we worked on the piece."

The timing was right for Palmer. By the time of "Toccata", he had begun to dabble with electronic percussion and expand his repertoire. "I had my sound spectrum, I was trying to think ahead and keep on top of any possible developments," the drummer explained. He was one of the first drummers ever to do so. This was in conjunction with designing his own custom-built stainless steel drum kit [3.] He had also begun to take lessons for the first time since schooldays, including studying timpani with Gilbert Webster at London's Guildhall School of Music.

"My main thing has always been to be a musical drummer. I've preferred a musical approach rather than the heavy rock rhythmic playing. I can't slate those kind of players, because they're good for what they do but I've always thought maybe I should use gongs and timps and tubular bells on stage...and I thought to myself that if I was going to take that approach I should have a very futuristic approach as well as developing the instrument I play. It just seems like a logical progression. My reason for doing it also lies with the fact that I wanted to be the first to record something on an electric drumset – which I did on *Brain Salad Surgery*. I don't believe in it totally, because I believe in symphonic, tuned percussion. I just have this thing in me that I like to do things first, whether I believe in them a hundred per cent or not."

Palmer's percussive piece on "Toccata" is not an ordinary drum solo, independent of the rest of the music, but a related section for tuned and synthesised percussion (plus a small number of interesting exchanges with keyboard and guitar), based on the thematic material of the Toccata. All the band members contribute, though Palmer obviously has the lion's share. The movement features one of the very earliest uses of synthesised percussion, using a custom-designed Moog system. The timpani and the tom-toms are at least as important as the unusual electronic sounds, however.

"Eventually we got the whole thing together," Emerson says. "I wrote a letter to Ginastera and sent it care of Boosey and Hawkes, the publishers. They read the letter and said that they understood that I wanted it doing very quickly, and they thought it would be much quicker for me to go and see him.

"The next day I was off the plane with Stewart Young and met Ginastera, and I was quite nervous about meeting the guy face to face and playing his music to him. I had dinner with him and he was quite familiar with this electronic equipment because he'd worked in Argentina on these things, and after dinner we got him to play the music. He couldn't quite believe his ears at the start of it, and then listening to it the second time through he said that it was fantastic, 'you captured the essence of my music!'

Ginastera is quoted on the lyric sheet of the album as saying, "Keith Emerson has beautifully caught the mood of my piece". "Toccata" quickly became a big concert favourite, though it was dropped after the world tour of 1973/74.

87

Track Three, "Still.... You Turn Me On", slows the proceedings to a tranquil pace. This song follows on from "Lucky Man", "The Sage" and "From The Beginning" as a typical Greg Lake solo spot. Though it's ostensibly a love song, Lake is at least partly addressing the audience here. The phrase "Still...You Turn Me On" is double-edged. He needs his audience literally to turn on the music because performing to them turns him on. And yet, *"it all gets so intense...It just doesn't seem to make sense"; "Every day a little sadder, A little madder"*. The price of fame and all that?... On the tour Greg was toying with another song called "You Can Sing My Song" for possible inclusion on the album.

While the song is musically uncomplicated, interest is maintained by Emerson and Lake's attractive textures. Lake's acoustic playing is fine as always, but he scores especially with his sad, delicate electric guitar phrasing. Emerson plays restrained accordion and harpsichord – as well as a small amount of synthesiser. There is also an intriguing echo/delay guitar effect in the refrain.

As Palmer didn't appear on the track, it couldn't be released as a single under the ELP name. However, it became a major radio hit in the States when the record company distributed special copies to the radio stations.

On "Benny The Bouncer" Emerson plays the first prototype of the Polymoog [4] synthesizer, and has a field day indulging his passion for boogie-woogie piano at the end. The honky-tonk effects were generated by using a piano with one string out of tune. However, the track's most distinctive aspect is the lyrics – "We knocked that out in a couple of days," Lake's co-lyricist on the song, Pete Sinfield [5], recalled. Inspiration no doubt came from direct experience of fights in clubs and concert halls – while the band plays on. The song is the first example since King Crimson of shared lyric writing credits by Lake and Pete Sinfield. In the same year, 1973, Sinfield released his solo album, *Still*[6], which included some tracks on which Lake performed and co-wrote. On *Brain Salad*, the association continues in the epic "Karn Evil 9", one of ELP's finest extended pieces to date.

The title was Pete Sinfield's, punning on his initial feeling that Emerson's piece was like carnival music. The number 9 was simply seen as having a "universal" character. This half-hour long magnum opus is in three long movements called Impressions, the central one being entirely instrumental. The first was divided between the two sides of the record when released, because of the format's time restriction. Indeed, the limitation is built into the piece itself: Part Two, opening the second side of the LP, has as its unforgettable opening line, *"Welcome back, my friends, to the show that never ends"*. Pete Sinfield revealed recently that line was his, and he joined Alex Fraser from the first album in not being credited. At that stage he was only dabbling in his old King Crimson pal Greg's new project, but a little later he was put on the payroll.

The song had originally got off to a shaky start. ELP had been rehearsing the First Impression upstairs at their Manticore HQ, but it hadn't quite taken off. Just by chance no one was renting the downstairs area, and on the big stage the piece sounded a lot more impressive. It was only then that it was up and running.

"Karn Evil 9" was built around a far more precise and coherent concept than *Tarkus,* to which it bears some relation. "In the First Impression there is a statement," said Emerson. "The statement tells of a loss of human value through man's so-called progress. Then there's a reaction to the statement. The reaction, I think, is very typical of what the people feel today when they read the news. The situation becomes almost laughable. People now are laughing about the Watergate thing. We've had the Irish thing in England and people are so bored with people being blown up and shot. It happens every day, and before you know it, it becomes old news. There's this whole impersonal thing. That is the reaction in the First Impression.

"So then there is the Second Impression... Really what that is, is a series of abstracts dealing mainly with time and travel, producing a disorienting feeling. That's sort of like because we are affected by travel as people, we travel so much. This alters the whole consciousness, I think, of people today. They lose their identity.

"The Third Impression is rather like being in the future and looking back at what we've come through. It deals with the evolution of creativity starting from the Stone Age. It goes right through, it continues up to where we are right now with computers. Now the world starts to turn full circle. The computer starts to make things. And then again begins the Stone Age created by a different source, and man has lost contact with what he has created. Now this could be either a computer or it could be referring to the morals or principles man has set himself and is trying to get out of. The two things are over-running each other, so there is like a running battle sequence in this Third Impression. Man is trying to get back his original identity. It ends with the computer having the last word, but it is left in the air who has succeeded or what has actually happened." In relation to computers, Pete Sinfield brought invaluable specialist insight to the final part of "Karn Evil 9". Back in the 60's he had worked with IBM.

ELP's publicity department pulled out all the stops to promote the album *Brain Salad Surgery*. One of the most notable experiments was the sponsoring of a nationwide schools art competition. 1,500 paintings on the theme of the album's title were submitted by teenage artists. DJ Alan Freeman – a tireless campaigner for ELP on radio, and a close friend of the band – presented a prize of a week's holiday on ELP's European tour. The best of the paintings were exhibited at Command Studios in London.

As ELP set out to promote the new album on the road, they were at the peak of their success and their power. Before long *Brain Salad Surgery* was at Number 2 on the UK charts. ELP's tour was designed to match their status and their aspirations. The publicity for the '73/'74 tour described it as "the most ambitious spectacular ever mobilised for a group", and for once the hype was probably true. ELP's touring party included 20 tons of equipment valued at $750,000 (requiring 40 roadies to shift it all), including a quadraphonic sound system and stunning light shows (there were over 100 spotlights, then unheard-of for a rock group, and lasers too). For a few gigs, there was also a piano which rose in the air and spun over and over while Emerson played Chopin's "Revolutionary Etude", a revolving drumkit with all kinds of extras including flashing dragons, state-of-the-art keyboard and percussion synthesisers, all manner of fireworks, a Persian carpet, organs to stab and beat up – and five sets of huge stage curtains. Three 40-foot trucks were needed to transport the specially designed and built proscenium arch and stage which was erected for every performance.

The Persian carpet appeared as a result of an incident during the European leg of the 1973 tour when Greg received an electric shock from his microphone while performing. At first he solved the problem by standing on an insulating rubber mat. Deciding that this was ugly, while in Germany he had one of his roadies buy an ornate £5,000 Persian rug. It has been his trademark and constant touring companion ever since – not to mention the butt of much critical scorn!

From November 1973 to March 1974 the band took this huge convoy across the US and Canada. In spring '74 they were in Europe before spending July and August touring America again. It was this extended touring that truly put ELP at the top of rock's first division in the US.

US tour highlights included two concerts at Madison Square Gardens, New York on December 17 and 18, 1973. The band played "Silent Night" as an encore, with a full choir. Snow began to fall at this point during the first concert, unforgettably creating the brief illusion that ELP had a hotline to God!

A month later Lake was arrested by Salt Lake City police officers. "We got [to the hotel] late that night," recalls Lake, "and didn't play until the next day. The pool looked so inviting but we didn't have any swimming stuff with us. We got permission from the guy at the desk and went in [naked]. The next thing we knew there were policeman. And dogs."

A woman on the 11th floor had seen the prime specimens of manhood frolicking in the pool far below and had called the cops. The errant bassist was fined $75 for "disorderly conduct" and wasted a couple of hours in the local jail.

At the San Francisco concert on February 2, 1974, one of the pyrotechnics in Emerson's ribbon controller backfired. He stood there hanging onto the still-droning instrument for about ten seconds, then walked back and said through the mike, "I just blew my thumbnail off!"

"Blood was everywhere," Emerson says. "All a roadie could do was put a bucket of water by the keyboards for me to dip my thumb in. It was very unpleasant and I was green by the end!" Lake and Palmer kept things together but Keith managed to play the entire set including all the difficult bits, especially the piano solo. "We're British, you know!" Emerson exclaimed with stiff-upper-lipped pride.

April 6, 1974 saw the staging of the first made-for-TV rock festival – the first California Jam, at the Ontario Speedway outside Los Angeles, co-promoted by ABC Television. Over 350,000 people attended and ELP shared top billing with Deep Purple – though only after a heated discussion with Blackmore and co., who delayed the other acts by refusing to appear until it was dark, so their light show could take full effect. In fact, Blackmore, still enraged by the argument with the network's producer, thrust his guitar into one of the cameras at the end of Deep Purple's set, the upshot being that ELP's set was shot with one camera less. Blackmore's antics also meant that ELP didn't take the stage until 1 a.m. Even though by this point it was freezing cold – the racetrack was out in the middle of the desert, which cooled rapidly after sundown – the band put on an amazing show that night; Palmer is convinced it was their greatest performance.

After the California Jam, the band returned to England for a string of dates. The band had booked two concerts at Wembley Empire Pool, plus others at the Liverpool Empire and Stoke's Trentham Gardens. The Wembley dates sold out so quickly that a third and then a fourth show had to be added. The press, however, were less impressed than the ticket-hungry fans.

The year 1974 saw press criticism of ELP's grandiose music and presentation reach an unprecedented level of vitriol. Until the *Brain Salad Surgery* tour, in spite of a number of detractors, the critics had often responded positively to their work. However now ELP had reached the pinnacle of success, the journalists' knives came out. Legendary proto-punk journalist Lester Bangs, writing in *Rolling Stone* and reprinted in *New Musical Express*, led the attack. While not averse to musical ambition *per se*, his main charge was that not only had technology taken over the act but that the band themselves were no more than robots. The Bangs article was very influential within the journalistic fraternity. Pretty soon, UK reporters were making wounding personal attacks on the band members and their stage act to the almost total exclusion of discussing the band's music. However, even before Bangs' broadside the British critics had been turning against the band. The previously enthusiastic *Sounds* now considered ELP "highly embarrassing" – their reviewer Matthew Gocher was particularly turned off by what he saw as the arrogance of *Brain Salad Surgery*'s Ginastera sleevenote. Gocher concluded that the album was "boring, hideous, insipid, vapid…" *Melody Maker* dismissed the record as "stale salad" and singled out Sinfield's "banal" and "pretentious" lyrics for particular criticism. *Music Scene* saw ELP's take on "Jerusalem" as "bloody sacrilege" while *Melody Maker* felt Blake "must be turning in his grave."

Nonetheless, the critical backlash against ELP has been overstated. *NME*'s critic began a December '73 *Brain Salad Surgery* review, "I can honestly say that I like all of this … It seems to me their most uncluttered and melodic album to date." *NME*'s James Johnson also saw the US tour as proof that "ELP are the one band who actively benefit from playing the largest halls with the maximum of presentation to heighten the rather staggering, overwhelming effect of the concerts." The *NME* also claimed that ELP's act worked so well out of doors it saved the California Jam from being an otherwise "lacklustre" event. Their writer Bob Edmands even rounded off a band profile in October '74 by stating that "the ultimate vindication of ELP is in their live performance, which vigorously rebuts most of the accusations against them… ELP are said to be sterile, clinical, lacking in emotional commitment…. Strangely, this sort of description appears at odds with evidence of the band's act…."

Also, many progressive rockers suffered similar press antipathy to ELP; Ian Anderson would take Jethro Tull out of circulation for a while because of press attacks. Writer Edward Macan makes a number of observations about why progressive rock attracted so much bile. His first major point concerns the musicians' aesthetic stand: their claim that their music was an extension of high art – and the concomitant arrogance. There was a certain aloofness about the genre's musicians which miffed many journalists. Macan's second main point is that many journalists considered black music to be the only authentic base on which to make popular music – pop had thus no right to stray from its roots and its rhythmic base.

The media coverage around the time of the Wembley Pool shows was so negative that Manticore Records "blacklisted" some of the more hostile publications, refusing to place advertising with them or give them interviews. As Greg Lake noted at the time, "We never get good press. I don't read reviews much any more."

After the UK gigs, ELP toured the stadiums and arenas of Europe before another trek across the US. The massive tour finally closed in August 1974 with some shows on the American East Coast. However the fans were given a tour souvenir in the form of the band's second live album, *Welcome Back, My Friends, to the Show That Never Ends*.

For a band operating on ELP's current massive scale, a second live album in just a couple of years had to be something special. So in an era of double live sets, with characteristically cavalier bombast they made it a triple – they needed three records to fit something approaching a complete concert, their gigs approached the three hour mark – and there were three members! When folded out, the package revealed three gleaming silver letters E, L and P, which were intended to retain the records. This was an inspired idea, although in practice the unwieldy sleeve had a tendency to fall apart.

The three disc set was a well-recorded document of a brilliant live band at their peak, featuring great versions of long-standing favourites, as well as new material in Emerson's solo spot. A fine "Hoedown", taken at a cracking pace, is an ideal opener. "Jerusalem" is perhaps a bit of a disappointment, but the band are settling in well by the end of a rollicking "Toccata". The latter two tracks are very similar to the original studio versions.

"Tarkus" too follows the original template closely, but with some great bonuses. At the end of "Battlefield" Lake plays and sings solo, adding a verse from King Crimson's "Epitaph". The "Aquatarkus" solo begins as a looser, less bitingly rhythmic variation on the original, and soon goes into a "free" improvisational synthesizer section, with bass and drums constantly bubbling away beneath, Emerson quoting substantially from an early Moog piece, "The Minotaur", by Dick Hyman.[7] It's one of the best things the band ever put down live

"Take A Pebble" is the framework for both Lake's and Emerson's solo spots. The beginning of the instrumental section is even better than the original, featuring some light, delicate trio work. In the middle of this track Greg's heartfelt, straightforward solo performances of the popular, "Still...You Turn Me On" and "Lucky Man" draw deserved applause – who needs a seminal Moog solo?

"Take A Pebble" is the jumping-off point for Emerson's "Piano Improvisations", but he opens with the Fugue from Friedrich Gulda's[8] "Prelude and Fugue". His performance stays close to Gulda's original, though lacking Gulda's swing and delicate touch. It's also, amazingly, faster!

Next up is Emerson's take on Joe Sullivan's 1937 number, "Little Rock Getaway". Sullivan was a versatile jazz pianist. Tutored at the Chicago Conservatory of Music, he was one of the first white pianists not only to understand but also to play the hard-driving kind of music produced by Fats Waller, Willie "The Lion" Smith, Earl Hines and others, blending his own aggressive style with theirs. The song is Sullivan's tribute to his wife, recalling their elopement in 1931 to get married in her Arkansas hometown.

Emerson's version is firmly based on Sullivan's own performance with the Bob Crosby Orchestra. The Emerson version is somewhat heavier, but it's no less subtle. Lake and Palmer join in for a racy jazzy section. Pretty soon the band are piling up musical quotes. Emerson throws in a few bars each of "The Star Spangled Banner", "Daisy, Daisy", and the Laurel and Hardy theme! Everything starts falling apart good naturedly before a quote from the Prelude to Respighi's "The Birds"[9], plus a standard tag bring the band section of Keith's spot to a close. After pausing for applause, the last verse of the song is announced with a huge piano glissando. At the end they dare the audience to hold back their applause, pausing for a full seven seconds before Greg finally utters the last phrase.

After rattling through a medley of "Jeremy Bender" and "The Sheriff", quotes from "Colonel Bogey", silent film music, Rachmaninov's "First Prelude" and a final twiddly bit, ELP finally come to the main event of the evening. "Karn Evil 9" hadn't had time to develop, so it's 95 per cent the same as the *Brain Salad Surgery* version. It sounds great live though – often better than the original recording – and features an explosive Palmer drum solo which showcases the unusual sound of his custom built steel kit. The final sequence begins extremely slowly. You can hear gasps from the audience as the sound accelerates quadraphonically, reverberating around the hall, and is brought to a sudden stop by the "explosion" of the computer.

On release, *Welcome Back...* raced to the upper echelons of the album charts. It was the biggest-selling triple album to date.

The tremendously successful *Brain Salad Surgery* album, tour and live LP signalled the end of ELP's first phase. They had gone as far as possible along their chosen electronic musical route. They had also endured an incredibly gruelling schedule of writing, recording and touring since the band's inception. After a benefit concert in New York City on August 24, 1974, it was time for the band to take stock.

Notes

1   Dan Nooger, *Circus* Magazine, USA 1977

2   Title shortened to "Mass" when recorded on *Tarkus*

3   The drum kit that Carl Palmer used from 1973 to 1978 is probably the most unique drum set ever built. If any drum kit could be considered a work of art, then this would be it.

    Constructed out of stainless steel, the complete rostrum set-up weighed about 2.5 tons. "Each drum was suspended by a rod that was angled at the exact position I wanted it," Palmer explained. "I would make a template out of cardboard and take it to the steel manufacturers with my specifications.... Every night that I set the drums up they're in the same position and my technique had got really good because I'm familiar with the distances."

    The kit comprised a 28" x 20" bass drum, 6", 8", 10", 12", 13", 14", 15", and 16" single-headed tom-toms, as well as an 18" floor tom-tom – also single-headed for projection – and a Ludwig super sensitive concert model 14" x 5.5" snare drum.

    For a personalised touch Palmer had an engraver working with a dentist's drill etch various hunting scenes he took from rifles across the drums. The kit took twelve months to complete, and involved input from the British Steel Corporation. The final cost of the kit came in at around $15,000. The only off the shelf items were the Gretsch hoops.

    Palmer's cymbals were all Paiste and comprised: 24" medium ride; 22" crash; 20" crash/ride; 22" china type; 16" very heavy ride; 7.5" tiny splash; plus five heavy little cymbals, 7", 5", 4", and 3", as well as a tiny 2". Palmer's kit also included: 26" and 29" Ludwig symphonic model timps; an octave and a half of Tubular bells; 50" and 38" Paiste gongs; a set of temple blocks; a row of camel bells and an atmospheric tray consisting of a vibraslap, a ratchet, a violin bow and cymbal and chain in a bucket plus an extra large triangle. Finally there was a 134 lb church bell mounted above his head. "I bought this from the Aldgate Bell Foundry," Palmer says. "It was a reject from a church peal, it being slightly out of tune."

Palmer also incorporated his drum synthesizers into the steel set-up.

As well as having a distinctive sound, set up on a revolving riser with its own light display, the drum set was visually breathtaking. The kit can be heard on *Brain Salad Surgery*, *Welcome Back My Friends*, *Works Vols 1 & 2*. It can be seen in the California Jam movie and the video, *Live '77*.

The kit is currently owned by Ringo Starr.

4   He toured with two thirds of the entire original unit, then known as the Constellation. It consisted of the Apollo, the early version of the Polymoog; the Lyra, a monophonic instrument that was never mass-produced; and the Taurus bass pedals – the component Keith never used; pity about that.

5   Spaced-out lyricist and multi-talented visionary, Pete Sinfield was born in Fulham, London, in 1943. His association with Greg Lake goes back to the early days of King Crimson. Jobs in computer operating and fabric design temporarily delayed a full-time commitment to the world of rock and pop, though he sometimes worked as a roadie and light show operator for bands.

"I'd looned around playing guitar and singing – both very badly – in Spain and Morocco, and when I started the band, Ian [McDonald] was one of the three guitarists who only stayed a few days because we were so atrocious. He asked me to write songs with him. He joined Giles, Giles and Fripp [the immediate precursor to King Crimson], and told them he had a guy who wrote words."

When Giles, Giles and Fripp failed to make a mark, Sinfield stayed on with Fripp as Crimson's roadie, lights man, and now the main lyricist. Fripp recalls that Pete built stage lights out of baking foil and plywood for the band's first rehearsal. When they got their first gig – a residency in Newcastle (still under the G,G & F moniker) – Pete and the other roadie got a tenner each for the week. "When Pete Giles left and Greg joined I became their pet hippie, because I could tell them where to go to buy the funny clothes that they saw everybody wearing. I acted as unpaid roadie for three months, because I believed in them as musicians. Bob says he used me as a barometer, and I also thought up the name of the band."

Sinfield was a member of King Crimson for their first five albums. Dissatisfaction with the demands of touring, and disagreement with the band's leader, led Fripp to ask him to leave after the 1971 U.S. tour. The last Crimson LP to feature his work was the live album, *Earthbound*, on which he plays VCS3 synthesiser for the long drum solo on "Groon".

In 1972 Sinfield produced the debut Roxy Music album, and invited Greg Lake to help on his solo album, *Still* (re-released with bonus tracks as *Stillusion* in 1993: see Discography). Greg did some singing and electric guitar playing for the album, as well as co-producing and having "a hand or three in the mixing". Sinfield sang, spoke, and played acoustic guitar and synthesiser. The album appeared on Manticore. A book of Sinfield's work, *Under The Sky – A Collection Of Lyrics And Poems*, was later published.

The first ELP song involving Sinfield to be released was "Brain Salad Surgery", initially available on the *NME* free flexi-disc and later to turn up on *Works, Vol. 2*.

In the same period as his work on *Brain Salad Surgery*, Sinfield contributed material to two albums by his Italian discovery, Premiata Forneria Marconi (PFM), whom he had Emerson sign to Manticore. Sinfield was also involved with many other artists, including (on Manticore) Angelo Branduardi, Keith Christmas and Esperanto Rock Orchestra.

Songs with lyrics co-written by Lake and Sinfield are as follows:

Brain Salad Surgery "Karn Evil 9"; "Benny The Bouncer"; *Works, Vol. I* "Lend Your Love To Me Tonight"; "C'est La Vie"; "Hallowed Be Thy Name"; "Nobody Loves You Like I Do"; "Closer To Believing"; "Pirates" *Works, Vol.2* "Tiger in A Spotlight"; "Brain Salad Surgery"; "Watching Over You"; "So Far To Fall"; "I Believe in Father Christmas". *Love Beach* "All I Want is You"; "Love Beach"; "Taste Of My Love"; "The Gambler"; "For You"; "Memoirs of An Officer And A Gentleman": Prologue/ The Education of A Gentleman/ Love At First Sight/ Letters From The Front. "Humbug", the instrumental B-side of Lake's solo single "I Believe In Father Christmas", was also co-written by Sinfield.

Other musicians for whom Sinfield has written or co-written songs include Gary Brooker, John Wetton, Chris Squire, Agnetha Faltskog and Cliff Richard. He had several stabs at penning a Eurovision Song Contest winner.

In 1982 he formed the Pete Sinfield Band with his old King Crimson friends Mike Giles and Boz Burrell, plus Gary Brooker, and they performed in Spain, where he lived for a number of years. Music from this concert can be heard on a four-song EP (see Discography) released in 1993.

Sinfield can also be heard on the CD re-release of the very-limited-edition 1979 album *In A Land of Clear Colours*, on which he narrated the text of writer Robert Sheckley – a fellow resident of Ibiza – to the accompaniment of music by Brian Eno. This is a must for Sinfield and Crimson fans. Sheckley and Sinfield (and Eno, for that matter) are concerned with language and the difficulties of communication, as well as the disturbance of rational expectations, the unease of the exile, and the instability of individuality and culture, and Sheckley's work expresses many of Sinfield's own themes.

In 1994, asked what his favourite self-composed song was, he chose "Heart of Stone", written for Cher. "'Heart of Stone' was a nice simple summary of 20 years in the rock 'n' roll business which obviously appealed to Cher as well," said Sinfield. "It summed up my feelings three or four years ago rather like 'Epitaph' did in 1969 when I wrote 'Confusion will he my epitaph'. It wouldn't be my epitaph now; 'Sometimes I wish I had a heart of stone' is more how I feel these days. I'm not that confused, I just find coping with the world a painful process". – GF: *I know how he feels!* There are echoes of "Hallowed Be Thy Name" and "Closer to Believing" in this great song: "Big crowd for the crazy house / Long queue for the joker's shoes."

6   See Discography

7   Dick Hyman (B. 1927), veteran American jazz pianist/organist/composer. A master of all forms of jazz, in the Sixties he cut two records of Moog music (the instrument was just gaining popularity in the wake of Walter Carlos' *Switched-On Bach*). The first of these, *Moog – The Electric Eclectics of Dick Hyman*, included as its first and probably best track 'The Minotaur'. The ELP version is faithful to it, though not a little heavier. The album (long deleted) was on COMMAND X5938, 1969. At this stage Hyman's tremendous piano and composing skills far outweighed his dabbling with the Moog, but he obviously had plenty of fun making it.

8 It's worth taking a longer look at the life and musical philosophy of the Austrian pianist and composer, Friedrich Gulda (b 1930), in view of his influence on Emerson. Gulda became internationally famous as a concert pianist early in his career, but a developing interest in jazz led him to found a jazz combo, and then a big band. Later he initiated a jazz competition and an International Music Forum. He hoped by mixing jazz with the classics in concert programmes to introduce the respective audiences to each others music and build bridges. A similar ambition was being cherished at about the same time by the young Keith Emerson, who it is clear, was strongly influenced by Gulda's ideas and practice.

9 Respighi's *Prelude* (which was derived from a piece of music by the Baroque composer Pasquini) was used from this tour onwards as the opening of the backing music accompanying the credits projected at the end of each show.

CHAPTER 7

Gold Drives Three Men To Dream

They believe in doing things in a spectacular way. Stewart Young, ELP's manager

In the aftermath of the colossal Brain Salad Surgery tour, Emerson, Lake and Palmer embarked on an extended period away from band duties. After so much time on the road, they took time out to relax and spend time with their families. Lake's wife, German model Regina, had recently given birth to his daughter, Natasha, and at the end of 1974 he and his family moved into a Tudor manor house set in fifteen acres of land near Windsor in Berkshire.

Emerson's life away from the stage was less contented. One of the factors behind his extended sabbatical was a fire at his Sussex home[1]. Many original scores and personal possessions were destroyed. The Emersons moved to Kent while the house was being rebuilt. "It was so depressing," Emerson explained, "not just from the personal aspect, but because that house had so much history. And I lost so many things – all my scores, tapes…" Depressed, Emerson hit the bottle and worse.

"I did drugs for a long time," Emerson confided later. "The lads were great. They helped me through it and got me over the withdrawal symptoms." In the end, Emerson managed to be phlegmatic about the incident. "You go through changes, and that is what experience is about." He was fortunate eventually to be able to afford to have the house completely rebuilt.

Meanwhile, Palmer moved to Tenerife in the Canary Islands with his girlfriend Maureen (since 1968 – they would marry in the 80s), in 1974. In fact all three members of the band became tax exiles in this period, with Emerson and Lake both acquiring houses in the Bahamas.

Although they weren't in the public eye ELP were still getting poll awards in 1975. Emerson won Best Keyboards and Palmer Best Drums in the *Circus* poll, and they both got Number 2 in the *Sounds* poll. Lake was also voted 5th Best Bass in that *Sounds* poll.

In the meantime, the band recorded some group material in the Manticore's Curzon Street HQ. However, in the main, the three musicians concentrated on their own long-planned personal projects, most of which by coincidence turned out to involve orchestras. Emerson had a piano concerto and some jazzier material in mind.

Lake worked with Pete Sinfield on some ambitious songs, and around Christmas 1975 enjoyed a major hit single with "I Believe In Father Christmas". Lake had actually completed the song the previous September, but his record company told him he had missed the Christmas deadline.

"I Believe In Father Christmas" got to Number 2 in the week of December 6, 1975, staying on the chart for 7 weeks. In normal circumstances it would have been Number One, but Greg was unlucky to come up against the extraordinary phenomenon of Queen's "Bohemian Rhapsody". (Years later it dented the Top 75 again, peaking at Number 72 for a week and in 1992 it was an apt money-raiser for the charity for the homeless, Shelter)

It was not conceived as a Christmas record: it started life, says Greg, as "a naive little piece of acoustic guitar music looking for a lyric". Then he noticed that "Jingle Bells" fitted nicely with the tune. Because it was around at the time of *Works*, grandiose schemes with orchestras were flying around, and it received an orchestral arrangement from Godfrey Salmon [2]. "As soon as the record company heard it, they cried 'Christmas single!'", says Greg, "And it took on a life of its own after that." The bitterness of the song – what *Sounds* saw as a "Lennonish sharpness" – probably comes more from Sinfield than Lake. According to Greg, "I've always loved Christmas. It was my favourite time of year as a kid, and I love to spend Christmas now with my own kid."

"We'll be hearing this one for years to come," prophesied *Cashbox* in the US and they were right. The single became a perennial Christmas favourite

In January 1976 Emerson turned up on the British TV show *Oscar Peterson's Piano Party*, playing a then-untitled boogie piece (later to become "Barrelhouse Shakedown") written in tribute to the jazz giant. He also ran through Meade Lux Lewis' boogie classic "Honky Tonk Train Blues" in duet with Peterson himself with Palmer on drums. When "Honky Tonk Train Blues" became a surprise hit single within a few month's of Lake's Yuletide smash, talk of solo albums and tours gathered further momentum. However, Emerson was lucky to release "Honky Tonk Train Blues" at all. All his tapes of the piece were in his house when it burned down. "Luckily the master tape survived," he explained.

Meanwhile, Palmer had extended his range of talents by taking lessons in tuned percussion from famed player, pedagogue and populariser James Blades [3], and was now able to add vibraphone, glockenspiel and marimba to the list of percussion instruments he had mastered. He also gathered enough material for two albums, including a ballet suite written with the help of Polish composer Andrzej Panufnik and a 20-minute percussion concerto, recorded with the London Philharmonic. For many years the status of this was "soon to be released." Now at last, it really is to be released on Palmer's upcoming anthology.

"I have been writing and rehearsing with a chap called Joseph Horovitz[4] for this percussion concerto which features about 60 players," Palmer explained at the time. "There's never been a concerto written for percussion before. We're going to feature all tuned percussion, such as marima, vibraphone, timpani and tubular bells. I'll be playing vibraphone, marimba, glockenspiel, timpani, tubular bells and possibly an enlarged version of a standard drum kit. I have a little cadenza.

"I have a complete theatrical idea in my mind to incorporate myself playing all these instrument with the orchestra, and using three females dancing in syncopation to what I'm playing…. There are a lot of things in this concerto that are fantastic. I've got this huge bucket full of chains that I pick up and throw at the gong, which is suspended four inches above the ground. It makes a terrific sound!"

Palmer hoped to perform the concerto at New York's Radio City Music Hall and also talked of eventually putting together a movie based on his life story, in which the concerto would strongly figure.

Palmer's various other projects included some big band jazz with Harry South and a conceptual vibraphone piece called "Lifeline". He also found time to produce Back Door's fourth album, *Activate,* in 1975.

Away from stage and studio, Palmer began to learn karate, working out with Geoff Britton, who for a short time had been drummer with Paul McCartney and Wings. "I'll spend an hour with him every morning," Palmer explained. "I see karate as very artful, like my drumming. I'm not into it as a hostile sort of thing. I see it more as energy than aggression although the animalistic part of me is quite strong." Palmer eventually acquired a high degree of skill and holds a black belt in the Wado Ryu discipline, though he recently retired from the art, as karate injuries were affecting his drumming.

For all this activity, in general Emerson, Lake and Palmer kept a pretty low profile from 1975–76. By the time they returned in March 1977 with a new album and tour, much had changed in the music world. The burgeoning punk scenes in England and New York were marginalising the 70s progressive rock giants. Punk fans were infiltrating the music press, bringing with them musical revisonism of almost Maoist fervour. Musical virtuosity was now out of fashion, replaced as the *ne plus ultra* of popular musical utterance by amphetamine-fuelled three minute bursts of adolescent anger. Hair was short and spiky, album covers were rough and ready – double albums were dismissed and gatefolds old hat. Worse still for bands such as ELP, not only did the new punk bands wear their lack of technical ability as a badge of Year Zero pride, they didn't *need* to be able to play extended guitar solos, as guitar solos of any kind were frowned upon; drum solos of course were beyond the pale! The sneering young guns had nothing but contempt for tax exile millionaire rock stars and stadium giants like Pink Floyd, Jethro Tull or Led Zeppelin – or so they made out at the time; some of them later attained that status themselves. With their classical arrangements, huge stage set, vast wealth and penchant for the grandiose, ELP were perhaps the most vulnerable of their generation to punk's attacks.

For all their noise, visibility and media presence, punks were still commercially feeble beyond the UK in 1977. ELP still had plenty of fans desperate for the follow-up to the classic *Brain Salad Surgery*. However, just as music had changed in ELP's absence, so ELP had changed while they were away from the spotlight. When they returned after their two and a half year break, it was with a radically different kind of album, *Works, Vol. 1*. The full band played only on the fourth side, while each individual took a side for his own orchestra-based "works" – the grandiose title signalling their desire to create music that would last, rather than, as they saw it at the time, easily disposable electronic rock. They also immediately embarked on a tour with a full orchestra. Against the changing musical landscape, this was a brave, almost self-consciously suicidal move. As the punks embraced the trashy and the disposable, ELP were out to build a grand artistic legary "Here," the band were saying to the critics, "kick our butts!"

Works, Vol.1 marked the beginning of ELP's association with a new record company, Atlantic, and the first stage of the winding down of Manticore, which became a publishing company, and was later – bizarrely – sold to Motown Records. "We set up Manticore to further the huge success we experienced and the considerable amounts of money we had to manage, thinking that in a certain way other artists could benefit from our financial means and our show business experience," Lake later reflected. "Then our careers became more and more demanding, and we realised we couldn't give these artists the time we had wished to give. And we reached a point where it wouldn't have been fair to go on like this. We helped them to find new contracts in the best possible conditions, and it relieved us of the responsibility of their future without prejudicing them. We could have kept them and tried to make money by selling our rights, but we preferred to release them and dissolve Manticore".

Atlantic Records were proud of their major new signing and promoted the new album with the slogan, "Individually, masters. Collectively, a masterpiece".

ELP's new direction had evolved out of a group reaction to the *Brain Salad Surgery* period and the subsequent solo projects. According to Palmer, "Originally what happened, is we all went off and recorded the pieces of music we each wanted to do. And after about six months we got together and said we've got this and that of individual stuff. So we played through the individual stuff and suddenly it all clicked. Everybody had used an orchestra, had something with like brass and strings and woodwinds. And Stewart Young came up with the idea of packaging it this way.

"We also knew the problems about releasing individual albums. If you release them too close to each other, one takes the sales from the other. So when Stewart said how about doing it this way, we thought that would be interesting and went ahead and packaged it as you have it now."

"We really wanted to make a break in the basic direction we were going in," Lake explained before the release of *Works, Vol. 1.* "We had flogged it to death from every standpoint. To make such a drastic change it did require a lot of rethinking. By bringing this album out we have exposed ourselves individually, and tried to show what makes up the group. It just took that long to hook it all out."

The band adjourned with their families to Montreux, Switzerland, to record the album. In every respect, ELP were sheltered from the outside world and the seismic shifts taking place on the rock scene.

The decision to record in Montreux was, in Emerson's anguished recollection, "the worst we ever made. It was like living in a padded coffin. There was nothing to do and nowhere to go to rave it up. I had ridden through there on my motorbike for the jazz festival the previous year, and it seemed great. But that had gone, there was nothing there.

"Being there made us feel so isolated. We had been off the road for a long time, and there was nothing there to give us the reassurance we needed very badly. But by the time we realized the effect the place was having on us we were too committed, with contracts on the houses and so on."

For Carl Palmer, "The thing that kept us going in Montreux was the quality of the studio."

Greg Lake told one reporter, "It was a long hard struggle to achieve what we wanted to achieve. The only question left is – are the people ready to listen to our idea of the future of music?"

There were some consolations. Emerson headed for Zurich on one of the five motorbikes he owned at the time, a Kawasaki 1100. "It is great biking country, that's one thing I can say for it. I also did quite a lot of water skiing, and Greg got into the pushbike scene. He bought himself a racing bike, a model with a plutonium frame that cost him about £1,000 [At least £5,000 at today's prices, some bike!], and then he bought all the gear on top of that …. Stewart Young, our manager, bought one as well, and joined him on rides. Carl spent his time running up and down the Swiss hills."

On their return, the band seemed unconcerned about losing fans because of staying away so long. "If there was a loss of fans, then for me particularly it might be a stimulus," Emerson said, "because I'd go out there with that added punch. The problem is going to be to get people to accept the new music."

They needn't have worried. Their long-time supporters were still with them and the "Long Silence", as Alan Freeman named it, had resulted in a great album. "I get bored with all these great authorities on music telling people what they should and shouldn't do, and pontificating away," he said. "It would be the easiest thing in the world for ELP just to put out any old album very quickly. A huge section of the public would buy it immediately, but they want it to be really worth the wait".

Worth the wait it was. In spite of everything ELP had done before, *Works Vol 1* was easily the most eclectic album they'd ever made. Emerson filled Side One with a piano concerto.

Emerson's growing frustration with ELP's direction had been a big factor in his desire to create something more substantial. "You get to the stage where you do things like 'Tarkus' and 'Karn Evil 9' and they come out and records eventually get deleted, and you think, what the fuck's it all about?" Emerson railed. "It's just not lasting. You feel you are banging your head against a brick wall, and it's all forgotten. Really, in this lay-off, personally I've been concentrating on writing my ideas down so other people can do it; doing something which is more meaningful. Let other people play the music, y'know? Therefore, when this next album is released, there will be orchestrations available for anybody to play. To me that is a lot more satisfying. That is working as a serious composer, rather than just churning it out.

"I had experimented with electronics. Helped out the Moog Corp and modified their instruments, and worked with every other electronic company developing their synthesizers. I helped Moogs develop their polyphonic synthesiser, advised them on how to set their controls...I'd gone through all that thing.

"And yet nothing is so satisfying as getting behind the actual *acoustic* instrument. It's all very well to have electronic instruments and try and copy acoustic instruments, but really it is not so rewarding."

In spite of all the solo projects, Emerson seemed happy to have the band back together. But he did say that had Lake and Palmer not wanted to go in an orchestral direction, he would have gone it alone.

"I'd have definitely done it on my own, 'cause that's what I was into. I didn't want to go back on the road unless there was an orchestra. I wouldn't go with anything less. After three years, I didn't want to go back with the same set-up. I needed a change, a new challenge.

"I think the orchestra really helps give my music the extra dimension it needs. As I listen back to all the ELP albums, I always hear them slightly augmented. Although an orchestra wasn't behind *Brain Salad Surgery* or *Tarkus*, I'd always hear it in my own mind. I wanted to hear the records bigger than they actually were, and I soon realized that I was fooling myself, and considered that orchestration was what I should be getting into.

"It was either strip everything down to the basics, like no thirteen keyboards, but just possibly piano, bass and drums. Go that route or one step further than what we've ever done before. I chose to go one step further. Everybody laughed when I mentioned it. Said, 'You're crazy, it'll never pay.' They've been proved right so far. It hasn't paid," he laughs. "But it's working."

Emerson composed the Concerto between 1975 and 1976, working with John Mayer, who exposed him to many new ideas in form, composition and orchestration.

"When I started I'd intended writing a set of variations," Emerson explained, "And it gradually got away from the original variation which I'd created, which gave me the clue that it would possibly be worked better into the concerto format. It may have not have anything to do with 20th-century music, but it has a lot to do with me, and the way I write is unhindered by what is going on in today's music. There are certain styles throughout the concerto which are intentional. Whereas I could put the first movement into a sort of pastoral context, the second movement went into a sort of baroque piece, and the last movement more into the modern way of writing – a very atonal sound...."

Emerson's key desire was "to show people that I was interested in things other than pop music. The concerto was meant to be a piece that proved I was a musician with some depth of musical thought".

The concerto's first and second movements are evocative and descriptive, in that they represent the composer's mood of contentment in his Sussex home, whilst the composition of the third was at least in part an exorcism of his anger about the fire. "I started writing the concerto when I moved in and it was nice and peaceful, happy, happy! And then, Bang! Fuck it... It was a pretty traumatic experience. I felt so damned ... frustrated... and I was really fucked up and could not give a shit about anything. And I think the music really comes across like that."

So strong were the memories of the havoc wrought by the fire on the Emerson family's lives, that Keith's wife was almost reduced to tears every time she heard the last movement. It is a potent cocktail of anger and libidinous sensuality, sometimes a little reminiscent of the mood swings of *West Side Story*, affording scope aplenty for the grand gesture, eventually finding a triumphant resolution. Principles of sonata form are discernable, but it is chiefly a movement of vivid contrasts and dramatic conflicts, a virtuoso showcase for *all* the players. It is, briefly, cinematic, technically and emotionally.

From the earliest days of The Nice, Emerson had been interested not only in classical music, but also in working with orchestras to realize his ideas. *Ars Longa Vita Brevis* and the *Five Bridges Suite* had been early attempts at this, but the Piano Concerto was the first formally 'classical' piece he had written, requiring only orchestra and soloist and owing nothing to rock or pop idioms.

"I am being a pioneer. There's no sense being modest about it, because nobody's done this before on this level. Way back in '68, I did it with the *Five Bridges Suite*. But technology wasn't what it is today, miking up every individual member of the orchestra. Back in those days it was eight-channel mixers, overhead mikes and a tremendous amount of overspill. The whole thing was a big battle where electronics drowned out orchestra."

The Piano Concerto was to become one of Emerson's favourite performing pieces, though he found working with a full orchestra occasionally frustrating.

"In classical music you have to read your parts rather like an office clerk, and I've found that, having worked with orchestras in America and England, it breeds a certain type of person rather like a bank clerk. I've been at concerts where I've seen guys reading the tennis results during a hundred bars' rest. "When I did the Sadler's Wells gig with The Nice, I was amazed to look down in the orchestra pit and see all the music stands with crosswords on them, all filled in. Obviously during the breaks they'd got their puzzles out. I can't work with people like that."

Emerson also wasn't sure that orchestra members were always clued into his way of doing things. "I'd already gotten to record the 'Bolero' with an orchestra and I'd realized how hard it was to play. You see, these trumpet players had been used to playing Bach and Beethoven. They only have to play in certain registers for that. And all of a sudden they had to scream out these high notes and they couldn't cut it. Their lips weren't up for that."

The musical language of the three-movement work is as eclectic as one might expect of Keith Emerson, beginning with twentieth-century serialism, and subsequently passing through Baroque, Romantic and jazz styles. The influences of Copland, Ginastera, Bernstein and others can be discerned. The piano part presents a great many difficulties for the performer, with its rhythmic complexities and rapid ostinato patterns. After the release of the album, Emerson was pleased to find a wide audience for his concerto, with both pop and classical stations prepared to play it. Even Britain's rather conservative BBC Radio 3 played it a couple of times. (BBC music critic Derek Jewell was a great ELP supporter).

"I'm pleased that all sorts of people have taken an interest in it," beamed Keith proudly. "Now I think a few other people want to have a go at it. I know the London Philharmonic are considering it as part of their regular repertoire. It would be ideal to hear someone else have a go at it. That's really a major goal of mine, because I don't want to be a performer all my life."

Emerson's "Piano Concerto No 1" is probably the best formally structured orchestral work ever composed by a rock musician. It would be unfair to compare it with anything by other major Seventies rock musicians, since none – even Clapton – has ever written a work of comparable seriousness.

The acoustic trend on *Works Vol. 1* set by Emerson was carried on into Lake's side with a number of ballads arranged for orchestra with help from Godfrey Salmon and Tony Harris [5]. Lake had been working on his own material, often in collaboration with Pete Sinfield, since the *Brain Salad Surgery* days. "I had so many ideas on the acoustic guitar," he said, "too many to go into ELP's music without making ELP unbalanced, I wrote them down all over the place, mainly while I was on tour, of course, because we spent so much time on the road. I usually compose on guitar, though some things I did on piano." Back then, Lake had been planning a solo album. "The aim is to meet, mix with and play with new musicians, so I doubt Keith and Carl and I will play on each other's discs."

Lake had begun to refine these rough compositions in the summer of 1974. "I wanted to do them soon after I'd written them, or else they'd become stale." Even at that stage, however, Lake stoutly affirmed that ELP remained his main priority. "The solo is a secondary thing, kind of like a hobby....What communicates for me is a band who have been together for a long time, and they're like a family communicating. It's very important that a family should stay together."

A collaboration between Greg Lake and Pete Sinfield made perfect sense as both writers had been covering similar lyrical territory since the days of King Crimson – dealing with the big issues such as religious hypocrisy, the futility of war, political corruption and poverty. However while Lake's tone tended towards anger and outrage, the laconic and highly intelligent Sinfield tended towards acid irony, bitterness and regret. Both returned frequently to the fear of death and God, though this existential dread is more acute and tortured in Sinfield's labyrinthine world: *"Blind stick blind drunk cannot see/Mouth dry tongue tied cannot speak...Lost soul, lost trace lost in hell"*[6]. Both seek rest, peace and "life to be", but doubt, confusion, fatalism and resignation tend to win out; love and passion tend to be the only consolation.

The hallmark of Pete Sinfield's writing from Crimson days onwards was, as one friendly critic[7] put it, "a terse epigrammatic style notable for its economy". This concise, witty, paradoxical expression of ideas both big and small, is evident in at least four of the five songs on Lake's side of the album – though Sinfield doesn't take it nearly as far as he did with King Crimson and on his own solo album. "Usually the ideas are mine," said Lake, "and Peter comes in halfway through the thing and we join together and finish it off."

Lake's fatalistic *carpe diem* "Lend Your Love to Me Tonight" kicks off his side. The orchestra here reinforces and supports the piece, providing an increasingly powerful motive force, before building to a frenzied climax at the end.

The next cut "C'est La Vie" was the first song that Lake and Sinfield worked on after the latter was taken on as a lyricist for the band. At the beginning of the chorus, Lake's voice is subtly multi-tracked to produce a choral effect, anticipating the arrival of the choir itself later in the song. The strings are lush, sultry and exotic. Reflecting the words *'Like a song/out of tune and out of time'*, the choir (sounding remote, icy and Russian), the group and the orchestra go out of synch with each other, blundering along confusedly – the overall effect is disturbing and moving.

The song's sad, romantic accordion solo is not Keith Emerson's. "I felt quite bewildered about that," says Keith with obvious regret, "because when Greg came into my house playing 'C'est La Vie' I got my accordion out and suggested that it might be a good idea to put an accordion solo on it. I think it was at a stage when we were being secretive about our solo projects. It was almost taboo for one of us to be in the studio when another of us was doing something for a solo album. I think that's why Greg brought in another accordion player. Anyway, on-stage I copy that solo. I don't even know who the accordion player was on the album."

"C'est La Vie" was released as a Greg Lake solo single, but with little success. Reviews were predictably mainly poor, with one writer describing the band as "the most fashionably redundant pachyderm in business" and the song as "obsolescent *in extremis*."

"Hallowed Be Thy Name" reflects the typical Sinfield and Lake themes of loss and resignation. There's not much right with anyone or anything – statesmen, thinkers, optimist, pessimist, the planet, God, least of all the protagonist himself. Failing to find "some truth he can use", he drowns his sorrows in drunken philosophizing and unhesitatingly embraces "temptation", "recreation" and "degradation." The song had originally been considered for *Brain Salad Surgery* and all three members of the band performed on it. Emerson's fractured speakeasy piano and the remarkable discipline of the string players' stabbing glissandos are the most notable features.

"Nobody Loves You Like I Do" elaborates the themes of Lake's first song, but is more upbeat in the way it sees love as offering redemption, with the music matching the more optimistic mood. "I'm not after conveying messages," Lake would later assert. "Messages are for Western Union. I'm after conveying feelings, because feelings are what people want. If they want messages they'll pick up a philosopher's book."

"Nobody…" is the first ELP song to feature Lake on harmonica and a good fist he makes of it- there's restrained electric guitar in the back of the mix too, the first time it is heard on the album – and a touch of accordion helping to fill out the soundstage with the orchestra as engine-room. However there was another disappointment for Emerson. "I did a lot of ragtime piano in the middle, but it's mixed so far down that you can't hear it," he grumbled.

The final cut on Lake's side is "Closer To Believing". First performed back in April 1973 at a German concert, this is one of Lake's and Sinfield's most dramatic songs. More than any other song, the process of its composition reveals Greg's perfectionism. Stewart Young once recalled that it took Greg and Pete 'two years' to complete it, and that he must have heard 'fifty versions of it' before they hit on the final version.

The recurring words *"I need me/ You need you/ We want us"* sum up the central import of the whole side's lyrics; Heaven may be lost, but human love remains. The music is basically very simple – just a few chords. The lush, sensitive orchestration amplifies the yearning lyrics. The painful metaphors of crashing on the shore, and of driftwood, are echoed in the rolling, lonely sea music produced mainly by the strings with some piano backing. Chamber textures – strings and oboe – reinforce the sense of loss at the end of the first two verses.

Interestingly enough, both Lake and Pete Sinfield view the lyrics as one of their greatest achievements.

The first half of the double album was overtly acoustic. However, the second half of the album would inch back towards the favoured electronic path. Although there are still flashes of the orchestral approach.

Palmer's pieces varied from adaptations of classical works by Prokofiev and Bach, the latter featuring his percussion tutor James Blades on marimba, to the low-down funk of "L.A. Nights". Meanwhile, "Food For Your Soul" is a big band number, and "Tank" returns from the first ELP album, rearranged for big band and orchestra. "I tried to find pieces which would please me, with the particular blend," Palmer explained of his selections of *Works, Vol 1*, "Be it classical, jazz-rock or whatever…. It's completely self-indulgent. It was as individual and as solo as I think you'll find. I didn't say I'm going to go for one particular style, or I'm going to hit the media this way. I decided I wanted to play some jazz, I wanted to play a classical piece, I wanted to write, and I also decided to re-record 'Tank'.

"They are all different pieces I wanted to play, a selection of tracks that portray me as a player. I don't have any particular style. I could go into a Max Roach approach or a Billy Cobham jazz-rock approach, but I try to cover a lot of things.

"For me it was something completely different that gave me a chance to experiment as a writer, and on different instruments. That's why there are such vast changes throughout. I had to play all those different things to get out all that was in me."

Palmer opens up with Prokofiev's incendiary "The Enemy God Dances with the Black Spirits" from the 1917 ballet score *Ala and Lolly*, later recast as the *Scythian Suite*. He uses the piece as a drum vehicle, but far from being intrusive, the drums enhance the original music, which is played straight, without alteration. It is one of Palmer's best ever recorded performances. "We were going to record 'The Enemy God' with the group originally," said Carl, "but found it sounded better with an orchestra. That was my classical piece."

The funky "L.A Nights" is one of the highlights of Palmer's side of the album. It was initially recorded in the early part of 1974, after Carl met The Eagles' guitarist Joe Walsh[8] and invited him to play on one of his songs, tentatively entitled "L.A. '74".

"I did the basic tracks in L.A. with Keith, and Joe Walsh on guitar," Palmer recalled. [The other guitar contributions came from Snuffy Walden, formerly with Manticore signings Stray Dog.] "I enjoy playing that kind of rock a lot," Palmer enthused, "and I wanted to try and capture energy if I could." He certainly did – it's superb good-time stuff – "Like a 90 mph ride down Sunset Boulevard", in the words of Dan Nooger of *Circus* magazine.

As with Lake's material, Emerson felt that his parts were reduced to low down in the mix.

Palmer had originally planned to record "New Orleans" with The Meters[9], but felt they were not up to the job. Instead he handpicked players, including Colin Hodgkinson and Ron Aspery from Back Door, whose album he'd produced, and Snuffy Walden. Palmer and Co. have obviously absorbed The Meters' distinctive brand of New Orleans funk, summoning up the Creole carnival atmosphere in this uncomplicated firecracker of funkiness.

The Bach piece Palmer chose was the "Two Part Invention In D Minor". Harry South [10] arranged it. While it comes across as a trifle amateurish, it's quite pleasant. Additional string parts have been added to Bach's two-part original, which is played virtually straight by Palmer and Blades, and there's a bit more interest from other occasional tuned percussion.

Palmer wrote "Food For Your Soul" for the previous song's arranger, Harry South. "[He's] like England's Quincy Jones", Palmer explained. "That was the jazz element I wanted to capture." The result is some great flashy big band stuff, with nice jokes added by triangle and gong, and a lightning-fast solo.

Palmer had wanted to re-record the closer "Tank" for ages, "because when we did it originally we didn't have the money for an orchestra; it was our first album, and we were an unknown band, really." Emerson put together the Moog parts while Harry South helped on the arrangements again. The new version is an effective reworking for orchestra and group. Brass and strings are prominent, not to mention a steaming soprano sax solo. The strings revel in the call and response section before the original entry of the drum solo.

Aaron Copland's "Fanfare for the Common Man" opened the full band side. Copland had been commissioned to write the piece as one of ten patriotic fanfares for the 1942-3 season of the Cincinnati Symphony Orchestra. It was originally composed for brass and percussion. Lake introduced the piece to Emerson.

"We were in the studio, blocked out of our skulls," Emerson remembered. "Greg picked up on the idea. He kept on playing it, and I said, 'What do you keep playing that for?', and very slowly I got used to it."

The discovery of the piece coincided with Emerson's experiments with a new type of keyboard, the three-manual Yamaha GX1 synthesizer, which he would use for the first time on this track with astonishing results. Yamaha had spent over two million pounds developing the new synthesizer, a £30,000 test-bed for systems which would soon be used in more modestly priced instruments. Stevie Wonder christened the GX1 the "dream machine".

"I heard about it through the Manticore office," said Emerson. "I was dubious about what they said it could do. About a week later my office rang me up and said, 'We've got it set up at the studio and it's incredible. Come along and play it.' So we wandered over to the studio (which was in Fulham at the time) and these two Japanese gentlemen were looking over it very excitedly. They explained to me what it did. I got more and more wrapped up as I went along. I'd be doing something and they'd say, 'How do you do that? How do you do that? Hang on a second. That's great. How do I do that again?'"

"…I said, 'This is fantastic, I'd like to use it a bit more.' [When] I found out how much it cost, [it] was a bit of a shock. But I played nothing else after I got it…I didn't use the organ or the Moog synthesiser setup on the group side of *Works*. That's all Yamaha. That just shows how much I liked it. I didn't need anything else. It was just so complete, even with its silly little drum machine, which seems very home-organish now, but was quite revolutionary at the time."

Unfortunately, the GX1 was as difficult to move as the Moog, requiring an improbable eight men simply to lift it, making it difficult for touring. Also, it was extremely delicate, with problems arising even if it was moved from one side of the studio to the other. Still, there were plenty of compensations. "The main thing about the GX1 was that it had such a good, fat sound that I've really been able to make it my own," Emerson pointed out, "Probably because most people won't ever be able to afford one." (Collectors can now pick them up quite cheaply in the US.)

The GX1 was just the instrument for an over-the-top distinctively ELP version of "Fanfare For The Common Man". Emerson made the fullest possible use of the GX1's potential for producing brassy, distorted sounds and bold solo voicings. "I've tried playing 'Fanfare' on the organ and it sounds really horrible," Emerson insisted. "It doesn't sound good at the piano either, yet it sounds all right at the Yamaha."

ELP follow the lines of Copland's piece, though it had to be altered sometimes to fit it into a swung rock rhythm. "It needed transposing, so I did that first", said Emerson. "I wanted to improvise in a key that was sort of bluesy." The band hadn't played together for a while at this point, and so "Fanfare" was thoroughly jammed in the studio. The band got a "dirty" live R&B sound by recording part of it on just one microphone. In fact the take that was used was a soundcheck that Palmer had asked the engineer to tape.

Now the band just had to get Copland's permission. "After doing 'Fanfare', says Keith, "I was a bit dubious about our treatment of it as opposed to 'Hoedown', because that was more or less straight through just as it had been done originally. So

I sent Copland the version of 'Fanfare' without the improvisation in the middle to begin with, and the message came back through the publishing company that he couldn't see why we want that version to come out because we'd really done nothing more with it than he'd done.

"So I got back to his publisher and said I didn't send the whole version because I thought Copland might find the other section a bit offensive, and they said, 'No, Copland is just a twelve year old at heart, he'd love anything like that' – so then I sent him the complete version and that he liked."

"Fanfare" went on to become ELP's first and only hit single, but it was nonetheless a formidable smash. They only just failed to shift Hot Chocolate from the U.K. Number One spot on 16th July, 1977. It undoubtedly did a lot for the sales of *Works, Vol. 1*. The track was also used by British Airways in a television advert at the time. Amazingly, "Fanfare" was originally going to be held back for the subsequent *Works, Vol 2*. It was only when Emerson pleaded to Atlantic Records boss and long-time friend of British prog-rockers, Ahmet Ertegun, that it was included on *Vol 1*,

As *Works Vol 1* only had one side allocated for full band pieces, the music had to be special. Fortunately, track two, "Pirates" kept up to the high standard set by "Fanfare". The piece was originally composed for the soundtrack of a Norman Jewison movie of the Frederick Forsyth novel about mercenary soldiers, *The Dogs of War*. Unfortunately the film was subsequently shelved[11] . Emerson had planned the piece for his solo side, but with the film score going nowhere, he approached Lake to write some lyrics along the theme of the book. Lake told him, "I don't want to write about mercenaries but let's see if we can't come up with something else." Lake got together with Sinfield and called Emerson with the idea of coming up with a lyric about pirates.

"The idea of pirates was good for my music," Emerson decided, "Because my music is very adventurous, much like an adventure novel. It demands to have visuals connected with it."

Lake and Sinfield used the pirate motif as the perfect metaphor for the rock world. It's all there – the adventuring, intrepid, devil-may-care spirit, setting out on brave voyages, seeking fortune, fighting, conquering all in sight, looting money and treasure, indulging in as much wine, women, song and gambling as possible along the way. In its – sometimes ironic – discourse of loyalty and heroism, "Pirates" is as much about ELP and their relationship with their fans, as it is about seafaring outlaws of old. The final line, "Gold drives a man to dream," was inspired by Ahmet Ertegun.

The music is very obviously cinematic, the broad sweep of the strings and triumphant punch of brass and percussion summoning images of buckles being lustily swashed, in the manner – vaguely – of Korngold's deathless MGM pirate-movie scores. (Incidentally, it's possible to discern a Korngold influence in the first movement of Keith's Piano Concerto No. 1.) Though Keith's synthesiser and the orchestra are often prominent, Carl and Greg play important roles. Their respective drumming and bass playing on this track is among the best they have ever done.

Coming after "Fanfare", "Pirates" more than any other ELP composition makes clear the strength the band derives from this apparent conflict of styles.

"I'm more of a romantic than anyone else in the band," reflects Lake. "In terms of music I believe in beautiful things rather than bizarre things. I'd rather have harmony than dissonance. I know there's a lot of dissonance in this band but it's that contrast that makes music dynamic. It's the combination and the battles between the romance of mine and that technical development of Keith's which make this an interesting and exciting group…."

All told, *Works, Vol 1*, was yet another fascinating, groundbreaking album. While commercially less successful than some of its predecessors, it was still a hit record, and just as with *Brain Salad Surgery*, it left both band and fans wondering where Emerson, Lake and Palmer could go next. Unfortunately, as would soon become clear on the *Works* tour, it appeared the only way was down.

The ambition inherent in *Works, Vol 1* was worth the risk; musically the album was a great success. However, taking the mammoth show on the road, complete with orchestra and all the requisite back up – a touring party of over 160 people – financially ruined the band. Although they would later recoup some of these losses, it was the first real sign of ELP's imminent disintegration.

Everything about the orchestra tour operated on by now familiarly mammoth scale. Equipment was to be carried by seven 45-foot articulated trucks (plus another three for the open-air dates, the first of which was at Chicago's Soldiers Field on June 4th). No less than *three* buses transported the orchestral players and choir. The 72,000 watt PA system, which included mixers and submixers, was designed by JBL, the company that had provided a similar sound system (only smaller!) for the 1976 Montreal Olympics.

In addition to the musicians, the touring party also included 63 roadies, assorted road crews, personal assistants, secretaries, two accountants (!), a doctor… The tour was indisputably the biggest logistical undertaking so far undertaken by one band in the history of rock. Even Bob Dylan's *Rolling Thunder* tour of 1975–76 had only employed a comparatively piffling 60 people. In fact, over $1,000,000 had been spent *even before the lights went down on the first show* at the Freedom Hall in Louisville, Kentucky, on May 24, 1977. Was it an omen that the lighting gantry almost caused a fatal accident on that first date?

Tour manager Tom Mohler relates how "one of the welds had broken and the lights could have smashed down on to the stage. It was noticed early in the morning, and if it hadn't been spotted, then it could have fallen on the band during their sound check or during the concert."

The stage set was uncluttered: speakers were hung from the ceiling, amps were hidden. The band themselves had a triangular stage surrounded by towering metallic tubes. Rather than being hidden away in a pit, the orchestra, eye-catchingly kitted out in white, were seated behind the band on modular platforms. Each orchestra instrument was individually miked with a revolutionary new device, a Frapp pick-up, and had to be custom-fitted to each instrument. For example, the mouthpieces of the trumpets needed a hole drilled for the insertion of the pick-up. Its function was simply to amplify the orchestral instruments to the high decibel level of the band. Although other devices of the time could do this, they tended to 'electrify' the sound; the Frapp kept the sound true to life, with all the original subtleties of timbre and intonation. The resulting sounds, including those from the choir, were then fed under the stage to a complex mixing system, and reduced to 12 different amalgams of sound (strings, brass, etc.), which were fed back via amps on the stage, to the musicians. "For the first time we can actually get the orchestra as loud as a group," Palmer enthused.

Huge rectangular lights (custom-designed by Nicholas Cernovitch, a major ballet and opera lighting expert) were suspended above the stage. In addition, 300 thousand-watt coloured lights were choreographed by a computer to form over 200 variations. For all this obvious, some might say gratuitous, expense, it would be the presence of the touring orchestra – key to the *Works* project – that would really be the money-pit that dragged the venture down.

Rather than employ a name orchestra or choir, the band set out to build one from scratch. Out of 1,500 original applicants, 350 had been auditioned worldwide for the 110 places in orchestra and chorus. With scaled salaries averaging $450 per person per week and a two year option on touring Europe and the Far East, there was a tremendous buzz of optimism among the orchestral players, none of whom was over 35 years old. "This is a watershed moment," gushed the shock-haired Godfrey Salmon, conductor of the orchestra, although with hindsight the statement was a little over the top. "It is the coming together of two ages. We are breaking new ground, and they will be talking about the tour for years to come." ELP joined the new recruits for three months of intensive rehearsal in Montreal to hone every detail. These were *very* expensive rehearsals!

The *Works, Vol 1* tour marked the culmination of all of ELP's grand stage gestures. While, especially during the punk era, the band were repeatedly castigated for the grandiose theatricals and the opulence of their live productions, they maintained that they were just investing more resources towards the audience's entertainment.

"I've always been conscious of the showbusiness aspect of performing music," said Lake. "A concert is all-around entertainment, whereas records are pure music... Theatrics should be used to complement the music rather than obscure it."

For Carl Palmer, "To get music across is one thing. To present it with some ribbon tied around it is show business, which is the glamour, the glitter and the lights. I think people like to see something up there which needn't happen to get the music across. We bring that element into the music when the music warrants it. I wanted to do something else while I did my drum solo, so I started turning it around. Keith does the same – throws the thing over... They love to see it."

Even the orchestra were astounded by some of ELP's live showmanship techniques. "When Carl was into his drum solo and the drum stage started revolving, the whole orchestra stood up in surprise to get a closer look," Emerson recalled. "They just had no idea it was going to happen."

Palmer remained defiant in the face of critical adversity. "They used the word 'pretentious' ... because of the amount of money we used to spend on our stage show," he said. "I'm sure that if you go to a concert you want your money's worth; yet when we give people their money's worth critics call us pretentious because we're so extravagant. On the other hand, if you didn't get your money's worth they would slag you off as well, so I don't take any notice about that. I enjoy making money and I enjoy the fame that goes with it. If that's being pretentious, then I love it!"

Keith noted the orchestra's delight in being part of it all: "For most of them it was their first real involvement with rock music, and I think the orchestra have been highly amused by it, especially the way American audiences come up with great cries of 'Yeah!', 'Wow!' and so on during the quiet bits. Although we had rehearsed solidly for more than a month with the orchestra, they had not seen the full show before the first night."

Behind the scenes, equally, no expense was spared. ELP traveled like aristocrats. Emerson set off with four cases of Dom Perignon '69 – to last two weeks before getting to a major city – and crates of his favourite Burgundy, the esteemed Montrachet (he liked to have a bottle or two handy during a performance). Lake had a specially ordered luxury bus complete with master bedroom, tape and video systems and movies from *Jaws* to *Deep Throat*. With admirable restraint, the relatively parsimonious Palmer settled for booking in his karate trainer as a member of the entourage – for practice.

It had been clear even before the start of the tour that full houses were essential every night just to break even. However, the money ran out earlier than anyone expected. Quite soon it became obvious that touring with the orchestra was bringing ELP to the edge of bankruptcy. The cancellation of just one gig – in Tampa, Florida, on July 1st, 1977, because of riots after a Led Zeppelin concert – brought massive problems. A promoter aborted the Cleveland gig (another auspicious venue), and (relatively) poor ticket sales put an end to the Pittsburgh outdoor show. Total losses from these cancellations alone came to $2,000,000. There was worse to come.

"There were a lot of unforeseen things that made us [jettison] the orchestra," Emerson explained. "One was a ruling by the union that musicians can't travel more than about 100 miles every day. But the thing is that people travel that far these days to see concerts. So we were packing places one night and then we'd travel 100 miles to the next place and we'd only have half the house filled. Of course, we were planning on having every place completely sold out so we could at least break even. And a lot of little things started piling up to put us behind. From then on it was impossible to catch up with the finances, so we just had to stop and go out as a three-piece."

ELP reluctantly decided that the orchestra would be used only for the very large venues. This saved the band $80,000, but it still cost $120,000 a week to keep the show on the road. After the final Madison Square Garden gig on July 9th, Stewart Young reported; "Keith told me he was prepared to sell his house if necessary, to get this tour together. We said it wouldn't work financially but they still went underway. There's such a great team spirit on this tour, it's like a big family. The musicians are really great, we've become close friends. It's fun." Young told his interviewer that the band planned to use the orchestra again at the Montreal Olympic Stadium and film the show for television [12].

Still, there was no disguising the band's disappointment with the state of affairs. "When we had to halt the whole thing for a period of time it was very hard," Emerson complained, "very upsetting." Even with the new arrangement, there were still plenty of hurdles.

"When we stopped using the orchestra we were faced with me working overtime to compensate for what the orchestra used to do," Emerson explained. "I'd really got my hands full. And even so, there were a few numbers we couldn't do without them – 'The Enemy God' and so on. There are so many orchestral lines in that, that it's impossible for one person to play it. And with ELP alone it's only possible to play the first movement of my concerto. Then I have to play some of the orchestra's lines. Luckily people have come expecting the orchestra and still haven't been too disappointed. In fact, a lot of people said we sound better without them. I'm inclined to disagree with that. I think some of them are under the impression that the orchestra is taking a lot of what we are meant to be doing away from us. It's really untrue.

"Actually, what the orchestra is enabling us to do is more of the ELP repertoire than we've ever done before. Like the 'Bolero' from 'Trilogy'. We tried doing that as a trio in all manner of ways. I even taught Greg to play keyboards [Mellotron and Minimoog] for it [on the *Trilogy* tour]. Then we had the strings on a tape recorder and Carl had headphones on. He played drums to that. It didn't work for too long.

The tape broke down one night and everything fell to pieces. So we never used that again. I think the only number that suffers without the orchestra is 'Pirates'. It sounds a bit too thin for my ears, but the audience still goes along."

However, ELP would have to get used to touring without the orchestra. The second phase of the US tour, from late '77 to March 13, 1978, was played entirely as a trio. Keith apologized many a time on stage, sometimes three times a gig, for not having the orchestra. It proved to be the final tour of ELP's 1970s career. A tour of the UK was tentatively planned, with four nights at London's Olympia planned over Christmas, as well as a few provincial dates. It was never really a viable option; even though ELP recouped a lot of their initial losses with the second tour, to embark on any more dates would have tipped the scales into debit once again.

"The mistake was taking the orchestra on a night-to-night basis straight away," Palmer reflected. "What we should have done was make a film or series of television concerts, maybe five altogether, which was my suggestion at the beginning and one which we now all wish we had done. Maybe Keith would have done his concerto. For the second show Greg could have sung more of his songs, then I could have played more of my pieces. The other two shows would have been totally group oriented – past and present.

"We had the facilities to get out the five shows in a period of three months, possibly even two, and then to go out with an orchestra. I think it would have opened people's eyes a lot quicker to what we were about to present. The television medium being as big as it is could have helped us bridge the gap the economy forced us into, that is, to stop touring with the orchestra. If we had hit all those people through television first, there might have been a way we could have toured with it a bit longer.

"Then again, it could only have been done in the major markets because the overhead of 120 people on the road is astronomical... By the time we allowed for everything it cost about $208,000 a week. We needed $3,000 a week just for incidentals."

Lake contended that, "it would have been better economically to go out as a three-piece, make a lot of money and then see if we could afford it or not. What's interesting is that instead of people telling us, 'I told you so', they're telling us how much they admire our courage and diligence."

Not surprisingly the whole *Works* debacle put an incredible strain on relationships within the band. By the time the tour was over the band was near to splitting. In some ways for Emerson, there was a sense of *déjà vu*.

"We had an awful lot of disagreements," Emerson explained. "Some of our repertoire needed orchestral ornamentation, and when we were playing as a three-piece group I sadly missed that looseness the orchestra gave me. I certainly had my hands full. The tour as a three-piece was long and very hard. We discussed what would happen afterward and what possibilities were open to us. One thing was certain: in order to continue we would have to do a lot of cutting down. We even discussed a piano/bass/drums format...more material like 'Show Me The Way To Go Home', I would think. Simplified things.

"Actually, there were quite a number of things we could have done. Carl would have had to use a smaller drum kit, and we would have played smaller places, more clubs and that sort of thing. But to me it seemed like history repeating itself, because I had been through that with The Nice. We broadened and expanded, and reached the ultimate doing the *Five Bridges Suite*. But it left the other members of the band behind. They didn't feel completely involved. This is more or less what happened with ELP. They felt it was more my thing than theirs, but they went along with it because that was the only way we could stay together...

"At the end of that tour we were considering a final separation. It was at the back of all our minds, but was left unspoken. The orchestra plagued Greg and Carl as a financial and artistic disaster – a view I totally disagreed with. I'd read enough from critics that I respected and heard enough from friends to assure myself that it was the contrary. The orchestra was the finest, most dedicated and trusting bunch of people I had worked with in that context. They were as disappointed as I was when they had to disband. We had a lot of fun."

In the middle of the touring debacle, ELP released another album, *Works, Vol 2*. It did little to buck the band's downward trajectory. At the time of its release it was felt by many to be something of a disappointment. There are some good things but there's a genuine feel that the record was less momentous than any previous ELP album. One critic slated it for being "a ragbag of out-takes". Some years later, Emerson offered a similar view, "It was really a bit of a let-down after *Works, Vol.1*, because it's really just a collection of old singles that hadn't been available on album before. We were really just trying to recoup some of the losses we incurred on tour with the orchestra."

While seven of the twelve tracks had never previously been officially released in any form, the presence of four previously issued tracks and one remix meant that there was under half an hour of really new music out of a total playing time of less than forty-four minutes. Many fans, inevitably, felt short-changed.

On the plus side, there was not a duff track on the album. Also, if the record wasn't all it could have been, it did serve the valuable purpose of highlighting the band's lighter side and once again demonstrated their versatility. The record takes in boogie-woogie, rock of various kinds, big band, ballad, novelty, lullaby – everything but classical! The album contained two new band tracks, the standard "Show Me The Way To Go Home" and the new composition "So Far to Fall". The former is a good Emerson work out and was used by the band to close their shows. The latter is quite a good song with a punchy orchestration and lyrics on the kinky side of risqué. One assumes that these two tracks were originally destined for side four of *Vol 1* when, in the early stages of planning, "Fanfare" was bound for *Vol 2*.

Other highlights included a lovely Lake ballad about his daughter, "Watching Over You". Palmer's "Bullfrog", featuring his mates Back Door, could be called spunky. It's quite the most unusual track ever associated with the band. "Tiger in the Spotlight" was originally recorded for *Brain Salad Surgery* and may have been one of the tracks to be used if Ginastera had refused permission to use "Toccata".

However, for all its charms, *Works Vol 2* represented something that ELP had never had before – an album that didn't sell. The record enjoyed almost no commercial success and did little to alleviate ELP's financial crises.

In spite of the difficulties and disappointments, the *Works* tour was grand, glorious and spectacular – an important milestone in rock history, both musically and in terms of pioneering staging techniques. However, the North American Orchestra Tour of 1977 really signalled the beginning of the end of ELP.

Artistically they could go no further. Had they played safe, they could have made potloads of money, touring their classic material as a three-piece. Instead they took a huge risk in taking such a massive show on the road. Corporate sponsorship has taken all the risk out of such ventures. Jagger, Richard, Bono and Gilmour et al, can now emerge from a world tour of even modest success and ring up millions of dollars in the kitty. ELP were one of the acts who blazed the trail for global stadium touring – and paid a heavy price.

Notes

1   The Tudor house, build in 1457, had a long and venerable history. It was for a long time the home of James Barrie, the author of *Peter Pan*. Keith's and Elinor's second son Damon was born there in 1975.

2   Salmon enjoyed popularity from 1973–75 as a viola/violin player in the Esperanto Rock Orchestra, which played classical-based music, largely on orchestral instruments. Session work, arranging and conducting for groups and soundtracks, prepared him for Emerson, Lake and Palmer's grand enterprise. In 1980 he conducted the orchestra for Keith Emerson's soundtrack to Dario Argento's *Inferno*. Ten years later they collaborated on another Argento horror film, *The Church*.

3   James Blades (1901–99) was a superbly sprightly 75-year-old when he recorded with Carl Palmer. He was more influential than anyone else in establishing the role of percussion in British music; a skilled lecturer, he wrote a standard textbook on playing percussion, was a regular performer on children's TV. Blades was the sound behind the Rank Organisation's movie intros (though Billy Wells was the muscle man with the gong.)

4   Born in 1926, Joseph Horowitz (not to be confused with the 19th century composer or the contemporary writer on classical music of the same name, nor the mercurial Russian pianist Vladimir Horowitz) is an Austrian-born British composer. His appealingly modern and highly individual style is laced with wit and humour. His many compositions include operas, ballets, a Toy Symphony, a Jazz Harpsichord Concerto – and a Horrortorio! He has also written a great deal of TV music including the theme of *Rumpole of the Bailey*.

5   Another viola-playing member of the Esperanto Rock Orchestra (see footnote on Godfrey Salmon). Soon after *Works Vol 2*, he played for Kai Olsson – her band included Ron Aspery, who had worked with Carl Palmer on *Works Vol 2*. How interesting these connections are. Oh, please yourselves.

6   From "Pictures of A City" on King Crimson's *In the Wake Of Poseidon* album 1970.

7   Richard Williams, writing in *Melody Maker*, February 2, 1971.

8   Born 1947; Walsh pioneered an early heavy metal guitar technique, and the "voice bag" from which his distorted voice was emitted after being sung into a plastic tube. To non-guitarists it is doubtless best known through its use by Peter Frampton on his 1976 double-album smash *Frampton Comes Alive*. He uses it on 'LA Nights'. Walsh has had a long and varied career since, including a stint with the short-lived supergroup 'The Best', in which Keith Emerson played keyboards.

9   A New Orleans based vocal R & B band, formed there in 1967. Their lean, funky harmony sound, full of tricky rhythms and understated vocals, made them attractive to rock artists; many big name stars used them as backing singers. By the time Carl Palmer was planning to record "New Orleans" in 1977, the Meters were divided by legal wrangles and artistic struggles over production, a fact of which Palmer was probably unaware. They split for good that same year.

10 A veteran arranger and bandleader, whose name was once found in the credits of, as it seems, half the big shows on British TV, including 70s cop smash *The Sweeney*; he also helped out on pop and rock records. In November '72, Carl was reported in *NME* as having "earned himself a fiver recently by playing at the Jolly Cockney pub in Lambeth, South London with Harry South, Les Condon and others" (Tony Stewart interview 18 Nov 72). Sounds like a good jazz bash.

11 Jewison did get *Dogs* made eventually. The film was released in 1980, starring Christopher Walken. The score was provided by Geoffrey Burgon. Watching the film, it's hard to see where music of the "Pirates" type could have been used. Emerson's expansive pirate music belongs to a grander, less gritty film altogether – i.e. the one that didn't get made.

12 The now legendary Montreal Olympic Stadium concerts were indeed filmed for television broadcast. The film was given a limited release in US cinemas, later being issued on video. In fact ELP still hold the attendance record for the Montreal Olympic Stadium – they attracted more people than any day of the Olympic Games!

CHAPTER 8

All Good Things Must Come To An End

After the extraordinary highs and lows of the *Works* saga, the question going through everyone's minds, not least the band's, was "How do you follow that?" Unfortunately, although they had ideas aplenty, many things conspired against them.

For a start, punk and disco, which had been emerging in 1976–77, were now holding sway; there was a general reaction against progressive music, which was seen by a new generation as remote from "real" concerns; Led Zeppelin and ELP were the chief scapegoats. Record companies played it safe in an economic climate very different from the boom years of the early Seventies. The bands themselves were beginning to realize that the glory years couldn't go on forever. There was uncertainty about what direction ELP should take.

One option was to strip back to basics – write shorter songs with less instrumental development, an approach very much in step with the times. But this risked losing a major part of the older progressive audience, which had an increasing amount of buying power. Another possibility was to lie low for a while and see how things developed. Then again, a band could just refuse to change anything about the music. Finally, a band could opt to make all manner of compromises and hope for the best. This is what ELP did.

"After meeting with Atlantic Records we were finally persuaded to make one more album," Emerson explained. "Much to my reluctance a commercial album was suggested, 'commercial' meaning we would compress all of the simpler ideas and make them into neat little radio-playable singles. Since Greg had felt repressed in the area of his writing, I eased up on my opinions to an extent, bit my nails, and gave him the freedom he kept asking for on Side One of *Love Beach*."

ELP recorded *Love Beach* in Nassau in 1978. Things did not go smoothly.

"Greg and Carl hated being in Nassau and just wanted to get out as quickly as possible," Emerson recalled. "Leaving me to more or less finish off the album single-handed." But it was the product of the sessions that would cause the real problems.

Love Beach is a schizoid album, half-commercial AOR, half progressive rock. A complete album of short Lake/Sinfield songs might have bombed, but at least it would have had some sort of overall coherence. Likewise, an out-and-out progressive concept album based on the excellent and under-appreciated concept piece,

"Memoirs Of An Officer And A Gentleman", might not have won many new fans – and there would still have been other problems – but it would have been recognized as a genuine attempt to create an album with a clear identity.

Instead, schisms in the group writing cast their shadow. Side One is very much Lake's, and for the most part not really Emerson's kind of thing; Side Two, while a brilliant group effort, is one of the best showcases for Emerson's talents the band ever recorded.[1]

Though full of good things, quite apart from the now-predictable critical savaging, the album was received with much less enthusiasm from many of the fans. This was in no small measure due to the sleeve, which has got to be one of the most embarrassingly awful in the history of embarrassingly awful album sleeves. The most ridiculous thing about the sleeve and title, however, is that they only represent the content of less than half of the album. There was no clue from the outside that Side Two would be dominated by an extended concept piece, "Memoirs Of An Officer And A Gentleman". The sleeve photograph had of course been calculated in all seriousness to help market the album. Pete Sinfield was not the only one who felt they looked like the Bee Gees. In addition, an insert with the album advertised tour gear: T-shirts, satin jackets...and jogging shorts!

The band were far from enthusiastic about the new look, and Emerson, for one, hated the title. "I even organized a survey to find out what people would think," he recalled. "We had people posted at O'Hare Airport in Chicago with a little questionnaire, asking people first off, 'Have you heard of this band?' and if they said yes, then, 'Which of these album titles do you think would suit their next album?' They weren't told what the music would sound like, but they all indicated that *Love Beach* was at the bottom of the list.

"So I said to the people at Atlantic Records, 'There you go. Doesn't that prove it?' But they were adamant about using that title. In the end I rang up Ahmet Ertegun [president of the company] and said, 'Look, man, it makes us appear like a bunch of beach boys, which we're not.' And he said, 'Oh, it doesn't really matter about album titles. What are titles, you know? Look at the name of the Beatles. What does that mean? It doesn't make any difference.' So I said, 'It makes a lot of difference to me because it doesn't fit the image of this band.' But they went ahead anyhow."[2]

Pete Sinfield got the sole lyric credit for the record's centrepiece, "Memoirs Of An Officer And A Gentleman". It was the only ELP track he scripted without Lake. In fact, at the time of *Love Beach* Sinfield wasn't working for ELP at all. Stewart Young had asked him to help Lake with the lyrics for their upcoming "contractual obligation" album. Sinfield was well aware of the frictions that had arisen between him and Lake and was reluctant to agree. Knowing that time was a factor, he told Young that he would do it only if he could write on his own. Young agreed.

Sinfield figured that two or three weeks in the sun would be good for him – and his new girlfriend – though in fact he actually spent the entire Nassau trip stuck in front of a typewriter. It didn't work – the lyrics on "Memoirs" get worse as the piece goes on. There are some good lines at the beginning, but there were plenty of banalities too. The lyrics were laid down piecemeal; the band would ask Sinfield for the next lyric simply so they could go and record some more. Even though Sinfield did put care into "Memoirs", the tension in the ranks meant a certain amount of underachievement was inevitable, and the album has a "demo" feel to it.

Still, "Memoirs", Emerson, Lake and Palmer's first concept work since "Karn Evil 9", is a substantial piece of work that marks a new approach. This story of a relationship between a soldier and his fianceé in the First World War is their first attempt to tell an ordinary human story in that form; in contrast to the mythical epics, "Tarkus" and "Karn Evil 9". It is also the first time that they treated the subject of war in such an intimately personal way. Musically, "Memoirs..." is as accomplished as anything ELP have ever done, giving all three members plenty of space to show what they can do; but it's also more musically balanced – while on "Tarkus" and "Karn Evil 9" the three members seemed to be in constant competition to outshine each other, here they blend their contributions in the service of the music. If only the rest of the album was as strong.

Chris Welch's review was, expectably, among the most positive; though a *Melody Maker* sub-editor gave it the title "ELP At Sea". It was, to be honest, a neat and accurate judgment, in spite of the excellence of some of the actual music. Chris Welch captured the album's mood with this description "*Love Beach* was laid down after a productive day drinking rum and coke, lazing on the beach and indulging the whims of native girls featured so prominently on the holiday brochure type album cover". Welch ends the review with the plea to the band to get down to the local Odeon, plug in and do what they always did best.

The deepest cut of all, though, came when the "commercial" album failed to succeed in the market place. ELP's farewell album was not a hit – a situation that would have a devastating impact on the band.

"We literally came off the road and went straight back into the studio – and tried to sell ourselves," Emerson explained, "Which really didn't suit the band. We just went about it with the wrong attitude and a lot of the morale went out of the band." Nonetheless, Emerson would defend aspects of the album: "The LP has had a lot of criticism because it's so MOR. Though I still think some of it stands up fairly well. On the other hand there's no way it could be called classic ELP.

"I feel there was a certain charm in 'Canario'. It had almost the same effect as 'Hoedown' or something. And the second side had a kind of concept about it. The lyrics are a bit gross, but it was all because everybody but me wanted to get the hell out of Nassau. There were a lot of bad things going down. We'd go into the studio and just rap all day because we hadn't got any music down."

"We actually decided to split around the time of *Love Beach*," Palmer confirmed. "I tried to organize a farewell tour and spent two months working on it....

"So I tried to get this tour together, and it was coming along well. Then there were internal problems within the band, such as what we should play and how we should play it. Who should pick what tune, who should do what and in what order. Although we were planning the end of ELP it really wasn't being done as well as I thought it should. I realized maybe I should just stop. You only have so much energy in life. I wanted the ending to be organized and with good feeling..."

Palmer, however, felt that the US tour with the ill-fated orchestra had not made a split inevitable.

"The tour with the orchestra was definitely the start of the downfall of ELP, but it never looked that way to us," he maintains. "The *Works, Vol.1* album went gold, which means it went platinum, because it was a double album. Everybody said we lost tons of money on tour — yes, we did lose a lot of money, but we only toured with [the orchestra] for three weeks, and then we went out as the dynamic trio for six weeks, and we made substantial amounts of money to pay the debts. We recorded an album with the orchestra and a film [see elsewhere], so all was not lost – the trio kind of put the books straight. It wasn't as grim as the press made out."

Palmer is very clear about the effect of *Love Beach*. "I think the album *Love Beach* really said 'That's it', because the record sales diminished...."

ELP never toured any of *Love Beach*, and eventually, after seemingly endless speculation, on the eve of a new decade they announced what everyone was expecting – that they were splitting for good. The earliest hard news of it was splashed on the front page of Chris Welch's then newly-established weekly *Musicians Only*: "ELP to go solo" was the headline of Steve Wall's article. It seemed to be clear that "all three are forming bands for recording under freshly signed, money-spinning contracts with the same company, Ariola". The debut album by Carl Palmer's new band PM was anticipated in the spring. Emerson was "now in Italy writing film scores". Lake was "expected to beat Emerson in the album stakes". There was some small hope held out for a re-formation in the fact that the three were all signed to Ariola.

Palmer was philosophical about the split, and perceptively pointed out the in-built obsolescence in the ELP project, "I don't regret any of it, and I don't hold any grudges for it breaking up, because it was inevitable. I don't regret anything we played together. We did jazz, classical, even a bit of folk: we drew on many elements, and that was fabulous. Looking back, I'd say the best albums were the first one and *Works, Vol.1*. The reasons are because if you listen to those albums you can see why the band was called Emerson, Lake and Palmer, and you can also see why the band broke up. You can hear the same questions and answers. Example: on the first album there's a track by Greg, 'Lucky Man', I had 'Tank', and Keith played 'The Three Fates'. On *Works, Vol.1* there is exactly the same format, except we took a side each, so that was the beginning and the end. The material on those two albums was the band. The seeds of destruction were there from the word go. But I think we did damn well – nine and a half years! Good God, how much more can you ask for? I just wish we had disbanded on an up instead of a down, but it wasn't going that way."

There was one more new album to come from ELP's first incarnation, *In Concert* (later re-released in expanded form for CD as *Works Live*), but by the time it saw the light of day in November, 1979, ELP had already split up. The live album also involved one more insult for the band. Faced with the changing musical background of punk, disco and new wave, Atlantic insisted it was a single album. They preferred not to risk a double on a band who had split and gone to other labels and whose last studio album had been a comparative sales flop (in 1993, a remastered *Works Live* 2-CD set would be culled from the tour). In spite of good performances the album was dogged by technical problems and hardly made a fitting memorial to a great band and a historic and extraordinary tour. The reviews were predictably poor – *Sounds* dismissed it as "arrogant and emotionless" while *Record Mirror* felt the ideas were "too ragged to make much of an impact."

In Concert was followed by a patchy single disc compilation album, named inaccurately: *The Best of Emerson, Lake and Palmer*. A double album package, at least, would have been needed to do justice to that title.

For all the talk of punk's overthrowing of the progressive rock "establishment", most of the seventies giants ploughed on, adapting to the changing times. Rock bands could still thrive if they followed the blueprint of hugely successful FM acts like Foreigner or Journey – short pop-oriented, catchy, drum-driven, guitar-laden rock with a minimum of instrumental breaks. In the same year as ELP compromised on *Love Beach*, fellow past masters of the concept album, Genesis, now reduced to a three-piece, hit the album charts with *And Then There Were Three* and scored a Top Ten hit single. Prog eggheads Gentle Giant also put out a complete album of short, more commercial songs in *Giant For A Day*. Even Yes did their best to hone things down on *Tormato*.

If ELP had stayed together and toured stoically in spite of the realization that a split was perhaps inevitable, things might have gone differently in the short term. If Atlantic had promoted *Love Beach* properly, perhaps ELP could have had another Top Ten single. Perhaps they might even have stayed together; perhaps just one more album, a really good one to crown it all; if, if, if...

In the end, the threatening punk revolution was shortlived, but it would leave disastrous consequences for bands like ELP in its wake. It led to a "dumbing down"

124

of music, and the upshot was the bland '80s. "In the '70s you had rock heroes," Lake would reflect years later. "In the '80s you had rock product". It's a blow that the industry has never really recovered from. One of the more depressing pieces of fallout from the postpunk years was the way punks, new wavers and the emerging New Romantics all marked the eclipse of the serious musician, especially the keyboard soloist, in all popular genres – not to mention the fragmentation of popular music.

In the light of all this, it is not surprising that the '80s were to bring Keith Emerson, Greg Lake and Carl Palmer very varied fortunes. It was to be twelve long years before ELP would return.

Notes

1   In George Forrester's opinion at least.

2   In G.F.'s opinion, again, the sleeve of *In The Hot Seat* is even worse, truly sterile and uninspiring.

CHAPTER 9

Separate Roads

After the demise of ELP, Keith, Greg and Carl now had the opportunity to turn their individual talents to very different musical areas. Each did more or less what might have been expected. Emerson entered the musically exacting world of film score composition. Lake put together a rock band. Palmer did the typical drummer's thing (cf. Alan White of Yes, Nick Mason of Pink Floyd) of forming a band of which he was director rather than songwriter.

Emerson enjoyed having greater control over his music, "I think one of the main things which excited me about doing soundtracks was being given the responsibility of taking on the whole work myself... What I really relished was ... being able to vary the type of music instantly and relaying this to a bunch of musicians. If you were playing jazz you got in some jazz musicians, if you played classics you brought in classical musicians, if you played rock then you got in a rock singer. So it really stimulated me 'cause I was able to play with a wide variety of people. I did feel limited by rock."

Undeterred by his experiences with the shelved *Dogs of War* project, Emerson tested the water in 1980 with a score for Dario Argento's controversial Italian horror movie, *Inferno*. Emerson went to town on it, keen to impress from his very first attempt. Godfrey Salmon, conductor of the ELP *Works* orchestra, was engaged to help. Emerson had always had a strong following in Italy and both film and score were resounding successes. The score won major awards and even produced an Italian hit single, "Taxi Ride – Rome".

The following year saw Emerson's most major project as a soundtrack composer, when he scored the big-budget terrorist thriller, *Nighthawks*, starring Sylvester Stallone. Emerson brought in friends from ELP's *Works* recordings – the Orchestra de l'Opera de Paris and conductor Godfrey Salmon, as well as veteran arranger Harry Betts. A fine band of session players, including Sky's percussionist Tristan Fry, lent support. For a chase sequence, Emerson adopted the recently developed sampling synthesizer, the Fairlight Computer Music Instrument. The score was distinctive and individual and Emerson even sang on a version of The Spencer Davis Group's "I'm A Man", which was released as a single.

After completing *Nighthawks*, Keith finished off his first non-soundtrack album, *Honky*, which he'd been working on at home in the Bahamas. It was a delight for all those who enjoyed the lighter side of Emerson's work. Released first by his Italian record label, Bubble, the front of the original gatefold sleeve illustrated the title by picturing an uptight-looking Emerson in a white suit, seated among a group of partying black Bahamians. The back photo was of Emo and a black friend lying drunk in the street in the pouring rain. Inside was a huge photo of Emerson in the bath pretending to be eaten by a shark, with his small son Damon looking bemused. The music was as much fun as the pictures. George Malcolm's difficult but entertaining fugal piano piece "Bach Before The Mast" was used within "Hello Sailor", which was followed by "Salt Cay", the theme music he had composed for an Italian TV programme. This, "Rum-A-Ting"[1] and other pieces show the influence of the local 'junkanoo' music. Meade Lux Lewis's "Yancey Special" featured veteran sax players Dick Morrissey and Pete King. The first of Keith's flirtations with Gospel music, "Jesus Loves Me", was a great idea which didn't quite come off, but was still a lot of fun.

After the success of *Nighthawks*, it was surprising that Emerson did no more soundtracks for mainstream Hollywood movies, though he was rumoured to have turned down *Chariots of Fire*. But he kept learning the craft of film scoring.

1983 was a busy year. Keen to start a new band, Emerson recorded briefly with American guitarist Pat Travers, drummer Ian Morris and bassist Mo Foster, recording a new version of "America" and Ian Dury's "Sex And Drugs And Rock And Roll". Next, Emerson scored another successful Italian horror movie, *Murderock*, before notching up a massive hit in Japan with the soundtrack to the biggest animated Manga film yet made, *Harmageddon*. Emerson provided seven of the thirteen tracks on the album, all of which were in true Emerson style, and was credited as Music Director. One piece, "Children Of The Light", with vocalist Rosemary Butler, was a hit single in Japan. The album was Number One in Japan for seven weeks and Korg Instruments promoted their new keyboard range with footage of Emerson playing tracks from the film.

Meanwhile rumours of a new Emerson band circulated. The names of Steve Hackett, Jack Bruce and Simon Phillips were thrown into the pot. Emerson and Bruce did in fact record yet another version of "America".

Emerson also came up with the theme music for the new ITV comedy show, *Up The Elephant And Round The Castle*, a showcase for his friend and fan, the British comedian Jim Davidson. The tune was popular, and was released as a single. When Davidson appeared on *This Is Your Life* that year, Emerson was one of the guests.

The keyboard player also found time that year to contribute "My Name Is Rain" to the compilation album, *Songs For A Modern Church*. Performed with the West Park

School Choir, it was co-written with Lorna Wright, wife of former Spooky Tooth keyboard player Gary Wright, who was a long-standing friend of Emerson's.

Emerson's biggest soundtrack project since *Nighthawks* was *Best Revenge*[2], a 1983 film about drug-running starring John Hart and former singer with The Band, Levon Helm. It was one of his best. The soundtrack album included a long orchestral suite, of which he was justly proud, based on the music of the whole film, and played by him with the National Philharmonic Orchestra. The other tracks were all excellent, with the piano-driven "Dream Runner" standing out as one of Emerson's finest lyrical compositions to date. Levon Helm sang on one track. Emerson spent some time in Morocco listening to traditional instruments – like the double-reeded Zoukra, used briefly on the *Trilogy* album – before writing the score. "I visited some out of the way music stores and bought some obscure folk albums of Arabian music and eastern drum rhythms." Sadly for Emerson the film was poorly received and didn't even earn a nationwide release in the UK.

Around this time Emerson began working with Sussex neighbour Roger Daltrey. "We were talking about music and he said if I wanted somebody to sing, he would have a go. He came in and sang and we both realized the potential." There were other, as yet unreleased, collaborations to make fans drool – another version of Ian Dury's "Sex & Drugs & Rock 'n' Roll" with former Earthquake vocalist John Doucas, and a re-recording of "America" with guitarist Pat Travers. "Captain Starship Christmas" (or was it "Starship Captain Christmas" at that stage?) was first recorded around this time, but record companies didn't want to know about this or any of his other schemes. It was a frustrating period.

In 1984, the year of his 40th birthday, Keith Emerson ran the London Marathon for the second time, improving on his previous time. He also completed the grueling New York Marathon in 3 hours 43 minutes – 17 minutes faster than his previous marathon best. Very satisfying. But he was not finding complete musical satisfaction in the film score business. He was disappointed by the trend in modern movies.

"I didn't like the way they were going," he explained. "I didn't believe in the story lines. They were just nonsense, you know? A lot of the films that were coming my way were just nonsense, and I just didn't believe in it any more. I got a bit tired of having my music squashed out."

1986 saw the release of a solo compilation, *The Emerson Collection*, on compact disc only, featuring two new tracks. "Chic Charni" was in fact a version of "Nighthawking" from the *Nighthawks* soundtrack. "Starship" was an instrumental ancestor of "Captain Starship Christmas". It's almost a composition in its own right, however, with an unaffected charm lacking in the vocal version – a great example of Emerson's ability to pace a composition.

The same year also saw a Peter Hammill album, *And Close As This*, include a track

Greg at the Roosevelt Stadium soundcheck, NJ, 20.8.74. *(Mary Ann Burns)*

Robert Moog gives Keith hints on technique at Roosevelt Stadium
soundcheck, 20.8.74. *(Mary Ann Burns)*

Carl and his stainless-steel drumkit, Roosevelt Stadium, NJ, 20.8.74.
(Mary Ann Burns)

Greg on stage, Universal
Amphitheatre, Chicago,
22.1.78. *(Steve Peterka)*

Keith in robes at the Hammond Organ, circa
1971. *(Pete Mould)*

The foam-spewing Tarkus tank.
(Pete Mould)

ELP with their orchestra outside Olympic Stadium, Montreal, Canada, one day before their concert, 25.8.77. *(Marc Eisenoff)*

Keith at Olympic Stadium, Montreal, 26.8.77.
(Marc Eisenoff)

Keith plus orchestra, 1977.
(Steve Peterka)

Greg enjoys a laugh with the roadies at the Montreal gig, July 1977. *(Marc Eisenoff)*

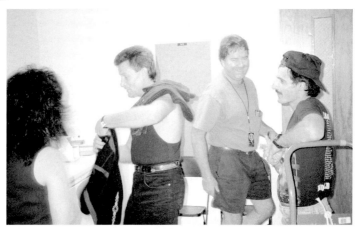

Carl doing his laundry on tour in the 90s. *(Marc Eisenoff)*

Carl in full concentration. *(Doug Anderson)*

At the end of their show, Royal
Albert Hall, London, 2.10.92.
(Craig Stuart)

ELP's last gig in Britain, to
date, Bristol, UK, 28.11.92.
(David Bentley)

Keith during 'Lucky Man', Waterloo Village
show, Stanhope, NJ, 31.7.92.
(Mary Ann Burns)

Carl at Waterloo Village, 31.7.92.
(Mary Ann Burns)

Greg during one of
the midwest US
shows, August 1992.
(Mary Ann Burns)

ELP during their *Black
Moon* Tour, 1992.
(Mary Ann Burns)

Pete Sinfield at King
Crimson's 'Epitaph'
playback, London,
February 1997.
(Liv G. Whetmore)

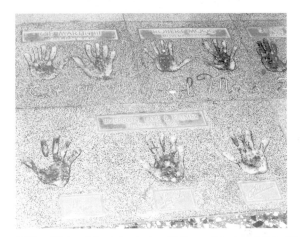

ELP and Robert Moog's handprints, Hollywood Boulevard, LA. *(Mary Ann Burns)*

Keith Emerson (top), Greg Lake (middle) and Carl Palmer (bottom), 1997. *(Mary Ann Burns)*

Keith fires the Moog Ribbon Controller, The Beacon, NYC, 9.10.97. *(Priscilla Eisenoff)*

The Chance,
Poughkeepsie,
NYC, 8.3.98.
(Marc Eisenoff)

Keith with Marc and Priscilla Eisenoff,
Jones Beach Amphitheatrer, 9.8.98.
(Marc Eisenoff)

credited to "Emerson/Hammill"," Hammill knew Emerson through Tony Stratton-Smith. "He needed some lyrics," Hammill explained. "I think mine were a bit too strange for him (even though I was being a pro, and working to a brief). I wrote three lyrics for him. I don't think the other two ever saw the light of day."

*****

"Maybe one day I'll make a catastrophic solo album," Greg Lake had said with a grin back in 1973. His first solo venture was anything but. Assembling a remarkable band – Gary Moore (guitars), Tommy Eyre (keyboards), Tristram Margetts (bass, formerly with the Lake-produced band Spontaneous Combustion) and Ted McKenna (drums) – Greg recorded his first solo record, Greg Lake, which was released in 1981. "When ELP broke up I started within a couple of months to record things and put down a tremendous amount of material," said Lake on its release. At first he had tried to do the album with session players only in Los Angeles. "They were great. But the trouble was, there was no personality in the music. They played fantastic – but it was three songs a morning, y'know?" He did, however, eventually enlist the support of some of the world's best session players. Helping out in the guitar department were Snuffy Walden of former Manticore band Stray Dog, and two other veterans, Dean Parks and Steve Lukather. Old King Crimson mate Michael Giles, and the late, great Jeff Porcaro, did some drumming. And one of Greg's biggest coups was to get Clarence Clemons of Bruce Springsteen's E Street Band to play saxophone.

Lake's second major coup was to secure an unfinished Bob Dylan song, "Love You Too Much", which the Big Zim, who was then "into his religious stuff", was quite happy for him to complete à la Lake (Bob's original title was "I Must Love You Too Much"). Dylan and Lake did not actually meet however; the fragment was provided by a mutual friend. This catchy song was released in October '81 as the first single. It was followed early in '82 by a top-notch Lake ballad, "It Hurts". Neither charted, but they sold respectably.

As for the album, every one of the ten songs is a winner, and the album should be regarded as a minor classic. The lyrics are as intense as you would expect of Greg Lake – love, war, madness, they're all there.

Lake's new band gelled quickly into a tight performing unit, and toured the UK and the States between August and December, opening boldly at the Reading Festival. A substantial amount of classic material was included in the set: "21st Century Schizoid Man", "In The Court Of The Crimson King", "Fanfare For The Common Man" (for which two trumpeters had specially re-recorded the opening fanfare) and the beginning of "Karn Evil 9, First Impression, part 2". Gary Moore featured his 1979 hit "Parisienne Walkways", and the old R&B hit "You Really Got A Hold On Me" was given a dusting-off. The tour was a great success. The Hammersmith Odeon gig was recorded for the American programme *King Biscuit Flower Hour*, and surfaced as a (now much-sought-after) radio station CD. Thankfully the show was released in 1995 on King Biscuit's own label. And a wonderful show it is.

Lake used the tour to switch back to six string but as he explained his opportunities to play lead were inevitably going to be restricted: "With Gary around I don't need to play much lead guitar anyway," he explained. "He's fantastic. We do a few duet things, but he's so fluent, he gets it right first time. His style and mine are just beautiful together. I play a lot of clean chords. Gary is the opposite. He plays few chords and mostly sustained lead style. We don't clutter each other." Gary's vital role in the band was recognized when the 1993 Japanese CD reissue of the album was credited to 'Greg Lake and Gary Moore' on the spine.

A second Lake album, *Manoeuvres*, came out in 1983, but there was no tour and practically no promotion. It's possible to argue that this album was better than the first – and many fans think so. It's different, anyway. However, it sold poorly.

The title track and "Too Young To Love" feature great choruses and strong hooks. "Paralysed" has some insights into Greg's feelings about performance, while Gary Moore's warmly romantic ballad "A Woman Like You" gives Greg an opportunity to sing in a style we don't often hear from him. "It's You, You've Got To Believe" – apparently clumsily-titled until one hears the lyrics – is something of a minor masterpiece, a moving seven-minute call to personal courage and living in the present moment. It's a more intimate follow-up to "For Those Who Dare" on the previous album. Driven by fanfare-like synthesizer, it seems an obvious candidate for the ELP treatment! Also worthy of special note is "Haunted", a fine and beautiful song that tugs at the heart-strings. That unique Greg Lake voice is full of soul as he delivers the line "*Silence is pain*".

As an interesting aside, "Famous Last Words", the only bought-in song on the album, was co-written by The Sweet's Andy Scott. In the late '80s Scott shared a band with one Susie O'List – sister of Davy from The Nice.

"I did the solo albums as a breather from playing in a keyboard-dominated situation like ELP for so long," Lake explained. "Remember, I was originally a guitar player and I wanted to play guitar music. It was refreshing to play to a different vibe of fans."

In the intervening years, music took a back seat for Lake, as he took on the role of country squire, rearing sheep and keeping bees. "I went home to Dorset and bought a Georgian mill house and a stretch of river," he says, "Fishing became an obsession. I also rebuilt the river, the sluice gates and even resculptured the river bed."

* * * * *

Carl Palmer's initial post-ELP band was called PM. "I didn't want to call the band the Carl Palmer Band," quoth he. "I want the guys to feel they're in a band, not a backing group. The album we've done is called 1 PM and the group is called PM because calling a band by their surnames, or 'Warhorse' and the new album Energy, is all a little dated. PM are initials you hear daily and see written down a lot." Palmer envisaged a more stripped down, back to basics, approach with his new band.

"To get this sound I wanted younger musicians. I thought energy coming from someone else might be a gas for a change. I received 300 cassettes from all around the world. I'd advertised in a very professional way. It just so happened that most of the people I enjoyed from a writing point of view happened to be American – it was a pure coincidence that the band became American, I just had more of a choice. I wanted writers who could produce a band sound, and these days a superstar musician is disliked generally on the street by the layman."

The musicians were: Todd Cochran on keyboards, who had been a member of Automatic Man and had also toured with Peter Gabriel's backing band; Erik Scott on bass, who had worked with Alice Cooper; Texan John Nitzinger on guitar and vocals; and on lead guitar, Barry Finnerty who was with Blood Sweat and Tears for a while and the Chico Hamilton Group.

"The music that I'm playing with P.M. has no influence from ELP," Palmer was keen to stress. "What I've tried to do [is] stay away from any influence I picked up from ELP, because I tried to appear as fresh as possible with my new product. I didn't want to be criticized for re-hashing what ELP had done, because as far as I'm concerned there is only one ELP, and the music ELP played should be left to them to play as a unit. People shouldn't try to recapture that magic." [The only ELP number the new band would have performed was "Fanfare", which would have featured Carl's solo.] "When I put my new band together I completely turned around and went in a different direction, a more song-orientated direction instead of an instrumental direction which ELP were. I really didn't want to go into jazz-rock, fusion-rock or classical music. Although I appreciated that with ELP, it was a unique situation. I really wanted something a little lighter musically and heavier vocally."

1 P.M. has its flaws – it is weak musically and lyrically – but this was a new band, working out its own sound. PM needed time to get things together – just as ELP had, a decade earlier. On some tracks, such as "Dreamers", the band really get into gear. Others like "Dynamite", "Go For It" and "Children Of The Air Age" feature catchy hooks.

But despite Carl's obvious enthusiasm for the project, the album proved a commercial disaster. A tour was planned, but because of poor record sales it was called off. PM made a few TV appearances in West Germany, and then quietly disbanded. Carl was philosophical about it: "The record didn't sell – it was pathetic in actual fact, but I could live with that, because I've been exceptionally lucky in my life."

Palmer's next collaboration was with studio genius Mike Oldfield. "I recorded a couple of pieces with him for a solo album," the drummer explained at the time. "One side has already been recorded – the percussion concerto. On the other side will be a sort of electronic classical music – not a concerto but small sections. Mike Oldfield seemed to be the ideal person for me to work with. Anyway, he called me up and asked me if he could use one of the pieces for an album of his, and I said fine. The piece was called 'Mount Teidi' – on his album 'Five Miles Out' – and it was named after a volcano where I live. It was during that period that I took some time off, stayed at home, did a little bit of studying and tidied up some of my personal business."

Around this time, Palmer got a call asking him if he would like to join a new band featuring Steve Howe. "Well, I'd known Steve for a long time," he said, "And I'd known the manager for a long time. I came along and played – there was John Wetton, Steve Howe and myself, but no keyboard player. I wasn't too happy with that, because I feel with the amount of technology available, not to have a keyboard player is a bad idea. Steve Howe, having played with Geoff Downes in the last configuration of Yes, suggested that we try him. It seemed good to me, so the four of us played and we decided to be a band after about a week, because it felt so good."

The group called themselves Asia. It later turned out that Rick Wakeman was the band's original choice for keyboards and Simon Phillips was approached to fill the drum stool. Wakeman never made the rehearsal stage. Phillips wanted a straight wage, which proved unacceptable. Carl asked for 25 per cent of everything (advice he had received from his father many years ago, suggesting he be part of a band, take a percentage and watch it grow). Phillips would later have plenty of cause to rue his decision.

Palmer explained Asia's new approach: "This is different because we've gone for that overall group sound rather than create individual styles, which is what's interesting and good about it. And it means we're all going for the same thing, and a group sound is the only way you can really do it."

Asia confounded the critics in 1982 by blasting to fame and fortune with their triple platinum eponymous debut album released on the Geffen label. Produced by *Dark Side of the Moon* Engineer Mike Stone, it held the US number one spot for nine weeks and ensured a sell-out world tour. Asia surprised many people with their album of short, pop-oriented, commercial rock, since the individual musicians,

Palmer no less than any other, had come to be associated with long conceptual pieces of music. "Heat of the Moment" is probably the best known song from the album and became a Top Five hit in the US charts. "Only Time Will Tell" was another popular single.

The new approach would require a slightly simpler style of drumming than the ex-ELP man was used to. Indeed, listening to the album it was be hard to imagine this was the same man who had drummed away so intricately on *Brain Salad Surgery*. From a drummer's point of view, the most interesting tracks on *Asia* were "Sole Survivor," which featured some clever time changes and double bass drum work towards the end, and "Time Again" with a "Fanfare..."-like shuffle and some tricky big band phrasing. "Wildest Dreams" featured an opening drum rhythm reminiscent of *Tarkus* (although this was in 4/4 and not 5/4) while "Cutting It Fine" had some very nice snare /hi-hat work.

Although Palmer's approach to the songs was simpler, his solos were still bringing the audiences to their feet. "Of course, in all the songs there are instrumental passages where there is the room for the indulgence factor," Palmer added. "Obviously there's not a lot of room for that in our music on record, but on stage you'll probably see more of that develop – which is what a lot of people would expect! I think from a live situation we have a lot to offer in a different kind of way, where we can use things from our past more in the space of an hour and a half performing." As Geoff Downes put it, "Anyone can go out and buy a Linn drum machine, but anyone cannot go out and buy a Carl Palmer." Thundering away on his awesome gongs, timpani and revolving drumkit, and still rattling out faster-than-lightning rudiment work and juggling his sticks, he could hardly fail to bring the house down night after night.

On the 1982 tour, Asia played all of the album plus two new tracks, "Midnight Sun" and "The Smile Has Left Your Eyes", which were to appear on their next album. Palmer took his solo in "Here Comes the Feeling." There was no reference to their past bands, apart from Steve Howe's guitar solo known as "The Clap".

Asia's follow-up album, *Alpha* (again produced by Mike Stone), repeated the debut's formula. Though less successful in the charts, it was far from a flop. However, many fans were disappointed and felt the songs lacked the quality of the first album. There were some high points, most notable "The Heat Goes On" which featured an Emerson-esque Hammond solo, and "Open Your Eyes". "Don't Cry" was a successful single taken from the album. In the accompanying video Palmer appeared in his first acting roll, swinging through the jungle on ropes, sinking into a swamp and then finally taking an early bath in a vat of liquid gold!

During 1983 the band continued to enjoy success, although they had to cut their tour short. But before long, tensions developed within the band, and ultimately due to personal problems, John Wetton was asked to leave by the record company (not the rest of the band). It was the worst possible time for this turn of events. Considering Wetton's central roles as the chief songwriter and a distinctive vocalist, the band would be seriously diminished without him. To compound the difficulties, Asia were contracted to perform a live 'simulcast' TV show from the Budokan Theatre in Tokyo in December, to an estimated audience of twenty million[3]. With four weeks to go, the band's label invited Greg Lake to fill Wetton's shoes.

Lake stepped in, the concert went ahead, and all went well. It was the first time in over five years that two members of ELP had been seen on stage together. However, it was not to last. "Greg did really well," Palmer acknowledged, "He learnt all the bass lines and everything worked OK. After the Budokan show we all took a break and regrouped some weeks later. However, Greg had not written any material and I knew he was going through some personal problems, so he was asked to go."

"With Asia," Lake explained, "it eventually got down to whether I would join the band as a permanent member, and my response was to tell them I thought their musical direction was wrong. They were going in an extremely overt commercial path – a 'corporate rock'-type direction, and I told them it would all end up in shreds unless they made a more progressive album. Since they disagreed with me and opted to go straight for the commercial vein, I didn't want to be a part of it."

Shortly afterwards, Wetton was asked to return. He agreed, on condition that Steve Howe should leave. Obligingly, he did. Ex-Krokus guitarist Mandy Meyer was recruited, and work began on the third album.

In the meantime, Carl Palmer had more pressing matters at hand when his girlfriend Maureen gave birth to their daughter, Carissa. Carl would marry Maureen in 1985.

Asia's 1985 album *Astra* was critically well-received, but despite all the ingredients which made their debut album a hit – strong material, a big sound (again produced by Mike Stone), an inspired Roger Dean cover painting – it failed to match the high sales of its predecessors. Carl had co-written two of the tracks, "Hard On Me" and "Too Late". Both were very upbeat and snappy but were not a vehicle for Carl's drumming. The addition of Mandy Meyer on guitar gave Asia's sound a harder edge, very different from Steve Howe's more jazz-like approach. The opening cut, "Go", was issued as a single but flopped – a shame, as it was a strong single in the vein of Van Halen's "Jump" and was accompanied by a striking video.

Other strong tracks include "Voice of America", on which Wetton sings about the changing face of American rock music, and "Countdown to Zero" and "After the War", which indulges in a slice of anti-nuclear war campaigning. Perhaps one track above all stands out – the epic "Rock and Roll Dream" featuring the Royal Philharmonic Orchestra.

However, by now the Wetton/Lake saga had left cracks in the band. The poor sales made things worse and no tour was scheduled. Things went quiet in the Asia camp. Meanwhile, for Greg Lake, the experience had given him a new impetus. "Doing the Asia stint made me realize just how valuable the relationship between Keith and myself was, because he's such a pleasure to work with."

In the Summer of 1984, Keith Emerson got a call from Jim Lewis, Vice President of Polydor Records, suggesting an ELP reunion. Emerson reportedly threw the phone in his pool! However, when he met up with Lake to discuss it, his former bandmate was newly enthused by the Asia debacle. As Palmer was still contracted to Asia, Emerson and Lake would have to find a new drummer.

By the end of the 80s ELP would have appeared in every duo combination possible.

Notes

1   A piece which has never been included on CD releases of the album – why?

2   Emerson recorded an Elvis Presley song for *Best Revenge*, but could not use it. "In order to put 'Don't be Cruel' on the film, one had to pay around $10,000 for the licence. The budget was almost exhausted, and all they needed in the film was about one and a half minutes. So I spliced off the intro, used the synthesizer solo in the middle and the end, which were mine, and ended up with music to fit the scene, and it sounded pretty good." The full track may eventually appear on a solo album.

3   Released on video as *Asia in Asia*

CHAPTER 10

To The Power Of Two

With Carl Palmer committed to Asia, the reunited Lake and Emerson auditioned respected ex-Yes sticksman Bill Bruford – with the exception of Palmer, perhaps the most innovative and musical drummer in progressive rock – but it didn't work out. Reluctantly, they recorded demos with a session drummer, and nearly decided to make an album using session players as and when needed. However, they really knew that only another great British drummer could fill the bill. Enter Cozy Powell.

Powell's drumming skills had been constantly in demand since the beginning of the 70s, when he first came to attention with Tony Joe White. After a couple of early bands, he cut his first single with a band called Youngblood in 1968. The following year he was recruited as Jeff Beck's drummer. Next, he became a hard-working session musician, working with all Mickie Most's RAK Records artists – Hot Chocolate, Suzi Quatro, and CCS included. After a stint with a band called Bedlam he had a hit with his first solo single "Dance With The Devil", before forming his own band, Cozy Powell's Hammer.

In 1974, disillusioned (not for the last time!) with the pop business, Powell took a year out to indulged his great passion for motor racing for a year. Then Rainbow, the Michael Schenker Group and Whitesnake brought him massive success, and his powerful, musical drumming graced many an album by other rock bands, his reputation perhaps even rescuing some which might otherwise have failed to make an impression.

Powell tells how he became the new "P" in ELP: "The Whitesnake situation was very hectic and we did a lot of American touring. The last tour finished it off really. The aggravations were brought to a head on that little jaunt. I parted company with them and came onto the musical transfer list again.

"I didn't know whether to take another sabbatical or whether to carry on. Then a phone call came through saying that Keith and Greg wanted someone to come down and help them do an album. They had already tried two or three drummers, apparently. I've known Keith for years anyway and he said "Come on down and let's have a blow". I had just got back from Rio and I went down to his house, only to find I'd left my sticks at home. I felt a right prat!"

In February 1985, Powell made his way through the snow to Emerson's Sussex mansion to work on new material. "Then Keith said, 'do you fancy having a bash through "Fanfare For The Common Man?" '" Powell recalled. "We started playing, one thing led to another, and the next thing I knew, they'd asked me to join!"

"It wasn't the only offer I had at the time," Powell insists. "I could have done a number of other things, but obviously when you get the chance to work with musicians of that calibre, you take it. I've been with guitar-based bands for ten years, so it was nice to get into a keyboards trio. I've always wanted to work with a trio ever since I saw Ginger Baker years ago with Cream."

For all the outside impressions of ELP's ego battles, Powell found working with Emerson and Lake, "the most pleasurable working relationship I've ever been in." He also found the music an excellent challenge, combining bits and pieces of Palmer's style on the old material with his own personal stamp. "I've had to work hard with them, learning a lot of the old stuff," he acknowledged. "It's not just a three-minute 12-bar blues you have to learn. It's been interesting working out on *Tarkus*. It's opened up my musical vocabulary. They are clever pieces of music, and Keith isn't exactly a three-chord wonder. He comes up with some very clever stuff; and Greg as well. To play this stuff you need a lot of experience and confidence. It's not beginners' music, that's for sure, and I probably couldn't have coped with it twenty years ago."

The fact that Cozy's surname conveniently ended in a "P" meant that while the new band would be called Emerson, Lake and Powell, it would also be referred to by commentators as ELP. Not surprisingly, this new combination provoked some dry comments from the original "P"!

"I think it's a great idea," Palmer told the press, tongue in cheek, "And I'll tell you why. I made ten albums with that band, really good material, and it still holds water today. Now, with Cozy Powell joining that band it will make people buy albums of the past because they like what's happening now – and that is doing me a big favour.

"I was never asked, anyway," Palmer added more with a little more asperity, "They knew I wouldn't go. They're digging up something that is fifteen years old and has been dead for six."

Emerson maintained that Palmer joining was not an option due to his contract with Geffen Records. "I think he must have felt a little hurt to have made those statements," the keyboardist observed, "But certainly I don't think they've lasted. I think his reaction was one of hurt, but he couldn't have done it anyway. We were dubious about upsetting Carl, who greatly helped the sound of ELP in the 70s. For this reason we do not refer to ourselves as ELP. We are Emerson, Lake and Powell."

"I won't knock Carl," Lake added at the time. "The question of using him in this group never came up. We wouldn't have had a comfortable future working with him again..."

"Anyway," Emerson explained, "it was not our intention to recreate a Seventies band. Our intention was for it just to be Greg and me, filling out the sound with other players. We did want another influence, and we've got that with Cozy."

On September 14, 1985, *Sounds* ran a story about ELP's first low-key gig at Emerson's local, the legendary Six Bells pub in his home village of Chiddingly, West Sussex. The album details were at this stage 'being kept firmly under wraps', but in a brief interview, Cozy described the group's sound as "very powerful – sort of Led Zeppelin meets The Nice". This intrigued everybody, and it was amusing to find on the release of the album that such statements had been nothing more than red herrings! What was clear was that Cozy, who was confidently predicting the demise of the electronic drum[1], would bring the band a heavy sound which had long been absent.

Certainly though, the band made few concessions to the mid-Eighties musical climate. "We've stuck to our roots on this album," Emerson explained. "But with the new technology offered by the keyboards – the Kurzweil etc. – the scope for direction is widened and the possibilities in live performance are broadened, the sound is much bigger."

Meanwhile, the return of two thirds of the old ELP prog warhorse brought out plenty of critical cynicism. Emerson and Lake would never live down that the drummer's surname began with a P. It didn't help when the critics found out that Simon Phillips was auditioned. Emerson joked, "we also checked out Ringo Parr."

There was one major delay. Emerson's run of bad luck continued in improbable and spectacular fashion in 1986, when a runaway tractor carrying a ton of logs crashed through his barn studio. Emerson's state of the art musical and recording equipment ended up buried beneath the collapsed roof and the demolished walls. It caused a staggering £250,000 worth of damage. The GX1 synthesiser in particular was badly damaged. The forestry contractor who had been in charge of the tractor said afterwards with some understatement, "It's so bloody embarrassing. A pin on the tractor broke – and I was through the barn. I didn't see Mr. Emerson but his wife ranted and raved and said they had been working for months on a world tour and now it would have to be cancelled." The sessions recorded up to that point were eventually scrapped and new recordings undertaken.

Emerson, Lake and Powell's eponymous debut album was released in 1986. The working title "Principles of Science" had been dropped.

The record opens with a rousing cut, "The Score," which has more than a passing reference to the past. Keith explains: "That was one of the numbers I had prior to meeting Greg, and I think we needed a heraldic theme to say, hey look, we're back again!"

From the opening track, it is evident that the band had judged their sound very well, both to appeal to fans of the previous group and to take it forward into new areas. The triumphal blasts from the GX1, Lake's powerful underpinning bass lines, several contrasting sections, lots of interesting side-stepping chord changes and modulations, and direct allusion in "The Score"'s lyrics to "Karn Evil 9" – "You're welcome back, my friends/ To the show that never ends" – all hark back to former days. What's different is the huge sound. ELP's sound was always big, and got bigger, but here it is *massive*: partly because of Powell's heavier, less busy, drum style and also because of the background washes of string-like MIDI keyboard; and a crystal clear, thundering bass guitar sound.

"The Miracle" with its spine-tingling Tolkeinesque lyrics, was another highlight, picking up from the sword-and-scorcery motifs Lake conjured on "Knife Edge" and other early ELP songs. "I love the imagery that Greg creates on that," says Emerson. "We discussed a lot of different directions and ideas on that prior to settling on that one route that he chose. It just seemed a very majestic piece, really revolving around those big chords that I discovered. The big chords that run the tune."

For the obligatory classical adaptation, ELP chose Holst's jaw-dropping opener to his 1916 *Planets* suite, "Mars, The Bringer of War". The piece had, for years, been the basis for Powell's solo spot on stage. "Funnily enough, I did that to a backing tape with Whitesnake," remembered the drummer. "So when I brought it along, Keith said he'd like to play it himself. He learnt it in a few minutes. Makes you sick, doesn't it? Why use a tape when Keith can play it?"

"It was literally a drum solo to a tape recorder," Emerson says. "There he was with all his pyrotechnics going off, bombs and lightning flashes, and I was very impressed. I figured, 'Hell, let's give it a go!' So I got the music, tried it at rehearsals, and it worked out pretty well.

"It definitely falls into the category of "music to have sex by". It's kind of like *Bolero*. It's one of the hardest pieces in *The Planets*. It might sound easy on record, but it was just the three of us playing on that, and it was not easy to accomplish."

The four shorter tracks were also strong: from the mellow "Lay Down Your Guns", and the jazzy "Step Aside" (Emerson: " Any excuse to play jazz is fine by me.") to the two rockers "Learning to Fly" and "Touch and Go"- the latter a US radio hit that a reformed Emerson, Lake and Palmer would later rerecord at Palmer's insistence.

Sales were reasonable, despite an expectable critical drubbing. The new band set off on a major US tour. It wasn't quite the triumphant return the band had hoped for. Some dates had to be rebooked in smaller venues due to lower than expected demand and a scheduled Australian leg had to be cancelled. Still, the American shows were a great success, though planned support act Yngwie Malmsteen dropped out after just one show, complaining that by the time ELP had all their equipment set up, there was scarcely room for him to play. During the tour, Emerson found time to perform "America" on the major US TV show *Late Night With David Letterman*.

The UK would not be seduced, however; press coverage bordered on the contemptuous. Powell responded lamely that "America has gone potty about it. The album is 28 in the *Billboard* charts within four weeks, and every major magazine is interested in us. And yet over here ELP is a dirty word. I just don't know why. None of the reviews (except in *Kerrang!*) talked about the music, they just criticized the individuals. We weren't sulking, we just thought, What is the point of talking to anybody?"

A second Emerson, Lake and Powell album never materialised. In spite of their popularity on tour, the band was a financial catastrophe. "I must have gotten back with less than $500 in my pocket," groused Emerson. Before long Powell was on his way out.

"The next thing was an article in a London paper which said I was going to join Led Zeppelin," Powell recalled. "Apparently Keith read this and thought it was true. He didn't actually phone me, just presumed it was the case. Brian Lane, who is Carl Palmer's manager, wanted to get the original ELP together again and told Keith that Carl was available for... weddings and bar mitzvahs." With Palmer's contractual commitment to Asia at an end, he was free to join Emerson and Lake.

Powell wasn't unduly surprised. The atmosphere of the rehearsals, blessedly free of ego clashes, had vanished. "Keith and Greg decided that they hated each other so much at the end of that first album and tour that they didn't want to do another one," he said. "The whole damn thing was a big mistake. I did enjoy it musically, though. Musically it was a great band. And I think the tour we did, although it wasn't a sellout tour, some of the dates we did were very successful, and I thought it'd be a good vehicle for me to show I could play some other styles of music, not just heavy rock. But unfortunately, financially it was a disaster- ELP had a couple of different managers, some very heavy commitments to the record company and to the merchandisers, which weren't fulfilled, and lots of people sending writs through the post – it all got very unpleasant."

After ELP, Powell recorded an album with a new band, Force Field, an Australian outfit who also roped in the wayward brilliance of urbane Dutch guitar whizz Jan Akkerman (ex of Focus) and then continued as a session player. In late 1991 he was seriously injured when a horse he was riding had a heart attack and threw him into the path of an oncoming car. Powell suffered a fractured pelvis and other injuries, and took some time to mend. He returned in 1992 with a solo album, *The Drums Are Back* and went on to work with a variety of bands, including Peter Green's come-back group.

There is a tragic coda. On April 5, 1998, not long after quitting Green's outfit, Powell was involved in a motor accident on the M4 motorway near Bristol. He died in hospital from his injuries. Rock had lost one its greatest heroes.

*****

After Powell's departure from ELP, Emerson and Lake got together with Palmer for some rehearsals. However after just two weeks Lake walked out. "I think for Greg, to be in this type of band is something he wasn't ready to focus in on," said Carl Palmer shortly afterwards. "I think after Emerson, Lake and Powell it had come to an end for him. I don't think he wanted to pursue the amount of work you have that goes on within a group. We're still the best of friends, we have lunch and all that. I got asked to play in ELP again because we thought we owe it to ourselves to try the original format, but I think it's a case of it lived for nine to ten years, and it was good. To have carried on any longer as ELP at that moment in time was not on the cards, and it didn't feel good to everybody, though that's not to say it will never be done. Going back to ELP didn't seem fresh to me."

Palmer's manager Brian Lane suggested the drummer collaborate with Californian multi-instrumentalist Robert Berry, and Three was born.

Berry had begun his career drumming on covers of British Invasion songs in high school band Fourth Street Exit, and progressive rock numbers in other high school bands. Later he took up bass and guitar as well, influenced by Jeff Beck and Eric Clapton, playing in more pop-rock, guitar-based bands.

Berry went on to be the main composing member in pomp band Hush, who recorded three albums between 1978 and 1982. In 1985 he released his first solo album, *Back To Back*, which met with little success, but demonstrated that he had continued to refine his song writing skills. Meanwhile, back in 1982 he had founded recording studio, Soundtek, in his home town of Campbell, San Jose, which he would continue to run. Level-headed and professional, he was a thoroughly dedicated – perhaps workaholic – musician. "There is no 'not-doing-music for me'," he boasted.

Although the ELP reunion hoped for in 1987 had not come about, Palmer was still keen to work with Emerson. However, Emerson was not in at the beginning of Three, as Palmer explains: "It's wrong to think Keith and I were looking for a guitarist and got it together. I got it together, and Keith liked it immediately. Robert's tape was one of the first I heard, but I thought I should really listen to the other four hundred. At first I was worried, because he's American and I've had experiences working in all-American bands [namely, PM], but after working with him, he's the most un-American guy I know. His attitude is completely different."

Berry's tape had already found its way to Lane and Palmer through Geffen Records' John Kalodner – via Steve Howe, then working with the AOR-prog abortion of GTR with Steve Hackett, who invited Berry to London to work with that group. But after six months this turned out to be a blind alley.

Berry was a bit bewildered at suddenly finding himself in a band of major players: "I wasn't expecting this at all. I was writing songs. I had a local band, a recording studio. I wanted to expand, but I wasn't looking for anything in particular. Then Carl called and I flew to New York, and we met in the lobby of a hotel. Total strangers, but we hit it off straight away."

He also made an impression on Emerson. "I was not only impressed with his writing abilities. What inspired me with this project was what Robert had done in the past, and what you probably don't know is that Robert is pretty multi-talented, he plays drums and keyboards, and that is a tremendous advantage." It wasn't long before Keith's extended pieces were pared down to smaller, more concise units.

For Berry, it was the perfect opportunity. "When I first started in bands I'd play covers of ELP, Yes and Genesis. I was a keyboard player in that band[2]. I played more Genesis and Yes because Keith's parts were so hard! I got away with it because no-one else dared cover that music. Then I started writing more formatted pop music because everyone was into the "hit song", that three-and-a-half-minute song. Now I can go back and combine progressive rock, but with the experience of having written songs. This is incredible. This is an opportunity I couldn't have dreamed of having. To write things I enjoy and have Keith arrange them into these epic pieces. Working with both of them has opened me up a lot."

After the difficulties with the ELP reunion, both Palmer and Emerson enjoyed the fresh approach of a new group. "We're trying to keep things light," averred Palmer, ever the spin-doctor. "Three is a happy band. Obviously it's serious, but we like to keep a lighthearted flow with it. It's the only way we can survive in this industry. We've been through the serious years, and now it's down to having fun."

They tried to make the recording of their debut album, *To The Power of Three*, a much quicker and less stressful experience than previous projects. "...The music was organized and put together before we went into the studio," Palmer says, "and we knew where we were going So there were no musical decisions to be made, they were purely on a production level... we could get to points very quickly. It saves a lot of time and money – and the most important thing, it becomes very enjoyable, and as Keith knows, although we've made quite a few albums together in the past and we are proud of all of them, some of them did take too long to make, and music should be spontaneous." The band even found room for their own take on The Byrds' "Eight Miles High".

The differences between Emerson, Lake & Palmer/Powell and the new band are apparent from the start. Firstly, Berry's wimp-rock vocal inflections. *Kerrang!* magazine's acidic "Wimpwire" column described his earlier band, Hush, as "legendary Californian slush puppies", and quoted one reviewer's assessment of them as "the tackiest pomp rock band he'd ever heard". Secondly, Berry's lyrics, less ambitious than Lake's. Thirdly, the essential simplicity of Three; they ham up the pomp-rock aspects which were only a part of ELP. This music is not grandiose, but more in the FM tradition of Kansas, REO Speedwagon and other such bands. Very bright synth chords and interesting rhythmic accompaniment compensate for the essential simplicity of the songs. Fourthly, Emerson's role is wholly rethought. When he comes to the fore it is for the most part with rhythmic or colouristic effects, even in the more progressive "Desde La Vida". He points up, accompanies, serves the lyrics rather than hogging the limelight as soloist. It is ELP's particular and unique lack of balance that makes those solos *interesting*. Three's music is, as Carl Palmer might say, more "democratic".

Fifthly, the guitar shines through. Lake fans have often been disappointed that Greg's guitar skills have not always featured strongly enough in ELP's recordings. Here the multi-talented Berry doesn't neglect to provide some fine examples of his electric guitar playing. Finally, Palmer continues his stylistic economizing; he could be playing PM, he could be playing Asia.

"Basically, I think the new album is just more concise and to the point," Emerson said. "This was affected by my period of writing film scores, where I'd have to fill 38 seconds, so I'd give those 38 seconds my best shot. I learned to say more with my music, within a shorter time, rather than being so self-indulgent."

Palmer saw a comparison with his previous band. "I would say the band is closer to what I did in Asia than what we were doing in ELP. Mainly because we are dealing with shorter pieces of music in Three. The first Asia album is similar to what is happening here – what we're trying to do here is have long pieces of music, not twenty minutes, but maybe seven to eight minutes long, so in other words we're trying to get our musical ideas over quickly and stay fresh on it, that's where it's different from ELP."

The album had its moments. There are some good tracks, but they leant just a bit too far to the commercial for most ELP diehards. Reviews were predictably mixed. The anonymous name of the band, under-promotion by the record company, and the severe sleeve artwork and photography which gave a corporate impression far removed from the sheer fun of the live band, can't have helped. Ever faithful on the home front was Chris Welch, who gave the album four K's in *Kerrang!*.

Three played a warm-up concert in Los Angeles on January 21, 1988, but the tour did not start till April. Two girl backing singers, Debbie Parks and Jennifer Steele, were hired – something which must have pleased vocal-loving Carl!. Debby Parks was fired before the tour. One of Robert Berry's colleagues in Hush, Paul Keller, played guitar. The group decided to play in smaller venues, and thus sold out everywhere.

Three completed their tour on May 20 at New York's Madison Square Gardens, as one of many artists celebrating Atlantic Records' 40th Anniversary. Grumpily and gracelessly introduced by Phil Collins as "Emerson and Palmer", with no acknowledgment either of Lake's part in Atlantic's history or of the new member, they played "Fanfare", and the medley of "America/Rondo" to an enthusiastic audience reception. (The only other ELP number played on the tour was "Hoedown".) "America" included Carl's drum solo, which justifiably raised the loudest cheers and applause.

There was no European tour. The home fans were used to this by now. Nor were they surprised when it transpired that because of slow album sales (strange, in view of the commercial nature of the album, and the success of the tour), there would be no follow-up album. Towards the end of 1988, Three quietly disbanded.

One main reason for Three's eventual failure was, undeniably, Keith's relegation to the role of team member, not featured soloist. "I realised that too late," admitted Keith the following year. "When we did go out on the road, we ended up having to accommodate that... at the end it started heading in that ELP direction. Robert was great about it because he realised where the audience was coming from. Robert and I still talk and exchange tapes, but now is the time to pursue my solo career. I really don't want to fight with anyone anymore. I don't want to have to say "sing this or don't sing that". All I really want to do at the end of the day is play. It's as simple as that, really."

Had they gone on to another album, it's very possible that Three might have found considerably more commercial success. They had laid the foundations by going out and touring small venues and gradually winning a following. Reviews had been no worse than ELP's, and some critics expressed approval of the new direction. There was a rumour that the second album was going to lean toward a more progressive bent. Meanwhile, Three's rise and fall only succeeded in stoking up those perennial rumours. On the basis of Three's "bloody amazing" sound, *Kerrang!*'s Derek Oliver was not the only person to wish for "a full-scale ELP reunion"... He would have to be patient. An ELP reunion was becoming more likely, but the time was not yet quite right.

Notes

1   On the tour, he did make some use of an electronic kit. "It was a nightmare from start to finish. The kit was forever going wrong, and the feel of the pads was nowhere".

2   Berry's band Hush, based in San Jose, California, cut three rather good albums between 1977 and 1982 and enjoyed some success on the West Coast. See Berry entry in Discography for further details.

CHAPTER 11

Close To Home

The aftermath of Three marked the beginning of a long period of uncertainty for ELP fans. Emerson released a great solo album, *The Christmas Album*, in 1988, and contributed tracks to another Dario Argento horror soundtrack. Palmer toyed with Asia again. Robert Berry formed a new band with Gary Pihl (ex-Boston), Alan Fitz (ex-Night Ranger) and David Lauser (ex-Sammy Hagar Band) but nothing came of it and he returned to obscurity. Lake was rumoured to be on the way back with a new project – a collaboration with Asia's Geoff Downes to be known as Ride The Tiger. In the end, however, the dreamed of – but by now virtually despaired of – Emerson, Lake and Palmer reunion sneaked up to take both the band and their fans almost unawares.

****

Christmas often brings out the worst in musicians. 1988 was the year Bros jumped all over "Silent Night" and the Simon May Orchestra combined "Glory Be To God On High" with the *Eastenders* theme. More creditably, the eternal Cliff Richard got to Number One in the UK with "Mistletoe and Wine". Keith Emerson however got nowhere with "Captain Starship Christmas" from his latest, rather surprising, project, *The Christmas Album*.

Emerson had first conceived the idea of recording an album of Christmas music back in the Emerson, Lake and Powell days. "It was a culmination of events," he explained. "On Christmas Day I was having a drink with my neighbours, and we decided to go out to my barn studio. I stumbled upon an old carol book, pulled out my Yamaha GX1 and started improvising on some of the traditional songs. I was reminded the next day of how great it sounded, and it was suggested that maybe someday it would be a good idea to make a record of it.

"I didn't really think about it again until the following Christmas when I was digging through my records, looking for something suitable to play. The only things available were things like 'The King's College Choir Sings Bach' or 'Rockin' Around The Christmas Tree', which I didn't find very satisfactory."

"But the final motivation came while I was working on a video [early in 1988]. The producer said, totally out of the blue, 'Y'know, Keith, you should make a Christmas album'. It was like, 'Funny you should say that...'. Another thing that prompted me was that Greg Lake had some measure of success with 'I Believe In Father Christmas'. So, at the end of the Three tour, I decided to see what possibilities could come out of seriously rearranging Christmas carols. "I started with 'Little Town Of Bethlehem' and managed to immediately create six variations – a jazz variation, a classical variation, and so on. I had so much fun doing that one, I just kept going."

Emerson was aware of the dubious quality of most Christmas records. "It's not overtly a 'Christmas album'," he would maintain. "I think it's important to state there are Christmas themes used, but they have been adapted and arranged by myself, and the overall effect that we end up with is 'seasonal' rather than 'Christmassy'.

"I'm avoiding the syrup by expanding and exploring the harmonic content of the tunes. Aaron Copland did a similar thing when he borrowed from American folk melodies. The trick is to flesh them out and make them big and strong.

"A good example is 'We Three Kings'. If you hum the melody, it's a little silly. I had to toughen it up and give it some balls...

"The biggest challenge is finding an original way to approach each piece. These tunes are very simple, and it's difficult to give each their own twist. For example, on 'It Came Upon A Midnight Clear', my original intent was to imitate the acoustic guitarist Leo Kottke[1], on the keyboard. I tried to create what a guitar player might do if he had the potential of the keyboard at his disposal. In effect, it doesn't copy any guitar style; rather, it gave me another keyboard style. On the Bach 'Oratorio', the first step was to get the orchestral and choir score, then I tracked down a solo piano arrangement and studied all three. I absorbed as much as I could and decided to base my version on the orchestral score...

"'Snowman's Land' evolved in a very interesting way through the direct assistance of some Yamaha programmers. Yamaha invited me to check out their London recording studio. I spoke with the studio's engineer, Guy Gambel, and he suggested that I play 'Snowman's Land' straight-out on one of the MIDI-ed grand pianos and fuss with the sounds afterward. I knocked out the piece in three takes while they recorded the MIDI information. After I completed the third take, we went into the control booth, auditioned different sounds, and created the overdubs and orchestrations from the original performance. It was very quick."

The result of all this was perhaps Emerson's best solo album, soundtracks included. Reviews were often surprisingly favourable: "A bona fide and sometimes successful attempt to do something creative and original with traditional carols," said one critic.

However the relatively modest sales could be put down to Emerson's serious artistic approach to the project. "Some people have complained that the record isn't 'Christmassy' enough!" he bemoaned. "They expected to hear jingle bells and soppy little frills."

In Christmas 1988 the people of the Soviet republic of Armenia weren't in much of a position to debate the merits of Christmas albums. An earthquake on December 6 killed perhaps 100,000 people, and made five times that many homeless. It was one of the worst earthquakes anywhere on the planet this century.

One of the charities set up to help was 'Life Aid Armenia'. They decided to record a charity single, under the title 'Rock Aid Armenia'. Deep Purple's 'Smoke On The Water' was chosen as appropriate for a superstar rock single. Gary Langan and Asia's Geoff Downes produced, and a galaxy of legendary rock musicians provided voluntary support, including Brian May, Roger Taylor, Dave Gilmour, Chris Squire, Ian Gillan, Paul Rodgers, Tony Iommi and Ritchie Blackmore.

Keith Emerson joined the likes of Bryan Adams, Bruce Dickinson and Ian Gillan for the collective's fourth session, on Sunday, September 10. He was the only one who came along with something worked out – having adapted the "Fanfare For The Common Man" theme to fit round the 'Smoke On The Water' riff. "It's amazing that you worked out a way of fitting that in," commented Geoff. "I'll get it in somewhere!" chuckled Keith from behind his Korg M1 synth. Emerson enjoyed the session so much he felt the group should make an album. "Just one record is not enough," he said at the time. Unfortunately, Emerson's "Fanfare" trickery is very hard to discern on the resulting single, which didn't sell as well as the charity had hoped.

Emerson's next move in 1989 was to turn in a half-hour set for an Italian TV show, accompanied by old mates Frank Scully and Kendal Stubbs. Emerson restricted himself to a Steinway grand piano and a Korg M1, a recent acquisition which had become a favourite. An enthusiastic Italian audience was treated to three old warhorses, "Fanfare For The Common Man", "America"/ "Rondo" and "Honky Tonk Train Blues". The trio also performed a fine version of Charlie Parker's classic "Au Privave", which Keith had recorded many years before with Jon Hiseman and the New Jazz Orchestra for a never-completed solo album.

Ten years on from *Inferno*, the film's Italian director Dario Argento asked Keith to write some music for his new film, *La Chiesa* (*The Church*), which was premiered in 1990. Emerson spread the grand-guignol atmosphere over three tracks, adding Bach's 24th Prelude on organ as a fourth. Although it's not his strongest work, it does go splendidly with the film's dark atmosphere.

Ever popular in Italy, in the year of *Inferno*'s release, Keith was enlisted by that country's pop sensation Giovani Jovanotti to help out on his debut album. He contributed Hammond to two tracks and "Sheriff"-like piano to another. All three tracks sound like he had fun performing to a brief.

Emerson also still enjoyed immense popularity in Japan, and 1990 saw him tour the country with a little known combo called The Best.

"I was doing some jams with Jeff Baxter [ex-Steely Dan] and Joe Walsh every week at the China Club in Los Angeles," he explained. "Then John Entwistle showed up to one of the jams. A guy from the Japanese music industry attended one jam and said it would be very popular in Japan. I got a call from Jeff Baxter. He asked me to play keyboards in a new group. I wanted to know what kind of music they would play. Jeff said we should each prepare three pieces that we had done in the past. Then we could get together and decide what to play together. I played several times at the China Club, but we were not well prepared. I went to England to John Entwistle's house. Simon Phillips was there and we played together. They are special players to me. The fundamental members of the band were established but we still had to decide what to play."

Emerson selected "Fanfare For The Common Man", "America" and a piano solo, Ginastera's "Creole Dance." He also came up with the idea of incorporating the *Jaws* theme into John Entwistle's "Boris The Spider". "After mentioning this to John over the phone, I said, 'Let's check out all the other classical pieces that have that chung-chung-chung-chung rhythm'. *The Rite Of Spring. Night On Bald Mountain.* I should have stuck 'Pirates' in there as well [laughs]. John loved that arrangement."

The Best played a short series of gigs in Japan and Hawaii. One was broadcast live on Japanese TV. "I loved touring with The Best," said Keith in 1992. "It meant that I had to play keyboard parts that were written by some other guy, and I had to play them exactly. They were all songs I had heard before on the radio, like 'Rikki Don't Lose That Number', but when you actually have to learn the keyboard parts and play them onstage, you get a deeper understanding into why that song was a hit. It's a clever business to craft a song. I've never really been good at it."

Emerson also collaborated with ace young American guitarist Marc Bonilla. One night in 1991 Emerson found himself in a bar listening to Bonilla perform an impressive new number. He offered to play piano on it and the result, "White Noise", can be heard on Bonilla's 1991 debut album. Emerson matches Bonilla's virtuoso power and brilliance, and pounds out a wild solo.

Sadly the rumour that Emerson was to join Joe Walsh, Nils Lofgren, Jim Keltner and Todd Rundgren in the latest line-up of Ringo Starr's All-Starr Band, came to nothing.

*****

Musically, nothing was heard from Greg between the demise of Emerson, Lake and Powell and the Emerson, Lake and Palmer reunion. His collaboration with Geoff Downes under the name Ride The Tiger never really got off the ground. However, while the two musicians never released an album, four out of the six songs they worked on would surface on records by a reunited ELP, Asia and others.

During 1989 Carl Palmer was elected into the *Modern Drummer* Hall Of Fame. This is the most prestigious award in the magazine's annual poll, reserved for players who have made a special contribution to the history of drumming. Past winners have included such giants as Buddy Rich, Gene Krupa, Billy Cobham and Steve Gadd. Carl received his award from jazz great Joe Morello (famous for his drumming with Dave Brubeck and in particular "Take 5"). He made a gracious acceptance speech and performed a blistering snare drum solo. So touched he was with his award that he took out a full page advert in the following issue thanking all the readers for their votes.

In the summer of the same year, Palmer met up with John Wetton to discuss the possibility of an Asia reunion. "I was talking to John and we realized that with Asia we were musically compatible," Palmer explained. "We'd broken up too soon. So we got together for a couple of weeks and went out on a tour, opening for the Beach Boys in Europe. It was an odd sort of combination, but the response we received from the audience was so fantastic – we had no idea! So from there we decided that we should keep going… I don't get off playing jazz-rock instrumental music – not because I can't play it, because I can play it incredibly well – but it just doesn't suit me. What inspires me musically is to play melodic, tuneful, pull-on-your-heartstrings songs."

Geoff Downes wasn't available to play keyboards on the European tour so session man John Young filled his spot. Steve Howe no longer entered into the equation. Pat Thrall, ex-Automatic Man, took the guitar role.

The band had originally intended to tour on the back of a "Best of" album.

"As time went on, we found that we had two [new] songs, three songs and finally four songs. So we put it to [the record company], 'How about releasing a 'Best Of' with a little bit of something else in there?'" Outside songwriters were brought in to collaborate on the new material – including, rather bizarrely, David Cassidy of The Partridge Family fame!

The 1990 Geffen album was titled appropriately, *Then And Now*. It contained six songs from their previous albums, plus four extremely good new ones. A succession of guitarists played on the new tracks.

Asia toured parts of Europe and Japan, this time with Geoff Downes, and even sold out two nights at the Moscow Olympic Stadium in November 1990.[2] But despite the enthusiasm for the Asia reunion, John Wetton and Geoff Downes parted company and John Payne was drafted in to replace Wetton.

Palmer was working on the next completely new Asia studio album when the ELP reunion was suggested. In the end, he opted for ELP, and by the time of the May 1992 release of *Aqua* – which would incidentally feature the fine Lake/Downes song, "Love Under Fire" from the Ride The Tiger sessions – Asia had undergone a radical transformation. Carl was on just three of the tracks, the drum stool being filled elsewhere by Simon Phillips and Nigel Glocklar. The 1992 touring incarnation of Asia, featuring only Geoff Downes from the original line-up, was a pale imitation of the original group. It was a disappointing turn in the band's history. Meanwhile, Palmer had gone on to better things. The star of the rejuvenated Emerson, Lake and Palmer was in the ascendant.

Notes

1   As long ago as 1972, Keith had included a Kottke piece among his Radio 1 "My Top Twelve" selection.

2   See Discography and Videography

CHAPTER 12

Welcome Back, My Friends

This company will return one day. Lake/ Sinfield, "Pirates", 1977

In 1991, Keith Emerson was approached by former Atlantic employee Phil Carson – the president of a new record label, Victory Records – ostensibly to compose a new film score.[1] Emerson suggested that Lake and Palmer might help. Palmer was working on a new Asia album, but decided to throw in his lot with his old cohorts. The three musicians went into rehearsal, and worked on "Tarkus" – "just to get back into shape". It was during this time that they rediscovered the zest for music that had driven them to such great heights in their halcyon days. Consequently, all three were convinced the time was right for a full-blown reunion album.

Carson was delighted with the decision and saw the band as an ideal flag-bearer for his new label. Palmer quickly extricated himself from the Asia line-up and Emerson, Lake and Palmer were duly reconvened. (The film score story has subsequently been mooted as a smoke screen to cover up a reunion that was motivated by financial reasons).

Before long, the word was going around that ELP's comeback album was not only a return to form, but perhaps one of their best to date. This was soon confirmed with the arrival of *Black Moon* in May 1992. For most fans, their first hearing of the new Emerson, Lake and Palmer was the album's title track, which was released as a single. Those who were hoping for a classic progressive sound wondered if a desire for Nineties commercial success might have led ELP to opt for a safer, heavy AOR route. However, a brief period of familiarization was all that was required to lay all such doubts to rest. The album proved to be a superbly judged balance of the styles of music ELP had built their reputation on: ten tracks (plus one extra for the Japanese release available elsewhere only as a track on the "Black Moon" single), each one unmistakably ELP in sound and feel, delivered with a renewed intensity. Indeed, new advances in instrumentation and equipment helped propel *Black Moon* several steps beyond any of their previous classics in terms of power, textural complexity and dynamism.

Every track has a "live" feel but the overall sound is incisive and crystal clear, with an excellent balance between instruments. Full marks go to producer Mark Mancina and everyone responsible for engineering and mixing – this, after all, was the first time that ELP had conceded overall production responsibility to someone else. Keith Emerson acknowledges the band's debt to him. "It really helped to have an objective voice involved. [Mark's] a good keyboard player and writer himself, and he really understands ELP's background. He knows what makes this band tick and knows how to pull the best out of all of us."

The band had got closer than ever to the ideal ELP sound – a "three man orchestra", as Chris Welch described it. Emerson, Lake and Powell had attempted a massive, sweeping sound with instruments such as Elka and PPG synthesisers. Also, *Black Moon* benefited from Emerson's film score work, which had enabled them to write more concisely. The songs are for the most part short – certainly no-one could any longer accuse them of excessive soloing! – but much is said in a short time. There was one new compositional element: their producer, Mark Mancina, wrote one song, "Burning Bridges", specially for them.

Keith's incomparable virtuosity was reconfirmed throughout, particularly in the piano solo "Close To Home"; his Hammond, now sounding fiercer and brighter than ever, brought out some of his most aggressive and exciting organ playing for years.

Lake's voice was even more rounded and mature than six years before, with an occasional huskiness bestowing some edge. Lake's contributions both on bass and electric guitar were as sharp as ever. Palmer continued the modern, stripped-down approach to drumming he had adopted as early as 1978's *Love Beach*, taking it further than ever; veteran fans were pleased to hear his classic style at its best on Emerson's complex instrumental "Changing States".

In many ways *Black Moon* can be considered the debut album of a new band, and though tracks like "Black Moon" itself and "Paper Blood" have echoes of the past, they are very contemporary, while "Burning Bridges" and "Better Days" are unlike anything we have heard from ELP before. Nonetheless, the album is full of things which bring to mind the greatest moments of ELP's 70s heyday: a classical rearrangement, some vintage Lake songs, a top-notch Emerson piano solo, and, in "Changing States", an extended instrumental which is among the finest things they've ever recorded.

"There's no compromise in this new album," Palmer maintained. "For better or for worse, no one could ever mistake *Black Moon* for anything other than ELP, and I personally approached it as if we'd never stopped making albums. We were able to work on outside projects, and then could bring those outside experiences into ELP. It's not as if we sat around twiddling our thumbs since we did our last album."

Palmer in particular seemed to have returned to ELP with a crusading zeal, keen to right the wrongs of the nineties music scene. "I think what we hope to bring back into the music industry is the sound of a group," he said. "People actually playing their instruments, a real positive side of music – unlike a lot of music that came out in the eighties which was computer driven with a lot of button pushing – and I think it's now time to get that identifiable sound of a band actually playing together. We were always a live band. We designed the music to be played in a live situation and then transfer it to record. Also, now with the technology that is now available to us, which we didn't have in the seventies, it is a very positive time for a progressive band to come back."

Palmer also felt that the ELP reunion allowed all three members an opportunity to look at each other in a new light and appreciate each others' talents. "In the early seventies when we started, we never realized the chemistry that existed. We made an album every fourteen months, toured virtually every year, so time went very quickly and we just never realized what it was. Then coming back and playing together we thought, 'wow', this is just like we played yesterday. It just happened, a bit like putting on an old pair of shoes, and I think what we've grown to appreciate individually and collectively is the contribution we've made to this situation – not just musically, but to the ambiance of the whole thing. We're all older and wiser, and thus appreciate each other more..."

Lake was pleased at how well the reunion had panned out, "There was a thrill, and a genuine feeling that we could make a great record. I think we all heard something none of us had heard for many years. So many bands today seem to have no recognizable sound or personality. Well, we do, and we're not going to apologize for that."

This new creative period even ushered in a conciliatory attitude to past mistakes. Emerson admitted that he had been too overbearing when presenting new pieces to Lake and Palmer and that this tension had spilled over onto the tours. Now he was just happy to win both of them over first. If not, the piece would be dropped. Certainly, the presence of Mark Mancina as outside producer helped to create a more democratic atmosphere in the studio. This left the band free to focus on writing and playing.

Giant steps had been made in music technology since ELP last convened and the band were determined to use this technology creatively, not least the advent of MIDI and its impact on Keith's sound and thinking. Now, finally, he could combine the piano with the Hammond.

If anybody wanted any evidence about the effectiveness of this new technology, then "Pictures" live would provide it. Palmer & Lake also got in on the act. Palmer could store up to twenty drum programmes digitally. So at the push of a button he could have a new drum set all with consistent sound. Lake would also employ a versatile MIDI bass. Such developments were manna from heaven for the band. Emerson had been frustrated in the 70s because instrument technology didn't keep up with the band's musical ambitions.

The new album pushed Lake into new lyrical territory too. Without the restrictions of a "Tarkus" or a "Karn Evil 9" theme, he could concentrate on contemporary issues. "A lot of the album was written during the Gulf crisis. 'Black

Moon' came when I saw the oil wells burning in Kuwait. I was watching television one day, and I saw this report about all these oil fields being set alight, and this picture had the sun blacked out by all this smoke, but you could still see it, and it looked like a moon, and then a black moon, and that started me thinking."

"Black Moon"'s music is powerful enough to conjure up these images. The ominous opening is reminiscent of the beginning of *Trilogy*'s "The Endless Enigma" – a few doomy chords wind up on an E-pedal, over which Emerson spins a tortuous improvisational line followed by a sparkling arpeggio-like phrase descending again to a low E. "I composed that in London," Emerson recalled. "I remember that I went out for lunch, and when I came back Greg and Carl were hammering out this heavy solid rock thing. Without saying a word, I went up to the keyboard and struck this chord. That prompted me to do the main figure of the song. Next thing I know is that Greg and Carl are going, 'That's great! Do that again!' I looked back at them in disbelief and said, 'That? Is that all you want?' There were lots of times that I had to be held back from doing too much in the very early stages. The ending of this piece took a lot of crafting, though. I wasn't satisfied at the idea of ending with a heavy, head-banging piece of music."

A trip to Venice supplied the opening images of the romantic ballad, "Affairs of the Heart", another product of Lake's and Downes' Ride The Tiger sessions, which was chosen as the very different follow-up single to 'Black Moon'. "I was there on a holiday," recalls Lake, "and Venice is such a beautiful and romantic setting, a lovely place and full of art and the history of art, so it's a great environment to write a song. There is a hotel there called the Danieli[2], and in the lobby is this huge and beautiful chandelier, and there was a beautiful girl sitting across the other side of the lobby, and for some reason it all added up – Venice, the chandelier, the girl. The whole opening of the song just wrote itself, there and then."

"Out of all Greg's tunes, I really loved this one," Emerson enthused. "I suggested that this could be the new 'Lucky Man', so we made a more acoustic arrangement of it than the one he had done with Geoff [Downes]. Geoff's arrangement was great, but it was very horn-like, with a lot of synth padding. Greg sang it live with the acoustic guitar and then I added the keyboard parts. It was important that the keyboards should not be intrusive. We were looking for little hook-lines that would be as simple as possible and not interfere with the song. Your focus should be on Greg's singing and the acoustic guitar. It was difficult to play that sparsely. We had all the synths there, and we just did combinations to get different textures here and there."

The album's one classical piece is a powerful rendition of the "Dance of the Knights" from Act 1, Scene 2 of Prokofiev's ballet "Romeo and Juliet". "What struck me about this particular music was the similarity between it and the way that

Jimi Hendrix started 'Purple Haze'," said Emerson. "The rhythm was so similar that I was sure I could make it work with the Prokofiev. Amazingly, you don't have to force too many changes to make it happen. It works quite naturally, the same as the shuffle rhythm works with 'Fanfare For The Common Man'."

An early shorter, faster version of the track, known as "Montagues and Capulets" after the story's feuding families was aired in 1990 on local American radio by DJ Greg Stone, along with "Another Frontier", an early take on "Changing States." Kevin Gilbert, producer of the solo album which Emerson was planning at the time, came in to give a progress report on the album.

The Prokofiev number is followed by the stirring anti-war song "Farewell to Arms", which featured a wonderful Emerson solo. The string effects keep growing and growing in intensity, until the listener desperate for the big climax – in Lake's words, "When it gets to the chorus you think it's gonna go – but it just stays there simmering." The phrase "May the reign of freedom be released" is planted in the chorus, and when finally Emerson enters with a magnificent lead synth solo flight, the sense of release is enormous. "I used the Minimoog with the Korg 01/W to get that big modular sound," says Emerson. "The funny thing about this was that it was an overdub. We had recorded all of 'Farewell To Arms' before in England, but the ending had been left a bit empty. So when we got to Los Angeles, everybody started looking to me to put the icing on the cake.

"I got the sound up in the studio and started jamming. It's an easy chord sequence to jam over, so I was doing jazz licks and blues licks all over the place. Every time they played the tape at me, I came up with a different idea and looked over for some positive reaction from Greg and Carl. But they were going, 'Too complicated. Too jazzy. Too this, too that. Do it again.' After about an hour I said, 'Okay. Leave me on my own. I want you all out of the studio.' I sat down, and it came to me all of a sudden: Why am I trying to do jazz licks? Why am I trying to do blues licks? The theme was stated on piano right at the beginning of the song, so why don't I try to develop that in the way I would play it on the Moog – put in the portamento leaps and stretch it from there? It's a very honest solo. It comes through very strongly as a final statement."

In terms of vinyl, *Black Moon*'s first side is perhaps stronger than the second – which borne out by the way all of the above mentioned tracks were included at the beginning of the World Tour. However, the remaining tracks are still good. "Changing States", originally known as "Another Frontier", is a particularly strong instrumental. "Another Frontier" is raw and exciting instrumental progressive rock, though it lacked the grandeur provided by the final version's orchestral textures, and Emerson improved the central section for ELP.

"I went to a church in Pasadena to work on the fugal development of that piece," Emerson explains. "I had developed the theme at my house in Sussex. I had the verse and fugue themes written out. It was a proper fugue, so my intention when I went to the organ in Pasadena was to play it like a legit fugue, as Bach would have done. But when I took it back to the band and played it with Greg and Carl the fugal development didn't work out. There were lots of spaces in it that left Greg and, I guess, Carl feeling uncomfortable. There were a few gaps in the piece where there were no parts for them to play at all…. I think they felt embarrassed at the thought that they'd be standing around on their own during some of those sections. Since it was important to project this as a piece for the whole band, I changed those parts. In the original version, I got to a point with the theme where we faded on the B flat chord. That didn't quite work with ELP, so in the new version I broke into another tempo and introduced another theme.

"The middle part was meant to be a fugue, but that didn't work. We still have a lot of the counterpoint, though now there's much more energy in that passage than there was when I wrote it. There's a lot more force with the way that ELP does it than I would have gotten on my own.

"The original key was C, but it goes to B flat and then to E flat. I really stretched the piece to make it work for the band. That's why I ended up with the title 'Changing States', which was also appropriate because of what was happening in Europe at the time.

"All of what I write is based on emotions. Everybody I meet, my feelings about an individual, what is going on in the world, all become a direct force on my music. Sometimes they're opposing forces. If I'm happy, I'll write a sad piece of music . If I'm sad, I'll write a happy piece of music. There's always a sense of opposition in my music. It's the same in a live context. If I get some bad news before I go onstage, it might be the best concert I've ever played in my life. But if I go onstage feeling thoroughly confident that this is going to be the best show, it can be the worst show I've ever played. 'Changing States' is really the whole perspective of the way I live my life.

"I'm always very optimistic. If I'm down, I don't want to bring everybody else down with my music. I want them to be up. 'Changing States' leaves you with that feeling that you've just visited Disneyland and, hey, everything's okay. It's kind of sombre in places, but it doesn't drag you quite down into the blues."

"Burning Bridges" was producer Mancina's songwriting contribution. ELP must have counted themselves lucky indeed to have a producer who could present them with a specially written song of this standard, and they rise to it, giving as powerful and committed a performance as anywhere else on this album.

"When I heard his demo tape," says Emerson, "I began by copying his Hammond organ line, since that's all I heard. But Mark was insistent that we develop the piece a bit more." So Emerson brought in his Steinway Grand.

This track is the first which falls within the umbrella of commercial AOR, but it's so strongly ELP in character and interpretation that there can be no charges of compromise. Never mind categories: if there's one thing ELP have always sought to do, it's both to fulfil and subvert expectations.

"Close To Home" is the first instance in some time of Emerson performing a self-composed piano piece of such quality on an ELP album, though there have been many short tracks on solo and soundtrack records. "This wasn't one of those late-at-night compositions," Emerson commented. "I woke up one morning, did the octave part at the piano, and then filled the rest in. After I composed it at the piano, I took it into my studio in my barn and did an arrangement on synths. I did another recording with Kevin Gilbert, where Kevin played an acoustic guitar in unison with the piano theme, and we overdubbed some strings. But then I thought, No, this is a very honest piece of music. It just needs one instrument. I don't want to mess about with this piece. So I adapted it for solo piano, nothing more."

The end result is a delight for the listener, who can enjoy the lovely, subtle turns of the melody, and marvel at the extraordinary fortissimo descending runs. It begins in nostalgic mood, and then summons up a great burst of energy to continue the journey with a beautifully elaborated second theme of great strength and resolve. The return of the first theme is brief, and home is reached all too soon.

"Better Days" begins with the rumbling of a train and the distant noise of a railway station heralding the first line, "*I was walking on this station...*"

"That piece went through so many changes," recalls Keith. "It started off as a Hammond organ solo in the style of Procol Harum. But it got funkier when Greg and I started interchanging ideas about the storyline behind this piece. I happened to say to Greg that one Christmas I was at Victoria Station. I'm not a charitable person per se, but when I saw this lady who was obviously there for the night, I put some money in her hand and walked away. She wasn't begging – I hate people who come up to me and beg – but I did give her quite a large sum of money. I walked back into the cafe, sat down, and looked at the way that she revived as she looked around to see where the money came from."

Emerson got the the Clavinet sound from a JD-800. He now feels the organ sounds like "My Funny Valentine". The lyrics aren't entirely convincing, but new for ELP is the driving hi-energy drumming throughout the song, something normally reserved for instrumentals. There's some stirring organ and synth work here too, and the old gents work up a real sweat as they go for broke.

Chris Welch described Lake's "Footprints In The Snow" as "the final rebuke for those who see ELP solely as some sort of bombastic machine." Certainly, this poignant, simple ballad is one of Greg's finest songs to date. It is comparable in many ways – the very simple verse/chorus structure, few and easy chords, little else but acoustic guitar and voice – to the more naive "Lucky Man", composed thirty years before. Sparse string sounds from Keith and a final soft bell-tree ripple from Carl enhance the wintry atmosphere.

The Japanese edition's bonus track, "A Blade Of Grass", is a lyrical, melodic, Emerson solo piano miniature. We're so used to hearing Emerson in busier modes that this oasis of calm and peace comes as a shock. It makes you realise just how good a composer and pianist he is, how fluent in a wide variety of styles. For years he has been expressing his ambition to record a solo album which could show off his ability to play in many styles. "A Blade Of Grass" and "Close To Home" whet the appetite even further for a piano solo album.

On 24 July, 1992, Emerson, Lake and Palmer embarked on an ambitious world tour. The opening show was their first concert together for fourteen years and four months. They went down a storm across the United States, Japan and Europe. So successful, indeed, was this tour, that they had to add extra dates in the United Kingdom. During the final leg of the British tour, they played Newcastle City Hall, where "Pictures" had been recorded. "The atmosphere was electric," recalls one fan, Adam Fenton, as Emerson announced, "*And twenty years on, Pictures!*". For the final show of the tour, at Bristol's Colston Hall, Emerson played a short piano piece that he had written that day on the way to the hall; this was much appreciated.

"We certainly hadn't anticipated this sort of response to the tour – not in the UK anyway," Emerson confessed. "The reaction of the audiences in America has been fantastic. Nothing seems to have changed with regard to audience reaction. We're a little different, of course. There's no room for partying after the show, as we may have done in the Seventies. Things like that you've got to be aware of. We're older and wiser now, and we keep ourselves in pretty good shape."

The following January, ELP embarked on a second tour that would take in South America. "We played in Buenos Aires," recalls Palmer, "in a theatre that was below street level and it was flooded at the time! It was the last concert that we played after doing something like 140 dates. We had two days in this theatre and they kept pumping the water out [laughs]. There was unexpected torrential rain and we had to cancel a day. We ended up playing two concerts in one night. We went on at 8.30 pm, finished at 10.30 pm, went back on at 11.30 pm and finished at 1.30 am. It was fantastic. The people were incredible. Chile was also a nice place to play. We were surprised how young the people were that came to see us."

With everything going so well, there was little doubt that ELP would record a second studio album. But before that, there were two more releases to keep things ticking over: a live album of their Royal Albert Hall concert[3] and a long-awaited box set, *The Return of the Manticore*.

The Albert Hall recording was released in the middle of the world tour and contains a fair sprinkling of *Black Moon* along with old favourites like "Pirates". It may well be the best live album Emerson, Lake and Palmer have ever released – with the exception, of course, of *Pictures At An Exhibition.*

What else could they start with but the opening excerpt from "Karn Evil 9, 1st Impression, Part 2" (though by the end of the first tour, this had been dropped)? The first three parts of "Tarkus", "Eruption", "Stones Of Years" and "Iconoclast", somewhat miscast as a medley, set the pace for a fast, furious and heavy – with the sole exception of Lake's two-song solo spot – selection from the set. In "Stones Of Years" a vicious, biting, frenetic organ solo over a rock steady rhythm support is particularly notable; and "Iconoclast" is the cue for Emerson to leap into the crowd spitting fire from the ribbon controller.

This leads directly into "Knife Edge", where sampled orchestral strings enhance the power of the ending, reminding one of the *Works Live* performance. "Paper Blood" here is riveting. On the chorus, Lake's voice is synchronised with pre-recorded backing singers while Emerson gets in some fine kickin' organ playing. All in all, this number is even better live than on the album. The same is true of "Romeo And Juliet" – taken a little quicker than the studio version and with a screaming "electric lead guitar" solo courtesy of Emerson's Roland JD800. The roar of the crowd only goes to heighten the energy.

Emerson has been promising a recording of his arrangement of "Toccata" composer Alberto Ginastera's *Creole Dance* for some time. The *Suite de Danzas Criollas* – to give it its correct name – for solo piano dates from 1957, and consists of five dances of varying styles and speeds, with a concluding Coda (Presto ed energico), which amounts to a separate dance. Ginastera's Coda, which is only a little over a minute long, forms the basis of Emerson's arrangement. Emerson makes the most of the first idea, which in the original occurs only at the beginning and end: he repeats the first twenty bars. After this he deviates substantially from Ginastera's score; the typical improvisation over an ostinato bass in the middle bears little relationship to the composer's work, though there are a couple of brief references.

It's appropriate that his first recording of this long-standing live solo piano tour de force should be a live performance. Featured in Emerson's solo piano spot on both the Emerson, Lake and Powell and Three tours, as well as during the concerts by the short-lived supergroup The Best at Yokohama Arena in Japan, this is Emerson's hottest, most on-the-edge solo piano work of recent years, giving him a chance to display not only some fantastic finger work, but also an unusually ferocious assault force of forearm crashes and other trickery.

"Still...You Turn Me On" and "Lucky Man" provide the oasis of calm in an otherwise high-octane set.

The live "Black Moon" can't quite match the perfection and dynamic variety of the studio recording, but it's as good as six hands can do. The "Finale/ Encore (Medley)", which takes much the same form as it has since the late 70s, includes "Fanfare For The Common Man", "America" and "Rondo", as well as Emerson's foray into playing the organ from behind in the brief extract from the Bach "Toccata & Fugue in D minor". All the band's raw energy and high spirits seem to have been funnelled into this one performance. The heat really builds up in "Rondo", which they play with such delirious violence you'd think they'd come up with the idea yesterday. It's almost as if The Nice had been reborn. These guys were not in their forties, surely? All in all it's a storming conclusion to a great live album. In fact, listening to this album is almost as good as being back at the concert, as anyone who was present will attest – and especially those in the front few rows like the authors of the present work.

ELP's box set involved the novel idea of new recordings of old material. Hitherto, box sets had been used to showcase old material and unreleased studio tracks that at the time were not considered good enough for release. The band came up with the idea of re-record things from their pre-ELP days, just to show how they arrived at ELP. The original idea came from Keith, who dreamed of a live show featuring all the bands ELP emerged from. "I discussed this with Harvey Goldsmith and he thought it was a great idea," says Emerson. "The first half of the show would be The Nice doing ten minutes, the original King Crimson doing ten minutes, then the original Crazy World of Arthur Brown, then afterwards ELP come on stage to do the next half. We all thought it was a good idea, except for Greg: I think his relations with Bob Fripp were somewhat strained." While the show never got further than the drawing board, it provided the impetus to incorporate it into the box set. So there were versions of Arthur Brown's "Fire", The Nice's "Hang On To A Dream" – with no piano! – and Crimson's "Schizoid Man". New producer Keith Olsen's production on these tracks was very earthy, with few overdubs, and it gave hope that the new album would be in this vein.

The box set included "Touch and Go" transposed from C minor to G minor, to take Lake's now even deeper voice into account. The track is also played a little faster and with more of a biting organ. An alternative version of the re-recorded piece was used by the American National Football League (NFL). Explains Carl, "The NFL people always liked the lyric 'Touch & Go' for the obvious reasons, so we allowed them to use it for their games."

The triumph of the box set is a truncated version of "Pictures", recorded in Dolby Surround Sound. It sounds *huge!* The frequency spectrum is so wide that, at certain points, above a medium volume the room will actually shake and the CD may jump out of the machine and run sobbing into a corner. In terms of content, the major difference here from the earlier versions is "The Sage". Emerson accompanies Lake's more metronomic guitar picking. Greg provides a wistful, far less complex solo, and the choir lend a little support. Keith and Greg add a little instrumental coda which rounds it off perfectly.

The Nice committed "Rondo" to vinyl twice, so it's hardly surprising that ELP thought there was no need to do it a third time. A quarter of a century later, it's interesting to hear this very early ELP version, recorded only a few months after the demise of the Nice at the 1970 Lyceum show filmed for the *Pictures* movie, before an audience hoping they wouldn't be let down by this band that had been responsible for the splitting of three other great groups. The audience had no cause for complaint. Emerson, Lake and Palmer make "Rondo" their own from the word go: Emerson is as brilliant as ever, while Lake beats hell out of those repeated bass notes, and the 20-year old Palmer drives the whole thing along with every drum technique in the book, including a wonderfully fresh solo. At a little under four minutes, it's just perfect.

"Bo Diddley" is a real rarity – ELP cutting loose on a studio jam tribute to the blues legend, and playing with such complete freedom and lack of restraint that they seem hardly aware the mike's tuned on. Emerson is in the sort of 60s jazz mood we haven't heard from him for years. Lake has an all-too brief killer electric guitar solo, while Palmer covers every inch of the kit.

The box set's final rarity was a 1971 cut of Gulda's "Prelude and Fugue". It's a difficult piece, and while Emerson's performance doesn't have the sparkling delicacy of the composer's, he certainly matches Gulda's vitality. Emerson is accurate – there's only a couple of barely noticeable slips, and he plays it, astonishingly, faster than Gulda. To play any fugue at high speed is an achievement in itself. The added difficulty with this one is the many 'swung' notes. For a start, these are not individually notated in the sheet music, so it's hard enough to work out what you're meant to be playing. Also, one of the main challenges of the piece is to bring out the separate voices of the fugue while retaining the swing.

This recording, impressive as it is, doubtless fell short of Emerson's very high standards, and in the event he decided to content himself with the looser live performance of the Fugue alone.

The box was rounded off with an interesting selection of thoughtfully sequenced remastered versions of classic ELP tracks.

On top of a vintage comeback album and an enthusiastically received tour, the live album and box set kept ELP on a successful role. Unfortunately, things would soon take a turn for the worse. For the time being the band literally stayed in the studio after the box set recordings and went straight into the new album. But a storm was coming.

Notes

1 Keith told the Japanese *Keyboard* magazine in July 1992, "I wrote a theme song for an English movie, *Soul Scapes* before Christmas (1991)."

2 The Hotel Danieli is a magnificent restored palace just off Saint Mark's Square, Venice. The Palazzo Dandolo, named after its designer who was head of the family which first owned it, was itself built in the 14th century to meet the demands of Europe's travelling nobility. Described in its own brochure as 'a protected architectural treasure in Venetian Gothic style', its architecture and interior decor are among the most splendid in a city of splendours. The chandelier which helped inspire the song is no less impressive than the lobby of which it is the central feature.

3 A vital note for collectors – the Japanese release features the first of the Albert Hall concerts (2 October), whereas the CD released in the Europe and the USA, under the same title, was of the 26 October concert. The Japanese version also has a different cover, 1992 tour dates, more photos in the booklet, and song lyrics. "There was a time limitation on it," explained Emerson early in 1993. "The Japanese apparently wanted it in a big hurry, and we played three nights in all at the Albert Hall. I haven't actually heard the whole of the Japanese release so I don't know what that is, but it was pretty well mixed and released before we even knew anything about it. I think they spent a little more time getting the stereo perspectives a lot better and the Dolby's better and all that sort of stuff." The 2nd October gig was broadcast live on BBC Radio 1.

CHAPTER 13

Defeat Snatched From The Jaws Of Victory

In the 60's/70's record companies didn't question anything..... But these days, before you even get in the studio, you have to go through this whole lot of people who don't really understand what you are about. Keith Emerson

Remaining in the studio after the triumphant box set recordings, Emerson, Lake and Palmer started work on a new album with the working title, "The Best Seat in the House". The band was so pleased with the way the re-recorded "Pictures" turned out they decided to record the whole of the new album using the nascent Dolby Surround Sound technique. In fact the title was lifted from a Dolby advertising campaign for home TV systems.

However, somewhere along the line – no one is quite sure when – the initial project was abandoned. Lake later blamed Emerson's problems with his hand. The band came up with a new working title, *In the Hot Seat*. It summarised the band's predicament.

Victory Records was in dire financial straits. Their two big heavyweight acts, David Bowie's Tin Machine and Yes, had delivered flop albums. Consequently, Victory put pressure on ELP to recoup the label's losses by steering the band – through producer Keith Olsen – into a new more commercial direction. Olsen and Victory told Emerson bluntly: "Look – you may have done classical adaptations in the past, but you really must change!" The band were also told that the record would include *no* Lake acoustic piece, *no* conceptual piece and *no* Keith piano solo. The promise of a concept follow up to *Black Moon* given on the 92/93 world tour would not be honoured.

Additional pressure on ELP came from the fact that Emerson was just recovering from an operation on his right arm. During the *Black Moon* tour he noticed a weakness in his fingers. After a period of searching for alternatives to surgery, he relented and underwent the operation. When Emerson came out of hospital, he could only play to fifty percent of his normal ability[1]. It was, however, his mental state that was really suffering. In the initial post-surgery period, Emerson feared his playing days might be over. Or at best, he might never approach his old standard.

As Emerson was ELP's main musical source, it was critical for Olsen and Victory to convince him of the virtues of the more commercial approach. Emerson's hand condition may have made him less inclined to argue. Fortunately, the band had managed to record some tracks before his surgery.

In the meantime, while ELP had no choice but to go along with Olsen and Victory, they weren't sure where to begin. "It's very difficult for us to sit down and try and write something that is commercial," Palmer lamented during the early stages of recording. They had been in a similar position in the late 70s when they came up with *Love Beach*, though in fact that much maligned record is closer to a mainstream ELP album than people give it credit for, featuring as it does a classical adaptation, a concept piece and some prominent piano work. Olsen's and Victory's solution to this commercial conundrum was to seal the fate of the album. They drafted in a small army of writers to give the band a 'helping hand'. Olsen himself eventually took four writing credits, while his friends and associates came up with the rest. Olsen's partners helped to eliminate all but a few vestiges of ELP's musical character from the album.

About halfway through the recording sessions, Palmer gave an insight into the progress made: "We are not totally committed to any one direction. We have about six tracks recorded and another three we are looking at. We're not dealing with any long conceptual pieces, but we do have songs which are about seven minutes. There is nothing in the twenty-minute area as of yet, but that could change tomorrow. We have some ideas we'd like to try, but it depends on how the writing comes along. We have four or five tracks recorded that are four to five minutes long, but whether or not we are going to tie them together in any way really depends on how the lyrics turn out. It's too early to say." The ambiguous nature of that quote wasn't very reassuring.

The recording sessions dragged on into 1994. Just before completion Keith appeared on a local American radio show and surprised people by telling host Mike Kellie, his arm was on the mend. "I hope the new ELP album will show that," he continued. "It's a different direction, it's too early to really say what direction the new ELP album is taking. But we hope it gets completed in the next month." It was on this show that Emerson premiered some tracks from the vaults: a recording of "The Church" from his then unreleased solo album; "Au Privave" from the 1972 sessions for his first solo album and a late '80s studio version of "Creole Dance". Overall, Emerson sounded in upbeat mood as he spoke about past glories, even telling a wonderfully self-deprecating story of his meeting with Bob Dylan. Dylan maintained he had never heard of Emerson, and even after the introductions, Dylan seemed to forget where Emerson came from halfway through the conversation!

At the end of the show Emerson played down a recent "Will Emerson ever play again?" *Keyboard* Magazine cover story. The interview was done shortly after the operation – at the playback party for the box set – so it's not surprising that he was then in despair. Hearing past glories while worrying about the state of his arm,

Emerson was like a top runner watching footage of all his great races while sitting with a leg in plaster. Preparing himself for the worst was no doubt an effective defence mechanism.

In fact, the operation wasn't Emerson's only worry at the time. 1993 was a bad year for the keyboard player. A number of financial problems unravelled as a consequence of some tax efficiency plans hatched in the 70s. Barclays Bank demanded a repayment of a loan he had personally guaranteed to his company Emersongs, serving him with a writ for £145,000. As a result of non-payment, Emerson was banned from holding a company directorship for seven years. He had to sell the Tudor mansion in Sussex where he and his family had lived for over twenty years. Shortly after this Emerson and his wife split up.

Another low point was when Emerson appeared on US shock-jock Howard Stern's radio show, only to be mercilessly baited by Stern. No wonder Emerson would look back to this period of his life as a hell on earth. "It was just a tough time to make a record," he later commented.

In the meantime, things got worse! In the summer news filtered out that ELP's planned tour of Japan and the States had been cancelled. Then *In The Hot Seat* appeared.

ELP fans who had followed all the developments must have felt some trepidation as they put the CD on. In fact, there were a few clues in the booklet to alert any fan that things were not quite right. Firstly, they would have noticed the supplementary writing team. Secondly, Emerson's name comes after Lake and Palmer in the publishing credits. Lastly, the photo of the band was an old one, from the *Black Moon* video.

All such concerns aside, the album gets off to a rousing, explosive start, with the extended stirring introduction to "Hand of Truth", punctuated with Emerson's exhilarating synthesiser flourishes. The song was originally called "We Have The Power" – fitting with the song's environmental plea – but Emerson hated the title. Towards the end of the track Emerson takes one of the best solos on the album – actually one of the few. It took him numerous takes to get it right, but the end result is compelling. "Hand of Truth" is the best track on the album because it showcases ELP doing what they do best. Interestingly, the lyrics fit with Palmer's 1995 description of the themes for ELP's next concept album: "A global concept – political and topical."

The next track, "Daddy", took on a life of its own and dominated the album. It all started late in 1993 when Lake caught an item on *America's Most Wanted* show about young Sarah Ann Wood who disappeared from home, presumed dead. "I wrote the song originally just to get it out of my system," Lake explained, "Not intending to record it, because I thought it was a very morbid thing to do... It was a very disturbing story.... but what really hit me was when Robert Wood, Sarah's father, began to talk about Sarah's loss and about the fact that he wanted to be close to her and he believed she wanted to be close to him." He was even moved to write to Robert Wood. This is an excerpt from the letter:

****

Dear Robert

I am a musician by profession and for the past 25 years have played in a band called Emerson, Lake & Palmer. My reason for writing this is that back in January I saw the television programme that told the story of Sarah's disappearance. Having a daughter of my own it had the most deep impact upon me. So moved was I by yours and Sarah's story, that I felt a desperate need to try and help in anyway I could.

I am not a wealthy man and the only real skill I have lies in my ability to write songs. The song you will hear on tape was written directly after seeing the programme. I have been able to persuade Victory Records to do a special cassette version of the song, the proceeds of which will be donated to your charity. I can assure you I'm not doing this for any reason other than being genuinely moved by Sarah's story. I want to help in anyway I can.

Please feel free to contact me personally.

Kind regards

Greg Lake

****

The listener cannot fail to be disturbed by the unfolding tale, told through Wood's eyes: the first news, his desperate combing of the streets posting thousands of flyers appealing for help, his loss of hope – and throughout, the pleading ghostly echo of his child: "Daddy, come and bring me home". One is left with the thought, "There but for the grace of God go I".

Most striking is the integrity of Lake's storytelling: he never succumbs to cheap, supermarket-media sentiment. Key to this is his omission of a name for the "victim" of the song's abduction. Given the difficult subject matter, it's nothing less than a triumph for Greg, and one of his finest lyrical moments. Olsen's low key production ensures the music is never allowed to overshadow the lyrics. A chilling ambience is maintained throughout. Incidentally, the young girl who provides a ghostly echo to the chorus is Keith Olsen's daughter Kristen.

A version of Dylan's "The Man In The Long Black Coat" was a surprising inclusion. While this was the first time ELP had tackled a Dylan song, of course The

Nice had recorded "Country Pie", "She Belongs To Me" and "My Back Pages', and Lake had included his version of an unfinished Dylan song, "Love You Too Much" on his first solo album.

Emerson had been strongly affected by this disturbing and brilliant song from Dylan's 1989 return-to-form *Oh Mercy* album. Recalling the atmosphere of his earlier *Pat Garrett and Billy The Kid*, Bob weaves a typically enigmatic tale, unfolding in both interior and exterior worlds, of a meeting between a "Man With No Name" and a young woman – an ideal chance for Lake to conjure with the master's ambiguous language of threat and disturbance.

By the time ELP were in the studio, Emerson wanted to use "The Man…" as the basis of a new long concept piece – "a kind of Western with a screenplay written by Dylan and of which I was the producer." Moving in a more melodic direction than the original, Emerson arranged the piece in the style of a Western movie soundtrack. Adding parts of his own he came up with about twenty minutes of music. But he was later encouraged to separate his music from Dylan's. According to Emerson, "unfortunately, Olsen only wanted to have the screenplay and not the whole movie." Emerson also felt pressure from the rest of the band, because all the royalties on the long piece would have to go to Dylan. It was an argument that meant nothing to Emerson, but in the end, he gave way and his beloved concept was torn asunder. Some of the excess material was put together, with the help of Olsen, and became "One by One", the third song on the album.

For the Dylan cover itself, ELP wisely made no attempt to imitate the Daniel Lanois-produced evocative original. Here, it's a straight down the line arrangement, far from Lanois' oppressive, impressionistic ambience.

It's hard to find a relationship between the music of "The Man In The Long Black Coat" and "One by One'; but both mine a philosophical vein. "One by One" is one of the album's best cuts – no solos but an intriguing arrangement. It has obvious lyric references to "Knife Edge', and atmospherically is also related to "In The Court Of The Crimson King" and "Epitaph". As Keith later explained, the nine-eight meter changes made it lean more towards progressive rock. It's teasing to speculate how Emerson's original concept would have turned out. One can only lament this divisive episode.

"Thin Line" is an interesting experiment. Emerson composed a shuffle beat which Palmer took up with a vengeance. Originally it was an instrumental with lots of synths and Hammond. But after some Olsen surgery it re-emerged with horn-like synths, backing vocals, Mark King-style bass and guitar licks by the uncredited Tim Pierce from Toy Matinee. The angry lyrics about love and violence, in combination with a rather funky style, make it a rewarding song – though initially under-appreciated by some.

"Gone Too Soon" does a wonderful imitation of the late Genesis period. It's the sort of song Phil Collins would have sung oh so sincerely. Only later, somewhat sensationally, did it emerge that Emerson and Palmer are not on it! Someone else played keyboards, and a drum machine accompanied. Emerson and Palmer departed after their contribution, leaving Lake and Olsen in the studio for a few more weeks to "finish off". This was when the majority of the second half of the album was created – a parallel with *Love Beach*, when it was Emerson who was left "holding the baby". Apparently Lake does provide some great Fender Strat playing on this, though.

The album signs off powerfully with "Street War" – a straight rocker with Lake delivering his apocalyptic lyrics from what sounds like a telephone booth. ELP have increasingly been staking out this classic heavy anthem territory. "Street War" was originally written in the late '80s as part of Lake's and Downes' "Ride The Tiger" project, when it was known as "Street Wars" (plural). The song was clearly changed around enough to omit Downes from any credit.

Written years before the L.A. riots, it's about the violence inherent in American society – children taking guns to school, curfews, burning ghettoes, militias.

Towards the end of the cut, there's a fearsome keyboard solo performed with a Korg Wavestation, which produces a shrieking combination of guitar and police siren. It's one of the inspired cameos on this album, perfectly evoking the violent bassline that underpins urban life. "They're burnin' in the ghetto...You can't paint over anger".

One striking aspect of the entire album is the minimal nature of Palmer's drumming. Olsen had recoiled against what he saw as *Black Moon*'s overproduced drum sound. Also, Palmer was having trouble with his hands. He had developed a problem known as Carpal Tunnel Syndrome[2], a condition which manifested itself in a numbness and stiffness in the fingers, especially in the morning. Like Emerson, Palmer sought alternatives to surgery but had to go under the knife in the end. Thankfully, it was successful.

Even though Olsen and Victory Records were intent on making *In the Hot Seat* as unlike an ELP record as possible, the band did try to include some typical ELP elements. However, the piano piece that Emerson submitted, "Hammer It Out", for some reason only appeared on the Japanese version. (In 1996 Keith played this at some gigs as a tribute to the memory of his friend and producer Kevin Gilbert who had passed away early in the year.)

Surprisingly, a classical adaptation was also recorded for this album. ELP had cut a version of the "Karelia Suite" – which Emerson had recorded before with The Nice. (Stravinsky's "Firebird Suite" was also considered). However, there was a problem. "We wanted Trevor Rabin to put some guitar on it," says Palmer, "And

Keith Olsen messed up again and didn't get the tape to him in the format he wanted, so the guitar part was never done." Given Olsen's feelings about classical adaptations, it's not surprising there was this "mix up" with the tape. "Karelia" could have been the seven-minute track Palmer was talking about in the early stage of recording

The omission of the "Karelia Suite" is even more incomprehensible when faced with the addition of the Dolby-treated "Pictures" from the box set as a bonus track on the CD.

Once the album was in the can, it was time to consider promoting it. This would have to be a major operation if the album was to justify Victory's high hopes for its commercial potential. However, even before the record's release, the band had effectively scattered. Lake was on his own. Emerson was off composing the music for thirteen *Iron Man* cartoons he'd been commissioned to do and Palmer was nowhere to be seen. The errant sticksman did however appear on one obscure cable TV show, where the presenter introduced the interview by stating that *In The Hot Seat* was one of ELP's best albums. Steadily, by degrees, Palmer set him right on this count.

With Lake left to carry the mantle, he embarked on a solo tour with his own band to promote the Sarah Ann Wood Rescue Centre. Backed by Victory Records he appeared on TV shows and even shot a promo video for "Daddy". The trek climaxed with the Concert for Sarah, which Lake performed on W10 cable television. He played five songs, including two from *In the Hot Seat*.[3]

All of this was quite confusing. The longer Lake continued to promote the album on his own, the more *In the Hot Seat* would be associated as a Greg Lake solo work.

Without an ELP tour or a co-ordinated promotional campaign, the album came and went virtually unnoticed. Reviews were thin on the ground. The American *Keyboard* magazine could only say it was not as bad as *Love Beach*. Others would begrudge the record even such faint praise. *Keyboard*'s critic also noted the perfunctory nature of Emerson's keyboard work. The only UK review was on Channel 4's teletext, where it was compared to Pink Floyd's *Division Bell* because both comprised shorter tracks. The song-length was not the only untypical feature. For much of the time, the album's only resemblance to an ELP album was Greg Lake's voice. Otherwise it could have been any number of bands.

Predictably, ELP's fanbase hated the record. They acknowledged that it had good moments, but these were not sustained for any length. The album's stronger songs tended to be interesting rather than great. Bearing in mind that the band had all the elements in place to make a good ELP record, but were stymied by the label and producer, this was a real lost opportunity. Worse still, however, was the album's poor sales. Considering all Olsen and Victory's attempts to make it a hit, the record flopped. Victory Records would never recover from the blow and went into receivership afterwards.

In The Hot Seat marked the point where the real commercial music world finally caught up with ELP. For all their previous groundbreaking successes, they became victims of a system that makes a virtue of pandering to supposed "mass" tastes.

The only silver lining during this period came when ELP were inducted onto the Hollywood Rock Wall on Sunset Boulevard. On November 23, 1993, they put their hands and signatures into cement, taking their place with just 52 other similarly honoured artists. For one day at least, it was all smiles.

As time passed, ELP became more candid about the whole dreadful *In the Hot Seat* debacle. "I didn't really like the album very much in the end," Lake opined. "The sun has shone a little more for me in the past," Emerson commented with measured understatement.

"When you're in L.A., you're gonna get L.A.'d as I call it and you've had it really," Palmer would reflect. "You're running with the pack and the minute you're running with the pack and doing what everyone else does, you're fucked."

Notes

1   The problem was a compression of two nerves, The ulnar nerve at the elbow and the radial nerve at the back of the forearm. Both nerves had been pinched. Basically, this meant the impulses from the brain were impeded. This manifested itself as an unresponsiveness in the fourth and fifth fingers. This lead to both fingers curling up, thus making it impossible to use them. One expert from the Study of Tension in Performance suggested that Keith played with too much weight. In the Albert Hall video from 1992 one can see Keith exercising his fingers in-between songs. Keith tried all sorts of treatments to avoid surgery , including splints and anti-inflammatory drugs. He had the operation at Cedars Sinai Hospital, Los Angeles, on October 5, 1994. The aftermath of surgery created a lot of stress for Keith, and, as time went on it began to cast a shadow over his future as a musician.

2   Drummers are very prone to this because of high usage levels of the wrists, which puts strain on ligaments and tendons. It affects the nerve endings and diminishes the "feel" in the hands. NB. The aftermath of surgery created a lot of stress for Keith, and as time went on, it began to cast a shadow over his future as a musician.

3   Concert for Sarah December 17, 1994. Greg- guitars, Keith Wechsler – Drums, Rob la Vaque – Keyboards, Robbie Robinson – Bass, Guitarist – John Angard. They played: "From The Beginning," "Daddy", "Lucky Man", "I Believe In Father Christmas", "Heart on Ice". A video of the show was made and proceeds went to the Rescue Centre.

CHAPTER 14

Crossing The Rubicon

By early 1995 things looked very bleak for ELP. The uncertainty created by Emerson's recovering arm gave no hope for an immediate return to the stage. Tentative plans for a 25th anniversary tour were shelved.

Around this time Emerson made two big decisions. The first was to emigrate to Los Angeles. This relocation gave a clue as to where Emerson felt his future lay – the film capital of the world was the best place for soundtrack work. The second was to auction off some of his musical belongings. Both decisions were prompted by Emerson' recent divorce, which he admitted had "skinned" him. Some of the choice items for sale included Emerson's two Yamaha GX1's, and his blue and silver leather fishscale suit from the debut performance at the Isle of Wight. Other lots included the Clavinet used on "Tank" and memorabilia such as music books, rare videos and so on. All in all this would help in his fresh start over the water. However, the most symbolic item in the auction was Emerson's pair of Hitler Youth daggers, which he had acquired from Lemmy, one time roadie for The Nice. These had been used in the Hammond surfing section for many years. The triple whammy of bad blood during the making of *In the Hot Seat*, Emerson's arm operation and the auction led ELP fans to the logical conclusion that it was curtains for ELP.

Meanwhile, spring saw Emerson release an album that had been in the can for six years. *Changing States* had been produced by the "sickeningly talented" – to use Emerson's term – Kevin Gilbert. There were some interesting things on the record, including a new version of the "The Church". Encouraged by Gilbert to revisit this track with a high octane Hammond attack, Emerson produced a stunning, frenzied performance that ranks with classics such as "Knife Edge" and "Hoedown".

The album is also interesting because it casts new light on *Black Moon*. Some fans had been aware that "Another Frontier" and "Montagues and Capulets" had become "Changing States" and "Romeo and Juliet" respectively. Now another connection was discovered. "Ballade" was an earlier version of "Close to Home" with acoustic guitar. Considering that Lake had brought two tracks recorded prior to the album sessions, this helped establish that most of *Black Moon* had been written before ELP got back together.

Changing States is a fine album. Some good vocal tracks were included to increase the chance of getting a record deal, and there's the exciting bonus of a studio version of "Abbadon's Bolero" with the London Philharmonic Orchestra, taken from the *Works* period and remixed with Gilbert on tuba. According to Emerson the orchestra took over 50 takes to get it right!

In the meantime, Palmer had started a project with old buddy John Wetton. Adding Croatian guitarist Michael Calvin to the equation – the first "balls-to-the-wall" guitarist Palmer had ever worked with, he said – they called themselves K2. The new band recorded about a dozen cuts, reminiscent of The Police, Rush and ZZ Top. There was some record company interest, but it never got off the ground.

Lake had already started writing songs for a solo album. Asked about whether any famous guests would be on the album, he was reticent. "I'm beginning to think that there is also a value in a very personal thing," he said. "Not that I want to play everything myself. I think the concept of bringing in this person and that person and that all this makes a wonderful record, more often than not it doesn't. It's all about homogenous personalities." Referring to Gary Moore, he pointed out that the Irish guitarist only came to do one track and it was only when the chemistry was shown to be right that he was invited on board.

*****

By late summer 1995, ELP was in the process of changing record companies. As a result of Victory's demise the back catalogue was taken over by retro specialists Rhino Records. The press release gave hope: "The deal gives Rhino control of the masters for five years and includes..... live recordings, and unissued masters cut during the classic 1970–1980 period." One of the first projects to be announced was that all band members would have individual anthologies. This would give an opportunity to release some rare material. As a way of marking this union Rhino rushed out a rather pointless "Best Of".

Around this time, Castle Communications released the long awaited video of the 1970 Isle of Wight festival. ELP's segment is the last part of "Rondo" with the famous cannon firing sequence at the end of "The Great Gates of Kiev". Hitherto, hardly any photos of the performance had surfaced. ELP had almost been missed from the video footage altogether – the film crew had taken a break for the simple reason ELP were a new, untried act. It was only because ELP were going down so well that the camera crew started filming!

Meanwhile, September 9th saw the first ELP fan convention take place in Birmingham, England. One of the highlights was the premiere of an untitled piece of music that Palmer had recorded during the *Works* period (known by fans as "Crimzoid"), a pastiche of King Crimson's "21st Century Schizoid Man". While

173

none of the band could attend, they sent a personal video message to the Convention. To the delight of the congregated 400 or so fans, it proved that contrary to all rumours, Emerson, Lake and Palmer was still a going concern and coming to the end of a period of inactivity.

"There are some plans," Palmer explained, stressing that they were still at the drawing board stage. Sitting relaxed in a rugby shirt, Lake provided the confirmation that many had waited to hear: ELP were in the process of negotiating to make another studio album. Emerson was clearly still smarting from the *In Hot Seat* debacle. "In future we should stick to our guns and do our own thing, as we did in the seventies," he added.

Palmer also revealed that Rhino Records planned to put out his unreleased percussion concerto and Emerson's piano concerto on one CD (In fact, as we go to press some years later, although Rhino are now scheduling a release date for the percussion concerto, it will not be accompanied by Emerson's work). Palmer's major classical piece has taken on legendary status over the years. "Nobody has heard the Percusssion Concerto yet and it is lovely," Emerson commented. "The last movement is really haunting, really incredible."

Emerson also outlined other plans for a possible reunion of The Nice, and an ELP orchestral project for Sony. The centrepiece of this project would be "Tarkus", which would be made even more threatening. The Sony project was conceived as a "world music" concept with Brazilian bands and the Chieftains to be involved. The best news, however, was saved for last. The previous day nerve conduction tests on Emerson's arm showed no restriction. In fact, the doctors had told him they were the best results they had ever seen after such an operation.

A week after the convention, on September 16th, Keith Emerson appeared at Chicago's Gand Musitech. In front of 400 people he discussed his surgery, told anecdotes from his "forthcoming" autobiography and premiered a new piece of music. Early in the proceedings Emerson played "Eruption" from Tarkus, but with a twist – he handed out kazoos to facilitate noisy audience participation!

"I found it a bit daunting, to say the least!" Emerson confessed "....getting up talking about myself in front of 400 people for two hours, well , I thought I'd only be up there for 30 minutes, as I didn't think I'd have much to say." His original intention was that he would just talk. However when he sat down and thought of all the people coming to see him he felt it would be wrong not to play. The ice had been broken. Emerson was now back performing in public.

Emerson's talk included two funny incidents relating to Leonard Bernstein. Emerson had arranged for Bernstein to come to the studios in Paris where they were mixing "Pirates" and the Concerto for the *Works Vol 1* album. Emerson told the band to be on their best behaviour, but this obviously didn't cut any ice with Lake. As Bernstein entered the room, Lake was leaning back in a chair with his feet on the console. Smoking a joint, and clearly stoned, he greeted the great man, "How they hanging, Lenny?" Emerson, for his part, cringed, but Lake's goading got worse. The topic naturally got onto music with Bernstein confessing that he was worried about sounding like Beethoven. Quick as a flash, Lake told him, "I wouldn't worry about that Lenny, you'll never sound like Beethoven."

"Glorietta" was a new piece of music aired in Chicago. Dedicated to his mother, Emerson revealed it would be on his revamped *Christmas Album*. Clocking in at over nine minutes, with strongly contrasting sections in an A-B-A-B form, the classical sound of the "A" sections was somewhat reminiscent of his orchestral work with The Nice. And though the other parts of the piece have a very Celtic feeling, with a slight hint of "Abaddon's Bolero", the idea came to Emerson on a beach in Mexico.

Finally, Emerson revealed that he had got his Green Card and was now an American citizen. The last piece of the jigsaw was in place. It was now possible to envisage ELP back on the stage. Sure enough, to gulps of anticipation from the faithful, Emerson announced that ELP were planning to tour with Yes.

Strangely, the autobiography that Emerson was ostensibly pre-promoting has yet to see the light of day. Even back in 1996, it was almost two years since he had told Mike Kellie on *Nightwatch* that it was almost complete. "I never realised it would be such a complicated project," he confessed around this time. He was inspired to embark on the book by comments from friends he'd shown his diaries to, and was also able to call on the family scrapbooks that his mother Dorothy had religiously kept when fame first came calling. Dorothy Emerson likes most of her son's manuscript, it should be noted, but there are a few somewhat carnal episodes of which she does not approve. Emerson found the writing therapeutic. However, frustrated by publishers who suggested changes, he eventually passed the book to old pal Chris Welch, who began the massive task of editing. Perhaps in 2001?

Meanwhile, King Biscuit Flower Hour released a live recording of the Greg Lake Band from their November 5th 1981 London show. After the two studio albums, it gave the chance to assess just how good the band were on the boards. The album is split into three parts, ELP, King Crimson and his solo period. The choice of material is excellent, and the playing and the sound are nothing short of stunning. From the opening gambit, a guitar driven "Fanfare for the Common Man", to the closing notes of "Schizoid Man" guitarist Gary Moore and the rest of the band are extremely impressive. All in all, it's a welcome addition to the oeuvre.

December 1995 saw Emerson re-release his *Christmas Album*, as promised, in Chicago. In addition to the inclusion of "Glorietta", Emerson had added his version of Prokofiev's "Troika."

Meanwhile, Carl Palmer was also keeping busy. As well as the K2 project with Wetton there were also his drum clinics – he usually did about five of these a year.

An important one was at the Percussive Arts Society in London, October 1995, when the PAS presented Palmer with a certificate for his contribution to percussion. Even though using a relatively new kit he gave a virtuoso performance, in spite of an injury caused by catching his hand in a door. Palmer also had another project on the go with his friend Robert Berry. "We might do a little bit of recording together," he commented. "John Wetton might be involved with that too." Palmer also discussed the idea of touring with a jazz band playing instrumental jazz arrangements of ELP numbers.

A few months later, the planned ELP-Yes double-header tour fell through and instead it was announced that Emerson, Lake and Palmer would tour the States, as support act for Jethro Tull. This was an ideal way for Emerson to feel his way back. All in all 33 dates were announced. After the US dates, the band would do 10 shows in Japan where they would play a full set. Emerson's return to live work would thus take place at the Darien Centre in New York State on the 18th August.

In fact Emerson had been gigging at LA bars with Stuart Smith, formerly of The Sweet, in an occasional band called Aliens of Extraordinary Ability. "It was really just a bit of fun at the time!" Emerson explained. "And we popped up in the most unlikely clubs in L.A..... It was really like going back to the old days." As well as 50 dollars each there was the added bonus of free drinks!

The tour came about as the result of an invitation from Tull mainman Ian Anderson[1]. There was, however, something of the "walking wounded" about it. Apart from Emerson and Palmer's operations, Ian Anderson had also recently been in hospital. The Australian leg of Tull's tour was cancelled when he was taken seriously ill with a life-threatening blood clot in the leg. In spite of all the rumours of backbiting that was usually associated with main/support bands, relations on the tour were cordial. Emerson remarked how the two bands complemented each other and credited Tull's "cruel, but fair" road manager (Ian Anderson's wife), with the lack of friction. Tull's frontman reciprocated by stressing that "The ELPs were thoroughly nice people to work with." Anderson was impressed with ELP's professionalism and their "willingness to treat their fans with all decent respect," and it was his idea for them to play for an hour instead of the support act's usual 45 minutes. One evening Anderson jokingly remarked on stage, "It's great to be working with a band who still has all its own hair. Bastards!"

"The tour with Jethro Tull eliminated a lot of possible pressures that I anticipated after not having played on stage for such a long time," Emerson reflected afterwards. "And having gone through surgery,... It actually gave me the confidence to go to Japan."

Christmas saw ELP's music turn up in a rather unexpected location when UK comic Jim Davidson incorporated some of the band's songs into a risqué new version of the traditional pantomime *Dick Whittington*. The new show opened in Bristol on Friday 20th December and drew on most phases of Emerson's career. The opening piece was "The Score", while Davidson made his entrance to "Eruption" (he had chosen "Eruption/Stones of Years" in his top ten for a radio show, though he has said elsewhere that "Pirates" is his favourite ELP track.) "Captain Starship Christmas" even made a comeback in the panto. Emerson attended the opening night and was suitably impressed.

Early 1997 was dominated by Greg Lake activity. Using state of the art technology, Robert Fripp's company, Discipline Global Mobile, had mastered original King Crimson live material from 1969. The playback was at the Intercontinental Hotel, London, on the 15th March. The event was given an extra spice because it was the first time all five members of the 1969 band had been in the same room since they split. Resplendent in his bright red jacket, Lake turned up with his family and his new manager, former journalist Bruce Pilato. At the end of the playback the band all signed autographs. This was to be the only time the line-up would all be together. A repeat playback in New York saw Pete Sinfield cry off with illness.

1997 also saw Rhino Records finally get around to releasing the Greg Lake Anthology. It had been delayed for a year, but proved well worth the wait. The package as a whole is outstanding: from the title track of King Crimson's ground breaking debut album to 1994's "Heart On Ice" taken from *In the Hot Seat*. All of the ELP ballads are there, along with most of his first solo album, and there are a few rare gems too: Pete Sinfield solo material; "Take A Pebble" from ELP's 1972 Puerto Rico Mar Y Sol performance; and lost tracks from the abortive late '80s Ride The Tiger project also feature.

Shortly after the release of Lake's album, a new ELP tour was announced. The 50-date itinerary took in the US, Europe and Latin and Central America.

Emerson, always famous for his keyboard pyrotechnics, actually saw his own Hammond organ catch fire this time round, in Boston, USA. Lake and Palmer both looked on laughing as Emerson pulled it away from the rest of the equipment while a roadie gingerly sprayed it with a fire extinguisher (the ruined organ was donated to the Rock & Roll Hall of Fame & Museum). Another tour incident saw the band held hostage in Peru, when customs officials refused to allow them to leave the country as the Peruvian show promoter hadn't paid his tax bill. The band were held, effectively as an indemnity, in the hotel for two days without a word from The British Embassy. "You could disappear there, no problem," Lake commented ruefully after the Peru ordeal.

In the meantime, a controversial live CD surfaced. In early 1998 the band allowed a Polish promoter to release a *Live in Poland* CD recorded in 1997. The release was agreed as a strictly local limited edition and appeared to be sanctioned by the band to help the promoter recoup money he had lost on the gig. Suspiciously, the promoter "somehow" acquired an export licence and soon the CD was being sold all over the world, much to the chagrin of ELP, who had planned to issue the recording on Manticore at a later date. They were also concerned at the quality of some of the performances. An "official" live album followed in October 1998, double CD *Then & Now* on Eagle Records. The second CD was made up of 1997 performances far superior to the Polish show while disc one comprised the California Jam and a few tracks from the 1998 Deep Purple tour – the highlight of which was a storming version of "A Time and a Place".

In May 1998, Lake's manager announced on America On Line that Emerson, Lake and Palmer were working on a new album. This encouraging report was followed by a summer tour of the States and Canada with Deep Purple and Dream Theatre. Reports from the Deep Purple web site suggest that Purple fans were quite impressed with ELP. The greatest hits-dominated set included, for the first time since 1974, the whole of "Tarkus", as well as a new instrumental, "Crossing the Rubicon."

The train hit the buffers in late 1998. With a British tour already booked for the spring, promoter Jim Davidson had a shock when ELP failed to sign contracts. It appears that Davidson had run ahead of himself while the band were in turmoil over future plans. By December, ELP had split again.

Greg Lake was the first out of the blocks to issue a public statement, claiming that ELP had only made *Black Moon* because he had given ground on the producer issue. Now, however, he wanted the producer's chair back and blamed ELP's recent creative dearth on his absence from the role. Emerson and Palmer flatly refused.

A week later Emerson and Palmer issued their reply. Basically, they argued that it had been known for some time that the producer role was going to be a bone of contention. Therefore, it would have been prudent to compromise. Emerson and Palmer only based this request on the values of input equalling output. For example, they revealed that Lake had not presented any tangible new material for band audition – they knew he had material, as he had been writing a solo album for a couple of years.

Lake felt he had to be at the production helm to save ELP from creative and commercial oblivion. However, the *In The Hot Seat* debacle had already proved that a producer had little power against a recalcitrant record label like Victory Records who just wanted a commercial album.

Emerson and Palmer's stand was supported by the band's management, but it was a sad way to end.

*****

This super-talented company of musicians will return one day: that much is certain. The prospect of an ELP reunion may look bleak as the year 2000 finally bleeds over into a new millennium, but then, things have looked bleak for ELP on more occasions than anyone would like to remember! Emerson, Lake and Palmer have warred and quarrelled and split and reformed and split again throughout their career – as Chris Welch suggests in his excellent Foreword to this book, that is an essential factor in the rare nature of their creativity.

Thirty years since they first convened to break new ground by bringing rock and classical music together in a virtuoso three piece, rumours of a reunion tour persist; judging by their track record in this regard, as time passes, and the wounds of the last traumatic split heal, the odds are getting stronger by the day. The most recent evidence for this came in September of 2000. Carl Palmer, touring the United States on a drum clinic tour, was consistently – if unsurprisingly – asked when ELP would get back together. His upbeat answer to that question gave all ELP fans hope.

And as musical creative forces, they continue to thrive! Keith Emerson, Greg Lake and Carl Palmer continue to work on solo projects which have ELP stalwarts drooling in anticipation.

Keith Emerson has been recording with Rick Wakeman. The precise status of their plans is uncertain, but a "huge production" concert tour – of the US and Europe – has been envisaged, with a twenty-piece orchestra. Studio and live albums, video and DVD will be part of this mouthwatering package. Keith's and Rick's sons will be involved.

Also, Rhino Records have said there will be an Emerson Anthology including rare and unreleased material. This may well be concurrent with the publication of his long-promised autobiography *Pictures of an Exhibitionist*. Again, the exact form in which these things will appear is as yet unknown. Emerson also plans to record a solo piano album – well, it's been on the cards ever since 1972.

Another (slightly less) longstanding project that sounds as if it would be his personal dream come true at last, is that he's working on an orchestrated repertoire to perform as a guest with a variety of prominent orchestras in Europe and the USA. Emerson has also recorded a live album with Glenn Hughes and Marc Bonilla – he is really pleased with their version of "Tarkus" and has said the band really cooks. And of course speculations continue as to the possible re-formation of his pre-ELP band The Nice.

Greg Lake is completing a solo album with *Black Moon* producer Mark Mancina. He has also produced and contributed to an album by the British comedian Jim Davidson, which includes Jim's take on Lake's classic "Watching Over You" – Davidson has already been seen singing "Watching Over You" on British TV's *The Generation Game*, which he hosts. Greg's second solo album *Manoeuvres* will be released on CD for the first time – and not before time, either, it's an unjustly neglected album. Lake also featured as a guest star in the British TV special "Top Ten Greatest Christmas Songs". Lake discussed the writing and production of the song. The show also included excerpts from the original video and a short clip of ELP performing the song in 1993.

Meanwhile, Palmer has been collaborating with a number of musicians, including old sparring partner John Wetton. In the summer of 1999 an Asia re-union featuring Palmer, John Wetton and Geoff Downes had been aborted due to a dispute over rights to the name. Ex-member John Payne, leader of the most recent incarnation of Asia, by now owned the name and took umbrage at its unauthorised appropriation by the leading lights of the original band. Palmer and Wetton subsequently formed a new band Qango (sic). Publicity posters for their initial shows in London and the Midlands slated for November '99 promised ELP and Asia material would feature alongside new songs. Sadly, both dates were cancelled when Wetton fractured a wrist. The rescheduled shows took place in February 2000. Keith Emerson even guested on "Fanfare" at the London Astoria show, apparently surprising the band as much as the audience. In fact Emerson only got to hear of the occasion at the last minute (from Liv Whetmore of the *Impressions* ELP magazine), and roared up on his motorbike to get in on it for himself!

Qango played more dates in May, yielding a live CD *Live at the Hood*, recorded at the Robin Hood, Brierley Hill in the West Midlands and The Brook in Southampton.

Carl Palmer also has a Rhino anthology slated. It will include his Percussion Concerto – since 1977 a major cause for speculation. He has just formed a new band – titled simply "Palmer"! – featuring Shaun Baxter on guitar and Dave Marks on bass. Palmer plays ELP instrumentals, but with no keyboards! Baxter and Marks are acclaimed London musicians who have worked in music education at various universities.

Rhino Records' programme of re-releases of Emerson, Lake and Palmer albums commences in October 2000 with a *Very Best of ELP*, and the rest of the albums follow.

*****

This is the end of the book. It's not the end of the show. You can listen to the music, you can watch the videos, you can play from the music books, you can let in the unique musical energy of ELP. And more than that! – Emerson, Lake and Palmer have astonished us with all their creative energy over thirty years, so let's give them back our appreciation. Let's say to Keith, Greg and Carl, "Thank you for everything. And if you've got more music, whatever the form it takes, we want to hear it. Because even in the face of difficulties, you've always produced music worth hearing, music that bears listening to time and again. Play it live, and we'll support you steadfastly. We'll come and see the show – the show that never ends."

Notes

1 Coincidentally, Keith had recorded "Living in the Past" on the Jethro Tull tribute album.

Musical Analysis

George Forrester

Due to the complex nature of ELP's music, much of it demands a deeper level of technical study than is possible in the context of a musical biography. For this reason, this appendix comprises a more detailed analysis of some of ELP's most challenging and musically interesting pieces.

Thanks also to Blair Pethel for his permission to use his doctoral thesis in discussion of the Piano Concerto, and other pieces.

Emerson, Lake & Palmer

"The Barbarian"

"The Barbarian" set a high standard for the band's classical rock workouts. ELP demonstrate their barbaric power with an increasingly virtuosic endurance test, while sticking close to the notes if not the manner of Bartók's music. It is arranged in three parts: the outer parts for a heavy rock line-up, and the central section for piano trio. The tonal centre is F sharp, with a combination of Phrygian, Dorian, Lydian and non-diatonic modes. Three thematic ideas are freely developed and fragmented.

Greg's ferocious speaker-shaking fuzz bass line, based on the melodic contours of the piece, opens the 16-bar introduction. "The bass part is very difficult to play, because it doesn't stay on the same chord for long," he commented. The intro continues with 8 bars during which Keith enters with a similar organ melody line played over a tritone (diminished fifth). This introduction is four times the length of Bartók's plain four-and-a-half bar intro on the F sharp minor chord which is the piece's tonal centre.

Bars 5-100 are played with little fundamental alteration by organ/ bass/ electric guitar/ drums, with drums and fuzz electric guitar strongly featured. The thematic ideas begin at bars 5, 34 and 58 . Bars 58-100 are written in a call-and-response style, with alternating segments of a few bars each. In ELP's version, the organ alternates with drums/guitar/bass, and the last segment, which is a diminuendo into the middle part, is simply replaced by an almighty low F sharp on fuzz guitar, decaying away as the brushed drums fade in for the central section.

In the acoustic section Carl plays rapid sixteenth-note brushed drums in a constant rhythm (the original has regular brief decelerations). Apart from the addition of the drums and bass guitar, this section is pretty much the same as the original from 101 to 213 (12 bars before the end), except for the omission of a five-bar phrase (175-179), and the extension of 156-174.

Carl ceases the brushwork at 174, returning to full kit. As Keith rushes up the piano in octaves Carl brings the second part to a dramatic close with a massive crash on the gong on the first beat of 213.

The final section returns to the opening idea, with an extended coda giving Carl in particular a chance to demonstrate his skills. There is fuzz guitar as in the first part; indeed this whole part is similar to the first, only much heavier and busier. Bars 5-34 are repeated almost the same as before, then there is a 40-bar section more loosely based on the music. After this it's back to the five-beat motive (5-9) which opens the first 14-bar theme. This is repeated over and over for 48 bars by the organ and bass as Carl plays up a thunderous storm. "Barbarian" ends with three tritone chords (F sharp/C), whereas Bartók uses just two F sharp minor chords.

"Take a Pebble"

The opening strummed chords are played by Emerson on the piano strings, followed by a three-verse instrumental section in which the tune is cheerfully elaborated upon.

In his solo, with background effects of drops of water and gleeful handclapping and shouting, Greg plays pastoral acoustic guitar. This deceptively simple meditation involves the retuning of the 3rd and 6th strings of the guitar, enabling much of the solo to be played on open strings. It remains firmly anchored to a D chord throughout its 74 bars, with an occasional "blue" flattened third thrown in. In contrast to the complexity of the piano solo, the pleasure here comes from impressions of mood swings, and even of the skimming stone, conjured by the ever-changing intonation and dynamics.

In live performance this was the cue for a Greg Lake solo including a song, the complete lyrics of which went, "I had a dog and his name was Blue / Bet you five dollars he's a good dog too". As Greg concludes with the same six notes with which he began, Keith opens the lengthy improvisatory piano solo section with an ostinato left-hand accompaniment based on material from the open strings of the guitar and expanded from the very opening chords.

Bars 223-233 are a quotation (minus a few ornaments) of part of Bach's "2-Part Invention no. 1", in C major. The solo continues in an ever more varied manner until, followed by a grand pause, the song returns, announced dramatically by timpani, for a final vocal verse.

Carl demonstrates restrained good taste whenever he plays. In the first part he just plays cymbals, and towards the end he uses pure jazz phrasing.

"Knife Edge"

This is not an arrangement as such of the Janácek *Sinfonietta*'s first movement. The main *Sinfonietta* theme is not quite the same as that famous ELP riff. Janácek writes for several overlapping brass parts, giving an impression of a complete melodic theme. Emerson distils these parts into a 6-bar riff which never precisely occurs in the course of the original. The tonal centre is altered to D major.

The pattern of the song is straightforward. At certain points non-Janácek material is introduced. The instrumental passages following each verse have new organ material derived from the theme. At 1'50", after the instrumental passage following verse 2, the organ part is similar to parts of bars 34-58 of Janácek's work, but the melody of the vocal line based on rising broken chords is not found in the score.

Before the last verse, the instrumental section featuring Emerson is in two parts: first, an improvisatory solo over the main riff; then a Bach quotation on churchy Hammond. Carl plays an almost Latin type rhythm on the cowbell. One would think this would clash with the main theme but on the contrary, it in fact enhances it. Of the Bach section Greg adds: "The church organ sound was very difficult to get. We had to take out the bottom to make it reedy, and I tried to make the bass guitar sound like a bass pedal on an organ."

"The Three Fates"

Clotho is for solo organ. An impressive piece, of great contrasts, it makes the fullest possible use of the organ of the Royal Festival Hall on London's South Bank.

Lachesis is an entertaining free fantasia for solo piano, though Emerson gives it a vaguely rondo-ish structure: intro, section A, transition, section B, section A1, transition, section C, coda. He has done little of this kind of thing in his post-Nice career, and it would be nice to hear more. It is one of the first ELP pieces to show Emerson's preference for the interval of a fourth (as well as the related interval of a fifth), used both harmonically and melodically. Its theme is restated three times in succession (bars 5-10), on a series of roots related by minor thirds (G, B flat, D flat). This is a fairly frequent device in Emerson's music. A comparable passage occurs in bars 57-64, with different harmonisation of roughly the same material, a common variation technique. This same passage has an example of melodic variation, the original statement of the idea in 5-9 being syncopated and rhythmic, while this version is smooth and flowing. The tonality is changing most of the time. *Lachesis* also uses a whole-tone scale in parts, something not found much elsewhere in Emerson's music.

After an organ link, *Atropos* brings in the rest of the band for a relentless bash which becomes ever more desperate until suddenly extinguished. Featuring a typical heavy ostinato by Keith, its fatalistic frenzy anticipates "Infinite Space" on the next album, *Tarkus*.

"Tank"

Carl's solo feature is framed by a jazzy group piece, with Keith leading on clavinet. A call-and response section between keyboard and drums leads to the famous solo.

"Lucky Man"

The song has a simple and powerful chord structure. What made the song go down in rock history, however, was the Moog solo added at the end by Keith Emerson.

Tarkus

"TARKUS"

As mentioned elsewhere, Keith Emerson had heard the First Piano Concerto by Alberto Ginastera while still with The Nice and continued to be fascinated by the extreme percussive effects achieved by the piano. "I wanted to be able to get that kind of sound from the instruments I was using, and "Tarkus" was the result. I had also always wanted to write atonally, although I wasn't sure what that was, and that album allowed me the freedom to explore some things I had never really done before: percussive keyboard sounds, strong rhythm, atonality."

"Eruption" (Emerson)

The first five bars consist of an ominous "choral" crescendo chord. The notes of this chord (F-G-B flat-A flat-C-D) are not arbitrary, but relate to quite a bit of what follows. From bar 6 there is an incredibly powerful left-hand keyboard ostinato in 5/4 time (although they referred to is as 10/8 because of where the accents fall), based on perfect fourths, and a little later another figure – a theme – enters in the right hand. The sound is very heavy indeed, partly because of the rich sound of the Hammond, partly because of the overdubbing of the keyboard bass lines.

We're never quite sure of the metre – in fact it changes no less than 29 times in the printed score! At various times it passes through 4/4, 5/4, 3/4, 2/4, 7/8 and 6/8. From what Emerson said at the time it seems often he and the band weren't too clear about what time they were in either: "I think we can reproduce the sound on stage. Parts of it have no relative key and there are different time signatures in every bar. In the end, we had to ignore time and key. We had a discussion in the studio which lasted an hour, whether a bar was in four or not. In the end we had to abandon time signatures and just go by the feel. The piece has a logical beginning and end. It was planned out on paper and we had various songs for the different sections.

There is quite a lot of arrangement and not an awful lot of improvisation."

Comparing the score and the recording, it's obvious that there are points where the tempo could have been written differently or where it was unnecessary to change. Further clouding the issue of metre is the frequent syncopation. The key is basically F minor until about halfway through, when quite a lot of modulation and shifting sideways start happening.

In spite of sounding like a very free fantasia-like piece, "Eruption" is quite highly unified. The opening chord is influential in several places, while the 5/4 ostinato is mainly significant in the rhythmic development of the piece. There's also a lot of interest created by parallel lines, block chords, syncopation, unisons, long held chords, odd dissonances, cross-rhythms, unusual runs of notes – and that's without mentioning the weird sound of it all..

"Stones Of Years" (Emerson/Lake)

"Eruption" merges neatly into the first song. It stands in clear contrast to the instrumental "overture", being very straightforward in time (4/4), form (blues-rock) and key (C minor). The Hammond solo reaches a climax at the same point as Carl's drums – an impressive effect.

"Iconoclast" (Emerson)

A typically perverse, jagged descending Hammond run (rather Thelonious Monk-like too) makes a very appropriate opening for a piece called "Iconoclast".

The "Eruption" ostinato returns, now in 5/8. Only four tempo changes in this piece, though! The disturbing interval of an augmented fourth separates the parallel left and right hands here (as compared with a perfect fourth in "Eruption'): "Iconoclast" is a harsher, more brutal variation on the opening piece. There are traces in the bass-line of the first chord of "Eruption".

"Mass" (Emerson/Lake)

The shape of the melody bears a close relationship to some phrases found in "Eruption", and of course it's got those perfect fourths in it which are such a favourite of Keith's. After a metallic synth intro, there's an astonishing, percussive, biting Hammond solo – like a breathing machine – with frenzied drums and wailing double-tracked guitar entering before the end.

"Manticore" (Emerson)

A new, triple-time (9/8), ostinato idea, not far in spirit from "Eruption" and "Iconoclast", is the basis of this musically more straightforward instrumental section. It's fast and furious, with some unexpected twists, turns and false endings before the final stabbing repeated chords usher in the last song.

"Battlefield" (Lake)

Portentous chords, mostly based on major 7ths, introduce the song. Greg has an all-too-infrequent chance to shine superbly on electric guitar, here double-tracked. Keith largely fills on organ, while Carl creates a complex, staccato rhythmic counterpoint to Greg's long sustained notes. The "Aquatarkus" theme is briefly foreshadowed before the final verse.

"Aquatarkus" (Emerson)

The MiniMoog's three oscillators are tuned to sound a suspended chord, and the whole piece is founded on a very simple ostinato, giving wide scope for building to an increasingly embellished frenzy, which finally fades, leaving nothing but Carl's martial drumming. Now there's a return full circle to a repeat of the middle passage of "Eruption", and "Tarkus" concludes with fifteen crashing repeated chords and a triumphant fanfare based on the "Aquatarkus" theme.

"Jeremy Bender" (Emerson/Lake) and "Are You Ready Eddy?" (Emerson/Lake/Palmer)

The two "fun" tracks on the album – they don't fit in with the concept, but who cares? Just as "Jeremy Bender " is light relief after" Tarkus", so is "Are You Ready Eddy?". Keith does a touch of the Floyd Cramers in "Jeremy Bender", playing in the country style of Cramer's hit "On The Rebound". There's a trio of songs which belong together in ELP's output: "Jeremy Bender", "The Sheriff" (from *Trilogy*) and "Benny The Bouncer" (from *Brain Salad Surgery*), and this is recognised in ELP's first songbook, in which they are grouped together at the end. They all tell jokey stories, and all feature the piano, with "The Sheriff" and "Benny The Bouncer" ending with honky-tonk and boogie workouts.

Some thought the 50s rock 'n' roll – inspired "Are You Ready Eddy?" was a waste of space, but the fact is that over the years ELP have done all too few looser things like that, and one wishes now that they'd done more. Keith throws in a lot of show-tune references and everyone has a ball.

"Bitches Crystal" (Emerson/Lake)

This and the other three tracks are well in keeping with the mood of "Tarkus". We're back in the nightmare world of "Knife-Edge" and "Mass" in "Bitches Crystal" and "A Time And A Place", while "The Only Way" continues the theme of religious hypocrisy. There is some great piano work in "Bitches Crystal" – is that a substantial Thelonious Monk quote in the solo? The bass pattern of the heavy riff is all based on those fourths which are so important in "Tarkus" and throughout Emerson's work.

"The Only Way" (Hymn) (Emerson/Lake) and "Infinite Space" (Conclusion) (Emerson/Palmer)

The accompaniment to Lake's vocals is at first performed by Keith on the organ of St Mark's Church, Finchley (previously used on "The Three Fates" on the first album). The instrumental introduction is from Bach's Toccata in F major.

There is a move from organ to (studio) piano at the bridge section between the two parts of "The Only Way". The bridge itself is the opening of the Prelude from Bach's Sixth Prelude and Fugue (from the Forty-Eight).[1]

The left-hand riff of "Infinite Space" keeps going almost all the time, and when there is a break, there's a terrifying inevitability about the riff's return. Emerson and Palmer succeed in conveying a sense of despair at the awfulness of being condemned to go on for ever.

"Writing with Carl has been quite an inspiration to me," commented Keith, "because he can affect the piece quite a lot with his rhythmic ideas. When we wrote that piece "Infinite Space", on *Tarkus*, Carl was standing over the piano and hinted that one particular phrase would sound good played on the off beat. I tried it but it was difficult at first because I was playing 7/4 with my left hand, and he wanted me to play off the beat with my right hand. Anyway, he said try it, and this was in the recording studio and meanwhile Greg was mixing a track. I mean, we were writing that quickly. So I practised it and he said it sounded good, and we got a communication going and it was quite a knockout."

"A Time And A Place" (Emerson/Lake/Palmer)

Maybe life on the road was something to do with the inspiration for "Infinite Space"?[2] This might well be the case with Greg's lyrics for "A Time And A Place", another song very much in keeping with the general mood of the album:

"Save me from this shallow land...

Rest in a shade, No sound is made, Where silence is played."

Musically, *Tarkus* was the first work which clearly demonstrated Emerson's growing fondness for both harmonies and melodic ideas based on fourths. He continues to use ostinato patterns, unusual rhythms and classical ideas. After initial uncertainty Keith, Greg and Carl are by now playing as a tight, assured unit with confidence in their common musical direction.

Notes

1 Years later, in 1988 on the *Christmas Album*, Emerson used the same quote from Prelude 6 in "We Three Kings".

2 Well, it's possible. "Still...You Turn Me On" on *Brain Salad Surgery* is definitely on this theme.

Pictures At An Exhibition

"Promenade" (Mussorgsky)

Keith's solo Hammond version of the recurring piece – which represents the composer's perambulations through the gallery and past the respective pictures – opens the ELP version of "Pictures" in suitably grand fashion. By any standards this is an impressive rendition. In the earlier live performances Emerson divided left and right hand parts between two separate organs, largely for visual effect, one suspects, but certainly in part because the percussive effect obtainable from two separate organs is greater than with two keyboards on the same organ.

"The Gnome" (Mussorgsky/Palmer)

Carl kick starts "The Gnome" with a powerful drumroll. This is probably the most creatively arranged part of the ELP "Pictures", though they adhere closely to the original score, except for the very different instrumentation. Organ and snare drum often play beat-for-beat together, with the bass almost always reinforcing this, so there's a very powerful sound indeed. (There is a return to this unison technique in the second half of "Pictures", when "Promenade" and "The Hut Of Baba Yaga" raise the roof.)

Greg adds some witty wah-wah bass interjections which add to the comical side of the piece. Emerson adds an extra section at the point marked *Poco meno mosso pesante* in the score – a synthesizer lead with a Russian feel based on a scale that has a clear modal influence. What follows is very faithful to the composer's direction, but recombines and repeats phrases and sections with altered tempi and rhythms. Then there is a wild burst of sound, which progressively dies away before the beginning of the last section. The synthesised sounds here disperse into white noise, and then a pianissimo roll on a small cymbal accompanied by the bass guitar, with strummed damped strings producing an ominous effect like the thunder which precedes a storm.

The final *Poco a poco accelerando* section pulls a masterstroke: the left-hand trill originally assigned to the piano is played on the synthesizer, which is eerily tuned to sound like a pitched wind machine. Emerson plays only the right-hand part of the notoriously hard last five bars – which solves the problem nicely![1]

"Promenade" (Mussorgsky/Lake)

The second "Promenade" follows immediately. Apart from Lake's added lyrics it is very similar to Mussorgsky's. The differences are that Emerson repeats the first two bars using a rising scale accompaniment to the theme, and alters the chordal accompaniment to Greg's vocal line sometimes. Greg sings unaccompanied where Mussorgsky wrote a solo line, and is backed by Keith where the composer wrote chords. The words of the song are in the same spirit as those of "The Sage", and serve as a prelude to it.

"The Sage" (Lake)

Says Keith: "Greg had the idea of the minstrel singing underneath the castle". Greg has never repeated the experiment of "The Sage", which is far and away the hardest acoustic piece he's ever performed. It could so easily be played as a simple (and beautiful) folk song, were it not for the guitar solo, which is full of classical technique. It is constantly surprising in its changes of harmonies and rhythms – never complicated for the sake of it, just enough to convey the shifts of feeling expressed in the lyrics.

A short instrumental section played by Keith introduces the song. It can't be coincidence that the 4-bar theme (repeated once, a semitone lower) has its contour and intervals very much in common with those of the first couple of lines of the song. Keith's introduction is noisy, bright and jazzy, with a powerful synthesizer lead line in dynamic contrast to the gently reflective and even nostalgic mood of the song, whose atmosphere brings to mind "Take A Pebble".

The verses are in A minor; the solo passes through E major, its relative minor (C sharp minor) and E minor, by way of some lovely modulations and eventually some rather sad descending chords, before returning to A minor for the final verse. The solo requires a variety of techniques, and there are several obviously tricky passages. Lake was all too conscious of needing to play at his limits, and sometimes mentioned the difficulty of the solo in the middle of the performance (the filmed concert being one such occasion). In the version on the record it comes off very nearly perfectly – an absolute delight. Indeed, one gets the impression that all three members were really playing on the edge in those days, partly in competition with each other, and it would be great to hear real risks taken by all three of them on the writing front again.

"The Old Castle" (Mussorgsky/Emerson)

After a bit of Emerson showmanship, mainly in demonstration of the whoops and whistles obtainable with the Moog ribbon controller device, comes the piece entitled "The Old Castle" – basically a brilliantly fast and complex synthesizer solo with a swung rock rhythm backing from bass and drums. It hasn't got much to do with the original piece, however, and we have to wait for the opening of "Blues Variation" to hear more than a passing reference to that. Mussorgsky's piece is in a slow 6/8 – and another composition altogether!

"Blues Variation" (Emerson/Lake/Palmer)

'The Old Castle" is taken as a starting-point for a blues–jazz-rock fantasia for organ trio. This is a nice bit of ensemble work; their approach to "Nutrocker" is

189

comparable with it, especially in the use of the theme of the great jazz pianist/composer Bill Evans' "Interplay", which is substantially quoted, from nearly two minutes into the piece, as a contrasting middle section. "Interplay" is an unusual blues, based on the scalar approach which Evans loved – in this case the key-scale of F minor. Although the quotation lasts only about thirty seconds, it's very important to the balance of "Blues Variation".

The jazz-feel of Evans' original is retained, with Greg providing a lively bass line counterpoint to the organ theme, while Carl's swinging cymbal work is constant in the background.

"Promenade" (Mussorgsky)

The first piece on the second side of the original LP, this version of "Promenade" is played by the whole band. Organ, drums and bass play tightly together as if in preparation for the last push to the end.

"The Hut Of Baba Yaga" (Mussorgsky)
including "The Curse Of Baba Yaga" (Emerson/Lake/Palmer)

Carl Palmer's drumming is in large part responsible for driving along the second half of ELP's "Pictures". He propels "The Hut...", which is in strict time and keeps close to the original, by upping the pace to a frenzy with a subtle strategy of rhythmic confusion – is it in 2/4 (the tempo of the opening of the original piece), 4/4 or 12/8? The uncertainty, and the excitement, are increased by the bubbling, progressively accelerating drumming. When the brief main "theme" of the piece comes in at bar 33, Palmer reverts to strict tempo – a striking effect. The band takes Mussorgsky's piece at a rattling speed. At the "Andante mosso" Greg plays the bass melody through a "wah-wah" pedal – great music for a low budget horror flick!

This section is abbreviated, and segues immediately into "The Curse...". The new picture is the rawest, loosest and simplest of the lot, with everyone rocking out. Greg's wild lyrics are mostly impossible to decipher, but it sounds like we're back in "Knife- Edge" and "Bitches Crystal" territory. After a short introduction there's a new idea on organ which could be vaguely related to the riff from "The Gnome". Maybe there's also an echo of the descending chords which follow the opening ascending sequence of "The Hut". Carl's really having a workout as the band rushes to the final picture.

Mekong Delta (see "The Gnome", above) also took their cue from ELP when they recorded their own – utterly superb – version of "The Hut..." on the album *Mekong Delta* (also on AAARRG RECORDS, AAARRG 4). Definitely competition for the original!

"The Great Gates Of Kiev" (Mussorgky/Lake)

The structure of the piece needs to be tailored to the verses of Greg's song, but otherwise the band again stay close to the original.

Once or twice the chords are changed, but it's hardly noticeable – and the "choral" part is played at a different pitch. At the return of the (disguised) "Promenade" theme the band builds a massive crescendo to the end, Greg concluding the stirring lyrics of victory and aspiration to new life with what must be the perfect phrase to end the ELP "Pictures At An Exhibition': "Death is life". It also sums up much of what the band is all about: Emerson, Lake and Palmer were always an intense band, communicating extremes of experience on all fronts, in a way that no other band ever did, and those three words seem to take all that has gone before and roll it up into one final climactic blast.

"Nutrocker" (Tchaikovsky, adapted by Kim Fowley, arr. by ELP)

It's appropriate that a piece based on a work by another tragic Russian composer should be used for the encore. (A few years earlier, Keith Emerson had adapted the third movement *Allegro* of Tchaikovsky's Sixth Symphony, the "Pathetique", for The Nice.)

Kim Fowley (b.1942) was multi-talented and – in his own estimation – "a motherfucker". He produced/wrote a number of West Coast novelty hits in the early Sixties, including B. Bumble and the Stingers' "Nutrocker". This got to Number One in Britain in April 1962, remaining on the chart for fifteen weeks. Re-released in 1972, six months after Emerson, Lake and Palmer had made it famous again, it got to Number 19, staying in the Top 75 for eleven weeks.

Fowley used the March from Tchaikovsky's music for the ballet "The Nutcracker" as the basis of "Nutrocker". To have been inspired to create "Nutrocker" from the original March is amazing: the two couldn't be more different.

Tchaikovsky wrote the music to accompany a scene in the ballet where the children march playfully around the Christmas tree. A miniature fanfare on clarinets and brass is answered by a skipping dotted-note string phrase with a scale counterpoint, and ingenious variations of this make up the first section. The tiny middle section consists of pattering semiquavers on flutes and violins. The opening music returns with constantly changing accompaniment and orchestration.

In Fowley's piece, the middle section is not used, note values are altered, and pounding repeated notes and a rock and roll turnaround phrase are added. ELP's version is lighter and jazzier than Fowley's, but it never strays far from its overall structure.

Notes

1   By the time of *In Concert* he was playing both hands of this phrase.

Trilogy

"The Endless Enigma"

Although the two parts of "The Endless Enigma" are connected by a Fugue (in fact a Prelude and Fugue), the song and the piano piece have little if anything in common. While the instrumental parts of the song itself are impressive in themselves, there's no strong sense of an underlying structure. But there are in fact some unifying factors, and many aspects of the song are rewarding in themselves

The introduction, which sounds as if it could be used in a horror movie, has Carl opening with a "heartbeat" effect on the bass drum – while Keith plays some heart-stopping piano. At the entry of the bass guitar, Keith plays a couple of bars on an Arabian wind instrument called a Zoukra. Apparently it required a lot of lung power! Many years later he used it in the soundtrack of *Best Revenge*.

The driving Hammond triplet theme which begins about two minutes into Part 1 is inspired by the song's melody. In Part 2, there is a lovely overdubbed passage in which tubular bells, organ, bass and two related fanfaring synthesiser voices enter one after another, building to a grand crescendo introducing the final verse. The contour and harmony of the repeated descending figure here are more clearly derived from the melody and harmony of the song's tune.

The first part of "The Endless Enigma" ends on an F sharp chord, and the solo piano section begins with a free introduction with no tonal centre which ends on a dramatic diminished fifth progression – a C sharp major arpeggio going to an ominous G minor chord. The sweetness of the prelude comes as a surprise after this. Its melodic basis is the fugue's subject – which contains no less than eight of Emerson's favoured perfect fourths in its four-bar statement. While the fugue is angular and jagged, the prelude is smooth and flowing because those fourths are in a clear tonal setting (C major), with a sparse scalar accompaniment in the left hand, and its beauty lies in the contrast between the flowing line and the pleasingly abrupt, shifting harmonies.

The Fugue is written for three voices, two played by piano and one by bass guitar. It makes extreme demands of both the pianist and the bassist. Greg balked at the idea of playing it live, although he did relent in the end.

Exposition: From a dominant G chord followed by a short pause, the Fugue takes off at high speed. The subject is stated by the piano in the soprano voice (upbeat of bar 41 to downbeat of bar 46, played by the right hand). As this opening statement ends, the subject is taken up in the alto a fifth below (at bar 45), while the soprano continues with a counterpoint including parts of the subject. There is a three-bar chromatic interlude leading to a false (incomplete) entrance of the subject in the soprano (bar 50).

This is closely followed by the third full entrance of the subject. The third entry is traditionally the same as the first, at a higher or lower octave – but Emerson does not keep to this rule. The first half (doubled in the alto) is stated in the bass by the bass guitar, which enters at bar 51 and continues playing to the end of the fugue, and the statement is transferred to the soprano, where it is completed. A false entrance in the soprano in bars 55-6 brings the exposition to an end.

Development: This section is based on figures taken from the subject. There's a period of tonal instability until bar 67-8, where a dominant pedal (B) in bass and alto prepares E major in bar 69. The complete subject (with modified intervals) is stated from 69 to 72, followed by a false entrance from 75–6. From 74 to 84 the tonality is again unstable. The final complete statement of the subject, in the alto voice, is heard from the upbeat of 82 to the downbeat of 85.

Coda: A dominant (G) pedal from bar 85 prepares C major in bar 89, as the coda returns to the prelude's style. The coda begins with a false entry of the subject over the start of five bars of a pedal C, and the piece concludes with a long melodic line over a simple accompaniment.

Finally...the last chord of "The Endless Enigma, Part 1" is F sharp and the last chord of the Fugue is C; the interval between the notes F sharp and C is very prominent indeed in bars 32 and 33 of Part 1 and also in bars 63-6 (just before the end) of Part 2.

"Hoedown"

Keith Emerson's arrangement takes as many liberties with the original as one would expect – but then Copland himself delighted in altering old folk material, especially rhythmically, to suit his purposes. To transfer the varied colourings and textures of the original to keyboards, bass and drums would be impossible, and although Emerson reproduces some of Copland's orchestrational subtleties, in effect he rewrites and edits it to make it into a storming rock instrumental. In the process he greatly simplifies the rhythms in particular, and leaves out music which, though vital to the contrasting moods of the original, would dissipate the excitement of the rocked-up version.

Emerson deviates from the original from the word go, adding at the beginning ten portamento "whoops" on the synthesiser – a nice touch, in keeping with the raucous atmosphere of a heavy rock hoedown! The music proper begins after a couple of these. Emerson omits the first four bars. At this point the original music mimics a square-dance band tuning up. But there's obviously no reason to attempt imitating this for a rock band. Similarly, the wildly syncopated first part of Copland's main hoedown tune acquires a driving, straight-ahead rock rhythm.

Emerson deletes a quieter 24-bar transitional section with a prominent piano part: important in conjuring up the frequent sudden changes of tempo in square dance, here it would just slow the pace. Instead, Emerson cuts to the first part of the main tune (bars 39–46), giving the melody to the organ, while bass guitar and drums add occasional punctuation. He repeats it (Copland doesn't) with full rhythm section. The complicated rhythm of the tune's first bar is simplified; this remains the case throughout. The second half of the theme (from bar 47) is effectively rearranged from the original, bass guitar and drums punctuating in fifths while the organ plays the melody. The first part of the melody is then repeated. Emerson reflects the thinned-out, softer original passage which follows with a corresponding change of instrumentation. Copland has the melody in the low violins and violas with punctuation in the lower strings and horns; Emerson puts it in a lower octave on the organ, with organ pedal, tom-tom and bass guitar punctuating.

Here, both Copland and Emerson go from soft to extremely loud. Emerson puts the melody in octaves on the organ and gives the cellos' part to bass guitar, achieving the same shock effect as the original. There is a brief melodic episode for oboe and clarinets in bars 105–13 of the original. Emerson uses a reedy organ setting here, the only occasion when there's a change in the organ tone.

Copland repeats the whole of the contrasting episode in 97–113; Emerson goes straight to bar 122, and follows Copland till 138.

Copland's original in bars 138–41 is full of wild rhythms and accents. Again, this isn't the effect sought for the rock version, so they are left out. The portamento sound from the opening of Emerson's version returns, and a section comparable with the transitional part near the beginning – also with an important piano part – is removed for the same reason as before. Emerson then follows Copland from 159–66.

At this point Emerson works in the theme of "Hoe-Down" by jazz saxophonist and composer Oliver Nelson (2'24"–2'48") to introduce an entirely new, improvisatory section which lasts 106 bars. The melodic improvisations include American folk-tunes, among which "Turkey In The Straw" and "Shortenin' Bread" can be discerned. The texture thickens out toward the end in anticipation of what Copland does at the end of his orchestration. Above the original second half of the melody, Emerson adds some figures of his own which are in keeping with the hoedown style. The final bars are slightly abbreviated.

"Trilogy"

Emerson has often composed with a single germ idea which he expands and transforms, but this is one of the few occasions on which he takes a song's melody as the basis of the entire piece, using variation techniques to transform it, with parts – especially the final section – quite distantly derived from the theme

The tune of Greg's song – a mixture of B major and B minor – is the thematic basis of "Trilogy". As the piece progresses, Emerson makes good use of this opportunity for the creation of ambiguity or tension. Each of the three main parts is divided into sub-sections.

After the string synth introduction of the theme the piano picks up on the idea, continuing the introduction based on the theme for another six bars. Part 1 proper begins with the start of Greg's vocal in bar 10, and continues to bar 59 – three slow, lyrical verses with a short middle section between the second and third verses – all acoustic; then a transitional piano passage leading to Part 2 (bars 60-85), a much faster piano section winding up the tension for Part 3, the fast rock conclusion of the piece which also includes three verses of song in a similar A-A-B-A-codetta form, this time to a melodically and rhythmically transformed theme.

Part One: This gentle, fervent love song is given a piano accompaniment which grows ever more impassioned. Keith's developing fondness for fourths is seen in bars 26 and 28, where the root moves in fourths (this is picked up again in Part Two). When the vocals end, he uses the descending broken chord of the verse's last two phrases as a basis for the acoustic piano transition passage which brings Part 1 to an end; he also uses the harmonically altered theme, which begins over a pedal B. In its last six bars, Emerson plays five dramatic alternating chords (briefly accompanied by arpeggiated synthesised strings), one of his favourite climatic devices. These signal the direction the rest of the piece is to take, for he makes clear the harmonic tension inherent between B major and minor in the theme, playing the chords F minor (the dominant chord of B), B major and F major (the dominant chord of B flat major and minor, which are used in Part 3).

.**Part Two**: The last two chords of this piano transition are B major and F major. The opening bars of the solo piano Part 2 are based on the tension between these chords. Bars 60-63 (the first four bars): a quintuplet pattern is stated eight times. The bottom note is B; the next four notes a broken second inversion F chord above. Bars 64, 66, 68: also based on the tension between these distant tonalities (a diminished fifth apart). Bars 69-70: another standard Emerson device – the tonality is left unclear by means of a suspension or a diminished chord or leaving out the chord's third; these bars anticipate a five-bar move to a tonal centre of D in 71. Bar 76: a slightly thickened-out version of bar 26 in Part 1, where the root movement is by fourths. Bars 78-83: the B major/B minor/B flat major tension is expressed in an upwardly wrenching series of syncopated chords. Leading into Part 3, two bars of descending triplets are based on alternating chords, the second of which can be seen as B with its root sharpened to C.

Part Three: This descending run ends on a clear B flat major chord for the opening 5/4 riff. It's on solo piano for four bars (from now on we're in 5/4 with only a couple of short exceptions). The riff alternates between B flat major and B major chords in the right hand, and when the full band enters, the bass line also changes to reflect the tonal ambiguity. This section is drawn to a halt by six repeated chords.

There is a six-bar link to the last section, in which the style changes again. A new bass line gets the guys into what is for them quite a funky groove! A carnival atmosphere is created. At times the percussive voice of the synthesiser sounds like steel drums (a sound which would be returned to in "Karn Evil 9, Second Impression"). The vocal melody, by now very different in character from the wistful atmosphere of Part One, reflects the cheerful acceptance and resolution of the lyrics, as does the "throwaway" tag.

"Abaddon's Bolero"

The theme begins in A minor and passes through A flat, G and E flat before returning to A minor. Instrumentation and accompaniment vary enormously through the eight statements of the theme which form the piece, but the theme is the constant unifying factor.

Carl opens with the familiar 2-bar rat-a-tat-tat rhythm, which is repeated ever louder throughout the piece. The theme, which enters in bar 3, is 32 bars long. It is played eight times; each statement lasts about a minute. The first time, only the first 23 bars are played. At each successive repetition it becomes more fully orchestrated. (There's no attempt to mimic orchestral sounds, but many of the sounds are like orchestral instruments.) At the sixth repetition, independent synthesiser lines (which could technically be termed obbligatos) begin to be added, their unusual colourings becoming ever more prominent.

First statement Keith plays a lone flute-like synth voice against the snare drum in this shortened version of the theme, with very soft thin organ harmonies in sevenths and major triads soon entering in the background.

Second statement Greg punctuates the same flutey voice with off-beat bass guitar accents, the organ harmonies continuing in the background (though the organ comes to the fore very briefly when there is a long held E flat in the theme). The bass guitar gives a counterpoint to the theme at one point before resuming the off-beat rhythm; this counterpoint idea returns in statement 6 as the first added synthesiser obbligato line.

Third statement Now the theme is taken up by a brass-like voice. Greg continues the same sort of bass guitar accompaniment, only louder. Likewise, the unresolved background harmonies become more prominent, with a bit more motion.

Fourth statement Keith expands the same brass voice by tuning the three filters of the Moog so that a major triad is sounded when one key is depressed. The same kind of tuning technique was used in "Aquatarkus".

Greg's bass begins doubling the drum rhythm. This gives an urgency and onward drive not hitherto felt. A sustained high violin-like sound suggests imminent take-off.

Fifth statement The reedy supporting harmonies which have been further down in the mix are brought forward. The suspended harmonies and different rhythm drive the piece along even more, heightening the anticipation, along with the continuing sustained high string sound.

Sixth statement By now things have gathered considerable force, and the bolero rhythm is emphasised in several lines. There's a very slight increase in speed at the beginning of this statement of the theme – it's so subtle that you'd think it would be unnoticeable, but in fact it's very much detectable. Previous statements have lasted almost precisely 1 minute 2 seconds each; from now on they last bang on a minute.

Whether this is a calculated effect or pure group instinct doesn't matter: it raises the excitement at a crucial point.

Now there is a dramatic change in texture. Keith replaces the brass sounds with a single-note voice like an oboe, still giving triad support with reedy voices below, however. The long notes from the high string sound continue. The first independent synth obbligato line – something like a tuba – enters with the beginning of the theme, well up in the mix. Further on, a second obbligato enters, played by the main melodic instrument: a couple of bars of the Revolutionary War fife-and-drum tune "The Girl I Left Behind Me", above the theme's held notes.

Seventh statement The orchestration is very full by now, the theme being played by several voices at once, with the lead line supported by triads. The sustained chords become more shrill and reedy.

The timpani have hitherto been used only for accenting. Carl states the rhythm on them for the first time, changing pitch as the theme demands. This presents great performance difficulties, since constant retuning during playing is necessary – unless you run between eight separate timpani! A tom-tom is added to the percussion line-up, and a new brass obbligato line adds a line of counterpoint to the melody.

Eighth statement The final section has a bombastically massive sound. The unchanging bolero rhythm is now played on timps, snare and side drum, bass guitar in octaves and low brass synth. The theme is in triads on brass/wind synth voices. The sustained chords remain, framing the whole. Like a banshee wail, the last new obbligato is so powerful it almost obliterates the rest of the music, including the theme. It is on a synthesiser with a fast portamento setting, which provides a smooth legato feel at odds with the music's style so far. The theme and the bolero rhythm struggle to get through this eclipsing, blatant, uncompromising, agonised shriek. The short tag at the very end parallels Ravel's Bolero in that it comprises an excitingly abrupt harmonic shift. In this case it's to a tritone harmony (F sharp – C:

heard that anywhere before on this album?) which resolves to a C chord. Compare Ravel, who suddenly goes from C to E right at the end of his piece.

Brain Salad Surgery

"Toccata"

In general the synthesiser plays the main melody and the piano line, while the organ and bass take the orchestra's parts.

Opening section Ginastera opens fortissimo with a two-bar motive constructed from four consecutive diminished 5ths played by the orchestra.

Incidentally, he writes them as two augmented 4ths and two diminished 5ths – there is a tension between fourths and fifths throughout the piece, which is an obvious reason for its appeal to Emerson. Emerson greatly expands upon this. Unlike Ginastera, he opens quietly, making four repetitions of the first two intervals. Palmer, playing on the timpani, which will be strongly featured in the percussion movement, makes interjections based on the minor third interval which is the foundation of the soon-to-be-heard main thematic idea (developed in the first two-thirds of the movement). The use of the main theme's characteristic interval in conjunction with the opening motive – which anticipates the second theme – at this early stage shows that Emerson wishes to make crystal clear the compositional structure of the movement. He reinforces this in his second statement of the motive by lengthening the end of Ginastera's original, almost casually rising a minor third to C and falling back again to A. Ginastera later combines the two thematic ideas; it seems that Emerson, recognising this unity, is planting the idea of the relationship even earlier than the composer. This vital motivic introduction builds to a scream, with the distorted complete opening motive played at double speed.

The repeated orchestral chords following the motive are taken by the organ. The main thematic idea (for piano in the original) in bar 14 is played on a metallic-sounding synth, with the bass guitar taking the orchestra's part. The theme is based on the melodic interval of a minor third, eventually expanding to a diminished fifth, the interval which is so important in the introductory bars. The theme returns, organ taking the orchestra's part.

Emerson replaces a passage with a descending octave scale with four descending synthesiser portamentos. The organ re-enters and the first large cut is made (of bars which merely expand on what we have just heard). Leaping from 61 to 75, Emerson plays organ unaccompanied for several bars, ending up on a diminished chord, which he holds while sounding a huge crescendo with the same synthesised portamento as a little earlier. This comes to an abrupt stop as the music jumps to bar 108. Just Greg's bass guitar is heard now, playing the timpani part. Emerson comes in on organ above, going into the thematic motive and slightly simplifying the score by leaving out a couple of bars. The motive's repeat is followed by another major cut, from 130 to 208. ELP's version of the following passage is similar to Ginastera's. At bar 208 a second theme is introduced. It is derived from the first two bars of the movement, with their tension between a fourth and a diminished fifth. There are four statements of this theme.

The first is like a transitional phrase and more ornamented than the next two, which are clearly based on the diminished fifth idea. The minor-third based first theme is added to the end of each of these two statements, making one long complete theme. Emerson recognises the difference between the first statement and the others by assigning them different synth voices. The statements are fairly similar to the original, though sometimes slightly abbreviated and simplified. The long held chords which accompany the second two statements are played on organ, while a powerful synth voice takes the lead melody. Emerson gives the organ the violent glissandos at the point in the original score when the piano soloist re-enters. The last, fortissimo, statement is similar, with more twists and turns like the first. At about bar 257 the passage peters out in a welter of screaming synth as Carl plays a crescendo on the timpani for the beginning of the percussion movement.

Percussion movement For nearly a minute Palmer plays rapid, complex, seemingly random rolls and rhythmic figures, with a little gong-bashing to announce his presence at the centre of attention even more clearly. Slowing this introduction to a close with a series of triplets, he softly plays the minor thirds of the main theme on two timpani, then adds tubular bells in parallel, and concludes the "paragraph" with a roll on the lower timp. As Emerson plays three dissonant rising chords based on the clash between the fourth and the diminished fifth, a wind noise compounds the eerie atmosphere.

Palmer now begins playing the timpani quite "loosely" again, and Lake introduces a new melody on synthesised guitar played through an Echoplex device, which further adds to the ghostly atmosphere by creating an echoey effect. Lake's melody is almost totally derived from the thematic material, mostly the diminished fifth – loads of them – though there are a few minor thirds in there too. A whole-tone scale at one point unhooks the sense of tonal centre and helps the spookiness along. This guitar interlude lasts only about thirty seconds. When it ends, Palmer starts laying into the synthesised drumkit. By striking the pads he is able to produce a wide range of sounds: first, a sequence so rapid that the ear cannot detect all its notes (but you can guess what intervals it's mainly composed of). There's also a portamento whoop, a low bouncing sound, a much lower rumbling sound, a wobbling sound and a low-pitched F, not to mention a lot of fevered work on snares, toms and bassdrum.

At the end of his solo spot he alternates the wobble with the low-pitched F; four repeated synth-drum Fs usher back the whole band.

Closing section The 208-257 passage is recapitulated, louder, brasher and harsher than previously. The final cut takes us on to the final ferocious bars of the arrangement. It is much like the original, except that Emerson doesn't use the climactic semiquaver piano part at all, taking only the orchestral part; admittedly it would have been hard to find a way for the band to play both.

This is probably the most exciting adaptation ever played by ELP. It also sets the mood for the major work of the album, "Karn Evil 9"; indeed, the percussion movement is structurally comparable with the middle section of the Second Impression.

Readers may be interested to know that Ginastera's music inspired the jazz saxophonist Jane Bunnett to write a piece of music, which is named after him. "Ginastera" can be found on the album *New York Duets* by Jane Bunnett and Don Pullen (Music and Arts CD-629, 1989). We look forward to the day when a composition called "Emerson, Lake and Palmer" hits the shops!

"Karn Evil 9: First Impression" (Emerson/Lake)

The opening presents a bleak vision of a future, or perhaps the present, in which the poor and refugee people of the world are exploited and betrayed – a long-time theme of Greg Lake's writing.

The scene changes to a circus, with the singer playing the part of ring-master. "Thrills and shocks" are cynically piled one on top of another for nothing more than entertainment: a magician pulling Jesus from a hat, and so on. He might have added megastar rock groups to the list.

Part 1 The introduction begins on solo organ playing in 2-voice counterpoint, and leads into a statement by the full band in the bars preceding verse 1 of the motivic idea which is the basis of the piece. The vocal lines of the three verses are connected by this recurring motive, which is also the basis of the instrumental links between verses. The vocal lines of verse 1 are driven onwards percussively: Keith plays loud, heavy, running eighth-notes in the lower register of the piano, while Carl taps the centre of a cymbal with a stick. The level of excitement builds throughout the piece; by the last verse the accompaniment is much more solidly chordal, with the bass line more to the fore. Greg's powerful supportive playing of the difficult bass part is notable throughout "Karn Evil 9". He often provides interesting lines in counterpoint or in answer to the organ; the instrumental links here provide examples.

The coda at the end of Part 1 ('To heal their sorrow", etc.) is accompanied by chords which both anticipate the Part 2 accompaniment and are possibly related to the Part 2 opening theme. Dramatic chords and the crash of a gong announce Part 2 – which begins on Side 1, though the sleeve doesn't refer to it.

Part 2 A new theme on lead synth opens this part. There's some call-and-response writing in the middle – and there will be a lot of that to follow in the next two "Impressions".

A nice example is just before verse 1, where lead synth alternates wildly with full band over Greg's pedal A flat. There are plenty of shock tactics, such as the eight bars of unaccompanied snare-drum roll introducing verse 2, and no less than seventeen of Keith's trademark organ glissandos piled up before verse 3 – not to mention the trick of momentarily stopping all the instrumental tape tracks on the words "thrills and shocks"! The electric guitar solo, over an introverted, off-beat accented organ accompaniment, is just right for the mood of the lyrics: exciting, impressive, but also curiously weary. The sample-and-hold synthesiser fade-out/fade-in takes us over to Side 2 for First Impression Part 2 (Part 2).

This final part comprises four more verses, with a keyboard solo and another electric guitar solo. Little need be said of this well-known and brilliant piece except to note the hints in the guitar solo of the song's melody and the opening theme, and the return full circle to the opening theme.

"Second Impression" (Emerson)

The title is brought to mind by the carnival (Karn Evil, geddit?) nature of the outer parts of this instrumental movement, and the central section evokes a horror movie – all of which continues the atmosphere already set by the lyrics in the First Impression.

After the piano trio has stated the quick main theme a few times, a synth voice like Caribbean steel drums builds to fever pitch over a typical Emerson piano bass ostinato. At the end of this Emerson appropriately quotes the theme of the calypso "St. Thomas" by Sonny Rollins, and there's a return to acoustic piano for a short coda to the section.

The middle part is pure mood creation in the classic early horror film manner. Piano plays mostly diminished fifths, alternating softly with bass guitar phrases. Carl produces a variety of unusual sounds with a metal sheet, a bell tree, etc.

This section ends with what is effectively an extended cadence: Carl on temple blocks, Keith and Greg providing the long-drawn out cadential material, including some Ginastera-like piano runs. In fact this section is somewhat similar to the part of the percussion movement of "Toccata" which features the electric guitar.

A modulatory section which refers to the original theme leads into a new bass ostinato, with another calypso idea over the top of it. Soon we're back to the original theme once more, which is stated once at the end. The Third Impression follows without a break.

"Third Impression" (Emerson/Lake/Sinfield)

Nine minutes of relentless drama here, the most coherent and extraordinary long piece ever yet produced by the group. It was hardly surprising that at the end of this album they didn't quite know where else to go musically. "Karn Evil 9" – and perhaps the Third Impression in particular – makes this the definitive techno-rock album, as even the hostile critics had to admit.

Greg Lake and Pete Sinfield here bring together all the images of a desolate and hopeless future that they had drawn on from "Schizoid Man" onwards, and crown it with a cybernetically Manichean vision of man as servant of the computer.

The main thing to note about it is the vast amount of imitative and call-and-response material. After the words "Let the maps of war be drawn", there's some "glory" music – heroic lead synth and marching-to-war Apollo comping. Then battle commences in earnest. From here on it's a perfect lesson, as cheerfully corny and knowing as any silent-movie improvising pianist in the racheting-up of tension. Eventually there is a series of synthesiser whoops and cheers, and finally verse 3.

In concert, at the conclusion of the verse the band would leave the stage, which would fill with clouds of smoke as the Moog sequence of 24 notes got faster and faster, panning quadrophonically around the audience until it reached an intolerable blur, at which point the computer set-up exploded with a flash.

An interesting footnote to "Karn Evil 9". On the label on the centre of the disk and in the accompanying foldout, Emerson is credited with vocals on the First Impression. This is clearly incorrect and was in fact referring to Emerson's "Bridge Computer" vocals on the Third Impression. Greg sang all the vocals.

Works Volume 1

"Piano Concerto no.1" (Emerson)

A large (82 piece) orchestra is required: 3+1-2-2-2+1/4-3-3-1/timp/ 2 perc (triangle, bell-tree, tubular bell, crotales, side drum, tam-tam, gran cassa, tambourine, whip, deep side drum, glockenspiel, snare drum)/strings (58)

"First Movement: Allegro Giojoso"

The main thematic and constructional force of the first movement of Emerson's concerto is 12-note Serialism. The basics of this need to be understood if the first movement is to be enjoyed and appreciated to the full. It's more than just mind games for the composer.

More than a footnote is necessary to explain 12-note composition, or dodecaphony, which has had little popular impact on rock, though artists like Frank Zappa to name but a thousand have used it frequently.

Only the basics of Serialism are needed to Emerson's thinking, because the link to traditional tonality is strong. One can only speculate as to the reaction of a rock audience to a movement of a piano concerto entirely composed on serialist principles!

Serialism is a method of composition, brought to its fullest development by the Second Vienna School of composers led by Schoenberg, Berg and Webern between 1906 and 1945 in which a fixed series (or "set" or "row') of elements, usually individual notes, is used as the basis of *every stage* of a musical composition. Originally intended to be a totalizing theory for the harmonic language exponentially forged in the 19th century by Beethoven, Liszt and Wagner, its absolute approach to the harmonic possibilities opened up by such artists has opened up fundamental fissures in musical thought in the 20th century, to the degree that some espoused the theory that 12-tone composition's deleterious effect on a nonplussed and uncomprehending public had "destroyed" classical music.

Serial theory and music can be intimidating at first because it is so different from the tonal music we are familiar. People often describe it as tuneless, and indeed, strictly speaking, it is. The essence of serialism is that the twelve notes of the ordinary chromatic scale are put in the order of the composer's choice, *each appearing only once*. No individual note may be repeated until all the others have been sounded. It is, essentially, taken to its *ne plus ultra*, a textually democratic form of music, which might explain why leftist cultural theoreticians such as Bloch and Adorno have compared it to the political liberation of the musical mind.

The series may have any of 48 forms. The basic four are forwards, backwards, upside-down and backwards-upside-down. These are referred to as:

Prime	–	**P**
Retrograde	–	**R**
Inverted	–	**I**
Retrograde-Inverted	--	**RI**

These four basic forms may furthermore be played at any of the 12 different levels of the chromatic scale – that is, you can start any of them on C, C sharp, D, D sharp, or whatever. As Emerson's concerto shows, it is possible to create strong and appealing melodies from such a "tone-row". (Some of the more extreme advocates of serialism would no doubt consider Emerson's use of the method in a tonal context to be a compromise.) ELP have always sought to break down musical barriers – but most of their music is still tonal.

The following matrix shows the possible forms of the note-row in the first movement of the Emerson Piano Concerto.

If the number 0 is assigned to the first note of the row, then, where C = 0:

C sharp/D flat	= 1
D	= 2
D sharp/E flat	= 3
E	= 4
F	= 5
F sharp/G flat	= 6
G	= 7
G sharp/A flat	= 8
A	= 9
A sharp/B flat	= 10
B	= 11

The original, Prime form of the row is found by reading along the P-0 line, to read 0, 8, 10, 5, 3, 7, 2, 9, 4, 11, 6, 1. In everyday musical terms, this translates into C natural, A flat, B flat, F natural, E flat, G natural, D natural, A natural, E natural, B natural, F sharp, C sharp – so you can see that every note of the chromatic scale is used once.

Again, if you want to trace the Inverted form of the row when it starts on F (5), follow the I-5 line. This gives you the following pitches: 5, 9, 7, 0, 2, 10, 3, 8, 1, 6, 11, 4.

In practice, only P-0 and P-5 are used complete, while some patterns, occasionally recurring, can be derived from their being pitched higher or lower. It is unsurprising that these two forms of the series dominate the piece, since it is firmly anchored in a traditional tonal context, with A flat major and E flat major (a fifth apart, like P-0 and P-5) its clear tonal centres. You could think of P-0 and P-5 as tonic and subdominant – you'd be wrong, strictly speaking, but it does help to look at it that way.

Prime	I-0	I-8	I-10	I-5	I-3	I-7	I-2	I-9	I-4	I-11	I-6	I-1	Inverted
P-0	0	8	10	5	3	7	2	9	4	11	6	1	R-0
P-4	4	0	2	9	7	11	6	1	8	3	10	5	R-4
P-4	2	10	0	7	5	9	4	11	6	1	8	3	R-2
P-7	7	3	5	0	10	2	9	4	11	6	1	8	R-7
P-9	9	5	7	2	0	4	11	6	1	8	3	10	R-9
P-5	5	1	3	10	8	0	7	2	9	4	11	6	R-5
P-10	10	6	8	3	1	5	0	7	2	9	4	11	R-10
P-3	3	11	1	8	6	10	5	0	7	2	9	4	R-3
P-8	8	4	6	1	11	3	10	5	0	7	2	9	R-8
P-1	1	9	11	6	4	8	3	10	5	0	7	2	R-1
P-6	6	2	4	11	9	1	8	3	10	5	0	7	R-6
P-11	11	7	9	4	2	6	1	8	3	10	5	0	R-11
Reverse Inverted (Retrograde inverted)	RI-0	RI-8	RI-10	RI-5	RI-3	RI-7	RI-2	RI-9	RI-4	RI-11	RI-6	RI-1	Reverse (Retrograde)

This movement – the longest – is in ABCA form. The A sections are based thematically on a twelve-note row and divided into three sub-sections. Section B is jazz-inspired, with the solo piano sparsely accompanied by the orchestra. Section C is made up of three variations on a lyrical theme, followed by a developmental bridge which includes a cadenza for the piano. When Section A returns, it is as a brief coda, the theme being played once only.

Section A

1. The first thirty bars are of staggering volubility; following a "shock" opening chord composed of eleven of the twelve notes of the row, the melodic row itself, on flutes and first violins, is presented in its Prime form in bars 1-3, followed by its three other forms (Retrograde, bars 3-4; Inverted, bars 4-6; Retrograde-Inverted, bars 5-7). The next 22 bars comprise an energetic four-voice fugal development of the note-row.

This dissolves into freer counterpoint in bar 30. A resolution is arrived at in bar 34, via a contrary-motion scale passage, whose whole tone nature has the effect of a magic wand, casting aside the busy disposition of the opening to replace it with a peaceful mood.

2. The time-signature is now 5/4, and the texture contrasts dramatically with the contrapuntal opening. Delius-like tranquillity is invoked [5]as the first clarinet states a meandering, plaintive transitional melody (similar in shape to the original tone-row), while flutes, oboes and strings supply soft, long chords in accompaniment. Crucial to the overall effect here are the percussion instruments, triangle and bell-tree add delicate crystalline tracery.

Beginning bar 45, the strings state in A-flat major the tone-row's first variant. Excluding repeated notes, it follows pitches 1 to 8 of P-5 exactly. Tension results from the violins playing quavers in 2/4 while lower strings play crochet triplets. This subsection draws to a close with an A flat major perfect cadence in bars 58-9.

This struggle is commandingly swept away [6] by unison low brass and basses. They portentously sound an A flat major scale, first descending, and then rising to the dominant E flat, anticipated throughout on the upbeats by an E flat tubular bell.

The piano makes its first entry on the upbeat to bar 70 with a tonal variation of P-0 in A flat major, given additional sparkle by crotales. This melody is the theme of Section A. It becomes the most important thematic material in the first movement, recurring in several variations.

The theme begins in A flat major and begins to modulate to E flat major in bar 72. It ends firmly in E flat major in bar 76, with a cadential phrase in descending semiquavers which assumes increasing motivic importance in the movement. Rhythmically and harmonically altered, the violin music already heard in bars 57-8, just before the bass/brass scale, provides a perfect cadence modulation to the dominant, E flat major, the bass descending in fourths.

The first piano statement of the Section A theme is followed by a joyfully "whistled" interjection in the high winds above a tonic pedal in the timpani. This little phrase, which is taken up by the piano from bar 93, recurs regularly in the opening A section, culminating in a fully orchestrated statement beginning at bar 110. Before this, however, the theme returns in the piano, ending with a variation of the cadential phrase, which here resolves from the dominant to the major mediant rather than to the tonic. The interjection which formerly sounded like little more than a cheerful whistle returns boldly, fully orchestrated, modulating back to the by now familiar "home" key of A flat major.

3. A simple right hand piano melody, with a left hand ostinato derived from similar piano music in 100-101, is accompanied by various scales in the piccolos, flutes and crotales.

The descending cadential figure in bar 138 leads into a bridge passage, beginning in bar 140, to Section B. The Prime form of the row is heard in the piano and woodwinds above a long sustained open fifth (A flat/E flat) in the strings. This resolves to an expectant crescendo chord of D over a low E in bar 148, with a B flat timpanum making a glissando up to E (a diminished fifth). The effect is to create the expectation of a cadenza.

Section B

Except for one four-bar phrase, the pianist plays throughout this section, and orchestral instruments play for all but five bars. The music is quick and rhythmically tricky for piano and orchestra alike. Groups within the orchestra take turns to punctuate, support and imitate the almost continuous flow of the piano part. One could therefore, consider this section a cadenza for soloist *and* orchestra.

In marked contrast to the preceding music of the work, this is light, somewhat jazzy, and written largely in semiquaver triplets. The metre is constantly changing, alternating between 4/8, 2/8 and 3/8.

After a descending solo piano run in bar 150, there is a 4-bar introduction reminiscent of the theme's intervals and outline. The melody scurries along anxiously, in close harmony with chords of three notes and two notes. Then the piano briefly alludes to the main Section A theme (for two bars) in A major. The nervous next four bars of the piano part are a link section based on pedals first of A and the E, with violins boldly sounding out long descending chords of A and E.

A busy, rhythmically complex variant of the theme, beginning in C minor in bar 161 and ending in E flat major in bar 167, is followed by the solo piano playing four bars of the link material just mentioned, now over a C pedal. The full orchestra alone leaps in to imitate it as if to say, "I can do better than you!" These four bars are very densely orchestrated. Finally, the full C minor thematic variant is restated, ending as before, on an E flat major perfect cadence. The actual notes are almost the same as those of the theme in its original form, but the effect is so totally different that one might not immediately see the connection.

Section C

The entire section is comprised of four statements, with varied accompaniments, of a strongly lyrical legato theme. It may be seen as being constructed from the P-5 form of the note-row, since it rearranges its first seven pitches. Remaining in A flat major throughout, it is harmonically simple and somewhat chorale-like.

The "Maestoso" first version is played straightforwardly by woodwinds, horns and trumpets. The second, "Con amore", emphasises the chorale nature of the theme, the piano gently stating the theme while flutes and oboes supply quaver accompaniment and the first clarinet picks out the bass line. Next, "Con espressione", the melody is expansively stated by the strings, supported by the piano's rippling broken chords with the lower brass reinforcing the bass line; a trumpet obligato lends an air of nobility.

The piano pattern continues in the final "Maestoso" pattern, but now including the theme above it. This is the most grandly orchestrated statement of the theme. It is played largely in unison by piano, violins, viola and one horn. Flute 2 and oboe provide a high obligato against the theme, and flute 1, clarinet, bassoons and contrabassoon are in counterpoint to this, sometimes following the line of the theme. (Unfortunately, these interesting wind parts are drowned out in the recording by the powerful melody being proclaimed by the other instruments. This seems to be more a deficiency of the recording than of the orchestration.) The three trumpets in unison sound out another obligato.

The weak V-1 cadence concluding Section C puts the music in limbo for a moment. It is as if the melody is allowing a breathing space to call attention to the following brief but noteworthy transitional passage back to the "A" material.

Transition and Cadenza

At only 15 bars long, this delightful solo opportunity for the orchestra might easily go unappreciated. The music is derived from the Section A theme, which was first heard from the piano when it made its initial appearance in bar 69. Strings, winds and brass yearningly romance each other, at first with tenderness, and ultimately with passion. Tchaikovsky comes to mind. It is better heard than analysed! The melody, strongest in the violins, suddenly expires, yielding expectantly to the firm and assured entry of the piano. Sadly, the score direction to the orchestra to suddenly play more softly on the long final note, is not really followed by the LPO.

For all the freedom and jazziness of the short (two minute) piano cadenza, it rarely strays from the movement's thematic material. In the first nine bars, it picks up on the altered A theme just heard in the transitional passage, with a stride left hand accompaniment. The pace then quickens with an eight-bar link to a further development of the theme, not in E flat, with a definite jazz feel due to added grace notes and blue notes. After a couple of phrases in bold fanfare-like octaves, there's a slowing-down before the last part, which sees a return to A flat major. An improvisatory right hand solos over a very tricky ostinato which keeps returning to a tonic open 5th (A flat/E flat). This section of the cadenza is more loosely based on the outstanding intervals of the theme – perfect fourth, perfect fifth, minor sixth. It also leads us to expect a return to what we have come to feel is the "home" key, A flat major, in the final part, which recapitulates the Section A material.

Section A1 (Coda)

The return of the "A" material takes the form of a very brief (only 9 bars) coda. A massive "fortissimo" statement of the main theme by strings (except basses), piano, clarinets and bassoons is given sold bass support by lower brass instrument, basses and timpani, with insistent crotales and side drum giving encouragement, and high woodwinds and horns filling out the soundstage.

Although we might have expected the theme finally to end in A flat major, it remains exactly as it was originally – that is, piano takes a solo for a bar and a half, with the extension already heard in bars 107-9 of the cadential idea in descending semiquavers. Finally, orchestra and piano state a "molto fortissimo" perfect cadence in E flat.

Second Movement: Andante Molto Cantabile

To write a central slow movement that only lasts two minutes (50 bars including a 3-bar repeat) is quite a brave move. If it succeeds, the primary reason is that it stands in extreme contrast to the previous movement, being tonal (in C major), straightforward and unchallenging.

Although it serves the traditional function of providing temporary relief between two demanding movements, the Andante's brevity and its relatively thin musical ideas at first give the impression that it may have been added purely to complete the usual three-movement form. But it sounds far better than the printed score would lead one to believe. It's simple, charming – first happy, then (as soon as the piano enters) sad. It provides the perfect link between the cheerful Allegro and the ferocious Toccata.

Section A

The movement is in the form A/B/A/Coda. It begins contentedly in C major, with a concise exposition including all the important musical material. The upper strings and an oboe provide the main semiquaver melody, and the lower strings give strong support. In bars 3-6 the strings and winds pleasingly echo each other, and a "stringendo" 7 passage from 9 to 15 seems to indicate an increasing purposefulness.

Section B

When the piano enters, it is with a disconsolate, meandering minor key solo derived from the theme. It's a smooth sequence of broken chords and scales. Although it has no particular melodic or rhythmic interest, the slow, deliberate ascent up the F minor scale is serious and dignified, solidly supported by basses and contrabassoon. After passing through several more tonal areas, the return to C major is delayed: in a 7-bar cadential passage, piano and basses alternate the main musical idea of the early stringendo passage with a two chord response from the woodwind and horns.

Section A1

The immediate return of the Section A material sees the piano taking up the opening orchestral music, with bare octave support from the lower strings and contrabassoon, and a rather unmemorable counterpoint from the first violins.

Coda

The final solitary piano chord of C is preceded by a double time rush of descending semiquavers, formed from the first half bar of the theme.

Third Movement: Toccata Con Fuoco

Every available percussive resource is utilised. Percussion is pre-eminent, whether used in support of the other instruments, decoratively, to provide motivic material (in the case of the tuned instruments) or simply as a powerful driving force. Many of them are used in the first "B" section, which demonstrates the percussive capabilities not only of the actual percussion instrument, but also of various conversing groupuscules of piano, percussion and other orchestral instruments. Percussion is the key word; pianistically and orchestrally.

The several sections of the movement, whose form can be thought of as A/B/C/A1/D/E/Coda, are closely related to the thematic and motivic material stated in the first 45 bars.

A(1-45) Introduction of the basic motivic elements ending with the first full statement of the theme.

B(46-97) Highly percussive "cadenza" for soloist and orchestra. Only loosely related to the theme, mostly for its percussive potential.

C(98-119) Slower section based on a lyrical variant of the theme.

A1(120-144) Return of the first section with a greatly extended version of the original theme.

D(145-176) Development section composed of theme-derived material, including anticipation of the final form of the theme.

E(177-233) Final triumphant transformation of the theme.

Coda(234-245) Conventional final flourish.

Section A

With the score directions "Martellato" (Hammered) and "fortissimo", a piano ostinato, solo for four bars and then accompanied by the full orchestra, opens the movement. When the orchestra enters, it is with fierce, rhythmic motives and rushing scales. In bars 15-16 a high, screaming chord cluster is followed by an immediate descent to the pit – a very low chord cluster with the added dissonance of the tam-tam and a bass drum trill.

A new pattern appears in the right hand of the piano part above the continuing ostinato, and at the same time trumpets and violins sound a new idea (derived from the theme and the fierce rhythm just mentioned).

Six bars of solo piano from bars 21-26 now anticipate the first full statement of the theme. Bars 30-32 are entirely permeated by the interval of a minor third, which features, strongly in the movement.

A bridge leading to the main theme is begun by the piano: a two-bar descending sequence leads into four bars based on an ostinato formed from the same intervals which characterise the main ostinato – minor second, minor third and diminished fifth. This introduces the main ostinato itself, above which piano and strings give out the first complete statement of the theme.

Section B

Over a pedal C in the low strings, repeated octave Cs on tubular bells and high woodwinds introduce the dramatic "cadenza" for soloist and orchestra. Whilst the bells continue to sound, there is a once-repeated exchange between bassoons and piano. The bassoons, fanfare-like rise from C to F sharp (a diminished fifth – another important interval in the movement), and the piano spits back a martial descending cadential phrase. One can imagine this passage being used in the Third Impression of "Karn Evil 9".

Low broken C Octaves from the piano presage the frenzied percussive conflict of this section. Section B begins very aggressively in bars 56-64. Rapid flurries of broken-chord piano work are accompanied by shrill winds and intrusive tam-tam, bass drum and tambourine.

Two short solo piano passages, separated by a brief rhythmic spat between orchestra and piano, are based on the second ostinato pattern. The second of these is followed by an eerie whole-tone passage.

An ascending piano scale introduces a lively tow-bar phrase for piano and high woodwinds which relates to the contours of the final form of the theme. This is repeated once, in alternation with a heavy answering phrase from brass, percussion and lower strings.

The descending solo piano run which follows is based on a diminished chord, and then there's an ascending run based on perfect fourths. The following two bars are a magnificent descending run of stacked fourths (that favourite Emerson interval, not given so much prominence in this concerto) for piano and wind. Lastly comes an ominous, heavy brass passage made out of minor thirds and diminished fifths.

Emerson's persistent usage of very simple elements makes highly impressive grandiose music. But more importantly, this section lays bare some of the fundamental building blocks of the movement: the intervals of minor third and diminished fifth, rapidly ascending and descending scales, dramatic battles between piano and orchestra and between groups within the orchestra, and almost relentless percussion.

Section C

The music of the previous section dies away, and a brief "blue" piano solo introduces a sad, lyrical melody for flutes and violin. Its long held high notes, accompanied by rippling piano, become more and more ethereal, until at the end of bar 119 there is a Grand Pause.

Section A1

Once again, the theme is preceded by the second ostinato pattern, now violently reinforced by side drum and cymbal. When the theme returns, it is far more staccato and harsher than before, with pizzicato strings and stabbing brass chords as accompaniment, fragmented in 138-140 and restated briefly in 141-144.

The piano takes up the last three-quaver rhythm and plays a powerful 10/8 accompaniment to a string statement of a broad theme-related melody.

Section D

This new melody is then developed: melodic fragments pass between brass and string instruments, with constant quaver accompaniment by piano and woodwinds. The ultimate transformation of the theme is briefly anticipated by the strings before these phrases coalesce into a descending four-note pattern played eight times by soloist and full orchestra, in a massive unison rallentando.

Section E

The original theme, which at the start was jagged and staccato, full of clenched rage, on meeting the light is changed into something entirely new; joyful, confident, expansive.

The effect is startling: until now the music has been restless, dissonant, in frequently changing metres and tempos, with the various parts of the orchestra either in conflict with each other or playing different roles. Suddenly everybody's playing the same bold, strong tune: all resources are poured into the "grandiose" statement of the theme.

It is not in 3/4 time, and is first played by the orchestra alone. The second, more subdued statement is by the piano with the unison high woodwinds providing a melody in counterpoint.

Struggle persists, as if a last fight has to be won, with reminiscences of the material of Section D. In one striking passage, as the strings and woodwinds wrench agonisingly upwards, the piano plays a disturbed three-against-two pattern. When the music reaches its peak, the theme returns arranged as in its first statement, but now propelled by the pianist's demisemiquaver ascending arpeggios. The final resolution is sealed with a descending rush of semiquavers and a rising scale of F with a piano glissando.

The last movement of the Concerto is for the most part convincing. It is only towards the end, with the transformation of the theme, that one feels Emerson was perhaps finishing it off quickly. The music of conflict earlier in the piece is far more satisfying than the triumphant conclusion, which is comparatively thinly scored, and lacks forward drive until the very end. However, this is a fairly minor deficiency in an otherwise highly impressive piece of music.

The most recent known performances of Emerson's Piano Concerto were given on May 12 and 13, 2000. Soloist Terry LaBolt, with the Northern Kentucky Symphony Orchestra under the baton of James R. Cassidy, was enthusiastically received on both occasions by audiences at these classical rock concerts entitled "Roll Over Beethoven" at Northern Kentucky University. *Cincinnati Post* reviewer Ellyn Hutton commented that it was "chock full of delicious references" and "should be performed more often". Also featured were Frank Zappa's "Dog Breath Variations" and Paul McCartney's "Standing Stone".

"Pirates"

Tensions are unleashed by a brief and spectral introduction for Yamaha GX1 synth and percussion. It avoids harmonic resolution, ending on a diminished chord. Indeed, the restlessness which characterises ELP's music results primarily from this determined avoidance of resolution, and "Pirates" keeps the listener on tenterhooks throughout.

By Keith's admission the clearest classical influence on the piece is Stravinsky. "There is one part that's vaguely Copland-ish, but in general I think it's pretty well integrated with all my musical influences; it's really hard to point out. I guess you might say there's more Stravinsky than Copland there. That was intentional, with all those pounding accents coming in. It wasn't exactly the same as *The Rite Of Spring*, but I had that in mind."

The main instrumental introduction, for orchestra and group, begins with a long series of repeated chords played by strings and synth. They launch "Pirates" with a fierce motivic power. Composed of the typically Emersonian piled-up fourth intervals, they recall the chords which open the first scene of Stravinsky's *Rite*. Above these chords the brass section plays a grand, rolling fanfare-like phrase in fifths.

There are several changes of pace throughout "Pirates", which was no doubt one reason for critical grumbles about raggedness; these are at least consonant with the twists and turns of narrative, as are the varying textures and densities of the arrangement. The score's first indication of tempo is "Moderately, steadily" for the instrumental introduction, at a voyage's beginning. At one point in this part there are repeated high notes from the GX1 which resembles, postmodernistically, Morse code! – incongruous for a tale of the Spanish Main; perhaps a sketch for a film score?

At the entry of the first verse the indication is "Slightly slower". This tempo is maintained until the middle of the piece, though the driving motive power ceases for a moment or two for "Anchored in an indigo moonlit bay", over a long sustained bass guitar note. The fourth verse, about the slaughter of the treasure ship's crew, is followed by a marvellously dissonant, harsh blast from the orchestra, leading into an instrumental interlude.

After the tag "This town is ours...tonight!", the indication is "Fast, with a strong beat" for the entry of the band alone. The effect at this point is one of the most wrenchingly dramatic in all of ELP's music. Some great instrumental work follows in the following highly syncopated section, which employs material already heard with the orchestra.

Towards the end the tempo slows again for the dramatic final verse, and then remains at Tempo 1 to the end.

Works Volume II

"Bullfrog"

A "ribbiting" performance from Carl Palmer with members of Back Door. Once described by John Tobler as "the Geoff Boycotts of jazz-rock", Ron Aspery (saxes/ flute/ keyboards) and Colin Hodgkinson (bass, electric and acoustic guitars/ vocals) were the two constant members of the band Back Door, who produced four very fine albums between 1972 and 1976, but never quite got the success they deserved. The Back Door input is instantly identifiable in "Bullfrog". Aspery's unmistakable crazed sax work and Hodgkinson's funky bass, plus judicious flavourings of flute and keyboards, complement Palmer's amazing all-round work on percussion and drums. Especially impressive is the terrifically accurate unison playing at high speed.

[**F.A.**: *Carl recorded another piece with Aspery and Hodgkinson which sounded very much like a Crimson track. The main riff is in 7/4 time and in my opinion the drumming is amongst Palmer's finest statements being, both fast, accurate and incredibly tight, with a wicked use of cowbells. He uses many of the drum rudiments in unison with the other musicians and in the drum fills. A great shame this track never made it onto an album. However, I am endeavouring to persuade Carl to rectify this situation.*]

"Barrelhouse Shake-Down"

Barrelhouses were rough country drinking joints, wooden shacks with dirt floors that had piano players banging out music till the small hours. The pianos found in the barrelhouses were usually poor. Players used the out of tune strings to imitate the sound of guitar blues. The music bred by these dimly-lit violent haunts came to be called "Barrelhouse".

Barrelhouse music may have developed as early as 1870. The untrained musicians were unfamiliar with the complexities of ragtime, and passed the riffs and techniques on by example. For this reason many Barrelhouse pieces are highly idiosyncratic; compositions vary greatly from performer to performer.

Early Barrelhouse does have certain common characteristics, however. The song forms are simple, e.g. AABA. There is little soloing other than right hand embellishment between lines; and not much improvisation. Harmonically, there is a minor, hollow sound that uses open fifths and octaves to outline the simple chord progressions. The dotted quaver/semiquaver pattern which is found in much boogie, including "Honky Tonk Train Blues", is usually absent. Bass lines tend to be pedal notes or simple alternating patterns which provide little rhythmic support.

"Barrelhouse Shake-Down" seems at first sight to have little in common with most Barrelhouse music: it is more complex and more elegant than you'd expect. Many of the harmonies are quite angular and subtle, and the feel is cheerful, unpressured and relaxed. In this respect, it's very different from Emerson's reading of "Honky Tonk Train Blues" (see below).

The rocking left hand pattern seems like one of the most basic of moves – it suggests itself naturally to the fingers. But with its dotted quaver/semiquaver rhythm it is more commonly associated with boogie-woogie (as in "Honky Tonk Train Blues'). The alternating bass of the piano section following the inspired clarinet solo is characteristic of later (though slower) Barrelhouse blues such as "Short Haired Blues" by Kid Stormy Weather. The relaxed accompaniment of the band, supported by Jon Hiseman's understated drumming, is just what's needed.

The title may be a convenient tag for a peculiarly Emersonian amalgam of devices, but the piece is none the worse for that. On the contrary, its individuality is entirely in keeping with the spirit of Barrelhouse, and it is one of the most entertaining of all Emerson's piano compositions.

"Maple Leaf Rag"

Harmonically simple, ragtime is usually, like "Maple Leaf Rag", in 2/4 time. While the left hand maintains a bass beat, the melodic right hand is derived from folk and minstrel banjo music and dances like jigs, cakewalks and marches. It's more a musical approach than a form: you can "rag" any tune. It is also strictly notated, unlike, say, boogie-woogie, which is primarily for performance. Ragtime was born in the late 19th century of West African and European elements, and was really a white man's music. The greatest and most prolific ragtime composer, however, was a Negro, Scott Joplin. "Maple Leaf Rag" may be Joplin's greatest composition – and check out Jelly Roll Morton's amazing version of it.

Joplin specified that his pieces should be played slowly – "*Not Fast*" or something similar is printed at the head of most of his rags – and piano rolls of his own performances demonstrate this. But his wishes were often ignored. Ragtime was often played at breakneck speed on player pianos in penny arcades.

"Maple Leaf Rag" was the biggest ragtime hit of all. It consists of four different tunes or strains, each 16 bars long, and in form is AABBACCDD. "March time" is indicated for it. Too slow a speed would be silly, but then again it's fiendishly hard to play it fast anyway. Keith "Fingers" Emerson, however, performs it at a devilish lick. Here, the keyboard blends with the orchestral instruments (strings and winds). It's unusual for Keith not to take a clear lead in such a virtuoso piece as this; however – as if it was necessary! – his almost impossibly fast and accurate solo piano version on *Works Live* confirms just as much as the Piano Concerto his exceptional dexterity and keyboard mastery.

"I Believe In Father Christmas"

This is a less over-the top remix of Greg's Christmas 1975 solo hit.

The instrumental hook played by Keith Emerson is from "Troika", the fourth movement of Prokofiev's music for the film *Lieutenant Kije* (1933, published as a concert suite 1934). The original music depicts a ride through the snow in a three-horse sleigh, accompanied by bells. Emerson had wanted to use the music with the Nice, and performed it live with them, but had been prevented from recording it by the Prokofiev estate (however, see Discography, "Classical Heads").

"Close But Not Touching"

The last of Carl's big band collaborations on the *Works* sessions is based on a powerful marching theme. After an initial statement by flutes and rolling snares, the theme is treated in various ways by brass and guitar/bass drums; the central section has a guitar solo over a rhythmic backing with a harmonic basis similar to that of the theme.

"Honky Tonk Train Blues"

Meade "Lux" Anderson Lewis (1905-64) was born in Chicago. The nickname is an abbreviation of "The Duke Of Luxembourg", a name he was often called during his childhood in Louisville, Kentucky. In 1929 he made a remarkable recording for Paramount Records, "Honky Tonk Train Blues", an impressionistic interpretation of the railroad trains that passed through the South Side of Chicago. Amazingly, although Lewis was consciously creating an urban version of the guitar picker's tune "Goin' Where The Southern Cross' the Dog", much of it was improvised on the spot.

Lewis gave a couple of versions of how the title came about. Talking to Alan Lomax for the Library Of Congress archive recordings, he said that while playing piano at a house party, possibly in 1923 (shortly after he had completed the choruses and decided on their running order) a guest asked him "What do you call that thing?" When Lewis replied, "That's a train blues", the man suggested, "Well, we're all together here. You ought to call it the Honky-Tonk Train Blues".

The other version is that Lewis was making the first recording for Paramount, and suggested the title of "Freight Train" to the engineer, who, having just heard it, said, "Oh no, that sounds like honky-tonk music – we'll call it The Honky Tonk Train".

Late in 1935 the great jazz critic John Hammond found Lewis, out of a gig, washing cars in a suburban Chicago garage. He persuaded him to re-record "Honky Tonk Train Blues" for release in Britain on Parlophone.

The Paramount recording had reflected the poor urban roots of the earliest boogie-woogie style: though fast, it was somewhat melancholy, even mournful. By the time Lewis re-recorded it, the sad undertones had gone. The train no longer ran on a little local line; now it was a big freight train intent on reaching its destination. Lewis was at his creative peak. Sparkling right-hand phrasing, more choruses and increased speed add to the excitement. Lewis would probably have loved Emerson's high-octane performance: his own performances of this and other pieces often thundered on for half an hour or even an hour! The other side of the 78 had a piece written and performed by Jess Stacey called "Barrelhouse" – interesting in view of Keith Emerson's choice of title for the B-side of his version.

The model for Keith Emerson's version is pianist Bob Zurke's quicksilver performance with the Bob Crosby Orchestra.

Emerson had originally intended the piece for his planned solo album. When he did release a solo album (*Honky*, see Discography), he included another Lewis piece, "Yancey Special'.

"Show Me The Way To Go Home"

"Irving King" was a pseudonym for Jimmy Campbell (1903-1967) and Reg Connelly (1898-1963), who wrote the song together. Failing to get any of the London publishers to accept it, they printed it themselves and touted it around on handcart, with demonstrations by the two of them, Connelly playing an upright piano mounted on the cart! It sold so well that they were able to set up their own publishing house with the proceeds. The team wrote many other successful songs, and Campbell, Connelly & Co. Ltd. became a major force in Denmark Street (popularly known as "Tin Pan Alley") for the next half-century or more. It is now owned by the giant Music Sales Ltd. 1

The whole of the melody of "Show Me..." falls within a four-note range, which must partly account for its great popularity ever since its publication and especially before and during World War Two.

The rather dull verse was usually omitted; it soon became a chorus-only song; few publishers now print the complete song. ELP's arrangement follows custom. Vocally, Greg gives it a happy late-night blues feel; Keith uses his solo as an opportunity to show off some great Tatum-style runs.

Notes

1   Most of the above information was supplied by the noted expert on early jazz and popular music, Brian Rust, to whom many thanks.

In Concert (later Works Live)

After a stirring Introductory Fanfare (Emerson/Palmer), the announcer proclaims, "Ladies and gentlemen, Emerson, Lake and Palmer!" and the band kick into the only new number on the album, a beefy arrangement of Peter Gunn by Henry Mancini (1924-1994). The piece is a prime solo opportunity for Keith. Some very nice synthesiser pitchbend work here.

Then comes "Tiger In A Spotlight". This is one of several tracks which show that ELP have always been first and foremost a performing band: if anything, the live version is better than the studio one.

Greg's solo spot includes both "C'est La Vie" and "Watching Over You", the latter being absent from "In Concert". "C'est La Vie" is an accurate rendition of the song – with Keith actually getting to play accordion on it this time! The surging strings, and the overall clarity, sparkle and sumptuousness of the song demonstrate as well as any track the validity of the orchestra. Greg gives a committed performance vocally and on acoustic guitar. "Watching Over You" is direct and sincere, benefiting from the simple acoustic guitar/vocal treatment; Carl adds a few cymbal strokes by way of decoration in the first verse, and Keith briefly solos on a synth voice which attempts to mimic harmonica.

Keith dives straight into a rattling "bar piano" performance of "Maple Leaf Rag" – an amazing feat of accuracy at this speed.

"The Enemy God Dances With The Black Spirits" is played by the band alone. The lads bring it off superbly, though some of the barbarism and decadence and a lot of the fine detail which can only be supplied by the orchestra is lost. This particular performance was taken from a show without the orchestra.

A thunderous performance of "Fanfare For The Common Man" is at first not quite as punchy as it might be in the keyboard department; but this is more than compensated for by Greg and Carl's aggressive rhythm backing. About six minutes in, they go into a shitkicking performance of Rondo. The Hammond is superbly captured – you can practically see and touch Keith as he heaves the thing about! Finally it's back to Fanfare, which in concert they always ended with Copland's own dramatic coda. The unison sound of band and orchestra here is staggering!

"Knife Edge" is perhaps the only number which doesn't excite as much as the original recording, though judging from audience reaction it went down well on the night, and it's a solid performance.

"Show Me The Way To Go Home" is given a sonorous, late-night blues feel at the start, then goes into a snazzy good-time groove. The absence of strings doesn't matter at all. Maybe this is better than the studio version, too. Why did we have to wait 14 years to hear this little gem?

The live orchestral version of "Abaddon's Bolero" is vastly superior to the studio version released on the radio show promo LP "On Tour With Emerson, Lake And Palmer". This is the curtain-raising piece of the evening, whipping up the excitement before the full band joins the orchestra for the final statement of the theme. The orchestral instruments are vivid, well-balanced and played with enthusiasm, and the choir increases the magnificence of the overall effect.

"Pictures At An Exhibition" in its abbreviated form doesn't come across on disc as well as it probably did live. It lacks the drive and thrill of the original album version. Orchestra and group don't really gel except for dramatic unison moments and one or two other occasions such as "Promenade/The Sage" and the final spectacular verse with band, full orchestra and choir united behind Greg's powerful singing.

"An impassioned rendition of "Closer To Believing", very faithful to the album version, is followed by the Third Movement, "Toccata Con Fuoco", of the Piano Concerto No.1. This again shows that the orchestral experiment was a great success: the balance of piano and orchestra is just right, every section of the orchestra is crystal clear – as should be the case, for this movement is a orchestral virtuoso showpiece, not just a showstopper for the soloist alone. The double CD would be worth buying for the incredible version of "Tank" if nothing else.

Love Beach

"Memoirs Of An Officer And A Gentleman"

1. Prologue/The Education Of A Gentleman (**Emerson/Sinfield**) Attention is focused from the start on Greg's voice. Keith provides a simple and noble grand piano accompaniment as Greg sings in praise of the fallen. Carl's snare/bass drum intro leads into the first verse of the second part of the prologue, which could be called "Comrades In Arms". Carl uses the clashing ride cymbal to good effect in the second verse – "Sword in his hand/In the face of the teeth and flame". The brilliant polyphonic Korg synthesiser sound might have been made for this piece. The musical accompaniment to the powerful vocal is very simple: sustained chords against a syncopated bass line with drums in parallel.

2. Love At First Sight (Emerson/Sinfield) This is not just the central section in terms of its position, but also musically. The opening eight bars are the first eight bars of Chopin's First Etude (from the opus 10 set), and form the basis of the song. The melody of the song is nicely fitted in with the harmonic basis of the Etude. This Etude is among the most difficult pieces in the classical piano repertoire. Keith plays Chopin's music excellently. His own music, which is derived from it, is also very challenging: lots of his favourite 4ths, well integrated into a smooth melodic texture. This kind of romantic piano style had not been heard from Keith since "Take A Pebble", and before that, "Hang On To A Dream" on The Nice's last album, "Elegy". We don't hear enough of Keith playing the instrument which is probably his greatest strength. The magic is enhanced when first Greg on acoustic guitar, and then Carl on glockenspiel, join in the central solo. One nice touch is a nostalgic, wistful little piano phrase commenting on the phrase "was it a dream?" at the end of the chorus.

After the central instrumental section the initial Chopin Etude material is reprised, accompanying the vocal line for the first time. This is an impressive example of controlled performance by all concerned.

3. Letters From The Front (Emerson/Sinfield) The only occasion that Keith Emerson used a Fender Rhodes piano on record. "I remember the Fender Rhodes being advertised as an electric piano. It sounded nothing like a piano – very muffled – and I think the people who made good use of it were people like Chick Corea, really not accepting it as a piano but accepting it in some other way. I didn't really get into that. I hated the Fender Rhodes because they said it was a piano and I knew it wasn't."

In the introduction, bare 4ths and 7ths in the piano riff alternate with an answering idea in octaves. The effect is very jazzy. The song itself is quite basic, but has a funky syncopated feel. At the dramatic words "The telegram dropped from my hands", time stands still as the music is suspended over a long pedal G, and the Rhodes plays bare staccato 4ths and 5ths – an effect guaranteed to send a shiver up the spine.

4. Honourable Company (A March) (Emerson) Just like "Abaddon's Bolero", this closing instrumental section starts off with a simple statement of the theme, which is then built up to a climax by progressively adding several extra layers. Also like the earlier piece, it would have been impossible for the band to perform it without the help of tapes, sequencers or an orchestra. Perhaps sequencers could have been used if they had chosen to perform it live in 1979, as they were probably by then sufficiently advanced to be able to do the job.

However – what a great opportunity for using an orchestra, or even a marching band in the middle of some huge stadium! The basic 9-bar theme is first stated by a simple flutey "organ" voice. The second statement repeats it with a fuller sound, adding an extension of 4 bars. This extension is doubled to eight bars in the following three repeats. Statements 6-13 repeat the original 9 bar theme. To a martial beat provided by Carl, the texture gets denser and denser, with increasingly triumphal lines added to the mix. One of these briefly alludes to the introduction to "Rule Britannia"; the next brings in glockenspiel. Eventually the impression is created of a military band marching off into the distance, as the music fades. It's rather a fitting swansong for Emerson, Lake and Palmer. For now, at least, the show really had ended.

Emerson Lake & Powell

"The Score" (Emerson/Lake)

After three resonating opening notes from synthesiser and percussion, making up a grand chord of C, the bass guitar throbs out a rapidly repeated pedal C, while the drums keep up a steady heavy beat, cymbals in time with the bass rhythm. Enter Keith on GX1 with a couple of series of fanfares based on C chords.

A one-off fanfare based on B flat, F and C chords announces the main theme, a bright, festive, typically Emersonian fanfare melody extending over nearly two octaves. This is repeated, and after a contrasting section, it returns. A brooding, minor mood – three ominous chords over an A flat pedal – is summoned in the middle section, before, via chord changes over descending minor thirds, four fanfares over G announce the return of the original idea.

Straight into the vocal of the first verse – as throughout the album, there's nothing redundant in this piece; the music is always, as Keith says, "concise and to the point". The music is basically the same as in the instrumental introduction. Each phrase is punctuated by a stabbing organ chord. The second verse's bass line is less busy. Over some very long organ chords, Keith adds multiple glissandos.

There's a shift to triple time and into F major for the new theme on which the celebratory final part, filled out with a sweeping string sound, is based. Unison passages highlight the underlying triplet rhythm.

"The Miracle" (Emerson/Lake/Powell)

Four ominous keyboard open 5ths (C/G) like a tolling bell announce this magnificent and ambitious piece of fantasy. It is fairly complex structurally, having five component sections in the pattern ABACDEECAC; it's a testimony to the band's increased skill at writing concisely and with balance – no doubt aided by Keith's film experience – that it's easy to grasp and enjoy at first hearing. It is enhanced by a few judiciously placed grand flourishes and illustrative effects such as the brief but terrifying organ solo after "the bishop takes the pawn" and the single stabbed organ chord after "the arrows fly/each one to its mark".

Just as in "Mars" later, the texture becomes brighter as the piece progresses, adding to the mounting excitement; and the final heavy repeated chord of the "C" sections (after the chorus line "We're searching for a miracle") are also reminiscent of the concluding bars of "Mars".

"Touch And Go" (Emerson/Lake)

The tune is everything here; it's simply harmonised with some nice bass support and simple drum patterns. Excellent material, in fact, for a single, which is what it became – though that was probably a happy accident, according to Keith: "'Touch and Go' was the last to be added to the album. It was during the time that we were rehearsing for the live show, and I was dabbling around in a motif on the organ and Greg had a set of lyrics around 'Touch and Go', so we put the two ideas together."

"Step Aside" (Emerson/Lake)

The song has a smooth late-night jazz feel, certainly – Cozy uncharacteristically provides light jazz cymbals and brushed drums. Greg's in delightfully relaxed and easy mood supporting Keith's gentle nocturnal swagger of a piano solo. The string wash enhances the urban late-night feel, as does the faraway whistling at the end. For what it's worth, the key centre is around C sharp/G sharp – which does tend to create a bright but moody feel. And let's all remember Greg's advice: "Get it straight before it gets too hard to operate!"

"Mars, The Bringer Of War" (from The Planets by Gustav Holst, adapted by Emerson/Lake/Powell)

Holst, who was very interested in astrology, composed The Planets between 1914 and 1917, though its conception was much earlier. Many have thought "Mars", which he said represented the stupidity of war, was inspired by the horrors of the First World War, but it was in fact completed before the outbreak of hostilities.

The original music of "Mars" requires a large orchestra, including sixteen woodwind instruments, fifteen brass, six timpani, three other percussion players, celesta, xylophone, two harps, organ and strings. It is characterised by the relentless barbaric rhythm, a march-like 5/4 or 5/2 often consisting of an incessant repeated note with dotted or syncopated rhythms heard against it.

The band stays quite close to the original arrangement. Some chords are beefed up, some brief sections are omitted – such as brief counter-melodies which are just too much even for Keith's two hands to cope with along with everything else (e.g. bars 50-53). The wonderful onrush of string semiquavers (bars 93-4) which brings the first main part of the piece to a climax before falling suddenly away to almost nothing, is simplified.

The following passage (96-109) is scored with many surging crescendos and diminuendos, but this interesting effect is unfortunately not picked up on – consequently, these forty seconds drag a bit. After this however, things really take off, so it looks like ELP are doing one of their oldest tricks – actually it dates back much further, to The Nice's "Rondo" – namely starting off fairly muted and monochrome in texture, and winding up extremely bright and snazzy – always a good crowd-pleaser! Earlier on this album, both "The Score" and "The Miracle" benefit from this touch.

"Mars" ends as "The Score" began, on a big C chord, thus rounding the album off nicely.

In concert, this piece was Cozy's solo opportunity. The solo was Cozy's best ever, a spectacular assault on all the senses.

"The Loco-Motion" (Goffin/King, arr.ELP)

The story goes that Little Eva, populariser of this party classic, was Carole King's babysitter. One day she was improvising dance steps to Carole's piano playing; in response to this Carole hit on the tune of "The Loco-Motion", and Gerry Goffin penned the lyrics. Thus it was that in the same year that the public were treated to "Twistin' The Night Away" and "Twist & Shout", Little Eva could be heard wailing "Everybody's doin' a brand new dance now" – while enthusiastically showing how.

Hardly surprising that it's been covered by many artists. In the 70s many heavy music fans took Grand Funk Railroad's version to their hearts, of course. Among the most striking recent re-workings are those by Dave Stewart and Barbara Gaskin, and Orchestral Manoeuvres In The Dark; and Kylie Minogue made it a worldwide chart hit again. Emerson, Lake and Powell showed that it could be rocked up a storm.

To The Power Of Three

"Talkin' 'Bout" (Berry)

Just like "Emerson, Lake & Powell", the first song on this album opens on a dramatic C chord. After a punchy slow rising fanfare motif, the song begins in earnest, setting the style for most of the rest of the album – short, up tempo pomp/AOR songs with a progressive leaning.

"Desde La Vida" 1) La Vista (Emerson/Berry/Palmer). 2) Frontera (Emerson) 3) Sangre De Toro (Emerson/Palmer)

Keith: "This is the nearest thing to a conceptual piece. I wanted to keep concepts out of this album because we wanted to get over a lot more ideas rather than be self-indulgent, and I'd been playing a piano solo prior to this album, and 'Desde La Vida' was the idea from that piano solo. Robert and Carl heard it and said, "This is an instrumental, and I said, "No, no, I'm sure you can get some lyrics on this one", so Carl, living in the Canary Islands, was a big help getting all the Spanish stuff together."

Robert: "This is the twelfth version of this song we went through. We went through quite a bit to refine it."

Carl: "It really was the twenty minute version when we first started off. Keith had lots of ideas and we had to go through everything to see what we could get from it in seven or eight minutes. We wanted to have everything musically there. If it took longer, it took longer. I think in a live concert situation it *will* be longer."

Lyrically, the piece begs comparison with "Pirates". Written by Berry with help from Palmer with the Spanish, the words are effective and sometimes stirring but hardly in the Lake/Sinfield league. Linguistic switches in songs are often ill-advised, and that rule is uncomfortably emphasised here. No doubt Hispanic-Americans winced. Translating the words as you go is an acme of naffness, particularly if grammatical literacy is lacking ('El tiempo es buena, the time is good'). A basic tutor would have at least helped.

The central instrumental section, "Frontera" gives Keith a chance to shine, though again, it's not really in the ELP manner – mainly lots of stabbing, repeated, very percussive chords. Into the gap between the two verses of the final section, "Sangre De Toro", Emerson solos ferociously on grand piano, with finger-breaking staccato runs and crashing chords, battling with Palmer's fierce snare rolls. "I found a very interesting combination with one of the sounds in the Yamaha TX816. It blended very well with the MIDIed Bosendorfer. You can hear it on the piano solo in "Desde La Vida". I also brought out the percussiveness of the piano by MIDI-ing it to a Kurzweil 250 and using a marimba sound. On some occasions, I even MIDIed it to the Korg Sampling Grand."

The song has a superb, rolling "glory on the ocean wave" main riff, but perhaps outstays its welcome. It might perhaps have been wiser to make no concessions to the hardcore progressive audience, and leave "Desde La Vida" off this album; judging from the band's comments, they were preparing for a second, more ambitious album, so perhaps it would have found a home there.

"Eight Miles High" (Clark/McGuinn 2 /Crosby, revised lyric Emerson/Berry/Palmer)

This song by The Byrds from their album "Fifth Dimension" was a hit on both sides of the Atlantic in 1966, reaching Number 24 in the UK. It marked their shift to a more "progressive", or "space-rock" style. "We had a tape that was Coltrane's 'Indian Africa', said co-writer McGuinn in 1973. "The other side was Ravi Shankar, and we played that one tape over and over again. When we got into the studio that's what came out." "Eight Miles High" was one of the first singles to be banned because of perceived references to drug usage. Prosaically, it was in fact partly about air travel, and also, in McGuinn's words, "I was trying to get spiritual... But it seems that very few people really understood what I was saying." However, sensitivity to the widely-believed misinterpretation led Robert Berry to revise the lyrics for the Three version. This no doubt accounts for the alteration of the beginning of the last stanza from the highly corrupting "Sidewalk scenes and black limousines" to "Sidewalks of dreams as far as one sees'! – an astonishing example of playing it safe. And one of the more intriguing lines of the song are wilfully altered: "Nowhere is there work to be found/Among those afraid of losing their ground" becomes "Nowhere near/What can be found/Among us we can't lose more ground" – hardly an improvement.

The fantastic brass sound, recalls Keith, "was a combination of things, probably the Oberheim Matrix MIDIed to the Yamaha TX816 and the Korg DSS-1, as far as I can remember. I found that solo at the end quite fun. I could have gone on all night, playing different solos, but I sort of fell in love with the one that's on the record."

"I found it interesting to deal with a classic from the rock and roll era. Basically, the arrangement started from a rhythm that I created on a drum machine; I think Robert may have added an accent here and there after I got it going. Then the brass riff [based on Roger McGuinn's 12-string guitar solo] came out of that. That needed a bit of playing around with, because McGuinn's solo is very free-flowing."

Live, "Eight Miles High" was taken as the opportunity for Keith and Carl both to come out to the front with their respective axes (Keith playing his Korg remote keyboard while a sequencer played the riff, Carl with his Dynacord Rhythm Stick3) and join with Berry on bass in a superb jam.

224

"You Do Or You Don't" (Berry)

Another cracking song, gradually building to a wonderful climax by way of a beautifully crafted central section for both keyboards and guitar. It has a simple tune, based on a descending chromatic line, which makes the impact of a modulation into a different key much more effective. "That's why I felt a key change was necessary," commented Emerson. It is a familiar sort of chord structure, quite similar to a few other songs, so I felt the arrangement needed a definite change. You don't want to overdo key changes, though, because that can come out sounding a bit like Chicago."

"On My Way Home" (Emerson)

Emerson wrote this track, which doesn't strictly belong with the style of the album, "in memory of Tony Stratton-Smith", the then recently-deceased former boss of Charisma Records, who had been both a good friend and, by signing the Nice when problems dictated their moving from Immediate, a major factor in Keith's career success. At the memorial service at St. Martins-In-The-Fields church in London, Keith played his "Lament for Tony Stratton-Smith'.

This is Keith's first contribution of lyrics to any record, witnessing to the fact that they were deeply-felt. They are strikingly simple and affecting. "It was Tony, actually, who introduced me to Carl Palmer when we formed ELP. Tony died last year. A very distressed Brian Davison broke the news to me over the phone. Then Lee Jackson called up and said he was going to come over for the funeral. I was very upset. My whole family was, in fact, because we really liked the guy. He was well loved in the recording industry. So I thought, "Hell, I'll use this emotion to write a piece of music". So I sat down at the piano and wrote this ballad. Tony's office rang up and said that there was going to be a memorial service. I told them I'd written a piece of music, and they said, "Would you like to play it at the service?" It's not an easy gig, quite honestly. You get up there and perform, and nobody claps. Everybody cries. Fortunately it was broken up by a lot of people from the entertaining industry who got up and said funny things. The Monty Python contingent, who'd been represented on record by Charisma, launched into 'Always Look On The Bright Side Of Life'."

The piano "introduction" is not technically an introduction, according to Keith. "In fact, the piano plays the theme, then the chorus comes in, and it's basically A-B-A-B all the way through. When I wrote the piano passage out, I stuck an extra chorus and some other modulations in too."

He had transcribed his own performance from the recording, a practice begun in 1979 when he was asked to do a variation of "Good King Wenceslas" for the American magazine *Keyboard*. "Since then, I do that a lot more with my own pieces. I'll listen to what I've recorded and say, The fact that I can play it that way is good, but maybe there's some other way to play it too. I had a go at one of Hoagy Carmichael's songs, "Skylark". I wrote an interesting arrangement of that. I used to play it in a pub," he laughs. "I wrote all the album out so that I could see on paper all the different lines I had put down on the record, and figure out how I could cope with them in a live situation."

The synth sound is warm and cheering, and Keith graces the song with a solo of impassioned quality. "When I wrote that piece, in the section where I go up to G, I incorporated a lot of themes from The Nice, because of the memories I associate with it. I came up with a brief idea, wrote it down on manuscript paper, went for a run, and finished it when I got back. "Rondo", "America", the "Five Bridges Suite" – I moulded all those themes together."

"On my way Home" is both a moving personal tribute to a man who was by all accounts one in a million, and a superbly anthemic ending for the album.

Another Shifrin song, "Business & Pleasure", was at one stage intended as the first single, but it was eventually ditched completely. It can be found on a bootleg CD. Sounds like PM + Emerson – who gets in a great piano solo at the end.

Notes

1   Sue Shifrin is a highly successful songwriter. Before Three, she had written for Tina Turner, Dionne Warwick, Heart and others. She is the third wife of David Cassidy.

2   The Nice had recorded a McGuinn song "Get To You", which was originally recorded by the Byrds on their 1969 "The Notorious Byrd Brothers" album, for a Radio One "Top Gear" session.

3   This device resembles a small fretless guitar without a head. Drum sounds are produced by hitting it where the pickups of a guitar would be. Palmer first used it live at the Marquee, London, on 4 June 1986, for a charity concert with John Wetton, Phil Manzanera, Don Airey and Robin George, during a cover version of "Honky Tonk Women" and an Airey/Palmer solo. On Three's tour, he got a fierce metallic sound out of it. Carl also used a Dynacord electronic drumkit, which he played as a complete and separate entity on the left of the Remo kit.

APPENDIX 1

DISCOGRAPHY

1: ALBUMS

OFFICIAL RELEASES
Every effort has been made to include all issues of each item, but any additional information will be welcomed. Albums and singles produced by E, L & P are included, even if they do not perform.

EMERSON LAKE & PALMER

Emerson Lake & Palmer
Island ILPS 9132 LP UK
Island 6339 026. Gatefold sleeve; inner picture of band on spiral staircase.
Cotillion SD 9040 LP USA
Cotillion M 9040 reel, USA
Atlantic Japan P-10111 A LP. Lyric insert
Atlantic 781 519-2 CD
Victory 828 464-2 CD (remastered, 1993) December 1970
Tracks: The Barbarian, Take a Pebble, Knife Edge, The Three Fates, Tank, Lucky Man

Tarkus
Island LIPS 9155 LP UK
Cotillion SD 9900 LP USA
Cotillion M 9900 reel, USA
Atlantic Japan P-10126 A LP. Lyric insert.
Atlantic 781 529-2 CD
Victory 828 465-2 CD (remastered, 1993)
Mobile Fidelity Sound Labs 1-203 LP (1993)
Mobile Fidelity Sound Labs Ultradisc UDCD 598 (1994) June 1971
Tracks: Tarkus – a) Eruption, b) Stones of Years c) Iconoclast d) Mass e) Manticore f) Battlefield g) Aquatarkus , Jeremy Bender, Bitches Crystal, The Only Way, Infinite Space, A Time and a Place, Are you ready Eddy?

Pictures at an Exhibition
Island HELP 1 LP UK
Cotillion ELP 66666 LP USA
Atlantic 781 521-2 CD
Mobile Fidelity Sound Lab MFSL 1-031 LP USA (remastered at half speed onto high-definition vinyl, 1981. Highly revealing and noise-free; better than the Victory CD remaster?)
Melodiya C 90-16383-4 LP USSR, 1981
Victory 828 466-2 CD (remastered, 1993) November 1971

Tracks: Promenade, The Gnome, Promenade, The Sage, The Old Castle, Blues Variations, Promenade, The Hut of Baba Yaga, The Curse of Baba Yaga, The Hut of Baba Yaga, The Great Gates of Kiev, Nutrocker

Trilogy
Island LIPS 9186 LP UK
Cotillion SD 9903 LP USA
Cotillion/Capitol Record Club SMAS-94773 LP USA, 1973
Atlantic 781 522-2 LP
Atlantic Japan P-10113 A LP; lyric/bio insert.
IANT TD-1138 LP CHINA
Atlantic 19123-2 CD
Victory 828 467-2 CD (remastered, 1993) June 1972
Tracks: The Endless Enigma Pt 1, Fugue, The Endless Enigma Pt2, From the Beginning, The Sheriff, Trilogy, Living Sin, Abaddon's Bolero

Brain Salad Surgery
Manticore K 53501. Lyric/poster insert.
MC 66669 LP USA. Insert as above.
P-10114 M LP JAPAN. Additional Japanese bio insert.
Atlantic 781 523-2 CD 19124-2 CD
Manticore 258174 CD W.GER. (Parts 1 & 2 of Karn Evil 9 1st Impression plays continuously with no fade.)
Victory 828 468-2 CD (remastered, 1993) December 1973
Tracks: Jerusalem, Toccata, Still...You Turn Me On,Benny the Bouncer, Karn Evil 9 – First, Second ,Third Impressions

Welcome Back My Friends...To the show That Never Ends
Tracks: Hoedown, Jerusalem, Toccata, Tarkus, Take a Pebble, Jeremy Bender/The Sheriff medley, Karn Evil 9

Works Volume 1
Atlantic K 80009 LP UK
SD 2-7000 LP USA
Atlantic Japan P-6311-2A LP. Japanese bio insert. 7000-2 CD
Victory 828 470-2 CD (remastered, 1993) March 1977
Tracks: Keith side – Piano Concerto No 1 , Greg side – Lend your love to me tonight, Cest La Vie, Hallowed be thy name, Nobody You Like I Do, Closer To Believing, Carl side – The Enemy God Dances With The Black Spirits, LA Nights, New Orleans, Two Part Invention in D Minor, Food For Your Soul, Tank, ELP side – Fanfare for the Common Man, Pirates

Works Volume 2
Atlantic K 50422 LP UK
SD 19147 LP USA
Atlantic Japan P-6403-A LP. Japanese lyric/bio insert.
781 538-2 CD
Victory 828 473-2 (remastered, 1993) November 1977
Tracks: Tiger in a Spotlight, When the Apple Blossoms Bloom in the Windmills of Your Mind I'll Be Your Valentine, Bullfrog, Brain Salad Surgery, Barrelhouse Shakedown, Watching Over You, So Far to Fall, Maple Leaf Rag, I Believe in Father Christmas, Close But Not Touching, Honky Tonk Train Blues, Show Me the Way to Go Home

Love Beach
Atlantic K 50552
SD 19211 LP USA
Ariola 200 249-320 LP W.GER. Lyric insert
AMCY-217 CD JAP
Victory 828 469-2 CD (remastered, 1993)
November 1978
Tracks: All I Want is You, Love Beach, Taste of My Love, The Gambler, For You, Canario, Memoirs of an Officer and a Gentleman a) Prologue/The Education of a Gentleman b) Love at First Sight c) Letters From the Front d) Honourable Company (A March)

In Concert (later Works Live)
Atlantic K 50652 LP UK
SD 19255 LP USA
19255-2 CD USA November 1979
Tracks: Introductory Fanfare, Peter Gunn, Tiger in the Spotlight, C'est La Vie, The Enemy God, Knife Edge, Piano Concerto Third Movement, Pictures at an Exhibition
Victory 828 477-2 CD December 1993
Works Live Extra *Tracks:* Watching Over You, Maple Leaf Rag, Fanfare for the Common Man, Show Me The Way to Go Home, Abaddon's Bolero, Closer to Believing, Tank

***Best of Emerson Lake & Palmer**

***The Atlantic Years**
Atlantic 7567-82403-2 CD May 1992

Black Moon
Victory 828-318-1 LP
828-318-4 MC
828-318-2 CD
VICP-5164 CD JAPAN (Bonus track – Blade of Grass) May 1992
Tracks: Black Moon, Paper Blood, Affairs of the Heart, Romeo & Juliet,

227

Farewell to arms, Changing States, Burning Bridges, Close to Home, Better Days, Footprints in the Snow

Live at the Royal Albert Hall
Victory 383-480-011-2 (CD)
Jan 1993
Tracks: Karn Evil 9 First Impression Part 2, Tarkus, Knife Edge, Paper Blood, Romeo & Juliet, Creole Dance, Still... You Turn Me On, Lucky Man, Black Moon, Finale of Fanfare for the Common Man, America and Rondo

*Return of the Manticore
Victory 828 459-2 4CD box set
November 1993
New *Tracks:* Touch & Go, Hang On to a Dream, 21st Century Schzoid Man, Fire, Pictures at an Exhibition, I Believe in Father Christmas

In the Hot Seat
Victory 828 554-2 (CD) August 1994 ?
Tracks: Hand of Truth, Daddy, One by One, Heart on Ice, Thin Line, Man in The Long Black Coat, Change, Give Me a Reason to Stay, Gone Too Soon, Street War, Bonus track Pictures at an Exibition

*The Best of Emerson Lake & Palmer
ESSENTIAL ESS 296 (CD) ? 1995

King Biscuit Flower Hour
King Biscuit 88025-2 (2CD) ? 1997
Tracks: Peter Gunn, Tiger in the Spotlight, C'est La Vie, Piano Imp, Maple Leaf Rag, Drum Solo, The Enemy God, Watching Over You, Pirates, Fanfare for the common man, Hoedown, Still..You turn Me On, Lucky Man, Piano Imp, Karn Evil 9, Fully Interactive CD

Live at the Isle of Wight Festival
Manticore M-CD101 ? 1997
Tracks: The Barbarian, Take a Pebble, Pictures at an Exhibition, Rondo, Nutrocker

Live in Poland
Metal Mind Records PROG CD0060 ? 1997
Tracks: Karn Evil 9 First Impression Part 2, Touch & Go, From the Beginning, Knife Edge, Bitches Crystal, Piano Solo, Take a Pebble, Lucky Man, Tarkus/ Pictures, Fanfare for the Common Man

Then & Now
Eagle EDL EAG 098-2 (2CD)
August ? 1998

Tracks: Then 1974 – Toccata, Take a Pebble excerpts, Karn Evil 9 First Impression Part 2 & Third Impression, Now – 1997/98 , A Time and a Place, Piano Concerto No 1, From the Beginning, Karn Evil 9 First Impression Part 2, Tiger in the Spotlight, Hoedown, Touch & Go, Knife Edge, Bitches Crystal, Honky Tonk Train Blues, Lucky Man, Fanfare for the Common Man, Blue Rondo a la Turk, 21st Century Schizoid Man, America

Emerson Lake & Powell
Polydor POLD 5191 LP UK
829 297-2 CD USA June 1986
Reissued:With bonus track, USA: 1992, same serial number as 1986 release.
Tracks: The Score, Learning to Fly, The Miracle, Touch & Go, Love Blind, Step Aside, Lay Down Your guns, Mars, Bonus tracks: The Locomotion, Vacant Possession

THREE

To the Power of Three
Geffen 924-181-1 (LP)
924-181-4 (MC)
924-181-2 (CD) February 1988
Tracks: Talkin' 'bout, Lover to Lover, Chains, Desde La Vida, Eight Miles High, Runaway, You Do or You Don't, On My Way Home

ROBERT BERRY

Solo Albums
Back To Back
BIG CHEESE RECORDS LPBC-1005 LP, 1984.
Now available on cassette from Leonardo Records (see below).
Tracks: Louie; Between The Lines; Eleanor Rigby (Beatles); The Man In Me; Could Have Started Over; You Can't Do That; Middle Of The Night; C'mon Everybody (Cochran); Life The Game; Allright; Subway.

Pilgrimage To A Point
LEONARDO LEN 6691 CD, 1993. The second solo album by ex-Three member Berry. "Shelter" is co-written with Carl Palmer; the epic "Last Ride Into The Sun" (certainly superior to "Desde La Vida") is truly a Three composition, by all members of the band. It "was born out of tapes sent to me from Carl and Keith to work over".
No mention is made of either Palmer or Emerson playing on the two tracks here; however, they were intended for a projected second Three album, and the sound is

unmistakeably that of Three. Some of the keyboard sounds are from Eye & I Voice Crystals, used by Keith on the album and tour.

With HUSH

Hush
GNOME RECORDS 62477 LP, 1977, USA.
Tracks: Who Holds The Light; Truth; Reunion; Wanna Dance; The Journey; Lies; Hollywood.
Robert Berry: keyboards, guitar, vocals.
Paul Keller: guitars, vocals.
Roger Bonasera: drums, percussion, vocals.
Gene Perrault: bass, vocals.
Reissued in modified form, ASI RECORDS 218 LP, 1978, USA, omitting tracks 2-4 of the original and adding: Ever Since The Beginning; Rock And Roll Babies; Got To Keep The Music Alive; Words.

Hush 2
1980. Now available thru Leonardo Records (see below).
Tracks: Let Me Live; Out On The Street; You Hold The Key; Intro/ It's Allright; Rendezvous; It's All Too Much; You; Another Saturday Night; A Room.
Personnel as first album.

Hot Tonight
1982. Now available thru Leonardo Records (see below).
Tracks: Hot Tonight; You Hold The Key; Out On The Street; Money; Gotta Get Back To You; Runaway; Let Me Live; It's All Too Much.
Personnel as before, except Peter Adams, drums.
Repeated titles are different versions.

All Robert Berry's albums available, from Leonardo Entertainment Network, 85 S. 2nd. St., Campbell, CA 95008, USA.

KEITH EMERSON

With GARY FARR & THE T-BONES

One More Chance
DECAL LIK 11 LP, 1987. "We played all over Britain and the Continent, but I never actually recorded with the band. Well, we did record, but no actual records were released at the time." This album of "the complete recordings" of the band is of interest for those who still choose

to disbelieve Keith, as well as for the background information in John Platt's sleevenotes.

With THE V.I.Ps

The V.I.Ps
FUNTONA V 8500, AUSTRALIA. Double album of their complete recordings. Spot the tracks Emerson played on, if you can! "I Wanna Be Free" and "Stagger Lee", which definitely include him, are here. Now also on CD.

With P.P. ARNOLD

The First Lady Of Immediate
IMMEDIATE IMSP 011, 1967;

Kafunta
IMMEDIATE IMSP 017, 1968.

It is not clear whether the Nice, with Keith Emerson, played on the first of these; however, they certainly contribute to several tracks on "Kafunta". Both were available on CD as "The P.P. Arnold Collection", LINE IDCD 9.00611 0 CD, 1988.

With THE NICE

The Thoughts Of Emerlist Davjack.
IMMEDIATE IMLP 016 LP, 1967, UK.
IMMEDIATE 52004 LP, 1967, USA.
Reissues:
CHARLY CR 300021 LP, 1978, UK reissue.
LINE IDCD 9.00228 0 CD, W.GERMANY.
Tracks: Flower King Of Flies; The Thoughts Of Emerlist Davjack; Bonnie K; Rondo; War And Peace; Tantalising Maggie; Dawn; The Cry Of Eugene.
Keith Emerson: organ, piano, harpsichord, vocals.
Lee Jackson: bass, guitar, vocals, tymps.
David O'List: guitar, trumpet, flute, vocals.
Brian Davison: drums, tubular bells, tymps.

Ars Longa Vita Brevis
IMMEDIATE IMSP 020 LP, 1968, UK.
IMMEDIATE 52020 LP, 1968, USA.
Reissues:
CHARLY CR 300019 LP, 1978, UK
CASTLE CLACD 120 CD, 1987, UK.

Tracks: Daddy Where Did I Come From; Little Arabella; Happy Freuds; Intermezzo from the Karelia Suite (Sibelius); Don Edito el Gruva; ARS LONGA VITA BREVIS – Prelude; 1st mvt.: Awakening; 2nd mvt.: Realisation; 3rd mvt.: Acceptance ("Brandenburger"); 4th mvt.: Denial; Coda – Extension to the Big Note.
Keith Emerson: organ, piano, harpsichord, vocals.
Lee Jackson: bass, vocals.
Brian Davison: drums, percussion.
Orchestra arranged and conducted by Robert Stewart.

Nice
IMMEDIATE IMSP 026 LP, 1969, UK.
IMMEDIATE 52022 LP, 1969, USA.
Reissues:
CHARLY CR 300014 LP, 1978, UK.
LINE IDCD 9.00233 0 CD, 1987, W.GERMANY.
Tracks: Azrael Revisited; Hang On To A Dream; Diary Of An Empty Day; For Example; Rondo 69; She Belongs To Me.
Emerson/Jackson/Davidson as before.

Five Bridges
CHARISMA CAS 1014 LP, 1970, UK.
MERCURY SR 61295 LP, 1970, USA.
Reissues: VIRGIN CASCD 1014 CD, 1990. (With five bonus tracks: The Thoughts Of Emerlist Davjack; Flower King Of Flies; Bonnie K; Diary Of An Empty Day; America.)
VIRGIN JAPAN VJCP-23029 CD, 1990 (no bonuses)
Tracks: The Five Bridges Suite (Fantasia 1st Bridge/ 2nd Bridge; Chorale 3rd Bridge; High Level Fugue 4th Bridge; Finale 5th Bridge); Intermezzo from Karelia Suite (Sibelius); Pathetique (3rd movement, Tchaikovsky's 6th Symphony); Country Pie/Brandenburg Concerto no.6 (Dylan/Bach); One Of Those People.
Emerson/Jackson/Davidson as before.
Sinfonia of London, conductor Joseph Eger.

Elegy
CHARISMA CAS 1030 LP, 1970, UK.
MERCURY SR 61324 LP, 1970, USA.
VIRGIN CASCD 1030 CD, 1990, UK. With six additional tracks:

Diamond Hard Blue Apples Of The Moon; Dawn; Tantalising Maggie; The Cry Of Eugene; Daddy, Where Did I Come From; Azrial.
VIRGIN JAPAN VJCP-23030 CD, 1990 (no bonuses)
Tracks: Hang On To A Dream (Hardin); My Back Pages (Dylan); 3rd Movement, Pathetique; America

Autumn '67-Spring '68
CHARISMA PERSPECTIVE CS1. Best of the first two albums, plus the original, hitherto unreleased version of "Daddy Where Did I Come From" with Davy O'List.

NICE COMPILATIONS
(Note this list is not exhaustive. There are approx 50-60 compilations featuring The Nice):

Amoeni Redivivi
IMMEDIATE IML 1003, 1976, UK.
Amazing art work on the gatefold sleeve: three pictures of a manic figure in a sci-fi landscape playing keyboard, drums and guitar, respectively.
Tracks: Rondo; Hang On To A Dream (first version); The Thoughts Of Emerlist Davjack; Karelia; America (single); The Cry Of Eugene; The Diamond Hard Blue Apples Of The Moon; Ars Longa Vita Brevis 3rd mvt.: Acceptance (Brandenburger); 4th mvt.: Denial.

The Best Of The Nice
LINE OLLP 5278 AS, 1983, W.GERMANY.
Loads of biographical background information on the back, by Allen Betrock.
Tracks: America (single); Little Arabella; The Diamond Hard Blue Apples Of The Moon; Karelia; The Thoughts Of Emerlist Davjack; War And Peace; The Cry Of Eugene; Brandenburger.

The Best Of The Nice, The Small Faces, Humble Pie, Eric Clapton and John Mayall.
IMMEDIATE 1C148-92661/662 LP
W.GERMANY. Attractive 2LP comp.

NICE TRACKS: America; Brandenburger; Hang On To A Dream. Keith Emerson With The Nice.
PHILIPS GDA 1115/6 LP, 1970, ITALY. Released to complement issue no.57 of the magazine "Il ROCK".

Tracks: from Five Bridges – Five Bridges Suite; from Elegy – Country Pie/Brandenburg Concerto no.6; America.Keith Emerson With The Nice. MERCURY 830 457-2 CD. Playing time 69.01.
Tracks: from Five Bridges – Five Bridges Suite; Karelia; Pathetique; from Elegy – Hang On To A Dream; America; My Back Pages.

Immediate Lets You In
IMMEDIATE IMLYIN 1, 1968. Nine album tracks by artists on the Immediate label. Two by The Nice: Happy Freuds; Rondo.

The Immediate Story
VIRGIN V 2165 LP, 1980, UK. One track each by 17 Immediate artists. The Nice: America (single). Worth tracking down for the detailed history of Immediate by Michael Watts.

In Memoriam
IMMEDIATE 2C 054-91.151, FRANCE. Brief sleeve notes in French.
Tracks: America (single); Rondo 69; The Diamond Hard Blue Apples Of The Moon; Karelia; The Thoughts Of Emerlist Davjack; Azrael Revisited; Hang On To A Dream; Brandenburger.

The Nice
BELLAPHON CR 3029, W,GERMANY. One of a series of compilations by various artists.
Tracks: Rondo; Hang On To A Dream (first version); The Thoughts Of Emerlist Davjack; Karelia; Ars Longa Vita Brevis.

The Nice Collection.
CASTLE COLLECTOR SERIES CCSLP106, 1985
CASTLE COLLECTOR SERIES CCSCD106, 1985 Playing time 56.42. Rare col. photos.
Tracks: America (single); Happy Freuds; The Cry Of Eugene; The Thoughts Of Emerlist Davjack; Rondo; Daddy Where Did I Come From; Little Arabella; Intermezzo From Karelia; Hang On To A Dream (first version); Diamond Hard Blue Apples Of The Moon; Angel Of Death.

The Nice Collection
LINE IDCD 9.00720, 1989, W.GERMANY. Playing time 72.05. Sleeve notes and rare b/w photos. Some unusual track selections.
Tracks: America (single); Daddy,

Where Did I Come From; Rondo; The Thoughts Of Emerlist Davjack; Brandenburger; War And Peace; Karelia/ Don Edito el Gruva; Azrial, Angel Of Death; Hang On To A Dream (first version); For Example; She Belongs To Me.

The Nice Featuring Davy O'List
SEAL RECORDS SLP 2, 1987, UK. See Appendix 7: Davy O'List for more details.
Tracks: The Thoughts Of Emerlist Davjack; Flower King Of Flies; Bonnie K; America; Diamond Hard Blue Apples Of The Moon; Tantalising Maggie; The Cry Of Eugene; Daddy Where Do I Come From (original recording, with O'List).

The Nice: The Immediate Years.
ACCORD 139239 CD, 1987, FRANCE.
Playing time 57.53. Sleeve notes in French and English.
Tracks: America (single); Hang On To A Dream (first version); Rondo; Tantalising Maggie; War And Peace; The Thoughts Of Emerlist Davjack; Karelia; Bonnie K; Diary Of An Empty Day; Ars Longa Vita Brevis, 3rd mvt.: Acceptance (Brandenburger).

Also

JOSEPH EGER/ SINFONIA OF LONDON

Classical Heads
CHARISMA CAS-1008, 1970. Although the Nice do not perform on this album, it is essential for any Emerson fan, as many of these classical pieces were all played at one time or another by the Nice, with Eger conducting the Sinfonia. The "Troika" eventually got used in "I Believe..." of course.
Tracks: BERLIOZ – Lelio (2nd mvt.: Chorus Of The Shades; 6th mvt.: Fantasia on Shakespeare's "Tempest"); Symphonie Fantastique 1st & 4th mvts.; 5th Century Plain Song; Symphonie Fantastique 5th mvt.; IVES – The Unanswered Question; GABRIELI – Sonata Pian E Forte; Prokofiev – Troika from Lieutenant Kije; STRAVINSKY – Infernal Dance Of Kastchei from The Firebird.
Arranged, produced and conducted by Joseph Eger.
The Sinfonia Of London and the Ambrosian Singers.
Words spoken by John Neville of X-Files fame.

with ROY HARPER/ The Nice
Flat Baroque And Berserk
HARVEST SHVL 766 LP, 1970. One track, Hell's Angels, features The Nice (Keith Emerson, Lee Jackson, Brian Davison) with Roy Harper on vocals. As Harper comments, "I would also like to congratulate myself for playing electric guitar on Hells Angels on which track I was accompanied by three very dear friends whose names I cannot give you because they belong to another label. Enough to say that they turned me on to rock and I turned them on to the Karelia."

with ROD STEWART
An Old Raincoat Will Never Let You Down
VERTIGO VO4, 1969.
Keith plays organ on 'I wouldn't ever change a thing'

with VARIOUS ARTISTS
Music From Free Creek
CHARISMA CADS 101, 1973. Excellent double super-session album featuring performances from various groupings of big name musicians including Todd Rundgren, Linda Ronstadt, Doctor John, Mitch Mitchell and many others. Eric Clapton goes under the name of A.N.Other for contractual reasons. Keith Emerson plays on three tracks: Freedom Jazz Dance (Eddie Harris); Mother Nature's Son (Beatles); On The Rebound (Floyd Cramer). The Harris tune is the stand-out. Essential listening. Soon to be reissued on CD.

KEITH EMERSON SOLO ALBUMS

Inferno
CINEVOX CIA 5022 LP, 1980, ITALY.
CINEVOX CD-CIA 5022, 1989, ITALY.
ATLANTIC 50753, 1980. Gatefold sleeve opens to reveal giant close-up photo of Emerson.
ARIOLA 202 079-320, 1980. Same as above.
Soundtrack music from the Italian horror film. Winner of the Italian equivalent of an Oscar in 1980.
Tracks: Inferno main title theme; Rose's Descent Into The Cellar; Taxi Ride (Rome); The Library; Sarah In The Library Vaults; Bookbinder's Delight; Rose Leaves The Apartment; Rose Gets It;

Elisa's Story; A Cat Attic Attack; Kazanian's Tarantella; Mark's Discovery; Mater Tenebrarum; Inferno Finale; Cigarettes, Ices, etc.

Nighthawks
BACKSTREET RECORDS thru MCA RECORDS, BSR 5196, 1981. Mastered at half speed.
BACKSTREET/ MCA RECORDS MCF 3107, 1981. Mastered at half speed.
Soundtrack music from the major American film starring Sylvester Stallone. Features Emerson's first recorded use of the Fairlight Computer Musical Instrument.
Tracks: Nighthawks, Mean Stalkin', The Bust, Nighthawking, The Chase, I'm a Man, The Chopper, Tramway, I'm Comin' In, Face to Face, The Flight of a Hawk

Harmagedon
CANYON INTERNATIONAL RECORDS C28Y0044, 1983, JAPAN.
A Number One hit in Japan, riding on the back of the huge success of the animated film for which it was the soundtrack. Emerson contributes 7 of the twelve tracks and is credited with the role of music supervisor; the other tracks are by Nozomu Aoki.
EMERSON TRACKS: Theme Of Floi; Toccata And Fugue In D Minor (Bach); Joe And Michiko; Children Of The Light; Sonny's Skate State; Zamedy Stomp; Challenge Of The Psionics Fighters. Track 4 co-written with Tony Allen.
(The UK version omits the Toccata And Fugue and the Aoki tracks, and adds eight soundtrack pieces by Derek Austin. CHORD RECORDS CHORD 3, UK.)
Keith Emerson: Korg synths – Polysix, Mono/Poly, Vocoder, EPS, Trident Mk. 2.
Drums: Jun Aoyama (tracks 1,4,7).
Guitars: Fujimaru Yoshino (track 7).
Vocal: Rosemary Butler (track 4).

Honky
BUBBLE BLU 19608 LP, 1981, ITALY.
CHORD RECORDS CHORD 2, 1983, UK.
CHORD RECORDS CHORD CD 002 (inexplicably omits Rum-A-Ting and adds Chic Charni).
The first Emerson solo album, excluding soundtracks. Great fun from start to finish.
Tracks: Bach Before The Mast (Malcolm)/ Hello Sailor; Salt Cay;

Green Ice; Intro-Juicing; Big Horn Breakdown (Taylor); Yancey Special (Lewis); Rum-A-Ting; Jesus Loves Me.
Keith Emerson: Yamaha CP30, Minimoog, Hammond C3, Korg 3100 & 3300, Steinway Concert Grand Model D, Vocoder.
Kendal Stubbs: bass.
Frank Scully, Neil Symonette: drums, percussion.
Mott: guitar.
Andrew Brennan, Dick Morrissey, Pete King: saxes.
Keith Emerson, Michael Hanna, Shelley Lightbourn: rudimentary vocals, track 3.
The Kayla Lockhart Singers, track 8.

Murderock
BUBBLE RECORDS BLULP 1819, 1984, ITALY.
CHORD RECORDS CHORD 4, UK.
CHORD RECORDS CD COLL 3, UK (Best Revenge and Murder Rock on one CD)
Soundtrack music from the Italian thriller film. Tracks 2-4 co-written with Doreen Chanter.
Tracks: Murderock; Tonight Is Your Night; Streets To Blame; Not So Innocent; Prelude to Candice; Don't Go In The Shower; Coffee Time; Candice; New York Dash; Tonight Is Not Your Night; The Spillone.
Keith Emerson: Yamaha GX1, Steinway Grand, Korg synths.
Tom Nicol, Derek Wilson: drums.
Mike Sheppard: bass/lead guitars.
Doreen Chanter: lead vocals (2-4).
Mike Sebbage, Doreen Chanter: backing vocals (4).

Best Revenge
CHORD RECORDS LP CHORD 1, 1983, UK.
JIMCO RECORDS CD JIM 0013
Soundtrack music from the thriller film.
Tracks: Dream Runner; The Runner; Wha'dya Mean; Straight Between The Eyes; Orchestral Suite To Best Revenge; Playing For Keeps.

The Christmas Album.
KEITH LP1, MC1, CD1, 1989.
Reissued 1995 on Amp Records CD No AMP CD018
Reissued 1999 on Gunslinger Records
Excellent Emersonian interpretations of well-known Christmas music, plus two Christmas pieces of his own – Snowman's Land and Captain Starship Christmas. The latter was co-written with Lorna Wright, wife of Gary. *Tracks:* Variations

on O Little Town Of Bethlehem; We Three Kings; Snowman's Land; Aria from Bach's Christmas Oratorio; Captain Starship Christmas (with the West Park School Choir); I Saw Three Ships; Petites Litanies De Jesus (Grovlez); It Came Upon A Midnight Clear; Silent Night (with singers from the London Community Gospel Choir).
The reissued version drops Captain Starship Christmas but includes two new tracks Troika and Glorietta.
Keith Emerson: Korg and Yamaha keyboards.
Frank Scully: drums, track 9.
Les Moir: bass, track 2.
Mike Newbon: drum program, track 6. with singers from The London Community Gospel Choir, track 9.

La Chiesa (The Church)
CINEVOX MDF 33.192 LP, 1989, ITALY.
Soundtrack music from the Italian horror film. Four Emerson tracks; others by Goblin, Martin Goldray, Zooming On The Zoo and Definitive Gaze.
EMERSON TRACKS: The Church main title theme; Prelude 24 from The Well Tempered Clavier (Bach); The Possession; The Church Revisited.
"Written, performed, arranged and mixed by Keith Emerson."

Changing States
AMP Records AMP CD 026, 1996
Recorded in LA in 1989 for solo album. Never quite finished. When ELP got together in 1991 they plucked a few tracks for themselves – new title in brackets.
Shelter From the Rain, Another Frontier (Changing States), Ballade (Close to Home), The Band Keeps Playing, Summertime, The Church, Interlude, Montagues & Capulets (Romeo & Juliet), Abaddon's Bolero – with orchestra, recorded in Works era, The Band Keeps Playing – aftershock mix

Chord Sampler
CHORD LP, no number.
Tracks from five Emerson albums, plus four tracks by Derek Austin.
EMERSON TRACKS: Intro-Juicing; Big Horn Breakdown; Chic Charni (Nighthawking, instrumental version); Not So Innocent; Candice; Love Theme from Best Revenge; Playing For Keeps; Joe & Michiko; Inferno main title theme; Mater Tenebrarum; Children Of The Light.

231

The Emerson Collection
CHORD CD COLL 1, 1986.
The first good Emerson
compilation, Released on CD
only. Orchestral Suite To Best
Revenge; Bach Before The Mast/
Hello Sailor; Salt Cay; Prelude
To Candice; Candice; Nighthawks;
Inferno main title theme; Mater
Tenebrarum; Starship (excellent
early instrumental demo for
Captain Starship Christmas,
unavailable elsewhere); Chic
Charni – the only form in which
any of the Nighthawks album
has been available on CD so far,
though this should be rectified
soon); The Dreamer; Playing
For Keeps.

The Manhattan Collection
CHORD CD COLL 2.
Compilation of music by artists on
Chord Records. Other artists
featured are Derek Austin, Steve
Cameron and Albert Alan Owen.
EMERSON TRACKS: The
Dreamer; Prelude To Candice; Hello
Sailor; Inferno main title theme.

Best Works Collection
JIMCO RECORDS JICK-89169
CD, 1992.
Japanese compilation; the best one.
Tracks: Inferno main title theme;
Hello Sailor; Cigarettes, Ices, etc.;
Prelude 24 (Bach); Playing For
Keeps; Wha'dya Mean; Candice;
Petites Litanies De Jesus (Grovlez);
Taxi Ride; The Church main title
theme; Variations on O Little Town
Of Bethlehem; Dream Runner;
Elisa's Story; Green Ice.

with VARIOUS ARTISTS
Songs For A Modern Church
CHARISMA CAS 1159 LP,
1983, UK.
One Emerson track is included in
this compilation album which,
according to Tony Stratton-
Smith's notes, seeks to indicate
"the many strands of religious
feeling which inform the work of
today's songwriters". "My Name
Is Rain" is co-written with Lorna
Wright, Gary's husband, with
whom he later collaborated on
"Captain Starship Christmas".
Keith accompanied the West Park
School Choir.

for PETER HAMMILL
And Close As This
VIRGIN CDV 2409 CD, 1986.
One track, "Empire Of Delight",
was co-written by Hammill and
Emerson. Emerson supplied

Hammill with a piano piece for
which he wanted lyrics, and
Hammill duly obliged.

with GIOVANNI JOVANOTTI
Jovanotti YO IBZ 467557 2 CD,
1990, ITALY.
Three tracks on this debut album
by major Italian star Jovanotti
feature Emerson: Giovane sempre
(Hammond); Diritti e doveri
(Hammond solo); Sceriffo o
bandito (piano).

with ROCK AID ARMENIA
The Earthquake Album
LIFE AID RECORDS AID CD
001, 1990.
One ELP track on this compilation
album sold in aid of the victims of
the devastating Armenian
earthquake of 1990: "Fanfare For
The Common Man" (single
version). Keith is also one of many
rock musicians contributing to a
reworking of Deep Purple's
"Smoke On The Water".

with MARC BONILLA
E.E. Ticket
REPRISE RECORDS 9 26725-2
CD, 1991, USA
Emerson heard guitarist Bonilla in a
club playing a piece of music
intended for his debut album and
asked if he could play on it. The
resulting "White Noise", the
opening track, and possibly the
best on the album, features Keith
on piano. Brilliant stuff. The whole
album is worth buying, though the
track was released as a single.

plus VARIOUS ARTISTS.
The Best Of The 01/W
KORG CD 01/W, 1992, USA.
Nineteen tracks specially written for
Korg's flagship synthesiser.
Keith's, "Katoh-san", is named
after the chairman of Korg, Mr.
Katoh. It's one of the best things
he's done in recent years, and
brilliantly displays the capabilities
of the instrument. Among other
composers are Geoff Downes,
Edgar Froese, Eddie Jobson, Dave
Stewart, Rick Wakeman and Joe
Zawinul.

**EMERSON, LAKE AND
PALMER**

Emerson, Lake And Palmer
AMIGA 8 55 724, 1980
Not the first album, but an East
German compilation. Side One of
"Love Beach" plus "Fanfare",
"Maple Leaf Rag", "L.A. Nights"

and "The Barbarian"..

Emerson, Lake and Palmer
EURODISC, XF 301 883,4,5,6,
1982.
A box set of the first four albums,
released in Spain. Has a nice front
cover of the group logo formed
from broken electric cables. Boxes
individually numbered. Good sound
quality. MANTICORE, compiled
and distributed by ARIOLA

Works
ATLANTIC PR 271, 1977. Promo
with edited highlights.
ARIOLA, W.GER, 1977. An
equivalent double promo EP
sampler.

plus VARIOUS ARTISTS
*Mar Y Sol: The First
International Puerto
Rico Pop Festival*
ATLANTIC K 60029, 1972.
ATCO SD2-705, 1972.
Double album of live
performances by The Allman
Brothers Band, J.Geils Band,
Mahavishnu Orchestra with
John McLaughlin, Nitzinger
(John Nitzinger would later join
Palmer in PM), Osibisa, B.B.
King, Dr.John, Jonathan Edwards,
Herbie Mann, Cactus, Long John
Baldry – and ELP (Take A
Pebble/ Lucky Man).

By Invitation Only
2-LP, K60112, 1976.
Karn Evil 9, 1st Impression, pts.
1 & 2 complete (no fade). Other
artists include Led Zeppelin, PFM
and Yes.

**EMERSON, LAKE AND
POWELL**

Emerson, Lake and Powell
Released in Russia, MELODIYA
C60 26463 008, 1988.

GREG LAKE

With THE GODS
Genesis
COLUMBIA SCX 6286 LP, 1968,
UK.

The Very Best Of The Gods
C5 RECORDS C5 537 LP, 1989,
UK.
Although Greg did not record on the
Gods' first album, it is worth
hearing to give some idea of the
kind of material he was playing with
them. Six of the tracks can be found
on the above compilation album.

with KING CRIMSON
In The Court Of The Crimson King
ISLAND ILPS 9111, 1969, UK.
ATLANTIC 8245, 1969, USA.
POLYDOR 2302 057 LP, UK.
MOBILE FIDELITY SOUND
  LABS MFSL 1-075, USA. Half-
  speed remastering.
Tracks: 21st Century Schizoid Man;
I Talk To The Wind; Epitaph;
Moonchild; The Court Of The
Crimson King.
Robert Fripp: guitar.
Ian McDonald: reeds, woodwind,
  vibes, keyboards, mellotron, vocals.
Greg Lake: bass guitar, lead vocals.
Michael Giles: drums, percussion,
  vocals.
Peter Sinfield: words and
  illumination.

In The Wake Of Poseidon
ISLAND ILPS 9127, 1970, UK.
ATLANTIC 8266, 1970, USA.
PODOR 2302 058 LP, UK.
VIRGIN EGCD 2 CD.
LAKE TRACKS: Peace – A
Beginning; Pictures of a City; In
The Wake Of Poseidon; Cat Food;
Peace – An End.

**for SPONTANEOUS
  COMBUSTION**
Spontaneous Combustion
HARVEST SHVL 801 LP, 1972,
UK.
Greg produced this album. Great
concept for the sleeve design,
which is in the form of a strip
cartoon. The last picture is of Greg
wearing headphones, telling the
band to hurry up and start playing.

with/for PETE SINFIELD
Still
MANTICORE MC 66667, 1973.
Greg "produced the vocals and had
a hand or three in the mixing".
Pete also acknowledges his
"encouragement and strength". He
plays on three tracks: Hopes And
Dreams (electric guitar);
Wholefood (backing vocal); Still
(joint lead vocal).
Reissued as Stillusion,
  VOICEPRINT, 1993, UK, with
  bonus tracks.

for KEITH CHRISTMAS
Brighter Day
MANTICORE K 53503 LP, 1974,
UK.
MANTICORE MA6-503S1, 1975,
USA.
Greg produced one track, and co-
produced three with Pete Sinfield.
Keith acknowledges Greg "for the
energy transfusions".

for THE KING'S SINGERS
Tempus Fugit
EMI EMC 3268 LP, 1978.
Includes the Lake-produced
"Strawberry Fields Forever" which
was released as a single. Cover
versions of twelve pop and folk songs
by artists including Elton John, Bob
Dylan, David Bowie and Neil Sedaka.

GREG LAKE SOLO ALBUMS

Greg Lake
CHRYSALIS CHR 1357 LP, 1981,
UK.
CHRYSALIS JAPAN TOCP-7623
CD, 1993.
Track 2 completed from a basic idea
by Bob Dylan.
Tracks: Nuclear Attack; Love You
Too Much; It Hurts; Black And
Blue; Retribution Drive; Long
Goodbye; The Lie; Someone; Let
Me Love You Once Before You Go;
For Those Who Dare.
Greg Lake: bass, guitars, vocals.
Gary Moore: guitars.
Tristram Margetts: bass
Ted McKenna: drums.
Other musicians: Steve Lukather,
Dean Parks, Snuffy Walden:
guitars. Bill Cuomo, Greg
Matheson: keyboards.
David Hungate: bass. Mike Giles,
Jode Leigh, Jeff Porcaro: drums.
Clarence Clemmons: saxophone.
Willie Cochrane, David Milner: pipes.

Manoeuvres
CHRYSALIS CHR 1392 LP, 1983,
UK.
Tracks: Manoeuvres; Too Young to
Love; Paralysed; A Woman Like
You; I Don't Wanna Lose Your
Love Tonight; It's You, You've
Gotta Believe; Famous Last Words;
Haunted; I Don't Know Why I Still
Love You.
Basic personnel as above.

King Biscuit Flower Hour
King Biscuit 8010-2
? 1995
Tracks: Fanfare for the Common
Man, Karn Evil 9 First Impression
Part 2, Nuclear Attack, The Lie,
Retribution Drive, Lucky Man,
Parisienne Walkways, You really got
a hold on me, 21st Century
Schizoid Man, In the Court of the
Crimson King

From the Underground
GREG LAKE GL-CD3001 ? 1998
Tracks: Touch & Go, A Man A City,
Don't go away little girl, Still you turn
me on/Watching over you, Daddy,
Retribution Drive, Heat of the
Moment, The Score, Love, Affairs of

the Heart, Learning to fly, Lucky
Man, 21st Century Schizoid Man

for ASIA
Aqua
(for catalogue details, see Palmer,
  below).
Greg co- wrote one of the songs,
"Love Under Fire", with Geoff
Downes. A passionate ballad, well
suited to the delivery of new
vocalist John Payne, it is certainly
one of the best tracks on the album.
In better times for Asia, it might
have been a major chart success.

plus VARIOUS ARTISTS
Acoustic Aid
KOME 98.5 CD, 1992, USA.
Sixteen entirely acoustic
recordings, sold in aid of the San
Francisco AIDS Foundation.
Greg contributes a fine "From
The Beginning". Other artists
include Queen, The Allman
Brothers, Jethro Tull, MSG, Nils
Lofgren, Justin Hayward and
Little Feat.

CARL PALMER

**with THE CRAZY WORLD OF
  ARTHUR BROWN**
*The Crazy World Of Arthur
Brown*
TRACK 2407 012 LP, 1968, UK.
TRACK 8190 LP, 1968, USA.
POLYDOR 833 736-2 CD
Although Palmer was for some time
an active member of the band, he
contributed nothing to the first
Arthur Brown album, leaving to
form Atomic Rooster.

with ATOMIC ROOSTER
Atomic Rooster.
B&C 1010, 1970.
Tracks: Friday The 13th; And So
To Bed; Winter; Before
Tomorrow; Banstead; S.L.Y.;
Broken Wings; Decline And Fall.

for BACK DOOR
Activate.
WARNER BROS. K56243, 1976.
Produced by Carl Palmer, with P.M.
1:P.M.
ARIOLA ARL 5048 LP, 1980.
Tracks: Dynamite; You've Got Me
Rockin'; Green Velvet Splendour;
Dreamers; Go On Carry On; Do
You Go All The Way; Go For It;
Madeline; You're Too Much;
Children Of The Air Age.
Carl Palmer: drums.
Todd Cochran: keyboards, vocals.
Barry Finnerty: lead guitar, vocals.
John Nitzinger: 2nd guitar, vocals.
Erik Scott: bass guitar, vocals.

with ASIA

Asia
GEFFEN GEF 85577 LP, 1982, UK.
GEFFEN GEF 2008 LP, 1982, USA.
Tracks: Heat Of The Moment;
Only Time Will Tell; Sole
Survivor; One Step Closer; Time
Again; Wildest Dreams; Without
You; Cutting It Fine; Here Comes
The Feeling.
Geoff Downes: keyboards. Steve
Howe: guitars. Carl Palmer:
drums. John Wetton: bass, vocals.

Alpha
GEFFEN GEF 25508 LP, 1983, UK.
GEFFEN 904 008 2 CD, 1989, USA.
GEFFEN GEF 85577 CD, 1989, USA.
Tracks: Don't Cry; The Smile Has
Left Your Eyes; Never In A Million
Years; My Own Time (I'll Do What
I Want); The Heat Goes On; Eye
To Eye; The Last To Know; True
Colours; Midnight Sun; Open
Your Eyes.
Personnel as before.

Astra
GEFFEN GEF 26413 LP, 1985.
GEFFEN 924072 2 CD, 1985,
USA.
GEFFEN GEF 26413
Tracks: Go; Voice Of America;
Hard On Me; Wishing; Rock And
Roll Dream; Countdown To Zero;
Love Now Till Eternity; Too Late;
Suspicion; After The War.
Personnel as before, except Mandy
Meyer, guitar.

Aurora
SONY / GEFFEN ISAP 3155
(Japanese only) 1986
Tracks: Too Late (co-written by
Palmer), Ride Easy, Daylight, Lying
to Yourself.

Then And Now
GEFFEN 7599-24298-2 CD, 1990.
Compilation plus four new tracks.
Tracks: Only Time Will Tell; Heat
Of The Moment; Wildest Dreams;
Don't Cry; The Smile Has Left
Your Eyes; Days Like These; Voice
Of America; new songs – Prayin' 4
A Miracle; Am I In Love?; Summer
(Can't Last Too Long).
Personnel: Wetton, Palmer,
Downes, + various guitarists.

Live Mockba 09-X1-90
CROMWELL PRODUCTIONS,
thru ESSENTIAL RECORDS,
ESS CD 174, 1991.
Recorded at the Olympijski
Stadium, Moscow, in November
1990 before twenty thousand
people.

Tracks: Time Again; Sole Survivor;
Don't Cry; Keyboard solo; Only
Time Will Tell; Rock And Roll
Dream; Starless; Book Of Saturday;
The Smile Has Left Your Eyes (Parts
1 & 2); The Heat Goes On (including
Palmer drum solo); Go; Heat Of The
Moment; Open Your Eyes; Kari-
Anne. Personnel: Wetton, Palmer,
Downes, + Pat Thrall, guitar.

Aqua
MUSIDISC 109284, 1991, UK.
By now, the band was Asia in name
only, in spite of the presence in the
line-up of continuing guiding
spirit Geoff Downes, and Carl
Palmer (who was included in the
list of members on the album
sleeve) and Steve Howe
performing on some album tracks.
But Palmer, as we know, ditched
the new project for the new ELP.
Tracks: Aqua pt.1; Who Will Stop
The Rain?; Back In Town; Love
Under Fire; someday; Little Rich
Boy; The Voice Of Reason; Lay
Down Your Arms; Crime Of The
Heart; A Far Cry; Don't Call Me;
Heaven On Earth; Aqua pt.2.

Live in Nottingham
BLUEPRINT BP 253CD originally
released in 1991
Tracks: Wildest Dreams, Sole
Survivor, Don't Cry, Voice of
America, Time Again, Prayin'
For a Miracle, The Smile Has Left
Your Eyes, Only Time Will Tell,
Days Like These, The Heat Goes
On, Heat of the Moment, Open
Your Eyes.

Archiva 2
RESURGENCE LV105CD
Various artists compilation album
includes The Smoke That
Thunders

The Very Best of Asia '82-'90
GEFFEN 069 490 554-2, 2000
Tracks: Heat of the Moment, Only
Time Will Tell, Sole Survivor,
Time Again, Wildest Dreams, Here
Comes the Feeling, Don't Cry,
Daylight, The Smile Has Left Your
Eyes, Lying to Yourself, The Heat
Goes On, Never in a Million Years,
Open Your Eyes, Go, Voice of
America, Too Late, Days Like
These, Ride Easy.

with MIKE OLDFIELD
Five Miles Out
VIRGIN EURO 204500 LP, 1982.
VIRGIN VVIPD 106 CD.
One track, Mount Teidi, features
Carl on percussion.

with ROGER DALTREY
Under A Raging Moon
TEN RECORDS DIX 17, 1985.
Recorded in tribute to the late Keith
Moon. The title track features seven
drummers playing eight bars each;
in order of appearance: Martin
Chambers, Roger Taylor, Cozy
Powell, Stewart Copeland, Zak
Starkey, Carl Palmer, Mark Brzezicki.

COZY POWELL

The late and sorely missed
Cozy Powell has recorded so
much, with so many different
artists, that it is impossible to
include everything here. Solo
albums only are listed here, and
solo singles later.

Over The Top
ARIOLA ARL 5038 LP, 1979, UK.
POLYDOR 6312 LP, 1979, USA.
Tracks: Dave "Clem" Clempson,
Bernie Marsden, Gary Moore:
guitars. Max Middleton, Don
Airey: keyboards. Jack Bruce: bass.
Cozy Powell: drums.

Tilt
POLYDOR 5047 LP, 1981, UK.
POLYDOR 1 6342 LP, 1981, USA.
Tracks: The Right Side; Jekyll And
Hyde; Sooner Or Later; Living A
Lie; Cat Moves; Sunset; The
Blister; Hot Rock.
Jeff Beck, Gary Moore, Kirby:
guitars.
Don Airey, John Cook, David
Sancious: keyboards.
Jack Bruce, Chris Glen, Neil
Murray, Francesco Aiello: bass.
Francesco Aiello, Elmer Gantry:
vocals.
Cozy Powell: drums.

Octopuss
POLYDOR POLD 5093 LP, 1983,
UK.
Tracks:
Gary Moore, Mel Galley: guitars.
Jon Lord: keyboards.
Colin Hodgkinson: bass.
Cozy Powell: drums.

The Drums Are Back
ELECTROLA 1C 564-7 99226 2
LP, 1992, NL
ELECTROLA 1C 560-7 99226 2
CD, 1992, NL
Tracks: The Drums Are Back; Ride
To Win; I Wanna Hear You Shout;
Light In The Sky/ Return Of The
7; Battle Hymn; Legend Of The
Glass Mountain (Rota); Cryin';
Classical Gas (Williams);
Somewhere In Time; The Rocket.

Brian May, Steve Lukather, Jamie Paige, Ray Fenwick, Steve Makin: guitars.
Geoff Nicholls, Don Airey, Jon Lord, Jeff Francis, John Sinclair, Ray Fenwick: keyboards.
Neil Murray, Don Airey, Billy Sheehan, Lawrence Cottle, John Deacon, Steve Makin: bass.
Cozy Powell: drums, timpani.

RADIO SHOW RELEASES

All radio show releases are American in origin unless noted. A limited number of each is distributed to radio stations, and although they are not officially for resale, of course there is a big business based on selling them at prices ranging from nominal to enormous. Bootlegging is greatly facilitated by the easy availability of these broadcast quality recordings.

RECORDS

KEITH EMERSON

JIM LADD INNERVIEW. 1981. Whole album interview/music; Keith is pomoting the Nighthawks soundtrack. Good story about the Nice "flag-burning" incident.

EARTH NEWS. Week of March 2nd, 1981. Five short interview segments. Keith talks about ELP, what happened to them, his stage act and accidents, the critics, and the new album "Nighthawks".

ROLLING STONE'S CONTINUOUS HISTORY OF ROCK & ROLL.
2LPs. vol.2, no.89, week of June 19, 1983.

ABC ROCK RADIO NETWORK Music, daily features. Brief snippet of Keith on fingernail accident. ELP TRACKS: Lucky Man; Karn Evil 9. ASIA: Soul Survivor.

THE ROCK CHRONICLES.
2LPs.
WESTWOOD ONE Show 86-31, week July 28, 1986. Music, features. Brief clip of Keith; Touch And Go.

PSYCHEDELIC PSNACK.
WESTWOOD ONE PP87-34, week of August 17, 1987. Brief Emerson interviews; Trilogy.

SOLID GOLD SCRAPBOOK.
November 4, 1987. Emerson interview; From The Beginning.

EMERSON, LAKE AND PALMER

ON TOUR WITH EMERSON, LAKE & PALMER
ATLANTIC PR 281, 1977. Promo for "Works": interview/ music. Includes two tracks Which were unreleased at the time – "Abaddon's Bolero" played by the London Philharmonic Orchestra, and "Tiger In A Spotlight". Interview recorded 14 May, 1977 at Marko Studios, Montreal. The back cover has a discography.

ROCK AROUND THE WORLD.
No.163, week of September 11–17, 1977.
Interview/ music from "Works, vol.1", plus "America" by The Nice.

RETRO ROCK.
Week of August 31, 1981. 1978 concert without orchestra.

PIONEERS IN MUSIC:
1. EMERSON, LAKE AND PALMER.
2LPs, 3 sides. Show 31, week of February 17, 1986. History of the band.
Tracks: NICE America; KING CRIMSON 21st Century; ELP Lucky Man; Bitches Crystal; Nutrocker; From The Beginning; Hoedown; Karn Evil 9 1st, 2nd.

2. BRITISH PROGRESSIVE BANDS.
Week of June 16, 1986. ELP, Jethro Tull, Yes. Greg Lake short interview, KE9 1st.

3. ROCKING NOW AND THEN.
Week of February 23rd, 1987. BOTH ELPalmer and ELPowell.
Tracks: Hoedown; Still...You Turn Me On (Palmer); Lucky Man; Touch And Go (Powell). Also Led Zeppelin, Black Sabbath, Ozzy...13

MUSICAL BIOGRAPHIES WITH ALISON STEELE: EMERSON, LAKE & PALMER. 2 LPs. Interview/ music show, covering the band's history up to and including "Works, vol.1".

ROLLING STONE CONTINUOUS HISTORY OF ROCK AND ROLL.
RSMP-82-45, 1981. Includes a bit of Eddy Offord talking about ELP and the recording of "Pictures"; Are You Ready Eddy.

EMERSON, LAKE AND POWELL WESTWOOD ONE IN CONCERT.

2 LPs. Show 86-22, week of November 3, 1986.
Tracks: excluding commercials etc.: The Score; Touch And Go; Knife-Edge; Still...You Turn Me On; Learning To Fly; Pirates; From The Beginning; Lucky Man; Fanfare For The Common Man; Mars; Karn Evil 9.

OFF THE RECORD WITH MARY TURNER.
WESTWOOD ONE, 2 LPs. Show 86-37, week of 8 September, 1986. Interview, recorded music.The insert refers to the fact that the tour is co-sponsored by Westwood One and Coke. "The ELP tour...includes in addition to the band's performance a nightly video appearance by Coke's computerised, cult figure spokesman — Max Headroom."
Tracks: excluding commercials etc.: Peter Gunn; The Miracle; Lay Down Your Guns; Love Blind; Tank; The Score; Learning To Fly; Lucky Man; Karn Evil 9 1st; Still...You Turn Me On; Hoedown; Fanfare; Mars.

TOUR SPECIAL.
WESTWOOD ONE, No air date.
Tracks: Mars; Love Blind; Peter Gunn; Lay Down Your Guns; The Score; Learning To Fly; Hoedown; Fanfare; Tank; Are You Ready Eddy; Still...You Turn Me On; Karn Evil 9 1st; Lucky Man; Touch And Go. Masses of Coke commercials.

JIM LADD INNERVIEW. Series 37, show 9.

GREG LAKE

JIM LADD INNERVIEW. 1981. Whole album interview/music. Greg is promoting his first solo album.

EARTH NEWS. Week March 22nd, 1982. Four brief interview clips. Greg talks about his first solo album, the rise and fall of ELP, his long-distance collaboration with Bob Dylan, and visiting radio stations. Other interview segments with Henry Small of Prism and TV actress Janine Taylor.

THE ROCK CHRONICLES.
Show 87-1, week December 29, 1986. One brief snippet of Greg; Touch and Go.

PSYCHEDELIC PSNACK.
WESTWOOD ONE
1. PP 86-34, week of August 18, 1986.

Brief Lake interview; Lucky Man.
2. SN 88-02, week of January 11,
1988. Brief Lake interview; Karn
Evil 9 1/2

CARL PALMER

ROCK STAR GUEST DJ.
3 LPs (3 sides Carl Palmer, 3 sides
Sammy Hagar).
Show RSG 82-11. Week of June 7–
13, 1982. Carl introduces his
choice of music.
Tracks: STEVE WINWOOD Arc
Of a Diver; EAGLES Life In The
Fast Lane; DAVE BRUBECK
Take Five; CREAM Train Time;
MADNESS Baggy Trousers;
FREE Fire And Water; BOSTON
More Than A Feeling; STEVIE
WONDER Superstition; HOLST
Jupiter from The Planets.

DESERT ISLAND DISCS.
MJI BROADCASTING, INC.
Show 37, week of September 17,
1990.
No relation to the BBC radio
programme! Carl introduces his
favourite music. Great show!
EAGLES Hotel California; WHO
I Can't Explain; FOREIGNER
Feels Like The First Time;
ANIMALS House Of The Rising
Sun; ELTON JOHN Lucy In The
Sky With Diamonds; CREAM
Strange Brew; STEVE
WINWOOD Roll With It; ZZ
TOP Legs; KINKS All Day And
All Of The Night; ROLLING
STONES Jumping Jack Flash.

ROCK TODAY!!
MJI BROADCASTING, INC.
Show 152, week of May 30, 1988.
Interviews/features/music. Carl picks
his Song Of The Week: STING "Be
Still My Beating Heart".

CLASSIC CUTS. MJI
BROADCASTING, INC.
Show 194, week September 10,
1990.
2 short interviews with Carl; Knife-
Edge/ Lucky Man.

PSYCHEDELIC PSNACK.
WESTWOOD ONE PP 87-11,
week March 9, 1987.
Palmer interview; Lucky Man.

THREE

OFF THE RECORD WITH
MARY TURNER.
WESTWOOD ONE, 2 LPs.
Show 88-21, week May 16, 1988.

Interview, music.
Tracks: Eight Miles High;
Hoedown; You Do Or You Don't;
Tank; Still...You Turn Me On;
Runaway; Karn Evil 9; Lover To
Lover; Lucky Man; Desde La
Vida; Talkin' Bout; On My Way
Home. * Westwood One recorded,
but did not release, a broadcast of a
Three concert.

LEGENDS OF ROCK.
2 LPs. Week of June 13–19, 1988.
Music up to and including Three;
interviews with Emerson, Lake
and Palmer.

ROCK OVER LONDON.
Music and longer interviews.
Week of March 20 1988.
Emerson/Palmer/Berry
interviewed together.
Show 88-17, weekend of April 23,
1988. Keith and Carl on pre-
Nice/A.Brown days. Good stuff.

COMPACT DISCS

EMERSON, LAKE AND
PALMER

THE KING BISCUIT FLOWER
HOUR.
Produced by DIR RADIO
NETWORK, New York. No serial
numbers.
1. Week of March 13th 1988.
Tracks: Hoedown; Tiger In A
Spotlight; C'est La Vie; Still ...You
Turn Me On; Lucky Man; Tank/
The Enemy God; Karn Evil 9;
Fanfare For The Common Man.
2. Week of September 2nd 1991.
Tracks: Hoedown; Still...You Turn
Me On; Lucky Man; Piano
Improvisation; Karn Evil 9 –
1st/1; Drum Solo; 1st/2; 2nd,
pt.1; 2nd, pt.2; 3rd.

SINGLES

KEITH EMERSON

with THE V.I.Ps
I Wanna Be Free/Don't Let It Go.
ISLAND WI-3003 7", 1966.

with THE NICE
The Thoughts Of Emerlist
Davjack/ Azrial, Angel Of Death.
IMMEDIATE IM 59 ps 7", 1967,
UK. STATESIDE HSS 1232 7",
1967, USA.

America/The Diamond Hard Blue
Apples Of The Moon.
IMMEDIATE IM 068 7", 1968,
UK.

IMMEDIATE IM-8597 7", 1968,
AUSTRALIA

She Belongs To Me.
IMMEDIATE AS 4 7", 1969.
Double A sided sampler from the
album "Nice", due for release on
5/9/69 – not for sale.

Country Pie-Brandenburg Concerto
no.6/One Of Those People.
CHARISMA CB 132 7", 1970,UK.

Country Pie-Brandenburg Concerto
no.6/ Finale – 5th Bridge.
MERCURY 73272 7", 1970, USA

SOLO SINGLES

Honky Tonk Train Blues/
Barrelhouse Shakedown.
MANTICORE K 13513 ps 7",
1976, UK.

Odeon Rag (Maple Leaf Rag)/The
Sheriff.
DISCHI RICORDI MAN 5409 ps
7", 1977, ITALY.
The Italian TV show "Odeon"
started using Emerson's version of
"Maple Leaf Rag" as its new
theme tune, and confusingly issued
it under the title "Odeon Rag".

Taxi Ride (Rome)/Mater
Tenebrarum.
ATLANTIC K 11611 ps 7", 1980.

I'm A Man/ Nighthawks main title
theme.
MCA RECORDS MCA 697 ps 7",
1981, UK.

Rum-A-Ting/ 3 others.
BUBBLE RECORDS BLU 61002
7", 1982, ITALY.
Promotional 12" E.P. Other tracks:
Black and White Co, Tony
Esposito, Europe. Label says
"Disco Mix", but "Rum-A-Ting"
is not audibly different from the
LP version.

Children Of The Light/ Challenge
Of The Psionics Fighters.
CANYON INTERNATIONAL
7Y0039 ps 7", 1983, JAPAN With
inserts.

Up The Elephant And Round The
Castle (instrumental and vocal
versions).
RED BUS RBUS 85 7", 1983, UK.
Theme music from TV comedy
series, starring Emerson's friend
and fan Jim Davidson. Side A is
Emerson and band with female
vocal backing; side B is the same

with additional comedy vocals from Jim Davidson. It was recorded at Ollie Recording Studios, and engineered by Mike Sheppard, just like the Murderock soundtrack, which may indicate that the same backing musicians were used.

We Three Kings/ Captain Starship Christmas.
EMERSON RECORDS KEITH 1, 1988, UK.

with ROCK AID ARMENIA
Smoke On The Water.
LIFE-AID RECORDS ARMEN 001 ps 7", 1989, UK.

Smoke On The Water/ Paranoid.
LIFE-AID RECORDS ARMEN T001 ps 12", 1989, UK.

Smoke On The Water/ Paranoid.
LIFE-AID RECORDS ARMEN CD 001 1989, UK.

Smoke On The Water (radio mix/ extended version)/ Paranoid.
See album section for further details.

EMERSON. LAKE AND PALMER

Lucky Man/ Knife-Edge.
ISLAND 10 203 AT 7", 1970, W.GERMANY.
Lucky Man.
COTILLION PR-44106 7", 1971, USA.
Promo. Long and short versions in mono. Also, with same serial no., in stereo.

Take A Pebble/ Lucky Man.
COTILLION promo PR-176 7", 1971.

Stones Of Years/ A Time And A Place.
COTILLION 44131 7", 1971, USA

Nutrocker/ The Great Gates Of Kiev.
ATLANTIC JAPAN P-1128A ps 7", 1972.

Mar Y Sol E.P. ATCO ps sampler PR 176, 1972.
Promo E.P. for the album "Mar Y Sol – The First International Puerto Rico Pop Festival" (see album section).
Side A: Take A Pebble/ Lucky Man. Side B: tracks by J.Geils Band, Jonathan Edwards.

From The Beginning/ Living Sin.
COTILLION 45-44158 7", 1972, USA. Taiwanese E.P.
4 TRACK FT. 918 ps 7". Three *Tracks:* Hocus Pocus (Focus);

Frankenstein (Edgar Winter Group); Hoedown (ELP).

New Musical Express promotional flexidisc.
LYNTONE LYN 2762 ps 7", 1973.
Tracks: Brain Salad Surgery + excerpts from each track on the album. Free with NME, November 10th, 1973; packaged in single-sized replica of the album sleeve.

Jerusalem/ When The Apple Blossoms...
MANTICORE K 13503 7", 1973, UK.

Still...You Turn Me On/ Brain Salad Surgery.
MANTICORE MC-2003-PR 7", 1973.

Fanfare For The Common Man/ Brain Salad Surgery
ATLANTIC K 10946 7", 1977, UK.
ARIOLA 17 977 AT, 1977, W.GERMANY.

Tiger In A Spotlight/ So Far To Fall.
ARIOLA 11 776 AT 7", 1978, W.GERMANY

Tiger In A Spotlight.
ATLANTIC promo PR-3641, 1977. Long/short versions.

All I Want Is You/ Tiger In A Spotlight.
ATLANTIC K 11225 7", 1978, UK.

All I Want Is You/ Are You Ready Eddy.
ATLANTIC K 11225 7", 1978, UK

All I Want Is You.
ATLANTIC 3555 7", 1978, USA.
Double A sided promotional copy.
Peter Gunn/ Knife Edge.
ATLANTIC K 11416 7",1980, UK.

Black Moon.
VICTORY LON 320 UK/ 869 453-7 INT ps 7", 1992.
Single edit/ album version
VICTORY LONX 320 UK/ 869 737-1 INT ps 12", 1992
Single edit/ A Blade Of Grass/ Album version.
VICTORY LONCD 320/ 869 737-2 international, 1992.
As 12". Affairs Of The Heart. Limited edition collectors' doublepack.
CD1: Affairs Of The Heart; Better Days;A Blade Of Grass; Black Moon.
CD2: Affairs Of The Heart; Black Moon(previously unreleased radio version); Fanfare; Jerusalem (both remastered)

VICTORY/LONDON LONCD 327/ LOCDP 327, 1992.

EMERSON, LAKE AND POWELL

Touch And Go/Learning To Fly.
POLYDOR POSP 804 7", 1986, USA.
POLYDOR POSPX 804 12", 1986, USA. With bonus hitherto unreleased track "The Locomotion" (Little Eva).

The Score (edit and album versions).
POLYDOR PRO 432-1 12", 1986. Promo only.

Lay Down Your Guns.
POLYDOR 885-277-7 DJ 7", 1986.
Double A sided promotional single.
POLYDOR PRO 441-1, 1986 12", USA. Double A sided promotional single.

GREG LAKE
for THE KING'S SINGERS
Strawberry Fields Forever (Lennon/McCartney)/ Disney Girls.
EMI 2851 ps/cv 7", 1978, UK. Side One produced by Greg Lake, as it says in big letters on the scratch 'n' sniff sleeve, a picture of a pile of strawberries on a woman's bare, shall we say, midriff. A very interesting version of the song, heavily over-produced a la "I Believe...".

with THE SHAME
Too Old To Go 'Way Little Girl (J. Ian)/ Dreams Don't Bother Me.
POPPY RECORDS thru MGM RECORDS, POP 501 7",1968, USA.

with THE SHY LIMBS
Reputation/Love.
CBS 4190 7", 1969, UK. Both sides are included on the compilation CD "Circus Days, vol.3", STRANGE THINGS STCD 10004.

(Lady In Black/Trick Or Two.
CBS 4624 7", 1969, UK. Lake doesn't perform on the second one, but it's included here for interest.)

SOLO SINGLES

GREG LAKE

I Believe In Father Christmas/ Humbug.
MANTICORE K13511 ps 7", 1975, UK ATLANTIC A7393 7", 1992; CD with bonus track, "Jerusalem". Sold in aid of the charity for the homeless, Shelter.

Cover art, "Peace At Night", by Catherine Brightly for Shelter.

Also available as one track on compilation "It's Christmas" EMI CD EMTV 49, 1989, UK. Other artists include John & Yoko, Band Aid, Roy Wood, Elton John, Paul McCartney, Bing Crosby. The video of "It's Christmas" did not include Greg Lake's song.

C'est La Vie/Jeremy Bender
ATLANTIC K 10990 7", 1977, UK.
Watching Over You/ Hallowed Be Thy Name
ATLANTIC K 11061 7", 1978, UK

Love You Too Much
CHRYSALIS CHS 2553 7", 1981, UK

CARL PALMER

with THE CRAIG
I Must Be Mad/ Suspense
FONTANA TF 715 7", 1966
Also found on some compilations of Sixties psychedelia, including "The Rubble Collection"
BAM-CARUSO RUBBLE CD1, 1986.

with CHRIS FARLOWE and THE THUNDERBIRDS
Yesterday's Papers / Life is But Nothing 1967

with THE CRAZY WORLD OF ARTHUR BROWN
Nightmare/ What's Happening?
(B-side only) TRACK 604 026 7", 1968, UK.
NOTE: The B-side label gave "Music Man" as the title, though the actual title was "What's Happening". For some reason it was only released as such in Germany. The band was poorly promoted at this time, and this was one reason for the eventual split.

with ATOMIC ROOSTER
Friday The 13th/ Banstead.
B&C CB121 7", 1970.

with ASIA
Only Time Will Tell/ Ride Easy
GEFFEN GEF 2228 ps 7", 1982

Heat Of The Moment/Time Again
GEFFEN GEF 2494 ps 7", 1982

Soul Survivor/ Here Comes The Feeling
GEFFEN GEF 2884 ps 7", 1982

Don't Cry/True Colours
GEFFEN GEF 3580 ps/pd 7", 1983

The Smile Has Left Your Eyes/ Lying To Yourself
GEFFEN GEF 3836 ps/cv 7", 1983

Go/After The War. GEFFEN 6737 ps 7", A6737 7", TA6737 12", 1985

THREE
Talkin' Bout/ La Vista
GEFFEN 7-27988 7", 1988,

USA. Talkin' 'Bout (both sides)
GEFFEN PRO-A-2914, 1988,
USA. Promo 12" single

With QANGO
Live in the HoodSTARCAST SCL CD 007, 2000
Tracks: Time Again, Sole Survivor, Bitches Crystal, D.K. solo, All Along the Watchtower, The Last One Home, J.Y. solo, Hoedown, Fanfare for the Common Man (inc C.P. solo), Heat of the Moment.

John Wetton – Bass, vocals
Carl Palmer – Drums
Dave Kilminster – Guitar, vocals
John Young – Keyboards, vocals

APPENDIX 2
VIDEOGRAPHY

Emerson Lake & Palmer

Pictures At An Exhibition
UK: 1982, Precision Video VAMPV 2575 (PAL format) Running Time: 45 minutes
Repackaged 1986, Channel 5 Video CFV 00502 (PAL)
JAP: 1990, Vap VPLR-70116 (NTSC format) Running Time: 92 minutes
UK: 2000, DVD D2 VISION LTD. DVDP 002
Taken from ELP's concert at the Lyceum Theatre, London, on December 9, 1970. First UK theatre release, February 1971, at the Regent Theatre, Piccadilly, London. First US theatre release, March 1974, Westwood, California. The full concert was comprised of The Barbarian, Take A Pebble, Pictures At An Exhibition and Knife Edge, but the video had Pictures only. This situation has never changed. However, in Japan the entire film was latterly released on both video and laserdisc. The laserdisc is of superior quality, and comes complete with insert about the band (in Japanese).
In 1986 the video was repackaged by Channel 5 Video, omitting the film credits previously given inside the Precision packaging.
In September 2000 D2 Vision Ltd released a DVD which included both the complete album and the complete film.

ELP – The Manticore Special – BBC Documentary of 1973 Tour
USA: 1998 Manticore Video
Running Time: 54 minutes
This video was widely available as a bootleg but has now been officially released with digitally re-mastered sound. It is a very watchable account of the band at the height of their fame whilst on tour in Europe. The only slight reservation being the brevity of the performance excerpts. This is only an issue due to the fact that there is no other offical video of the band in performance during this period. The only piece which is played in its entirety is Hoedown at the end of the film.

Live '77
UK: 1986, Hendring Video HEN 2 005 D Running Time: 90 minutes
USA: 1998 Manticore Video

Running Time: 84 minutes
Film of the legendary Montreal
Olympic Stadium concert on
August 26, 1977. An audience of
88,000 saw ELP perform with a
hand-picked orchestra, each
instrument separately miked.
As exciting as it is to have a record
of this event, the film is far from
what it could be. It is a direct
transfer of the television film. The
opportunity to immortalise the
concert in stereo was missed, and
the picture quality is uninspiring.
However, when all's said and done,
the performance remains as a
testimony to an historic event. We
shall not see its like again.
Tracks: Abaddon's Bolero; The Enemy
God; Karn Evil 9, 1st Impression, part
2; Pictures At An Exhibition; C'est La
Vie; Piano Concerto no. 1, 3rd
movement; Tank (including Palmer
solo on revolving stainless steel
drumkit – one very good reason to
have the video); Nutrocker; Pirates,
Fanfare For The Common Man.
This video was deleted for some
years but has now been re-released
under the Manticore Label with
digitally re-mixed (by K. Emerson)
and re-mastered stereo audio.

Welcome Back
USA: January 1993, Strand Home
Video 8121 (NTSC) Running
Time: 80 minutes
UK: 1992 Beckmann
Communications distributed by
Polygram (PAL) 087778-3
A "musical biography" of ELP
featuring vintage footage, concert
highlights of their sell-out 1992-3
world tour, and exclusive interviews.
"This is a collector's piece for all true
fans," says the blurb-writer. Indeed it
does justice to "one of rock's foremost
progressive bands", communicating
much of the atmosphere and
excitement of the tour.
As well as interviews throughout
with the band members, there are
brief interviews with Alan
Freeman and Chris Welch, and a
reminiscence from Robert Moog.
Tracks: Romeo & Juliet, Karn Evil
9 1st Imp. P2, Pictures at an
Exhibition, Paper Blood, Honky
Tonk Train Blues, Creole Dance,
Changing States, Hoedown, Black
Moon, Tarkus, Close to Home,
Pirates, C'est La Vie, Tiger in a
Spotlight, Watching Over You,
Lucky Man, Joplin Rag, Fanfare for
the Common Man, Improvisation.

ELP Live at the Royal Albert Hall
USA:
UK: 1996 Beckmann

Communications BMO015
Running Time 88 minutes
This is an excellent account of the
band on their comeback tour in
1992. The concert at the Royal
Albert Hall had special significance
as it was their first performance in
the UK since 1974. One of the
best live performances of ELP on
tape ever.
Tracks: Karn Evil 9 First
Impression Part 2, Tarkus, Kife
Edge, Paper Blood, Creole Dance,
From the Beginning, Lucky Man,
Honky Tonk Train Blues, Romeo
and Juliet, Pirates, Pictures, Fanfare.

Message to Love
USA:
UK: 1995 Castle Communications
PNV 1005 Running Time 137
minutes
This is a compilation showing
excerpts from the performances of
the many bands who appeared over
the five days of the Festival. The
clips of Emerson Lake and
Palmer's performance are very
disappointing. The first clip last
barely 2 and a half minutes and
consists of three clumsily edited
extracts from Rondo and Pictures.
The only saving grace is that you
get to see the cannon go off at the
conclusion of Great Gates of Kiev.
At the end of the video there is a
longer (but still incomplete) clip of
Rondo lasting 5 minutes.

**Feature Films with Keith
Emerson music soundtracks:**

Inferno
UK: 1993, Fox Video World
Cinema WC 1140 (Widescreen)
Running time: 102 minutes
A young woman, Rose (Eleonora
Giorgi) becomes involved with the
occult forces which inhabit the
crumbling neo-Gothic mansion in
which she stays. Her terrifying
descent into unseen horror also
affects her brother in Italy, and
their friends and neighbours.
Argento's films have always suffered
from erratic UK video distribution
due to ambivalent censor's ratings
and, frequently, unwillingness of
many video stockists to err on the
side of adventure, particularly
following a typically vague 1982
BBFC directive about the use of
violence in Argento's movies. Now
largely available on sell-through, the
available copies have, sadly, been
expurgated. Five minutes of the
film have been edited out. This was
Emerson's first soundtrack (although
he had originally composed the music

of "Pirates" for an intended film of
Frederick Forsyth's "The Dogs Of
War", which was never completed).
He was awarded the Italian equivalent
of an Emmy for the score.

Nighthawks
UK: 1981, CIC Video VHR 1091
Running Time: 95 minutes
When Wulfgar (Rutger Hauer), a
terrorist, explosively announces his
presence in New York, two
undercover cops, DaSilva (Sylvester
Stallone) and Fox (Billy Dee
Williams) are given the almost
impossible task of finding and
stopping him before he strikes again.

Murderock
ITA: 1984, Scena Films. Video
release unknown
A series of brutal killings take place
in a dancing school.

Genma Taisen (Harmagedona)
JAP: 1983, Haruki Kadokawa Films,
Inc. VAF-1088 VIDEO
AH009-35KD LASERDISC
(NTSC format) Running Time:
131 minutes
A dazzling animated sci-fi film,
comparable with, and no doubt a
major influence on the Manga
trailblazer "Akira" and others which
have recently made a worldwide
impact, there are plans to release
this in both the USA and the UK,
though no date is as yet fixed.
From the Japanese sleevenotes :
"The end of the ten billion year
old great universe has come. The
ruler of the dark world, Genma,
has at last extended his tentacles of
death over the galaxy. Princess
Luna has been chosen by the Good
One, Floi, to challenge Genma to a
fight to the death, helped by a
group of Psionics Fighters from all
over the world, who will try to
protect the known universe.
The sleevenotes inform us that
Keith also wrote the theme music
for "Ginga Tetsudo 999".
Information, please! There is an
interview /discussion between
Emerson (KE) and the executive
producer Haruki Kadokawa (HK)
and the director Rin Taro (RT).
This took place on November 30,
1982 in Kudan, Tokyo, just before
Keith returned to the UK.
HK: I listened to the main theme,
"Children Of The Light". My
first impression was that it
sounded like you were playing a
hymn with a synthesiser.
KE: Really? That's good.
HK: I think a hymn fits into a small
space though, like a church. This

is bigger than just a hymn, it's like a message to the whole universe. You used a synthesiser so the effect was more powerful.

KE: That's exactly what I wanted. When I wrote the theme I wanted to express the expanse of the whole universe. The other idea was that it should sound rather like a hymn. I started writing the music with these ideas in mind, so that's why you probably feel that way.

HK: My film theme songs have almost always been big hits. I like all the songs, but I like this one the best. I've received several awards as a music producer/director myself, and I think that the high quality of this film soundtrack is one of the best I've ever been involved in.

KE: I'm very pleased that you gave me this opportunity. Your compliments are very encouraging. The work has been a big step forward for me and your encouragement will help me in the future, thank you.

HK: To change the subject – about Sonny Link's theme, "Sonny's Skate State", it just creates a picture of a contemporary American boy, and with other characters you clearly express in music the differences between each individual character and theme.

KE: It helped me to be shown pictures beforehand. I feel that recently my musical activity has differed from when I was a member of ELP. Now I write what naturally comes up inside me. In that respect it's interesting that I do film work, so that I can show the creative side of me.

RT: Yesterday I listened to some of Keith's music which has been laid down. I feel there's no doubt that the music will give the film depth. Keith's music is exactly what I visualised for the film. I thought the music for "Genma Taisen" should be rock but also grand like Bach's music. Keith's music produces images as you listen to it. I'm amazed how you grasped the ideas and understood the content just from the rough pictures when they hadn't even been coloured yet!

KE: Well, that's my job! [laughs]

RT: You know, "Challenge Of The Psionics Fighters", at first we were going to play the music over the action scene in New York, but it has such a good tempo we're thinking of playing it over the climax scene of the film also, when Mount Fuji explodes, molten lava pours out and turns into a fire

dragon which then fights the seven Psionics Fighters.

KE: Thank you very much, please use my music as you like. Some of the tracks are composed by Nozomu Aoki, and some by Keith Emerson. Those by Nozomu Aoki are given in Japanese on the LP sleeve. The full track listing in English is as follows:

Harmagedon – Prelude (Nozomu Aoki)
Theme Of Floi (Keith Emerson)
Toccata and Fugue in D minor (J.S.Bach, arr. Emerson)
Psionic Princess (NA)
Joe and Michiko (KE)
Mission Revived (NA)
Children Of The Light (Tony Allen, KE)
The Devil's Angry Growl (NA)
Sonny's Skate State (KE)
A Far Off Time (NA)
Zamedy Stomp (KE)
Challenge Of The Psionics Fighters (KE)

Apart from Keith's music, the soundtrack features on two tracks (Harmagedon – Prelude, and The Devil's Angry Growl) the amazingly ferocious and "demonic" sound of a Japanese percussion instrument, the shime-daiko. Played here by the Sadonokuni Kodo drum group, this is a barrel drum with two laced heads. It is often used in Japanese folk music.

Best Revenge
UK: 1983, Polygram Video 041 160 2 Running Time: 91 minutes
Routine mob drugs-and-vengeance shoot-em-up.

La Chiesa (The Church)
ITA: 1990, Vivivideo DGVS 10018 Running time: 100 minutes
Another supernatural horror flick reunites Emerson with grand guignol master Argento. Another common element is the presence of Feodor Chaliapin, the legendary opera singer who turned to film acting in later life.
As with Harmagedon, Emerson does not supply all the music. He plays on four tracks, three of his own composition (The Church – main theme, The Possession, and The Church Revisited), as well as Prelude 24 from *Das Wohltemperierte Klavier* (The Well-Tempered Clavier) by Bach. Other tracks are contributed by the Italian prog band Goblin (a favourite of Argento), Martin Goldray (playing a Philip Glass

piece), Zooming On The Zoo and Definitive Gaze.

Iron Man
UK: 1996 Marvel Films distributed by Buena Vista Home Entertainement Ltd D271082 Running Time 62 minutes
This is a special edition telling the story of the origin of the Iron Man cartoon series and including the first episode with music scored by Keith Emerson. There were many more episodes shown on American television but it is not known if these are also available on video. Keith only wrote music for the first series.

Asia

Asia In Asia
UK: 1984, Vestron Music Video 11009 Running Time: 60 minutes
Relayed live around the world to twenty million people, this video relives part of Asia's concert at the Budokan Theatre in Tokyo, Japan on 6th December 1983, featuring Greg Lake. This was the first time in six years that 2 members of ELP appeared on the same stage.
Tracks: The Heat Goes On; Here Comes The Feeling; Eye To Eye; Steve Howe solo; Only Time Will Tell; Open Your Eyes; Geoff Downes solo; The Smile Has Left Your Eyes; Wildest Dreams; Carl Palmer solo; Heat Of The Moment; Sole Survivor.

Asia Live
UK: 1991, Virgin Music Video VVD959 Running Time: 62 minutes
The recently re-formed Asia played at Central Television Studios in Nottingham, England as part of a series of concerts featuring 70s and early 80s favourites. The original line-up performed, with the exception of Steve Howe, who was replaced on guitar by ex-Automatic Man guitarist Pat Thrall. The television broadcast lasted about 45 minutes. The video is longer by about a quarter of an hour.
Tracks: Wildest Dreams; Sole Survivor; Don't Cry; Voice Of America; Time Again; Praying For A Miracle; The Smile Has Left Your Eyes; Only Time Will Tell; Days Like These; The Heat Goes On (including Carl Palmer solo); Go; Heat Of The Moment; Open Your Eyes.

Live Mockba – 09-11-90
UK: 1992, Excellent Video EXC005 Running Time: 65 minutes
Asia played two concerts to 20,000 people at the Olympic stadium in

Moscow. This is an account of those shows, plus behind-the-scenes footage and interviews.
Tracks: Only Time Will Tell; Sole Survivor; piano solo from Cutting It Fine; Days Like These; Rendezvous 6.02 (by one of Wetton's former bands, U.K.); Kari-Anne (previously unrecorded); The Heat goes On (including Carl Palmer solo); Book Of Saturday (from another former Wetton band, King Crimson); Praying For A Miracle; Go; The Smile Has Left Your Eyes; Open Your Eyes; Heat Of The Moment.

Various Artists
Beat Club vol. 7: Frontiers Of Progressive Rock JAP: 1988, Laserdisc Corporation HMO48-3227 (videotape) (NTSC format) BMO48-3227 (laserdisc) Running Time: 56 minutes
One of a series of Japanese-released compilations of appearances by pop and rock groups on the great German TV show Beat Club.
Tracks: Emerson, Lake and Palmer – Knife Edge
King Crimson – Larks' Tongues In Aspic
The Nice – Hang On To A Dream (black and white)
Soft Machine – Composition Based On Three Tunes Yes – Yours Is No Disgrace Kraftwerk – Truckstop Gondolero
This version of "Hang On to A Dream" by the Nice is the only commercially available video of the band.

Rock Aid Armenia
Smoke On The Water: The Video Collection
UK: 1989, Virgin Music Video Running Time: 77 minutes
Members of top rock bands joined forces to record a version of Deep Purple's classic "Smoke On The Water" in aid of the victims of the Armenian earthquake of that year. Keith Emerson (at that time between bands), and Geoff Downes of Asia, were among those who contributed to the single. This video is a collection of those artists' finest work, in addition to the video of the single. The first video on the compilation is the single edit of ELP's Fanfare For The Common Man. Heat Of The moment by Asia is also featured. See TV Appearances, "The Making Of Smoke On The Water".

Related to this video:

Hard 'N' Heavy, Vol. 5
UK: 1989, Picture Music

International Video MVP 9912033
This volume of the regularly issued Heavy Metal video magazine included in this volume a short report on the recordding of "Smoke On The Water" (unaccountably in black and white). Keith Emerson is seen briefly, as are Geoff Downes and many others.

Supershow
UK: 1986, Virgin Music Video VVD 167 Running Time: 82 minutes
"The last great sixties musical event", it says on the cover of this, and when you check out the line-up you find out why: Colosseum, Buddy Miles, The Modern Jazz Quartet, Buddy Guy, Roland Kirk, Led Zeppelin, Steven Stills, The Misunderstood, Jack Bruce, Eric Clapton, Duster Bennett, Dallas Taylor.
"March 1969 at a disused lino factory in Stains [sic!]. The unlikely setting for a remarkable two day jamming session which brought together the great names of rock and jazz to improvise together...This is the end of the sixties. Intense and introverted, concentrated brilliant music, blending blues and rock with hard edged jazz. It was – to use a word which was 'old fashioned' then – funky."
One person present was Davy O'List, formerly of the Nice and now with no steady gig to play. When the Misunderstood played 'Bad Hat', Davy sat in on guitar.

Ampersand
Videos with computer graphics accompanying nine pieces of electronic music by artists on AMP Records, mostly in live performance. Keith Emerson's "I Saw Three Ships" from the Christmas Album is one of three actual album tracks. The computer graphics video specially created by Simon Maddocks to accompany the track is thrilling and inventive – a "must-see" for all Emerson fans, not to mention anyone with an interest in computer graphics. It gives the track a new perspective, and both complements and enhances the music.
The sequencer-driven electronic music of Chris Franke, Clifford White, Tim Blake and others which comprise the remainder of the tape are very different musically and visually.
Available from: Future Age Music Express, PO Box 387, London N22 6SE

APPENDIX 3

TOUR DATES

FIRST GIGS 1970
AUG 23 Plymouth Guildhall, Plymouth, England (DEBUT SHOW)
AUG 29 Isle of Wight Festival, Isle of Wight, England

EUROPEAN TOUR 1970
SEP 19 Winter Gardens, Watford, England
SEP 24 Town Hall, Watford, England
SEP 25 City Hall, England (With Wishbone Ash, Farm)
SEP 26 Starlight Room, Boston, England (With Wishbone Ash, Farm)
SEP 27 De Montfort Hall, Leicester, England (With Wishbone Ash, Farm)
SEP 28 Guildhall, Portsmouth, England (With Wishbone Ash, Farm)
OCT 1 City Hall, Leeds,England (With Wishbone Ash, Farm)
OCT 4 City Hall, Newcastle, England (With Wishbone Ash, Farm)
OCT 7 Dome, Brighton, England
OCT 9 Greens Playhouse, Glasgow, Scotland
OCT 11 Caird Hall, Dundee, England
OCT 16 Technical College, Waltham, England
OCT 17 Brunel University, Uxbridge, England (With Opal Butterfly)
OCT 19 Colston Hall, Bristol, England
OCT 20 Winter Gardens, Bournemouth, England
OCT 21 Town Hall, Birmingham, England
OCT 24 Fairfield Hall, Croydon, England
OCT 25 Royal Festival Hall, London, England
OCT 27 City Hall, Sheffield, England
NOV 13 Kinetic Circus, Birmingham, England
NOV 22 Liverpool, England
NOV 26 Bremen, Germany ("Beat Club" TV performance)
NOV 28 Jahrhunderthalle, Frankfurt, Germany
NOV 29 Zirkus Krone, Munich, Germany
NOV 30 Nuremburg, German
DEC 1 Vienna
DEC 2 Stuttgart
DEC 4 Limathaus, Zurich, Switzerland
DEC 5 Stathalle,Vienna, Austria
DEC 6 Festhalle, Boblingen, W. Germany
DEC 7 Manchester Free Trade Hall, Manchester, England
DEC 8 Bradford St George's Hall, England
DEC 9 Lyceum Ballroom, London, England (filmed for movie)
DEC 12 Leeds University, Leeds, England

Typical set list: Pictures At An Exhibition; The Barbarian; Take A Pebble; Piano Improvisations; Take A Pebble (reprise); Knife Edge; Rondo; Nutrocker.

UK TOUR 1970
MAR 4   ABC, Stockton
MAR 5   ABC, Hull
MAR 6   ABC, Licoln
MAR 7   The Regal, Cambridge
MAR 10 Capitol, Cardiff
MAR 12 ABC, Plymouth
MAR 14 Civic Hall, Wolverhampton
MAR 17 Odeon, Cheltenham
MAR 18 Big Apple, Brighton
MAR 21 ABC, Blackpool
MAR 22 Free Trade Hall, Manchester
MAR 23 St. George's Hall, Bradford
MAR 24 City Hall, Sheffield
MAR 26 City Hall, Newcastle ('Pictures at an Exhibition' LP recording)
MAR 28 Odeon, Lewisham
MAR 29 Winter Gardens, Margate
MAR 30 Guildhall, Portsmouth
APR 1   ABC, Wigan
APR 2   Green's Playhouse, Glasgow
APR 3   Caird Hall, Dundee
APR 6   Winter Gardens, Bournemouth
APR 7   De Montfort Hall, Leicester
APR 9   Odeon, Birmingham

USA TOUR 1971
APR 21 Theil College, Greenville, Pa. (US DEBUT GIG)
APR 23 Detroit Eastown Theatre, Detroit, MI
APR 24 Detroit Eastown Theatre, Detroit, MI
APR 25 Phila Spectrum, Pa
APR 30 Fillmore East, NYC (ELP headlines; Edgar Winter & Curved Air also on bill)
MAY 1   Fillmore East, NYC (as above)
MAY 2   Shea Theatre, Buffalo, NY
MAY 11 Guthrie Theatre (with Mott the Hoople)
MAY 19 Kiel Opera House, Kiel (Mott the Hoople support)
MAY 26 Carnegie Hall, New York
MAY 28 Upsala College, East Orange, NJ (Hog Heaven on the same bill)
MAY 29 Boston College, Boston, MA
MAY 30 Bucknell University, Lewisburg, PA

EUROPEAN TOUR 1971
JUN 1   Stadthalle, Karlsruhe, Germany
JUN 2   Meistersingerhalle, Nurnberg(Nuremberg), Germany
JUN 3   Konzerthaus, Vienna, Austria
JUN 4   Zirkus Krone, Munich, Germany
JUN 5   Zoffingen, Zurich, Switzerland
JUN 10 Stadthalle, Offenbach, Germany
JUN 11 Meistersingerhalle, Nuremburg), Germany
JUN 12 Festhalle, Oldenburg, Germany
JUN 13 Rheinhalle, Dusseldorf, Germany
JUN 14 Musikhalle, Hamburg, Germany
JUN 17 Philipshalle, Dusseldorf, Germany
JUN 20 Royal Theatre Drury Lane, London, England

USA TOUR 1971
JUL 17 Sports Arena, San Diego, CA

JUL 18 Berkley Community Center, Berkley, CA
JUL 19 Hollywood Bowl, Los Angeles, CA (with Edgar Winter and Humble Pie)
JUL 23 Argadone, Vancouver, Canada
JUL 24 Paramount Theatre, Seattle, WA
JUL 25 Paramount Theatre, Portland, Oregon
JUL 30 Music Hall, Houston, TX
JUL 31 Municipal Auditorium, San Antonio, TX
AUG 6   Pirates World, Dania, Florida
AUG 7   Pirates World, Dania, Florida
AUG 9   Hollywood Sportatorium, Miami, Florida
AUG 12 Stanley Park Stadium, Toronto, Canada
AUG 13 Place des Nations, Montreal, Canada
AUG 18 Syracuse Auditorium, Syracuse, New York (With Edgear Winter's White Trash)
AUG 20 Dayton, Ohio
AUG 21 Transit Auditorium, Chicago, IL
AUG ?? Syria Mosque, Pittsburgh, PA
AUG 30 Bushnell Auditorium
AUG 31 Alexandria, VA
SEP 1   Gaelic Park, Riverdale, NY
NOV 12 Music Hall, Boston, MA (free concert)*
NOV 13 Phila. Spectrum, Phila., PA (with Yes)
NOV 14 Transit Auditorium, Chicago, Il
NOV 15 Eastown Theatre, Detroit, MI
NOV 25 Madison Square Garden, New York, NY
NOV 26 Shrieveport, Louisiana

*ELP also played the famous Hatch Shell in Boston around this time

UK TOUR 1971
DEC 8   City Hall, Newcastle (With Michael Chapman, Spontaneous Combustion)
DEC 9   City Hall, Sheffield
DEC 10 Free Trade Hall, Manchester
DEC 11 Odeon, Birmingham
DEC 12 Capitol, Cardiff
DEC 13 London Pavilion (2 shows)
DEC 14 London Pavilion (2 shows)
DEC 15 London Pavilion (2 shows)
DEC 17 Caird Hall, Dundee
DEC 18 Edinburgh Empire
DEC 19 Greens Playhouse, Glasgow

Typical set list: The Barbarian; Tarkus; Jeremy Bender; Take A Pebble; Knife Edge; Pictures At An Exhibition; Rondo; Nutrocker sometimes encored with A Time And A Place.

USA TOUR 1972
(Preceded by March 10th show at Capitol Theatre, Cardiff, UK)
MAR 21 Denver Colosseum, Denver, CO
MAR 22 Long Beach Arena, Long Beach, CA
MAR 23 Civic Auditorium, Santa Monica, CA
MAR 24 Winterland San Francisco, CA
MAR 25 Winterland San Francisco, CA
MAR 26 Arena, St. Louis, MS

MAR 27 West Kentucky University, Louisville, Kentucky
MAR 28 Municipal Auditorium, Alanta, GA
MAR 29 Orlando, FL
MAR 30 Bay Front Center, St. Petersburgh, FL
MAR 31 Miami Beach Convention Center, Miami Beach, FL
APR 1   Colosseum, Jacksonville, FL
APR 3   "Mar Y Sol" Festival, Vega Baja, San Juan, Puerto Rico
APR 4   New Haven Colosseum, New Haven, CT
APR 5   Music Hall, Boston, MA (2 shows, Dr Hook supports)
APR 7   Utica, NY (Support, Mother Night)
APR 8   Shea Theatre, Buffalo, NY
APR 9   Wooster College, Cleveland, OH
APR 10 Academy of Music, NYC, NY
APR 11 Academy of Music, NYC, NY
APR 12 Bucknell University, Lewisburg, PA
APR 13 F&M College, Lancaster, PA
APR 14 Sports Arena, Hershey, PA
APR 15 Spectrum Theatre, Phila, PA
APR 17 Cobo Hall, Detroit, MI
APR 18 Hara Arena, Dayton, OH
APR 19 Arie Crown Theatre, Chicago, IL
APR 20 Kent State University, Kent State, OH
APR 21 Louisville Town Hall, Kentucky
APR 22 Tarrant City Convention Center, Fort Worth, TX
APR 23 Municipal Hall, Houston, TX
APR 25 University of Cincinatti, Cinc., OH
APR 27 Theil College, Greenville, PA
APR 28 Forum, Montreal, Canada
APR 29 Colosseum, Quebec City, Quebec, Canada

EUROPEAN TOUR 1972
JUN 4   Gruga Hall, Essen, Germany
JUN 6   Deutschland Halle, Berlin, Germany
JUN 7   Musikhalle, Hamburg, Germany
JUN 8   Falkiner Center, Kopenhagen, Denmark
JUN 10 Festhalle, Frankfurt, Germany
JUN 12 Meistersingerhalle, Nurnberg, Germany
JUN 15 Genoa, Germany
JUN 19 Olympia, Paris, France
JUN 24 Mehrzweckhalle, Wetzikon, Switzerland
JUN 25 Stadio, Bologna, Italy
JUN 26 Paleur, Rome, Italy
JUN 27 Stadthalle, Vienna, Austria
JUL 8   Pocono International Raceway, Long Pond, PA ("Concert 10" Festival which included : Three Dog Night, The Faces, Black Sabbath, Humble Pie, J Geils Band, Badfinger, Cactus, Edgar Winter)
JUL 12 Maple Leaf Gardens, Toronto, Canada

JAPAN TOUR 1972
JUL 22 Kourakuen Stadium, Tokyo, Japan

JUL 24 Koshien Stadium, Osaka, Japan

US TOUR 1972
JUL 27 Civic Auditorium, San Francisco, CA
JUL 28 Long Beach Arena, Long Beach, CA
JUL 29 (or30? or31?)Santa Monica, CA
AUG 11 Mecca Arena, Milwaukee, WI
AUG 13 Saratoga Performing Arts Center, Saratoga Springs,NY
AUG 17 Arie Crown Theatre, Chicago, IL
AUG 19 NJ Convention Hall, Ashbury Park, NJ
AUG 20 Convention Centre, Asbury Park, NJ
SEP 30 Oval Cricket Ground, Kennington, South London, England (Melody Maker magazine's Poll Winner Concert, featured other acts incl. Focus)

BRITISH TOUR 1972
NOV 10 Winter Gardens, Bournemouth
NOV 11 Gaumont Southhampton
NOV 12 Capitol Theatre, Cardiff (2 shows)
NOV 13 Free Trade Hall, Manchester
NOV 15 St. Georges Hall, Bradford
NOV 17 Greens Playhouse, Glasgow (2 shows)
NOV 18 Guildhall, Preston
NOV 19 Trenton Gardens ,Stoke
NOV 21 De Monfort Hall, Leicester
NOV 22 Top Rank Suite, Liverpool
NOV 23 Capitol Theatre, Cardiff
NOV 24 Birmingham Odeon, Birmingham (2 shows)
NOV 25 Sheffield City Hall, Yorkshire
NOV 26 Hammersmith Odeon, London (2 shows)
NOV 27 The Dome, Brighton
NOV 29 Odeon, Newcastle (2 shows)
DEC 1 Caird Hall, Dundee

Typical set list: Hoedown; Tarkus; The Endless Enigma; The Sheriff; Lucky Man; Take a Pebble; Piano Improvisations; Pictures At An Exhibition; Nutrocker; Rondo, sometimes opened with Abaddon's Bolero.

EUROPEAN TOUR "Get me a ladder" 1973
FEB 20 Kiel, Germany
FEB 25 Ludwigshafen, Germany
FEB 26 Freiburg, Germany
MAR 30 Ostseehalle, Kiel, Germany
MAR 31 Philipshalle, Dusseldorf, Germany
APR 1 Forest National, Brussels, Belgium
APR 3 Saint-Ouen, Paris, France
APR 4 L'Arena, Poitiers, France
APR 10 Friedrich Eberthalle, Ludwigshafen, Germany
APR 11 Friedrich Eberthalle, Ludwigshafen, Germany
APR 12 Stadthalle, Freiburg, Germany
APR 13 Sporthalle, Cologne, Germany
APR 15 Hallenstadion, Zurich, Switzerland
APR 16 Ernst Merck Halle, Hamburg, Germany

APR 17 Branby Hall, Copenhagen, Denmark
APR 18 Scandinavum, Goteborg, Sweden
APR 21 Oude Rai, Amsterdam, Holland
APR 22 Westfallen Halle, Germany
APR 23 Munsterland Halle, Munster, Germany
APR 24 Olympiahalle, Munich, Germany
APR 25 Stadthalle, Vienna, Austria
APR 26 Stadthalle, Vienna, Austria
APR 28 Velodromo Vigorelli, Milano, Italy
MAY 2 Studio, Bologna, Italy
MAY 3 Bologna Palasport, Bologna, Italy
MAY 4 Vigorelli, Milan, Italy

BRAIN SALAD SURGERY US TOUR 1973
NOV 14 Sportatorium, Hollywood, FL
NOV 15 Civic Centre, Tampa, FL
NOV 17 Jai Alai Fronton, West Palm Beach, FL
NOV 19 Municipal Auditorium, Alanta, Ga
NOV 20 Civic Center, Roanoke,VA (cancelled?)
NOV 21 Convention Center, Louisville, KY
NOV 22 Cincinatti Gardens, Cincinatti, OH
NOV 23 Civic Center, Charleston, WV
NOV 24 Colosseum, Indianapolis, IN
NOV 25 Municipal Auditorium, Nashville, TN
NOV 26 University of Illinois, Champaign, IL
NOV 28 State Fair Arena, Oklahoma City, OK
NOV 30 Memorial Auditorium, Des Moines,IA
DEC 1 Metropolitan Sports Arena, Minneapolis, MN
DEC 2 Amphitheatre, Chicago, IL
DEC 3 Amphitheatre, Chicago, IL
DEC 4 Cobo Hall, Detroit, MI
DEC 5 Cobo Hall, Detroit, MI
DEC 7 Maple Leaf Gardens, Toronto, Canada
DEC 8 Cornell University, Ithaca, NY
DEC 9 Montreal Forum, Montreal, Canada
DEC 10 Boston Gardens,Boston, MA
DEC 11 Spectrum Theatre, Philadelphia, PA
DEC 13 Nassau Colosseum, Uniondale, NY
DEC 15 Civic Center, Baltimore, MD
DEC 16 Lyric Theatre, Baltimore, MD
DEC 17 Madison Square Garden, NYC,NY

Typical set list: Tarkus; Karn Evil 9 (1st Impression, part 2); Jeremy Bender/The Sheriff; Take a Pebble; Piano Improvisations; Still...You Turn Me On; Take A Pebble; Lucky Man; Take A Pebble (reprise); Hoedown; Pictures At An Exhibition.

USA TOUR 1974
JAN 24 The Omni, Atlanta, GA
JAN 25 Memorial Colosseum, Tuscaloosa, AL

JAN 26 Little Rock, AR 28 Colosseum, Denver, CO
JAN 30 Salt Palace, Salt Lake City, UT
FEB 1 Sacramento, CA
FEB 2 Winterland, San Francisco, CA
FEB 3 Long Beach Arena, Long Beach, CA
FEB 9 Swing Auditorium, San Bernadine, CA
FEB 10 Anaheim Convention Center, Anaheim, CA; released as the official album 'Welcome Back My Friends To The Show That Never Ends'
FEB 11 Colosseum, Seattle, WA
FEB 12 Swing Auditorium, San Bernadine, CA
FEB 13 Colosseum, Portland, OR
FEB 14 Vancouver Gardens, Vancouver, British Columbia, Canada
FEB 15 Pulfman, WA
FEB 17 Cow Palace, San Francisco, CA
FEB 18 Cow Palace, San Francisco, CA
FEB 20 Fresno, CA21 Sports Arena, San Diego, CA
FEB 22 Activity Center, Tuscon, AR
FEB 23 University of New Mexico, Albuquerque, NM
FEB 26 Tulsa, OK or San Antonio, TX
FEB 27 Reunion Arena, Dallas, TX
FEB 28 Astrodome, Houston,TX
MAR 1 Louisiana State University, Baton Rouge, LO
MAR 5 St. Louis, MO
MAR 7 Civic Center, Tulsa, OK
MAR 26 Henry Lewit Arena, Wichita,KA
MAR 28 Los Angeles Colosseum, CA
APR 6 Ontario Motor Speedway, Ontario, CA; 200,000 people attended. Other acts included Black Sabbath, Black Oak Arkansas, Eagles, Rare Earth and Deep Purple.

EUROPEAN TOUR 1974
APR 18 Wembley Empire Pool, London, England (Back Door support)
APR 19 Wembley Empire Pool, London, England (as above)
APR 20 Wembley Empire Pool, London, England (as above)
APR 21 Wembley Empire Pool, London, England (as above)
APR 23 Stoke Trentham Gardens, England
APR 29 Empire, Liverpool, England
APR 30 Empire, Liverpool, England
MAY 1 Empire, Liverpool, England
MAY 2 Empire, Liverpool, England
MAY 6 Sporthalle, Munchen, Germany
MAY 7 Palau d'Esports, Barcelona, Spain
MAY 8 Palau d'Esports, Barcelona, Spain
MAY 13 Sindelfingen, Germany
MAY 16 Olympiastadium, Innsbruck, Austria
MAY 17 Stadthalle, Wien, Austria
MAY 18 Olympiahalle, Munchen, Germany
MAY 19 Olympiahalle, Munchen, Germany
MAY 20 Wetzikon, Switzerland

MAY 21 Wetzikon, Switzerland
MAY 23 Philipshalle, Dusseldorf, Germany
MAY 24 Philipshalle, Dusseldorf, Germany
MAY 25 Ahoy Halle, Rotterdam
MAY 27 Palais Des Sports, Paris, France
MAY 28 Palais Des Sports, Paris, France
MAY 31 Festhalle, Frankfurt, Germany
JUN 1 Festhalle, Frankfurt, Germany

US TOUR 1974
JUL 26 Rich Stadium, Buffalo, NY (James Gang & Lynyrd Skynrd support)
JUL 27 Saratoga Springs, Saratoga, NY
JUL 28 New Haven Civic Center, New Haven, CT
JUL 29 Providence Civic Center, Providence, RI
JUL 30 Cape Cod Colosseum, Yarmouth, MA (SNAFU support)
AUG 1 Capitol Center, Landover
AUG 2 Civic Center, Pitts, PA
AUG 4 Cleveland, OH or Municipal Stadium
AUG 5 Hershey Park, Hershey, PA
AUG 7 Norfolk Scope, Norfolk, VA
AUG 10 Charlotte Motor Speedway, Charlotte NC. Known as "August Jam"; Allman Brothers on the bill, 200,000 attended
AUG 13 Knoxville, TN
AUG 14 Dayton, OH
AUG 15 Hershey Park Arena, Hershey, PA
AUG 17 Roosevelt Stadium, Jersey City, NJ (Postponed because of rainstorm after sound check that ruined stage and equipment)
AUG 18 Performing Art Center, Saratoga, NY(Due to the problem with a storm the night before, the show was cancelled.)
AUG 20 Roosevelt Stadium (Re scheduled), Jersey City, NJ
AUG 21 Spectrum, Philadelphia, PA
AUG 24 New York: ELP played a benefit concert in a park in NYC

Typical set list: Hoedown; Jerusalem; Toccata; Benny The Bouncer; Take A Pebble; Still...You Turn Me On; Lucky Man; Piano Improvisations; Take A Pebble (reprise); Jeremy Bender/The Sheriff; Karn Evil 9 (complete); Pictures At An Exhibition.

ELP NORTH AMERICAN TOUR 1977 with orchestra(*)

MAY 24 Freedom Hall, Louisville, KY*
MAY 25 Freedom Hall, Louisville, KY*
MAY 29 Riverfront Colosseum, Cinc., OH*
MAY 31 Cobo Hall, Detroit, MI*
JUN 1 Cobo Hall, Detroit, MI *
JUN 4 Soldiers Field, Chicago, IL *
JUN 5 County Stadium, Milwaukee, WI * (J.Geils Band, Foghat and Climax Blues Band support)
JUN 7 Market Square Arena, Indianapolis, IN
JUN 9 Dane County Colosseum, Madison, Wi *

JUN 11 St, Paul Arena, Minneapolis, MN *
JUN 12 Memorial Auditorium, Des Moines, IA
JUN 14 Terre Haute University, Terre Haute, IN
JUN 16 Roberts Stadium, Evansville IN *
JUN 20 Spectrum, Phila., PA
JUN 21 Spectrum, Phila., PA
JUN 23 Omni Theatre, Atlanta, GA
JUN 25 Mobile, Alabama
JUN 26 Birmingham Civic Center, Birmingham,AL
JUN 27 Civic Center, Knoxville, TN
JUN 28 Greensboro Colosseum, Greensboro, NC
JUN 29 Charlotte Colosseum, Charlotte, NC
JUN 30 Colosseum, Columbia, SC
JUL 3 Scope, Norfolk, VA
JUL 5 Jacksonville, FL
JUL 7 Madison Square Garden, NYC,NY *
JUL 8 Madison Square Garden, NYC,NY *
JUL 9 Madison Square Garden, NYC,NY *
JUL 10 Hartford Civic Center, Hartford, CT
JUL 12 Boston Gardens, Boston, MA
JUL 13 Boston Gardens, Boston, MA
JUL 14 Civic Center, Providence, RI
JUL 17 Municipal Stadium, Cleveland, OH
JUL 19 Brown Stadium, Cleveland, OH
JUL 20 Boston Gardens,Boston, MA or Civic Center, Baltimore, MD
JUL 21 Boston Gardens,Boston, MA or Civic Center, Baltimore, MD
JUL 22 Cobo Hall, Detroit, MI
JUL 23 War Memorial, Rochester, NY
JUL 24 CNE Stadium, Toronto, Canada
JUL 27 The Corral, Calgary, Alberta, Canada
JUL 29 National Pacific University Center, Vancouver, Canada
JUL 31 Seattle Colosseum, Seattle, WA
AUG 2 Memorial Colosseum, Portland, OR
AUG 5 Arena, Milwaukee, WI
AUG 6 Almeida Colosseum, Oakland, CA
AUG 7 Almeida Colosseum, Oakland, CA
AUG 9 Phoenix, AZ (Journey support)
AUG 10 Sports Arena, San Diego, CA
AUG 11 Long Beach Arena, Long Beach, CA
AUG 12 Long Beach Arena, Long Beach, CA
AUG 13 Swing Auditorium, San Bernadino, CA
AUG 14 Long Beach Arena, Long Beach, CA
AUG18 Arrowhead Stadium, Kansas City, Missouri
AUG 19 Civic Center, Tulsa, OK
AUG 20 Memorial Auditorium, Dallas, TX
AUG 21 Sam Houston Colosseum, Houston, TX
AUG 22 Anaheim Convention Center, Anaheim, CA

AUG 23 Kiel Auditorium, St, Louis, MO
AUG 26 Olympic Stadium, Montreal, Canada* (movie, LP recorded)
AUG 27 Olympic Stadium, Montreal, Canada*
OCT 15 Ohio University Convocation Center, Athens, OH
OCT 17 Madison Square Garden, NYC, NY(WNEW-FM benefit show)
OCT 18 Hershey Park Arena, Hershey, PA
OCT 21 Eastern Michigan University, Ypsilanti, MI
OCT 22 University of Maryland, Columbia, MD
OCT 25 The Colosseum, Jackson, MS
OCT 29 Baton Rouge, Louisiana
OCT 31 Houston, TX
NOV 8 Dane County Colosseum, Madison, WI
NOV 10 Hartford,CN
NOV 12 Colosseum,Wheeling, VA*
NOV 14 Illinois State University, Normal, IL
NOV 15 Michigan State University, Lansing, MI
NOV 20 Memphis, TN
NOV 25 Colosseum, Wheeling, VA
NOV 26 Hollywood Sportatorium, FL
NOV 27 St.Petersburg, FL
NOV 28 Tampa, FL
NOV 30 New Haven Civic Center, New Haven, CT
*Greg Lake lists this show as Ahearn Playhouse, Kansas State University, Kansas

Typical set list (with orchestra): Abaddon's Bolero; Hoedown; Karn Evil 9, 1st Impression, part 2; The Enemy God; Tarkus; From The Beginning; Piano Concerto no.1 (1st and 3rd movements); Closer To Believing; Knife Edge; Pictures At An Exhibition; C'est La Vie, Lucky Man; Tank; Nutrocker ;Pirates; Fanfare For The Common Man/America/Rondo.

US TOUR 1978

JAN 16 Quebec Forum, Montreal, Canada
JAN 17 Quebec Forum, Montreal, Canada
JAN 18 Ontario Memorial Auditorium,Kitchener, Canada
JAN 20 Universal Amphitheater, Chicago,IL
JAN 21 Universal Amphitheater, Chicago,IL
JAN 22 Universal Amphitheater, Chicago,IL
JAN 24 Indiana Hulman Civic Center, Terre Haute,IN
JAN 25 Richfield Colosseum, Cleveland,OH
JAN 26 University of WA, Morgantown, WA
JAN 28 Capitol Centre, Largo, MD
JAN 29 Civic Center,Springfield, MA
JAN 30 Cornell University, Ithaca, NY
FEB 1 Memorial Autidorium, Buffalo, NY
FEB 2 Maple Leaf Gardens, Toronto, Ontario
FEB 2 Maple Leaf Gardens, Toronto, Ontario

FEB 4   Boston Gardens, Boston, MA
FEB 5   The Spectrum, Philadelphia, PA
FEB 6   Renselaer Polytechnic Institute, Troy, NY
FEB 8   Field House, Plattsburg, NY
FEB 9   Nassau Colosseum, Uniondale, NY
FEB 10   Nassau Colosseum, Uniondale, NY
FEB 14   South Illinois University, Carbondale, IL
FEB 15   Assembly Hall, Champaign, IL
FEB 16   West IL University, IL
FEB 18   S U N Y, Plattsberg
FEB 19   Lubbock Colosseum, Uniondale, NY
FEB 20   Civic Centre, San Antonio, TX
FEB 21   Assembly Centre, Tulsa,
FEB 22   Civic Centre Colosseum, Amarillo, TX
FEB 23   Civic Centre, El Paso, TX
FEB 24   Alladdin Hotel, Las Vagas, NV
FEB 26   University of Colorado, Fort Collins, CO
FEB 27   Kansas City, MO
FEB 28   Kansas City, MO
MAR 1   Checkerdome Arena, St Louis, MO
MAR 3   Boston Gardens, Boston, MA
MAR 4   Olympia Stadium, Detroit, MI
MAR 6   New Haven Civic Centre, New Haven, CT
MAR 7   Riverfront Colosseum, Cincinatti, OH
MAR 8   The Omni, Atlanta, GA
MAR 10   Freedom Hall, Johnson City, TN
MAR 12   Civic Centre, Springfield, MA
MAR 13   Civic Centre, Providence, RI

Typical set list (as trio): Peter Gunn; Hoedown; Tarkus; Take A Pebble; Piano Concerto no.1; C'est La Vie; Lucky Man; Pictures At An Exhibition; Karn Evil 9, 1st Impression, part 2; Tiger In A Spotlight; Watching Over You; Tank; The Enemy God; Maple Leaf Rag; Nutrocker; Pirates; Fanfare for the Common Man; Show Me The Way To Go Home

USA AND CANADA TOUR 1986:
Emerson Lake & Powell
AUG 15   El Paso County Colosseum, El Paso, TX
AUG 17   Lloyd Noble Center, Norman, OK
AUG 19   Lakefront Arena, New Orleans, LA
AUG 20   Summit Festival, Houston, TX
AUG 21   Reunion Arena, Dallas, TX
AUG 23   Municipal Auditorium, San Antonio, TX
SEP 1   Riverbend Center, Cinc. OH
SEP 3   Massey Hall, Toronto, Canada
SEP 5   Montreal, Canada
SEP 8   Civic Center, Glens Falls, NY (Bricklin support)

SEP 12   Mann Center, Phila, PA (Bricklin support)
SEP 13   Meadowlands Arena, EastRutherford, NJ
SEP 15   Performing Arts Center, Providence, RI
SEP 16   Greatwoods Center, Mansfield, MA (Man support)
SEP 19   Capitol Center, Landover
SEP 20   Madison Square Garden, NYC, NY (Bricklin support)
SEP 21   Syria Mosque, Pitts, PA
OCT 2   Fox Theatre, Atlanta, GA
OCT 4   Lakeland Arena(Civic Center), Lakeland, FL
OCT 5   Knight Center, Miami, FL
OCT 12   Charlotte, NC
OCT 14   Opera House, Boston, MA
OCT 16   Colosseum, Grand Rapids, MN
OCT 17   Fox Theatre, Detroit, MI
OCT 18   Square Market Arena, Indianapolis, IN
OCT 19   Fox Theatre, Chicago, IL
OCT 21   St.Paul, MN
OCT 22   Mecca, Milwaukee, WI
OCT 23   Stephens Auditorium, Ames, IA
OCT 26   Civic Auditorium, Portland, OR
OCT 27   Paramount, Seattle, WA
OCT 29   Kaiser Pavilion, Oakland, CA
OCT 30   Greek Theatre, Los Angeles, CA
OCT 31   Pacifica Theatre, Costa Mensa, CA
NOV 1   Open Air Festival, San Diego, CA
NOV 2   Phoenix, AZ

US TOUR 1988: Three (Emerson, Berry & Palmer)
APR 6   New York,NY
APR 7   Philadelphia,PA
APR 8   New York,NY
APR 10   Washington,DC
APR 11   Baltimore,MD
APR 12   New Haven,CT Toad's
APR 14   New York The Ritz
APR 15   Boston,MA Paradise Theater
APR 18   Ottawa, CANADA
APR 20   Montreal, CANADA
APR 21   Pittsburgh,PA, USA
APR 22   Cleveland,OH Bogart's
APR 23   Detroit,MI
APR 25   Cincinnati,OH
APR 26   St. Louis,MO
APR 27   Chicago,IL
APR 28   Milwaukee,WI
APR 30   Kansas City,MO
MAY 2   Denver,CO
MAY 5   San Francisco,CA Fillmore
MAY 6   San Jose,CA (Robert Berry's home town)
MAY 7   San Jose,CA
MAY 8   Los Angeles,CA The Palace
MAY 9   San Diego,CA
MAY 10   Phoenix,AZ
MAY 12   San Antonio,TX
MAY 13   Dallas,TX (cancelled)
MAY 14   Austin,TX
MAY 15   Houston,TX
MAY 17   Atlanta,GA
MAY 18   Jacksonville,FL
MAY 19   Orlando,FL
MAY 20   New York, NY Madison Square Gardens (Atlantic Records 40th Anniversary concert)

Introduced by Phil Collins as "Emerson and Palmer".

Typical set list: Fanfare For The Common Man; Desde La Vida; Lover To Lover; Hoedown; You Do Or You Don't; Talkin Bout; Emerson solo: Dream Runner, Creole Dance; On My Way Home; Runaway; Standing In The Shadows Of Love; America/Rondo - including Palmer solo; Eight Miles High.

USA TOUR 1992 Black Moon
JUN 22   Tower Theater, Upper Darby, PA (press only show)
JUN 24   Mann Music Center, Phila., PA
JUN 25   Jones Beach, Wantaugh, NY
JUN 26   Garden State Arts Center, Holmdel, NJ
JUN 28   Merriweather Post Pavilion, Columbia, MD
JUN 29   Great Woods, Mansfield, MA
JUN 31   Waterloo Village, Stanhope, NJ
AUG 1   Empire Center,Syracuse, NY
AUG 2   Palace Theatre,Albany, NY
AUG 4   Bushnell, Hartford, CT
AUG 5   L'Agora, Quebec,Canada
AUG 7   Montreal Forum, Montreal, Canada
AUG 8   Finger Lakes P.A.C., Canadaigua, NY
AUG 9   Kingswood Amphitheater, Toronto, Canada
AUG 11   Nautica, Cleveland, OH
AUG 12   Pine Knob, Detroit, MI
AUG 13   Riverbend Amphitheater, Cinn, OH
AUG 15   Riverport,Maryland Heights, MO
AUG 16   The World, Chicago, IL
AUG 17   Deer Creek,Indianapolis, IA
AUG 18   Chastain Park, Atlanta, GA
AUG 20   Starplex Amphitheater,Dallas, TX
AUG 21   Woodlands, Houston, TX
AUG 22   Sunken Garden Theater, San Antonio, TX
AUG 24   Desert Sky Pavilion, Phoenix, AZ
AUG 26   Open Air Theater, San Diego, CA
AUG 28   Universal Amphitheater, Los Angeles, CA
AUG 29   Bren Center, Irvine, CA
AUG 30   Thomas Mack Center, Las Vegas,NV
SEP 1   Cal. Expo Center, Sacramento, CA
SEP 2   Concord Pavilion, San Francisco, CA
SEP 4   Schnitzer Auditorium, Portland, OR
SEP 5   Summer Music Theater, George, WA
SEP 6   Orpheum Theater, Vancouver, BC

JAPAN TOUR 1992
SEP 10   Kyoikubunkakaikan, Kawasaki, Japan
SEP 11   Koseinenkinkaikan, Tokyo, Japan
SEP 12   Shi Kokaido, Nagoya, Japan

SEP 14   Koseinenkinkaikan, Osaka, Japan
SEP 16   Hitomikinekodo, Tokyo, Japan
SEP 17   Shibuya Kokaido, Tokyo, Japan
SEP 18   Shibuya Kokaido, Tokyo, Japan
SEP 19   Shibuya Kokaido, Tokyo, Japan

EUROPE TOUR 1992
SEP 26   Arena di Verona, Verona, Italy
SEP 29   Sportshall, Budapest, Hungary
OCT 2   Royal Albert Hall, London, England
OCT 3   Royal Albert Hall, London, England; released as 'Live At The Royal Albert Hall'
OCT 7   Huxley's Neue Welt, Berlin, Germany
OCT 8   Kuppelsaal, Hanover, Germany
OCT 10   Stadthalle, Vienna, Austria
OCT 11   Stadthalle, Heidelburg, Germany
OCT 12   Winterhur, Zurich, Switzerland
OCT 13   Neu Siegerlandhalle, Siegen, Germany
OCT 15   Oberfrankenhalle, Bayreuth, Germany
OCT 16   Eissporthalle, Halle, Germany
OCT 17   E. Werk, Cologne, Germany
OCT 18   Grugahalle, Essen, Germany
OCT 20   Philharmonie, Munich, Germany
OCT 23   Congresgebouw, Hague, aaholland
OCT 25   Apollo, Manchester, England
OCT 26   Royal Albert Hall, London, England
OCT 28   Kongresszentrum, Stuttgart, Germany
OCT 31   Cuartel Conde Duque, Madrid, Spain
NOV 2   Arena Auditorium, Valencia, Spain
NOV 3   Sports Palace, Barcelona. Spain
NOV 5   Elysee Montmartre, Paris, France
NOV 6   Forest National, Brussels, Belgium
NOV 7   Congresgebouw, The Hague, Holland
NOV 8   Falkoner Theatre, Copenhagen, Denmark
NOV 10   Centrum, Olso, Norway
NOV 11   Konserthuset, Stockholm, Sweden
NOV 14   Donauhalle, Ulm, Germany
NOV 15   Kulturpalast, Dresden, Germany
NOV 16   Palasport, Turin(Udine?), Italy
NOV 17   Palasport, Torino, Italy
NOV 19   Palasport, Madena, Italy
NOV 20   Palaghiaccio, Rome, Italy
NOV 21   Palatrussardi, Milan, Italy
NOV 23   Stadthalle, Freiburg, Germany
NOV 25   International Centre, Bournemouth, England
NOV 26   City Hall, Newcastle, England
NOV 27   Symphony Hall, Birmingham, England
NOV 28   Colston Hall, Bristol, England
NOV 30   Kongresshalle, Frankfurt, Germany

DEC 1   Congress Centrum, Hamburg, Germany

NORTH AMERICAN TOUR 1993
JAN 13   North Alberta Jubilee Auditorium,Edmonton, Alberta
JAN 14   South Alberta Jubilee Auditorium, Calgary, Alberta
JAN 15   Center of the Arts, Regina, Saskatchewan
JAN 16   Walker Theater, Winnipeg, Manitoba
JAN 18   Community Auditorium, Thunder Bay, Ontario
JAN 19   Sudbury Arena, Sudbury, Canada
JAN 20   Centennial Hall, London, Ontario
JAN 21   Congress Center, Ottawa, Ontario
JAN 22   Massey Hall, Toronto, Canada
JAN 23   Massey Hall, Toronto, Canada
JAN 25   Theatre Saint Denis, Montreal, Quebec
JAN 26   Salle Albert Rousseau, Sainte Poi, Quebec
JAN 28   Memorial Auditorium, Burlington, VT
JAN 29   Orpheum Theater, Boston, MA
JAN 30   Providence Performing Arts Center, Providence, RI
FEB 1   Paramount Performing Arts Center, Springfield, MA
FEB 3   Radio Music Hall, New York, NY
FEB 4   Radio Music Hall, New York, NY
FEB 5   Tower Theater, Phila, PA
FEB 6   Symphony Hall, Allentown, PA
FEB 8   Palumbo Center, Pittsburgh, PA
FEB 9   Palace Performing Arts Center, New Haven, CT
FEB 10   Mid Hudson Civic Center, Poughkeepsie, NY
FEB 12   Palace Theater, Cleveland, OH
FEB 13   Veteran's Memorial Auditorium, Columbus, OH
FEB 15   De Vos Hall at Grand Center, Grand Rapids, MI
FEB 16   Ervia J. Nutter Center, Dayton, OH
FEB 17   Fox Theater, Detroit, MI
FEB 19   Northrup, Minneapolis, MN
FEB 20   Riverside Theater, Milwaukee, WI
FEB 21   Chicago Theater, Chicago, IL
FEB 23   Masonic Auditorium, Toledo, OH
FEB 24   Civic Center Theater, Madison, WI
FEB 26   Adler Theater, Davenport, IA
FEB 27   Stephens Auditorium at Iowa State, Ames, IW
FEB 28   Peoria Civic Center, Peoria, IL
MAR 2   Music Hall, Omaha, NE
MAR 3   Midland Theater, Kansas City, MO
MAR 4   Brady Theater, Tulsa, OK
MAR 6   Kiva Auditorium, Albuquerque, NM
MAR 9   BSU Pavilion Arena, Boise, ID
MAR 11   Kingsbury Hall, U of Utah, Salt Lake City, UT
MAR 12   Pioneer Theater, Reno, NV
MAR 13   Wilson Theater, Fresno, CA

MAR 14   Warfield Theater, San Francisco, CA
MAR 16   Wiltern Theater, Los Angeles, CA
MAR 1   Wiltern Theater, Los Angeles, CA

SOUTH AMERICAN TOUR 1993
MAR 23   Rio De Janeiro, Brazil, South America
MAR 24   Rio De Janeiro, Brazil, South America
MAR 25   Sao Paulo, Brazil
MAR 26   Sao Paulo, Brazil
MAR 27   Sao Paulo, Brazil
MAR 29   Porto Alegre, Brazil
APR 1   Santiago, Chile
APR 4   Obras Stadium, Buenos Aires, Argentina (2 shows both days)
APR 5   Obras Stadium, Buenos Aires, Argentina (as above)

Typical set list: Karn Evil 9, 1st Impression, part 2 (beginning) - omitted on later dates; Tarkus; Knife Edge; Paper Blood; Black Moon; Emerson solo: Close To Home, Creole Dance; Lake solo: From The Beginning, Still...You Turn Me On; Lucky Man; Honky Tonk Train Blues; Romeo And Juliet; Pirates; Pictures At An Exhibition – including Palmer solo; Fanfare/ Rondo/America.

USA TOUR 1993: *The Return Of The Manticore* box set promotional tour
NOV 17   Beacon Theatre, NYC (The "Hungerthon" benefit concert) ELP headline; also Richie Havens, Southside Johnny, Roseanne Cash, Roger McGuinn, Janis Ian and Buster Poindexter)
NOV 23   Virgin Records store, Los Angeles (ELP did a small "unplugged" performance, 3 songs)
DEC 17   The Hollywood Palladium, Hollywood, CA (KLOS radio Christmas show - ELP, Marc Bonilla and the Dragon Band (Emerson joined MB&TDB on "Nutrocker")

NORTH AMERICAN TOUR 1996
with Jethro Tull
AUG 18   Darien Center, Darien, NY
AUG 19   Kingswood Music Theatre , Richmond Hills, Ontario, Canada
AUG 21   Montage Mountain, Scranton, PA
AUG 22   Garden State Art Center, Holmdel, NJ
AUG 23   Merriweather Post Pavilion, Columbia, MD
AUG 25   Meadows Music Theatre, Hartford, CT
AUG 26   Great Woods Center For Performing Arts, Mansfield, MA
AUG 27   New York State Fair Grounds, Syracuse, NY
AUG 29   Hershey Park Amphitheatre, Hershey, PA
AUG 30   Jones Beach Theatre, Wantauh, Long Island, NY
AUG 31   E. Center, Camden, NJ
SEP 1   Riverplex Amphitheatre, Pittsburg, PA
SEP 3   Nautica Stage, Cleveland, OH
SEP 4   Polaris Amphitheatre, Columbus, OH

SEP 5   Pine Knob, Clarkson, MI6 Riverbend, Cincinatti, OH
SEP 6   Riverbend Music Center, Cincinatti, OH
SEP 7   World Music Theatre, Tinley Park, IL*
SEP 8   The Mark, Moline, IL
SEP 10   Northrup Auditorium,Target Center, Mineapolis, MN
SEP 11   Marcus Amphitheatre, Milwaukee, WI
SEP 13   Riverport Theatre, St. Louis, MO
SEP 14   Sandstone Amphitheatre, Bonner Springs, KS
SEP 15   Riverfest Amphitheatre, Little Rock, AR
SEP 16   Fiddlers Green Amphitheatre, Englewood, CO
SEP 18   Desert Sky Pavilion, Phoenix, AR
SEP 19   Aladdin Hotel & Casino Theatre, Las Vegas, NV
SEP 20   Open Air Theatre, San Diego, CA
SEP 21   Irvine Meadows, Irvine, CA
SEP 22   Concord Pavilion, Concord, CA
SEP 25   Reno Amphitheatre, Reno, NV
SEP 27   The Gorge, George, WA
SEP 28   Labor Day Amphitheatre, Salem,
SEP 29   BSU Pavilion, Boise, ID

JAPAN TOUR 1996
OCT 8   Sun Palace, Fukuoka
OCT 9   Festival Hall, Osaka
OCT 10   Shi Kokaido, Tokyo
OCT 12   Shibuya Kokaido, Tokyo
OCT 13   Kosei Nenkin Kaikan, Tokyo
OCT 14   Izumi T 21, Sendai
OCT 15   Nakano Sun Plaza, Tokyo
OCT 17   Nakano Sun Plaza, Tokyo
OCT 18   Nakano Sun Plaza, Tokyo
OCT 19   Bunka Center, Saitama Urawa Shi

Typical set list: Karn Evil 9 , Part 2 (excerpt), Tiger in a Spotlight, Hoedown, Touch & Go, Bitches Crystal, Still....you turn me on, From the Beginning, Hammer it out, Take a Pebble, Lucky Man, Tarkus/Pictures medley, Fanfare for the Common Man/Rondo.

EUROPEAN TOUR 1997
(Preceded byJUN 12 The Joint, Hard Rock, Las Vegas, NV;JUN 16 Z-Ninety-Free, Atlanta, GA)
JUN 20   Kiss Stadion, Budapest, Hungary
JUN 22   Spodek, Katowice, Poland; released as 'Live In Poland'
JUN 23   Palace of Culture, Prague, Czech Republic
JUN 24   Tollowood, Munich, Germany
JUN 26   Patinore de Kockelschuer, Luxembourg
JUN 28   Stadthalle, Kassel, Germany
JUN 29   The Paradiso, Amsterdam, Holland
JUL 1   Serandadenhof Atrium, Nuernberg, Germany
JUL 2   Elysee Montmatre, Paris, France

JUL 4   Peisenitzinsel, Halle, Germany
JUL 5   Westfallen Park, Dortmund, Germany
JUL 6   Daytona Festival, Lahr, Germany
JUL 7   Montreux Festival, Montreux, Switerzland
JUL 11   Museumshof, Fulda, Germany
JUL 12   Grosse Freheit, Hamburg, Germany
JUL 13   Elbufer, Dresden, Germany
JUL 16   Cantania Jazz Festival, Sicily
JUL 18   Velodromo Quarto, Sardinia (Quartu), Italy
JUL 20   Piazza Olimpo, Mantiva (Castiglione Delle Stiviere), Italy
JUL 21   Foro Italico, Rome (Centralino del Foro Italico), Italy
JUL 25   The Kingdom Festival, Bellinzona, Switerzland

SOUTH & NORTH AMERICAN TOUR 1997
AUG 6   Teatro Guaira, Curitiba, Brazil
AUG 8   Gran Rex, Buenos Aries, Argentina
AUG 9   Gran Rex, Buenos Aries, Argentina
AUG 10   Avendia Das Hortensias, Gramado, Brazil
AUG 12   Estadio, Santiago, Chile
AUG 13   Estadio, Santiago, Chile
AUG 15   Mineirinho Gymnasium, Belo Horizonte, Brazil
AUG 16   Metropolitan, Belo Horizonte, Brazil
AUG 18   Olympia, Sao Paulo, Brazil
AUG 19   Olympia, Sao Paulo, Brazil
AUG 20   Olympia, Sao Paulo, Brazil
AUG 21   Gran Rex, Buenos Aries, Argentina
SEP 6   Wolf Trap Farm Park, Vienna, VA
SEP 7   Oakdale Theatre, Wallingford, CT
SEP 9   State Theater, New Brunswick, NJ
SEP 10 Beacon Theater, New York, NY
SEP 11 The Tower Theater, Philadelphia, PA
SEP 12 Harborlights, Boston, MA
SEP 13 The Sands Hotel & Casino, Altantic City, NJ
SEP 14 Tower Theater, Philadelphia, PA
SEP 17 Nautica, Cleveland, OH
SEP 18 The Palace, Auburn Hills, MI
SEP 19 Rosemont Theater, Chicago, IL
SEP 20 Riverside Theatre, Milwaukee, WI
SEP 21 Fox Theatre, St.Louis, Missouri
SEP 23 Union Hall, Phoenix, AZ
SEP 25 Universal Amphitheater, Los Angeles, CA
SEP 26 Concord Pavilion, Concord, CA
SEP 27 Reno Amphitheater, Reno, NV
SEP 28 Visalia Center, Fresno, CA
SEP 30 Humphrey's, San Diego, CA
OCT 4 Muelle Uno, Lima, Peru
OCT 7 Costa RicaTeatro Nacional, San Jose
OCT 8 Costa RicaTeatro Nacional, San Jose
OCT 10 Plaza De Toros, Monterrey, Mexico

OCT 11 Teatro Opera, Mexico City, Mexico
OCT 12 Teatro Opera, Mexico City, Mexico

Typical set list: Karn Evil 9 Part 2 , Tiger in a Spotlight, Hoedown, Touch & Go, Bitches Crystal, From the Beginning, Creole Dance, Take a Pebble, Honky Tonk Train Blues, Lucky Man, Tarkus/Pictures medley, Fanfare for the Common Man/Rondo.

NORTH AMERICAN TOUR 1998
with Deep Purple and Dream Theatre
AUG 1 Hampton Beach Casino Ballroom, Hampton Beach, NH (no DP or DT)
AUG 2 Flynn Theatre, Burlington, VT (no DP or DT)
AUG 3 The Chance, Poughkeepsie, NY
AUG 4 Chamberland County Civic Center, Portland, ME
AUG 6 PNC Bank Arts Center, Holmdel, NJ
AUG 7 Meadows Music Theater, Hartford, CT
AUG 8 Great Woods, Mansfield, MA
AUG 9 Jones Beach, Wantagh, NY
AUG 11 Bud Light Amphitheatre at Harvey's Lake,Wilkes-Barre,PA
AUG 12 E Center, Philadelphia PA (Cancelled - Ian Gillan of Deep Purple ill)
AUG 14 Finger Lakes Performing Arts, Canandaigua,NY
AUG 15 Pineknob Music Theater, Clarkston, MI
AUG 17 Coliseum De Quebec, Quebec City, QUE
AUG 18 Molson Center, Montreal, QUE
AUG 19 Molson Ampitheater, Toronto, ONT
AUG 21 Blossom M.C. Cuyahoga Falls, OH
AUG 22 World Musc Theater, Tinley Park, IL
AUG 23 Grand Casino Amphitheater, Hinkley, MN
AUG 24 Marcus Amphitheatre, Milwaukee,MI
AUG 26 Fiddler's Green Amphitheater, Denver, CO
AUG 28 Warfield Theater, San Francisco, CA
AUG 29 Warfield Theater, San Francisco, CA
AUG 30 Universal Amphitheater, Universal City,CA
AUG 31 4th & B, San Diego, CA DP or DH

APPENDIX 4

FRANK ASKEW'S 1996 JAPANESE TOUR DIARY

Friday 11th October
Flight Aeroflot SU581 leaving London Heathrow 12.30 pm. Each Aeroflot plane is named after a Russian composer – our plane was called..... *Mussorgsky!* Mussorgsky was our constant companion for 13 hours, save for a one and a half hour stop at Moscow.

Saturday 12th October
Arrived at Tokyo 10.45 a.m. local time. Billy Forshaw, my companion for the trip, had been feeling unwell during the latter part of the journey. When leaving the baggage reclaim area, Billy collapsed and split his head open on the marble like floor. 3 hours later, we left Tokyo General Hospital where Billy had received a brain scan, numerous checks for fracturing, 6 stitches and one bald patch for the bargain cost of 40,000 yen (appx. £240) – not the ideal start!!

Checked into the Akasaka Yoko hotel at 4.30 pm. Enough time for us to freshen up for the show – WRONG! I phoned Eric Barrett (tour manager) to inform him of our arrival and was greeted by "Where are you guys.... – the lads are on at 5 o'clock!!" (Apparently, concerts at the weekend in Japan start very early.) We dropped our bags, turned round and made our way to the taxi rank. We arrived at the Shibuya Kokaido at about 5.15 – the lads hadn't started. I'd like to think they hung on for us, but I doubt that was the case. Set list as follows:

Karn Evil 9 Impression 1, Part 2 (excerpt)
Tiger in a Spotlight
Hoedown (inc. Ribbon Controller solo)
Touch & Go
Knife Edge
Bitches Crystal (brilliant – the best number by far!)
Still...You Turn Me On
From the Beginning – as a band piece (problems for Greg with his on stage monitoring)
Emerson Solo, including an unnamed piece dedicated to the late Kevin Gilbert, and Hammer It Out
Take a Pebble (a band piece with a jazz link passage that reminded me of the jazz improvisations from the "Welcome Back" album)

Lucky Man
Tarkus (Eruption, Stones of Years, Iconoclast and Mass) – medleyed into...
Hut of Baba Yaga
Great Gates of Kiev

Encore:
Fanfare
Rondo – inc. Carl drum solo and Keith Hammond antics.

Running Time: 1 hour 35 minutes (Great Show, From the Beginning apart)

After the show, we made our way to the backstage catering area and were greeted by Keith, Greg and Carl, all of whom showed concern for Billy's injury. We shared drinks and food with E, L & P and were then offered a lift in their limo back to our hotel. Needless to say, it took very little time to accept their offer! We were glad of this and welcomed the early finish so we could catch up on some ZZZZs. NB! – Whilst back in our hotel, we experienced a small earthquake measuring 4.9 RCS.

Sunday 13th October
Arrived at Koseinenkin Hall at about 3 pm to observe the sound check. This was another "early start" show. During the sound check, they played a full version of "Touch & Go" (or Wash & Blow, as they call it!). They also were concerned about "From the Beginning', as the previous night's performance had been "dogged" with on stage monitoring problems resulting in timing difficulties for the band. To resolve this, Carl reverted to a more conventional drum beat (8th notes on the hi-hat and a rim shot on 2 + 4), rather than the bongos used previously. The sound man (Chris Beyer) had to come up with a solution to the situation, so that Carl could use the bongos. However it was decided that for this gig, Carl would employ the simpler rhythm. After the sound check, I conducted part 1 of the Carl interview. Show commenced at 5.10 pm. Same set list as previous, except Keith replaced "Hammer It Out" with "Honky Tonk Train Blues", where Greg and Carl joined in.

The performance wasn't quite as good as the previous night's, but still impressive (dodgy ending to "Touch & Go" and "Bitches Crystal" wasn't quite "nailed"). For this performance we stood in the auditorium.

Once again we attended the after-show party. What was evident to me was how well Keith , Greg and Carl were getting on and how enthused they were to be out there playing. To round off the evening, we checked out the Hard Rock Cafe which ELP had attended a few nights previously. Upon entering, there was a great autographed poster of ELP – what a good way of enticing customers in!

Monday 14th October
Day off for us – ELP played in Sendai (approx. 200 miles away).

Tuesday 15th October
The first of 3 dates at Sun Plaza. Arrived at the venue at approx. 3 pm. The show had a more conventional start time of 7 pm. This gave us the opportunity to chat with all four of the technicians, Will Alexander (Keith's), Keith Wechsler (Greg's guitar tech – he was also the drummer with Greg's band on the "Daddy" solo tour and he co-wrote the song "Gone Too Soon"), Mike Burns (Carl's tech – he'd also worked with other famous drummers such as Steve Gadd, Dennis Chambers and had been responsible for some of the drum loops used by Madonna) and Chris Beyer (sound engineer who was on his first major tour). E, L & P arrived at 5 o'clock for the sound check and ran through the usual "Touch & Go". They also decided to work out an ending for "From the Beginning'. Apparently it always just "sort of ended". So Keith would now nod to the others when the end approached. Keith was chosen because "he has the biggest nod in the band" (quote Carl Palmer). A personal high spot for me was a cymbal which Carl presented to me. He'd used it for over 20 years – it's an 8" bell type cymbal. It had developed a small crack and although this wasn't visible, it affected the sound – he even autographed it and it is something which I shall treasure.

The gig itself was superb. We sat at the side of the stage (to Carl's left) by the mixing desk – what a view!! It was the same set as before ("Honky Tonk Train Blues" again was the 2nd piano solo). During Keith's 1st solo, Carl joined us at the side. After the show, one of the guests was Carl's former karate teacher whom he hadn't seen for many years. Keith and Greg both knew him well. It was a nice moment to see. A funny footnote to this, a rather rotund Greg was greeted by the Karate teacher exclaiming, "Ah My Rake, Mr Rake!!" – they say great comedy writes itself.

Wednesday 16th October
Day Off for ELP.
Met with Carl in his hotel suite to conduct interview for *Impressions*. In his room he had a snare drum set up where he could practice his brushwork. I was interested in the drum, because it was a Gretsch 1965 (I think) model but was only 4" in depth. Carl told me that this was one of the first piccolo snare drums (okay, I'll take my anorak off now!).

Thursday 17th October
2nd Sun Plaza gig.
The day started more or less as Tuesday's. Arrived at Sun Plaza at about 3 o'clock. Had a bite to eat back stage and generally chatted to the techs. We took a few photos of the "team" and the equipment. Sound check as usual on "Touch & Go'.
The gig commenced at 7.10 pm and turned out to be the best show so far. We had our usual seats by the side mixing desk and again was joined by Carl during Keith's solo ('Honky Tonk Train Blues" *again* – not "Hammer It Out"). The only problem that marred this otherwise excellent show was that Keith's L100 Hammond decided to break down during "Rondo". After the Show, Keith's 2nd cousin attended the party (I think her name was Liz or Lisa). She told me that she had never heard ELP before and was quite surprised that we'd travelled so far to see him. When I asked her what she thought of Keith, she replied "Yes, he's quite good, isn't he!". Nice one! Probably the understatement of the millennium! The boys had to leave a little earlier than usual to have dinner with Udo, the Japanese promoter who incidentally promoted ELP on their first Japanese tour back in 1972.

Friday, 18th October
Third (and final) Sun Plaza gig and the penultimate show of the tour.
Arrived at Sun Plaza at about 3.30 pm (the equipment was already in place from the previous night). The sound check featured yet again "Touch & Go" – I was hoping they might play something different, you know, "Karn Evil 9," 1st, 2nd & 3rd Impressions! There had been talk of setting Keith up by doctoring his speech. Before his solo he would address the audience with some pleasantries in Japanese, but he didn't have the foggiest idea what he was saying. Unfortunately, I can't repeat here what the intended alterations were to have been – suffice to say that they made references to certain parts of the anatomy (female)!!
Greg had been having problems with his "Tune" bass guitar for the past couple of gigs, so a new one was delivered along with another make – a Vortex, I think. He would use both during the gig. It was Will Alexander's birthday and a surprise cake along with some champagne had been secretly arranged. The cake was presented to Will during the sound check with everyone singing "Happy Birthday" to Keith's piano accompaniment. Keith also asked me to video this for him.
Showtime was again at 7.10 pm. We had our usual seats once again. The performance not quite as good as the previous. There were a couple of hairy moments in "Tarkus" and "Pictures". I think fatigue was setting in and I know that everyone was looking forward to going home. I was hoping Keith would play "Hammer It Out" for his solo (I'd only heard it on one previous performance), but he stuck with "Honky Tonk". Once again the L100 packed up, despite Will's attempts to rectify it earlier.
The after show party was very busy. Carl gave me a snare drum batter head which he autographed (a good prize for Impressions!). Katoh San, the President of Korg, visited and once again I videoed this for Keith. We were invited back to ELP's hotel for another surprise party for Will. Carl told me he wouldn't attend as he was tired. I thanked him very much for his time and graciousness he'd shown us.
Back at the hotel, I was very pleased to meet up with Yoko Fukuma and a few of her friends. Yoko had arranged another cake for Will. Incidentally, Yoko had attended the Convention back in September 1995. Keith, Greg, Will, Keith (Wechsler), myself, Billy, Yoko and her friends sat around until nearly 2 am. Keith and Greg were on very good form. Upon leaving, Keith and Greg had some nice things to say to us and were genuinely touched that we had travelled so far to see them (To be honest, I'd have travelled *twice* the distance to experience this trip!!).

Saturday 19th October
"On our way home" Flight Aeroflot SU582 leaving at midday. (There was a one hour delay)

APPENDIX 5

ELP POLL AWARDS

1970

Melody Maker
British Section
ELP: Brightest
 Hopes 1

International Section
Emerson: Keyboards 1

Sounds
British Section
Emerson: Keyboards 1

1971
Melody Maker
British Section
Emerson: Keyboards 1
Palmer: Drummer 1
ELP: Band 1
Tarkus: Album 1

International Section
Emerson: Keyboards 1
Lake: Producer 1
Palmer: Drummer 1
Emerson/Lake:
 Composers 1

Sounds
British Section
Emerson: Keyboards 1
Palmer: Drummer 1
ELP: Band 1
Tarkus: Album 1

1972

Melody Maker
British Section
ELP: Band 1

International Section
Emerson: Keyboards 1
Palmer. Drummer 1
ELP: Arrangers 1

Sounds
British Section
Emerson: Musician 1
Keyboard 1
Miscellaneous
 Instrument 1
 (Synthesiser)
Lake: Bass Guitarist 2
Male Vocalist 8
Producer 1 (Eddy
 Offord - 6)
Palmer: Drummer 1
Emerson/Lake:
 Composer 2
ELP: Band 2
Trilogy: Album 2

Trilogy: Album Design 8
International Section
Emerson: Keyboard 1
Miscellaneous
 Instrument 1 (Moog)
Lake: Bass Guitarist 3
Producer 5
Palmer: Drummer 2
Emerson/Lake:
 Composer 5
ELP: Band 4
Trilogy: Album 7

1973

Melody Maker
British Section
ELP: Live Act 1

International Section
Palmer: Drummer 1
ELP: Arrangers 1

Sounds
British Section
Emerson: Musician 2
Keyboards 1
Miscellaneous
 Instrument 2
Lake: Bass Guitarist 4
Male Vocalist 7
Record Producer 1
Palmer: Drummer 1
Emerson/Lake:
 Composer 5
ELP: Band 2
Brain Salad Surgery:
 Album Design 3
Welcome Back:
 Album 3
Album Design 7

International Section
Emerson: Musician 3
Keyboards 2
Miscellaneous
 Instrument 2
Lake: Bass Guitarist 2
Male Vocalist 8
Record Producer 1
Palmer: Drummer 2
Emerson/Lake:
 Composer 3
ELP: Band 1
Brain Salad Surgery:
 Album Design 5
Welcome Back...:
 Album 1
Welcome Back...:
 Album Design 3

New Musical Express
World Section
ELP: Group 2
Stage Band 2
Brain Salad Surgery:
 Album 3

British Section
ELP: Group 3
Stage Band 2
Brain Salad Surgery:
 Album 3

General Section
Emerson: Keyboards 2
Miscellaneous
 Instrumentalist 2
Lake: Bass Guitarist 3
Producer 3
Palmer: Drummer 1
Emerson / Lake:
 Songwriters 6
Brain Salad Surgery:
 Best-Dressed Album 2

1974

Melody Maker
International Section
Palmer: Drummer 1
ELP: Live Act 1

Sounds
British Section
Palmer: Drummer 1

1975

Melody Maker
British Section
Lake: Male Singer 9
ELP: Band 6
Live Act 6

International Section
Emerson: Keyboards 2
Miscellaneous
 Instruments 5
Arranger 8 (tied with
 Genesis)
Lake: Bass Guitarist 6
Male Singer 8
Producer 3 (Eddy
 Offord -1)
Palmer: Drummer 1
ELP: Band 3
Live Act 5

Sounds
British Section
Palmer: Drummer 1

New Musical Express
British Section
ELP: Group 3
Stage Band 3

World Section
ELP: Group 4
Stage Band 3

General Section
Emerson: Keyboards 2
Miscellaneous
 Instrument 3

Lake: Bass 5
Producer 2

1976

Melody Maker
(Results September)
British Section
ELP: Band 10
I Believe in Father
 Christmas: Single 7

International Section
Emerson: Keyboards 2
Miscellaneous
 Instruments 4
Lake: Bass Guitarist 10
Producer 8
Palmer: Drummer 1

Sounds
Emerson: Musician 3
Keyboards 2
Lake: Male Singer 10
Bass Guitarist 5
Palmer: Drummer 2
I Believe in Father
 Christmas: Single 4

1977

Sounds
British Section

Emerson: Keyboards 1
Miscellaneous
 Instruments 4
Arranger 3
Lake: Bass Guitarist 4
Male Singer 7
Producer 2
ELP: Band 4
Arrangers 7
Fanfare for the
 Common Man:
 Single 1
Works, Vol.1: Album 1

International Section
Emerson: Composer 6
Lake: Male Singer 5
ELP: Band 4
Composers 7
Fanfare for the
 Common Man: Single
 1
Works, Vol.1: Album 1

SOURCES

In addition to the authors' own interviews, articles and reviews in thefollowing magazines were used as source material for this book: *BAM, Beat Instrumental, Billboard, Chicago Sun Times, Chronicle Herald (Canada), Cincinatti Enquirer, Circus, Crawdaddy, Creem, Daily News (NY), Dayton (Ohio) Daily News, Dallas Morning News, Disc, Downbeat, East Coast Rocker, The Entertainer (NY), Faces, Good Times, The Guardian, Guitar Player, Goldmine, Hit Parader, Houston Chronicle, Houston Enquirer, Hurricane, Illinois Entertainer, Journal for Area Musicians, Kerrang!, Keyboard, Keyboards (France), La Gniappe, Los Angeles Times, Madison Capital Times, Melody Maker, Metal Hammer, Mix, Modern Drummer, Music Now!, Music Scene, Music UK, Musician, Musicians Only, New Musical Express, New York Post, New York Times, Patches, The Pittsburgh Press, Playboy, Progression, Q, Record Mirror, Rock Express, Rock Scene, Rolling Stone, Smash Hits, Sounds, Stereo Review, Toronto Star, Trouser Press, Turku (Finland), USA Today, Variety, Washington Post* Special mention should go to a "Music Scene Top Ten Series" colour magazine about ELP, published in 1974 (32 pages)
The authors would like to thank the writers whose work was consulted. They include the following:
Keith Altham, Robert Ashmore, Lester Bangs (RIP), Jan Beckenroth, Joe Bivona, Pete Bishop, Howard Bloom, Caroline Boucher, Tony Brock, Roy Carr, Edie Chandlier, Chris Charlesworth, Barbara Charone, Paul Colbert, Jean Charles Costa, Cameron Crowe, Michael Dawson, Simon Decker, Ross Del Ruth, Steve Demorest, Dave Dimartino, Bob Doerschuck, Jan Dove, Bruce Eder, Jim Farber, Eric Gaer, H.R. Giger, Dan Golds, Nick Gould, Barbara Graustark, Richard Green, Mike Greenblatt, Shelley Harris, Allen Hester, George Hines, Richard Hogan, Dennis Hunt, Cheech Iero, Peter Jackel, Allan Jackson, Mike Jahn,

Tony Jasper, James Johnson, Allan Jones, Howard Jones, Grace Lichenstein, Nick Logan, Terry McGregor, Pete Makowski, Rick Mattingly, John Mendlesohn, Stan Mieses, Tony Norman, Jim O'Connor, John Orme, Pat Patrick, Peter Perkins, Bruce Pilato, Mark Plummer, Marty Raccine, Lisa Robinson, Richard Robinson, Rick Sanders, Janis Schacht, Keith Sharp, Robin Smith, Tony Stewart, John Storm, David Terralavoro, Nigel Thomas, Brad Tolinski, Tony Tyler, Dave Wagner, Martin Webb, Julie Webb, Chris Welch, P. Wiffen, Richard Williams, Charles Young, Tom Zito.

There were also a number of articles and interviews consulted where it was impossible to trace the original source.

Other sources

Macan, Ed, *Rockin' The Classics*,
Martin, Bill, *Listening to the Future*,
Martin, Bill, *The Music of Yes: Structure and Vision in Progressive Rock*
Pethel, Blair, *Keith Emerson: the Emergence and Growth of Style*
In 1983 Pethel conducted an interview with Emerson for his docotoral thesis, which covered all aspects of Emerson's music, with particular emphasis on the Concerto. It subsequently became available via U.M.I. (University Microfilms International, 300 North Zeeb Road, Ann Arbor, MI 48106-1346, USA), and I am among the very few people who shelled out for a copy.
Rees, David, *Minstrels in the Gallery: A History of Jethro Tull*, Firefly, London, 1998
Stump, Paul, *The Music's All That Matters: A History of Progressive Rock*, Quartet, London, 1997
Tamm, Eric, *Robert Fripp*, Faber and Faber, London

Mention should also be made of "Keith Emerson: Interviews" (1992) – a superb Japanese-only collection of Keith interviews with a discography and many colour contributions. ISBN 4-8456-0040-4

ELP Fanzines

Sukrat by Chris Lonsdale (3 issues to May 1985)
Tank by Nick Gould (4 issues to January 1988)
Fanzine for the Common Man by David Terralavoro (17 issues from August 1989 to July 1997, with more promised)
Impressions edited by Liv G. Whetmore with Frank Askew, Martyn Hanson, Robert Ashmore, Sue Pittard and Jacquie Dutton (8 issues from April 1996 to present)

ELP ON THE INTERNET

There's quite a lot of web space devoted to ELP! Room here for just a small selection.

Emerson, Lake and Palmer: The Show that Never Ends.
http://members.theglobe.com/aluckyman/exp_fan1.html

Regular updates about this book will be posted here, and an improved version of the site will be constructed. We hope to produce a second edition of the book eventually, and we welcome your comments and suggestions! You may leave messages in the Guestbook as well as send emails.

Also bookmark the page for our book at Amazon.co.uk - the URL's too long to quote here, just search the books section under Emerson, Lake and Palmer.

Official Emerson, Lake and Palmer Sites.
www.emersonlakepalmer.com
www.keithemerson.com
www.greglake.com
www.carlpalmer.com
The ELP WebRing
www.janie.com/elp.htm
Links interconnecting 27 ELP-related websites including one for this book.

ELP Digest.
www.brain-salad.com
The original ELP website.

Impressions.
www.interx.net/~jgreen/impressions.html
UK-based ELP magazine, fully supported by the band, with regular contributions from Martyn Hanson and Frank Askew among others.

The Karn Evil Kids ELP Page.
www.ecs.uci.edu/rwm/elp/elp.html
Robert Murray's informative site.

Two ELP discussion groups:
Portabello Towne - The ELP Discussion Board
www.freespeech.org/furgle/elp.html
ELP-DISC
www.angelfire.com/rock/MarkyDee/index.html

INDEX

Back Catalogue

No More Sad Refrains: The Life and Times of Sandy Denny: Clinton Heylin
Drawing on fresh interviews with Sandy's closest friends and musical collaborators, and with unprecedented access to her journals, diaries and unreleased recordings, Heylin has produced a portrait of a complex, driven and flawed genius who may well have been this land's greatest ever female singer-songwriter. Clinton Heylin is a highly respected historian of popular music, whose book Dylan Behind Closed Doors (1996, Penguin) was nominated for the Ralph J. Gleason award.
'No female singer of the last ten years could touch her.'
Greil Marcus, Rolling Stone, May 1978
256 pages/8 pages b&w photos/235 x 156mm ISBN 1-900924-11-2 Hardcover UK £18.99

Like a Bullet of Light: The Films of Bob Dylan: C.P. Lee
Using archive research and fresh interviews, C.P. Lee traces Dylan's celluloid obsession from his teenage adulation of James Dean through his involvement in documentaries like Dont Look Back and his enigmatic appearance in Peckinpah's Pat Garratt and Billy The Kid. It looks at the genesis of Dylan's dramatic directorial debut, Renaldo and Clara, and his starring role in mainstream Hearts of Fire. The author also presents an analysis of all Dylan's major appearances on TV and video. 'There is no doubt that C.P. has done it again … thanks for getting it right.' Mickey Jones, drummer with Dylan during the Dont Look Back era.
192 pages/8 pages b&w photos/235 x 156mm ISBN 1-900924-06-4 UK £12.99

Jethro Tull: Minstrels in the Gallery: David Rees
The first ever biography of the band published on their 30th anniversary. This dates the band's career from the Rock 'n Roll Circus with the Rolling Stones in the 60s, through their megastardom in the 70s with platinum albums such as Aqualung and Thick as a Brick, and on to their place in the 80s and 90s as one of the great enduring rock acts.
'Brilliant, independently minded … A fine read for Tull fans and non-believers alike.' Mojo
224 pages/24 photos/235 x 156mm ISDN 0 940719-22-9 UK £12.99

Dylan's Demon Lover: The Tangled Tale of a 450-Year Old Pop Ballad: Clinton Heylin
This is a fascinating journey along the lesser-travelled byways of popular song into the heart of the ballad and investigates the tale of a 450-year-old popular ballad, spinning all the way from Dylan's 1961 recording of 'The House Carpenter' back to the origins of popular song. Heylin unearths the mystery of how Dylan knew enough to return 'The House Carpenter' to its 16th-century source, and looks at the development of folk song in the British Isles along the way.
'Clinton Heylin is the maddest muso currently writing.' Time Out
160 pages/235 x 156mm ISBN: 1-900924-15-3 UK £12.00

Blowing Free: Thirty Years of Wishbone Ash: Mark Chatterton and Gary Carter
During the early 1970s golden era of progressive and heavy rock Wishbone Ash were one of Britain's most popular hard rock acts. Formed in 1969 around the twin-lead guitar attack of Andy Powell and Ted Turner, the group's music showcased blistering solos and a strong melodic sensibility. They became a staple favourite on the live circuit, and hit LPs quickly followed. In 1987, after a period in the wilderness, their original manager persuaded the band to reform and since then they have continued recording and touring to widespread international acclaim. The authors have produced a gripping account of the long and distinctive career of one of Britain's premier rock bands.
224 pages/8 photos/235 x 156mm ISBN 0-946719-33-0 UK £12.99

Get Back: The Beatles' 'Let It Be' Disaster: Doug Sulphy and Ray Schweighardt
Subtitled Divorce, Drugs and the Slipping Image, this is the no-holds barred account of the power struggles, bickering and bitterness that led to the break-up of the greatest band in rock 'n' roll. The Get Back recording sessions were an attempt by the band to return to their rock'n'roll roots, but carping and sniping and trudging through old hits, the Fab Four were coming apart. This puts the reader in the studio as well as reliving the glorious rooftop concert when they left their differences behind for one last impromptu performance.
'First class-detective work … Fascinating and revealing, this is a Must for every Beatles fan.' Goldmine 'One of the most poignant Beatles' books ever.' Mojo
256 pages/235 x 156mm ISBN 1-900924-12-9 UK £12.99

XTC: Song Stories: The Exclusive and Authorised Story Behind the Music: XTC and Neville Farmer
The information fans have waited decades for! Following their evolution album by album, it looks at the band's early 70s foundation, and at their lyrics melodies, as well as containing photos from the band's archives. It features cameo appearances by famous XTC fans River Phoenix and Keanu Reeves. Co-written by one of the most popular cult bands of all time, this book is timed to coincide with their long awaited new album. 'A cheerful celebration of the minutiae surrounding XTC's music with the band's musical passion intact. It's essentially a band-driven project for the fans, high in setting-the-record-straight anecdotes. Superbright, funny, commanding.' Mojo
306 pages/100 b&w photos/235 x 156mm ISBN 1-900924-03-X UK £12.99

Bob Dylan: Like The Night: C.P. Lee
In 1966, at the height of his popularity, Dylan plugged in an electric guitar and merged his poetic lyrics with the sound of one of the great rock'n'roll bands. The rock world was delighted, but the folk scene felt outraged and betrayed. That summer Dylan toured the world, and every show was accompanied by frenzied booing and catcalls – culminating at the Manchester Free Trade Hall where fans called him 'Judas'. This book documents that legendary world tour where Dylan waged a nightly war with his audience, and reinvented rock 'n' roll with an incendiary zeal never subsequently equalled.
'Essential Reading.' Uncut 'C.P. Lee was there, but the point is that he can put you there too.' Greil Marcus
192 pages/24 b&w photos ISBN 1-900924-07-2 Paper UK £12.00

Back to the Beach: A Brian Wilson and the Beach Boys Reader: Edited by Kingsley Abbott
A collection of the best articles about Brian and the band, together with a number of previously unpublished pieces and some specially commissioned work.
Features Nick Kent, David Leaf, Timothy White and others, with a foreword by Brian Wilson.
'A detailed study and comprehensive overview of the BBs' lives and music, even including a foreword from Wilson himself by way of validation. Most impressively, Abbott manages to appeal to both die-hard fans and rather less obsessive newcomers.' Time Out
'Rivetting!' **** Q 'An essential purchase.' Mojo
256 pages/235 x 156mm ISBN 1-900924-02-1 Paper UK £12.99

A Journey Through America with the Rolling Stones: Robert Greenfield
By 1972, the Stones had become the number one musical attraction in the world: the only great band of the 1960s still around who played original rock 'n' roll. This is the definitive account of their legendary '72 tour, catching them at the height of their powers and excesses.
'A merciless, brilliant study of Jagger-power at full throttle.' Daily Mirror
'Filled with finely-rendered detail ... a fascinating tale of times we shall never see again.' Mojo 'Strange days indeed.' Q ****
192 pages/235 x 156 mm ISBN 1-900924-01-3 UK £12.00

Bob Dylan: A Biography: Anthony Scaduto
Along with Elvis and Lennon, Bob Dylan is one of the three most important figures in 20th-century popular music. Scaduto's book is his first and best biography.
'Scaduto's 1971 book was the pioneering portrait of this legendarily elusive artist. Now in a welcome reprint it's a real treat to read the still-classic Bobography.' Q*****
'Perhaps the best ever book written on Dylan.' Record Collector
'I like your book. That's the weird thing about it.' Bob Dylan
312 pages/8 pages of photos/235 x 156 mm ISBN 1-900924-00-5 Paper UK £12.99